A Selection of Image Processing Techniques

A Selection of Image Processing Techniques

From Fundamentals to Research Front

Yu-Jin Zhang

CRC Press
Taylor & Francis Group
Boca Raton London New York

CRC Press is an imprint of the
Taylor & Francis Group, an **Informa** business

First edition published 2022
by CRC Press
6000 Broken Sound Parkway NW, Suite 300, Boca Raton, FL 33487-2742

and by CRC Press
2 Park Square, Milton Park, Abingdon, Oxon, OX14 4RN

Library of Congress Cataloging-in-Publication Data
Names: Zhang, Yu-Jin, 1954- author.
Title: A selection of image processing techniques : from fundamentals to research front / Yu-Jin Zhang.
Description: First edition. | Boca Raton : CRC Press, 2022. | Includes bibliographical references and index. |
Summary: "This book focuses on seven commonly used image processing techniques.
These are Image de-noising, Image de-blurring, Image repairing, Image de-fogging,
Image reconstruction from projection, Image watermarking, and Image super-resolution.
For each of these selected techniques, comprehensive coverage is provided"– Provided by publisher.
Identifiers: LCCN 2021028218 (print) | LCCN 2021028219 (ebook) |
ISBN 9781032148397 (hardcover) | ISBN 9781032148489 (paperback) | ISBN 9781003241416 (ebook)
Subjects: LCSH: Image processing–Digital techniques.
Classification: LCC TA1637 .Z5279 2022 (print) | LCC TA1637 (ebook) | DDC 621.36/7–dc23
LC record available at https://lccn.loc.gov/2021028218
LC ebook record available at https://lccn.loc.gov/2021028219

ISBN: 978-1-032-14839-7 (hbk)
ISBN: 978-1-032-14848-9 (pbk)
ISBN: 978-1-003-24141-6 (ebk)

DOI: 10.1201/9781003241416

Typeset in Minion
by codeMantra

Color figures are available for viewing on CRC Press website:
https://www.routledge.com/9781032148397

Contents

Preface

IMAGE PROCESSING IS A discipline that has attracted a lot of attention in the information community. Image processing technology has been widely used in many applications in our society. This book takes a new way, in combining the contents, characteristics and styles of both textbook and monography, to introduce image processing technology.

This book is different from a pure textbook on image processing; it is also not a theoretical monograph on image processing technology. In this book, the introduction is focused on several commonly used image processing techniques. Comprehensive coverage is provided for each of these selected techniques. The book starts with the essential concepts and basic principles, discusses the typical specific methods and practical techniques, and finishes with the research frontier trends and latest developments.

This book should be suitable for readers who do not have the complete foundation of image processing yet, but need to use image processing techniques to solve specific tasks. From this book, readers can quickly grasp the elementary knowledge for further study without the prerequisite of the relevant basis information; they can find a suitable technique for solving a practical problem, and then learn the latest development in the specific application domain.

The seven selected image processing techniques are image de-noising, de-blurring, repairing, de-fogging, reconstruction from projection, watermarking, and super-resolution. This book does not attempt to cover all branches of image processing technology; rather, it gives a comprehensive discussion on those selected techniques. The presentations and discussions on each of these techniques are self-contained.

The materials in this book are arranged in eight chapters with 49 sections, 118 subsections, with 168 figures, 29 tables, and 437 numbered equations. Moreover, over 200 key references are introduced and provided at the end of the book for further study.

Special thanks go to Taylor & Francis Group and their staff members. Their kind and professional assistance are truly appreciated.

Last but not least, I am deeply indebted to my wife and my daughter for their encouragement, patience, support, tolerance, and understanding during the writing of this book.

Yu-Jin Zhang

Color figures are available for viewing on CRC Press website:
https://www.routledge.com/9781032148397

Author

Yu-Jin Zhang is a tenured professor of image engineering at Tsinghua University, Beijing, China. He earned his, PhD in Applied Science from the State University of Liège, Liège, Belgium. He is a post-doc fellow of Delft University of Technology, Delft, the Netherlands. He is also a CSIG and SPIE fellow. Dr. Zhang has published more than 50 books and more than 500 research papers.

## CHAPTER 1

Introduction

*I*MAGE IS A WIDELY used concept. People generally regard an image as a visual representation of a scene or scenery. For example, the definition of *image* in the dictionary is "the expression, representation, and imitation of an object, a vivid visual description, something introduced to express other things" (Bow 2002). Strictly, images are obtained by observing the objective world in different forms and methods with various observation systems, which can directly or indirectly act on the human eye and produce visual perception entities (Zhang 1996). The *human visual system* is an observation system, and the image obtained through it is the image formed by the objective scene in the human mind.

The image contains a wealth of information. We live in an information age. Scientific research and statistics show that about 75% of the information that humans obtain from the outside world comes from the visual system, that is, obtained from images. The concept of image here is relatively broad, including photos, drawings, animations, videos, and even documents. There is an old saying in China, "It is better to see than to hear a hundred times." People often say, "A picture is worth a thousand words." All these show that the information contained in the image is very rich, and image is our main source of information.

This book mainly discusses images obtained by imaging natural scenes, which also have many categories. For example, photos (people, landscapes, etc.) taken with digital cameras, videos (family parties, football games, etc.) captured with digital video cameras, various sequences (traffic management, missile flight, etc.) recorded by surveillance systems, various electromagnetic radiation images captured by space telescopes, and the images formed by radar based on reflected waves, as well as X-ray images, B-ultrasound images, CT images, and magnetic resonance images (MRI) that are commonly used in medicine. There are not only grayscale and color images but also texture and depth images.

In recent years, images have been widely used in many fields of social development and human life, such as industrial production, smart agriculture, biomedicine and health, leisure and entertainment, video communication, network communication, document management, remote sensing mapping, environmental protection, intelligent transportation, military and public security, space exploration, and so on.

DOI: 10.1201/9781003241416-1

In view of the application characteristics of images in different fields, many image technologies covering a wide range have been studied. This book attempts to select some basic categories of the very commonly used image technology and gives an introduction from shallow to deep (including basic principles, practical technologies, and development trends).

The contents of each section of this chapter are arranged as follows.

Section 1.1 gives a general introduction to the basic knowledge of images. It includes the representation method and display method of image and pixel, the relationship between image quality and spatial resolution and/or amplitude resolution, as well as the half-tone technology and dithering technology commonly used in image printout. This section provides some fundamental knowledge about image.

Section 1.2 provides an overview of image technology. The overall framework – image engineering (IE), as well as its three levels – image processing (IP), image analysis (IA), image understanding (IU), are introduced first. Then, the image system block diagram and some modules in this system are discussed. This section makes it possible for the following chapter to be focused on IP that is mainstream of this book.

Section 1.3 discusses the features of this book. It elaborates and analyzes the three aspects of writing motivation, material selection and contents, as well as structure and arrangement. It not only gives the overall content and structural characteristics of the book but also helps the readers to know how to learn and use this book.

1.1 IMAGE BASICS

First, some basic concepts and terminology related to images are reviewed.

1.1.1 Image Representation and Display

Let's first introduce how to represent and display images.

1.1.1.1 Images and Pixels

The objective world is three-dimensional (3-D) in space, but the image obtained from the objective scene is generally two-dimensional (2-D). An image can be represented by a 2-D array $f(x, y)$, where x and y represent the position of a coordinate point in the 2-D space XY, and f represents the image value of a property F at a certain point (x, y). For example, f in a *grayscale image* represents a gray value, which often corresponds to the observed brightness of an objective scene. Text images are often *binary images,* and there are only two values for f, corresponding to text and blank space, respectively. The image at the point (x, y) can also have multiple properties at the same time. In this case, it can be represented by a vector f. For example, a *color image* has three values of red, green, and blue at each image point, which can be recorded as $[f_r(x, y), f_g(x, y), f_b(x, y)]$. It needs to be pointed out that people always use images according to the different properties at different positions in the image.

An image can represent the spatial distribution of radiant energy. This distribution can be a function of five variables $T(x, y, z, t, \lambda)$, where x, y, and z are spatial variables, and t represents time variables, λ is wavelength (corresponding to the spectral variable). For example, a red object reflects light with a wavelength of 0.57–0.78 μm and absorbs almost all energy of other wavelengths; a green object reflects light with a wavelength of 0.48–0.57 μm; a blue object reflects light with a wavelength of 0.40–0.48 μm. Ultraviolet (color) objects reflect light with a wavelength of 0.25–0.40 μm, and infrared (color) objects reflect light with a wavelength of 0.78–1.5 μm. Together, they cover a wavelength range of 0.25–1.5 μm. Since the actual image is finite in time and space, $T(x, y, z, t, \lambda)$ is a 5-D finite function.

The images acquired in the early years are mostly continuous (analog), that is, the values of f, x, and y can be any real numbers. With the invention of the computer and the development of electronic equipment, the acquired images are all discrete (digital) and can be processed directly by the computer. Someone once used $I(r, c)$ to represent a digital image, where the values of I, r, and c are all integers. Here I represents the discretized f; (r, c) represents the discretized (x, y), where r represents the image row, and c represents the image column. The discussion in this book is related to digital images. Images or $f(x, y)$ are used to represent digital images without causing confusion. Unless otherwise specified, f, x, and y are all taken their values in the integer set.

In the early days, the term "picture" was generally used to refer to images. With the development of digital technology, the term "image" is now used to represent a discretized "image" because "computers store numerical images of a picture or scene" (Zhang 1996). Each basic unit in an image is called an image element, and in the early days, when the "picture" was used to represent an image, it was called a *pixel*. For 2-D images, "pel" has also been used to refer to the basic unit. If one collects a series of 2-D images or uses some special equipment, one can also get 3-D images. For 3-D images, *voxel* is often used to represent the basic unit. Someone has also suggested to use "imel" to represent various image units.

1.1.1.2 Matrix and Vector Representation of Image

A 2-D image with $M \times N$ (where M and N are the total number of rows and total number of columns for pixels in the image, respectively) can be represented by either a 2-D array $f(x, y)$ or a 2-D matrix F (where each element corresponds to a pixel):

$$\mathbf{F} = \begin{bmatrix} f_{11} & f_{12} & \cdots & f_{1N} \\ f_{21} & f_{22} & \cdots & f_{2N} \\ \vdots & \vdots & \ddots & \vdots \\ f_{M1} & f_{M2} & \cdots & f_{MN} \end{bmatrix} \tag{1.1}$$

The above *matrix representation* can also be transformed into a *vector representation*. For example, the above equation can be written as

$$\mathbf{F} = \begin{bmatrix} \mathbf{f}_1 & \mathbf{f}_2 & \cdots & \mathbf{f}_N \end{bmatrix} \tag{1.2}$$

where

$$f_i = \begin{bmatrix} f_{1i} & f_{2i} & \cdots & f_{Mi} \end{bmatrix}^{\mathrm{T}} \qquad i = 1, 2, \cdots, N \tag{1.3}$$

It should be noted that array operations and matrix operations are different. Take two 2×2 images $f(x, y)$ and $g(x, y)$ as an example. Their array product is

$$f(x, y)g(x, y) = \begin{bmatrix} f_{11} & f_{12} \\ f_{21} & f_{22} \end{bmatrix} \begin{bmatrix} g_{11} & g_{12} \\ g_{21} & g_{22} \end{bmatrix} = \begin{bmatrix} f_{11}g_{11} & f_{12}g_{12} \\ f_{21}g_{21} & f_{22}g_{22} \end{bmatrix} \tag{1.4}$$

and their matrix product is

$$\mathbf{FG} = \begin{bmatrix} f_{11} & f_{12} \\ f_{21} & f_{22} \end{bmatrix} \begin{bmatrix} g_{11} & g_{12} \\ g_{21} & g_{22} \end{bmatrix} = \begin{bmatrix} f_{11}g_{11} + f_{12}g_{21} & f_{11}g_{12} + f_{12}g_{22} \\ f_{21}g_{11} + f_{22}g_{21} & f_{21}g_{12} + f_{22}g_{22} \end{bmatrix} \tag{1.5}$$

1.1.1.3 How the Image Is Displayed

The display of 2-D images can take many forms, and the basic idea is to regard the 2-D image as an amplitude distribution on the 2-D spatial position. Depending on various images and different types of equipment, the display methods can also be different.

In Figure 1.1, two typical public *grayscale images* (Lena and Cameraman) are displayed in Figure 1.1a and b, respectively. The coordinate system used in Figure 1.1a is often used in screen display (screen scanning is carried out from left to right and from top to bottom), the system origin O is at the upper left corner of the image, and the vertical axis marks the image rows and the horizontal axis marks the image columns. $I(r, c)$ can be used either to represent this image, or to represent the value of the image at the intersection of row and column (r, c). The coordinate system used in Figure 1.1b is often used in image calculations. The system origin, O, is at the lower left corner of the image, the horizontal axis is

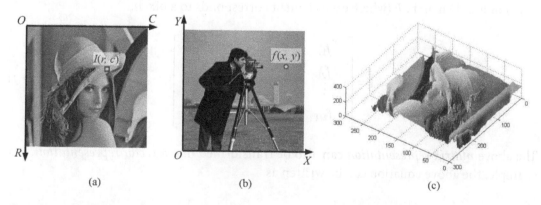

FIGURE 1.1 Grayscale image display examples.

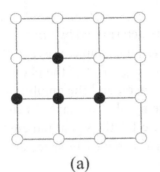
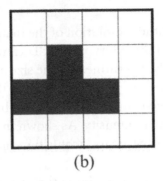

(a)   (b)   (c)

FIGURE 1.2   Three ways to represent the same 4×4 binary image.

the X-axis, and the vertical axis is the Y-axis (the same as the commonly used Cartesian coordinate system). $f(x, y)$ can be used either to represent this image or to represent the value of the pixel at the coordinates (x, y). Figure 1.1c shows the 3-D perspective display of Figure 1.1a, in which the grayscale of each pixel is also proportional to the corresponding vertical height.

Figure 1.2 shows three different visual representations of one same *binary image* (matrix). In the mathematical model of image representation, a pixel region is often represented by its center point. The representation form obtained in this way is a set of discrete points on the plane, corresponding to Figure 1.2a. If the pixel region is still represented as a square region, Figure 1.2b is obtained. When the amplitude value is marked at the corresponding position in the image, a result similar to the matrix shown in Figure 1.2c is obtained. Figure 1.2b can also be used to represent an image with multiple grayscales. In this case, different shades of tones need to be used to represent different grayscales. Figure 1.2c can also be used to represent an image with multiple gray levels. In this case, different gray levels are represented by different values.

1.1.2 Spatial Resolution and Amplitude Resolution

From the above introduction and discussion of image representation and display, it can be known that the content of a 2-D grayscale image is determined by the number of pixels (the number of rows of the image multiplied by the number of columns of the image) and by the number of gray levels for each pixel. The former determines the *spatial resolution* of the image, while the latter determines the *amplitude resolution* of the image. From the perspective of image acquisition, the acquisition of images is to record the spatial distribution of the light reflection intensity of the scene within a certain field of view. The accuracy in the spatial field of view here corresponds to the spatial resolution of the image, and the accuracy in the intensity range corresponds to the amplitude resolution of the image. The former corresponds to the number of digitized spatial sampling points while the latter corresponds to the quantization levels of the sampling point value (for grayscale images, it refers to gray levels; for depth images, it refers to depth levels). They are all important performance indicators of image acquisition devices.

1.1.2.1 Sampling and Quantization

The spatial resolution and amplitude resolution of the image are determined by *sampling* and *quantization*, respectively. Taking a typical CCD camera as an example, the spatial resolution of the image is mainly determined by the size and arrangement of the photo-electric sensing units in the image acquisition matrix in the camera, and the amplitude resolution of the grayscale image is mainly determined by the number of stages in the quantization of the electrical signal intensity. As shown in Figure 1.3, the signal radiated from the photoreceptive unit in the image acquisition matrix is sampled in space and quantized in intensity.

The sampling process can be seen as dividing the image plane into regular grids. The position of each grid is determined by a pair of Cartesian coordinates (x, y), where x and y are integers. Let $f(\cdot)$ be a function that assigns gray values to the grid point (x, y), where f is an integer in F, then $f(x, y)$ is a digital image, and this assignment process is a quantization process.

From the perspective of computer processing of images, an image must be discretized in space and gray level before it can be processed by the computer. The discretization of spatial coordinates is called spatial sampling (abbreviated as *sampling*), which determines the *spatial resolution* of the image; the discretization of gray values is called grayscale quantization (abbreviated as *quantization*), which determines the *amplitude resolution* of the image.

1.1.2.2 Resolution and Data Volume

If the size (spatial resolution) of an image is $M \times N$, it means that MN samples were collected during imaging, or the image contains MN pixels. If each pixel is assigned one of G gray values, it indicates that G gray levels (amplitude resolution) are quantized during imaging. In IP, these quantities are generally taken as an integer power of 2, that is (m, n, and k are all positive integers)

$$M = 2^m \tag{1.6}$$

$$N = 2^n. \tag{1.7}$$

$$G = 2^k \tag{1.8}$$

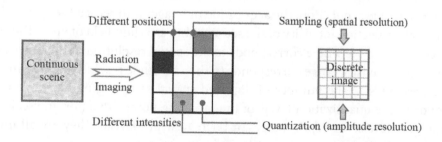

FIGURE 1.3   Spatial resolution and amplitude resolution.

Many image formats in actual use have different resolutions. For example, the resolution of the *source input format* (SIF) is 352×240, which is also the resolution of the NTSC SIF format; the resolution of the PAL SIF format is 352×288, which is also the resolution of the *common intermediate format* (CIF) format; the resolution of the *quarter common intermediate format* (QCIF) format is 176×144; the resolution of VGA is 640×480; the resolution of CCIR/ITU-R 601 is 720×480 (NTSC) or 720×576 (PAL); the resolution of HDTV can reach 1440×1152 or even 1920×1152.

The amount of data required to store an image is determined by the spatial resolution and amplitude resolution of the image. According to Equations (1.6)–(1.8), the number of bits b (unit is bit) required to store an image is

$$b = M \times N \times k \tag{1.9}$$

If $N=M$ ($N=M$ is generally set below), then

$$b = N^2 k \tag{1.10}$$

1.1.3 Resolution and Image Quality

Image quality is related to subjective and objective factors. In IP, the judgment of image quality often depends on human observation, but there are some related objective indicators. The most commonly used are the spatial resolution and amplitude resolution of the image.

The visual quality of an image is closely related to its spatial resolution and amplitude resolution. The following discusses the general situation in which the image quality deteriorates due to the decrease in the number of pixels and/or the number of gray-scale quantization levels.

Let's take a look at how the *visual quality* of digital images deteriorates with the reduction of spatial resolution and amplitude resolution, to give some link between *image quality* and *data volume*.

For an image having more details with 512×512 pixels, 256 gray levels, if the number of gray levels is unchanged and only its spatial resolution (by pixel copy) is reduced to 256×256, a square checkerboard pattern may be seen at the boundaries of each region in the image, and the pixel particles become thicker in the whole image, which has a great influence on the texture region in the image. This effect is generally more obvious in the image of 128×128, and it is quite obvious in the image of 64×64 and image 32×32.

Figure 1.4 gives a set of image examples of the changing effect of spatial resolutions. Among them, the spatial resolution, the number of gray levels, and the amount of data of each image are shown in the columns of Table 1.1; the ratio of the amount of data between two adjacent images is also given in the corresponding two columns. Here, each image keeps the number of gray levels unchanged, and in turn, the spatial resolution of the previous image is successively halved in both horizontal and vertical directions. The

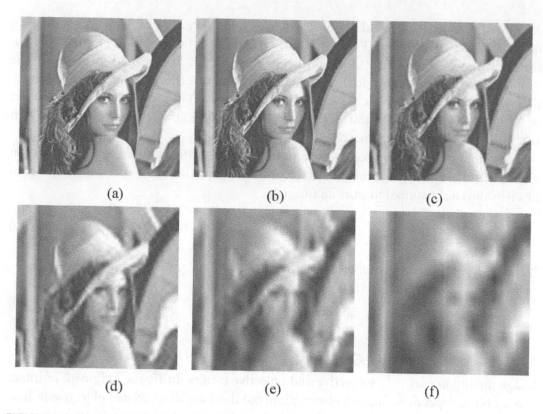

FIGURE 1.4 The effect of image spatial resolution changes.

TABLE 1.1 A Set of Images with Varying Spatial Resolutions

Figure 1.4	(a)	(b)	(c)	(d)	(e)	(f)
Spatial resolution	512×512	256×256	128×128	64×64	32×32	16×16
Number of gray levels	256	256	256	256	256	256
Amount of data/bit	67108864	16777216	4194304	1048576	262144	65536
Ratio of data volume		4::1	4::1	4::1	4::1	4::1

above-mentioned phenomena can be seen in Figure 1.4. For example, if the original image in Figure 1.4a is used as a reference standard, the brim of the hat in Figure 1.4b has become jagged; this phenomenon is more obvious in Figure 1.4c, where the hair has become thicker and provides the feeling of unclearness; the hair in Fig. 1.4d is no longer streaks; in Fig. 1.4e, the human face can hardly be distinguished, and in Fig. 1.4f, it is almost impossible to see what is in it when viewed alone.

Now the above-mentioned 512×512, 256-level grayscale image is still used to consider the effect of reducing the image amplitude resolution (i.e., the number of gray levels). If the spatial resolution is maintained and only the number of gray levels is reduced to 128 or 64, people generally cannot find any difference. If the number of gray levels is further reduced to 32, there will often be some very fine ridge-like structures that are almost invisible in the regions where the gray level changes slowly. This effect is called *false contours*, and it is caused by insufficient gray levels used in the gray-level smoothing region of the digital image. It is generally more obvious in an image with 16 gray levels or less than 16 gray levels of uniform gray numbers.

Figure 1.5 gives an example of the effect of a set of image gray level changes. Among them, the spatial resolution, the number of gray levels, and the amount of data of each image are shown in the columns of Table 1.2, and the ratio of the amount of data between two adjacent images is also given in the corresponding two columns. Here, each image maintains the same spatial resolution and sequentially reduces the gray levels of the previous image (the first two times are reduced to 1/4, and the last three times are reduced to 1/2). The above-discussed phenomenon can be seen from these figures. For example, Figure 1.5b still looks similar to Figure 1.5a as the reference standard,

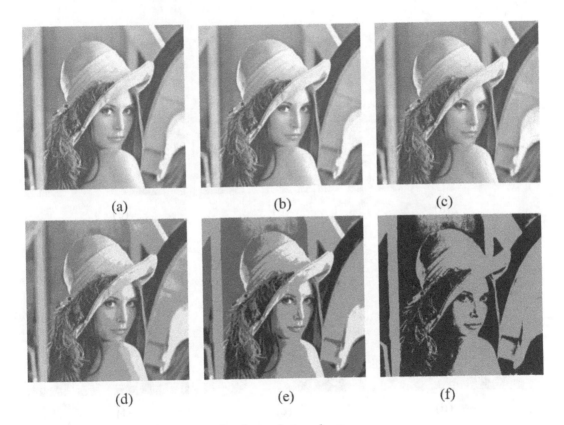

(a)   (b)   (c)

(d)   (e)   (f)

FIGURE 1.5 The effect of image amplitude resolution changes.

TABLE 1.2 A Set of Images with Varying Numbers of Gray Level

Figure 1.5	(a)	(b)	(c)	(d)	(e)	(f)
Spatial resolution	512×512	512×512	512×512	512×512	512×512	512×512
Number of gray levels	256	64	16	8	4	2
Amount of data/bit	67108864	16777216	4194304	2097152	1048576	524288
Ratio of data volume		4::1	4::1	2::1	2::1	2::1

and some false contours can be seen in Figure 1.5c. This phenomenon becomes obvious in Figure 1.5d, can be seen everywhere in Figure 1.5e, and Figure 1.5f has the effect of woodcut painting.

The previous discussion and results show the effects of changes in N and k on the image quality, separately, and they may also change at the same time.

Figure 1.6 shows a group of images with simultaneous changes in the spatial resolution and the amplitude resolution. Among them, the spatial resolution, number of gray levels, and data volume of each image are shown in the columns in Table 1.3, and the data volume ratio between two adjacent images is also given between the corresponding two columns. Referred to Table 1.3, the effect of simultaneous changes in image spatial resolution and gray levels can be seen from Figure 1.6.

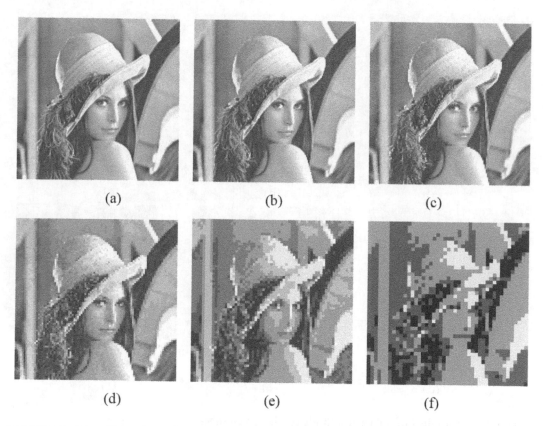

FIGURE 1.6 The effect of simultaneous changes in image spatial resolution and gray level.

TABLE 1.3 A Set of Images with Changes Both in Spatial Resolutions and Gray Levels

Figure 1.6	(a)	(b)	(c)	(d)	(e)	(f)
Spatial resolution	256×256	181×181	128×128	90×90	64×64	45×45
Number of gray levels	256	64	32	16	8	4
Amount of data/bit	16777216	2096704	524288	129600	32768	8100
Ratio of data volume		8::1	4::1	4::1	4::1	4::1

Since the spatial resolution and amplitude resolution of the image decrease at the same time, the image quality decreases faster here.

1.1.4 Half-Tone and Dithering Technology

To further understand the relationship between image spatial resolution and amplitude resolution and image visual quality, let's look at the half-tone technology and dithering technology commonly used in image printouts. Their principles are also very helpful for understanding the concept of images and pixels.

1.1.4.1 Half-Tone Output Technology

General printing equipment can only directly output binary images. For example, the gray-scale output of a laser printer has only two levels (either printing, outputting black; or not printing, outputting white). To output a grayscale image on a binary image output device and maintain its original grayscale level, a technique called half-tone output is often used.

Half-tone output technology can be regarded as a technology that converts grayscale images into binary images. It converts various gray scales in the intended output image into a binary point mode so that the grayscale image can be output by a printing device that can only directly output binary points. At the same time, it takes advantage of the integrated characteristics of the human eye, by controlling the form of the output binary point pattern (including number, size, shape, etc.) to give people a visual sense of multiple gray levels. In other words, the image output by the half-tone output technology is still a binary image at a very fine scale, but due to the spatial local averaging effect of the eyes, what is perceived is a grayscale image at a coarser scale. For example, in a binary image, the gray level of each pixel is only white or black, but from a certain distance, the unit perceived by the human eye is composed of multiple pixels, then the gray level perceived by the human eye is the average gray level of all pixels in this unit (proportional to the number of black pixels).

Half-tone output technology is mainly divided into two types: amplitude modulation (AM) technology and frequency modulation (FM) technology, which will be introduced separately below.

1. Amplitude modulation

In the beginning, the half-tone output technology proposed and used displays of different gray levels by adjusting the size of the output black dots, which can be called *amplitude modulation* (AM) half-tone output technology. For example, the pictures in the early newspapers used ink dots of different sizes on the grid to represent the gray scale. When viewed from a certain distance, a group of small ink dots can produce a brighter gray scale visual effect, while a group of large ink dots can produce a darker gray scale visual effect. In practice, the size of ink dots is inversely proportional to the gray scale being represented, that is, the dots printed in the bright image region are small, and the dots printed in the dark image region are larger. When the ink dot is small enough and the observation distance is long enough, the human eye can obtain a relatively continuous and smooth gray-scale image according to the integrated characteristics. In general, the resolution of pictures in newspapers is about 100 dots per inch (DPI), while the resolution of pictures in books or magazines is about 300 DPI.

In amplitude modulation, the binary points are regularly arranged. The size of these dots varies according to the gray scale to be represented, and the shape of the dots is not a decisive factor. For example, on a laser printer, it simulates different gray scales by controlling the proportion of ink coverage, and the shape of the ink dots is not strictly controlled. When the amplitude modulation technology is used, the effect of the output binary point mode not only depends on the size of each point but also depends on the size of the grid interval. The smaller the interval, the higher the output resolution. The interval size of the grid is limited by the resolution of the printer (measured in DPI).

2. Frequency modulation

In *frequency modulation* (FM), half-tone output technology, the size of the output black dot is fixed, but its spatial distribution (the interval between dots or the appearance frequency of dots in a certain region) depends on the desired gray scale. If the distribution is dense, one will get a darker gray; if the distribution is sparse, one will get a brighter gray. In other words, to represent a darker gray scale, many dots arranged in close proximity are used (they combine into a printing unit, also called a printing dot, which corresponds to a pixel in the image). Compared with the AM half-tone output technology, the FM half-tone output technology can better eliminate the Moiré mode problem caused by the superposition of two or more regular patterns in the AM half-tone output technology (Lau and Arce 2001). The main disadvantage of the FM half-tone output technology is related to the increase in dot gain. Dot gain is the increase in the size of the printing unit relative to the size of the original unit, which leads to a reduction or compression of the grayscale range of the printed image, and this reduces details and contrast.

In recent years, with the increase in printer resolution (>1,200 dpi), FM half-tone output technology has reached its limit. People began to study the combination of AM half-tone output technology and FM half-tone output technology to obtain a point set whose size and interval both change as the output gray-level changes. In other words, at this time, the size of the printing unit and the interval between the basic dots are changed with the required gray scale. In this way, the spatial resolution comparable to the AM half-tone output technology can be produced, and the effect of removing the Moiré mode similar to the FM half-tone output technology can also be obtained.

1.1.4.2 Half-Tone Output Mask

A specific implementation method of half-tone output is to first subdivide the image output unit and combine the adjacent basic binary points to form the output unit so that each output unit contains several basic binary points. Let some basic binary points output black while other basic binary points output white to get different grayscale effects. In other words, to output different gray levels, a set of masks/templates needs to be established, and each mask corresponds to an output unit. Divide each mask into regular grids, and each grid corresponds to a basic binary point. By adjusting each basic binary point to black or white, each mask can output a different grayscale so as to achieve the purpose of outputting grayscale images.

If a mask is divided into 2×2 grids, five different gray levels can be output according to the way shown in Figure 1.7. If a mask is divided into 3×3 grids, ten different gray scales can be output according to the way shown in Figure 1.8. If a mask is divided into 4×4 grids, 17 different gray scales can be output according to the way shown in Figure 1.9. By analogy, if a mask is divided into $n \times n$ grids, then $n^2 + 1$ different gray levels can be output.

Because there are $C_k^n = n! / (n-k)! k!$ different methods for putting k points into n units, the arrangement of black points in these figures is not unique. Note that if a grid is black at a certain gray level, it will still be black in all outputs greater than that gray level.

Divide the mask into grids according to the above method, then to output 256 gray levels, a mask needs to be divided into 16×16 units, that is, 16×16 positions are used to represent one pixel. It can be seen that the spatial resolution of the output image will be greatly affected. It can be seen that the half-tone output technology is only worth using when the gray value output by the output device itself is limited, and it is a reduction in spatial resolution in exchange for an increase in amplitude resolution. Assuming that each pixel in a 2×2 matrix can be white or black, each pixel requires one bit. Regarding this 2×2 matrix as a half-tone output unit, this unit needs 4 bits and can output 5 gray scales (16 modes),

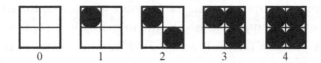

FIGURE 1.7   Divide a mask into 2×2 grids to output five gray scales.

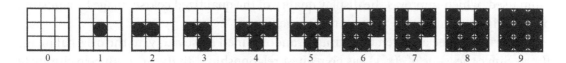

FIGURE 1.8   Divide a mask into 3×3 grids to output ten gray scales.

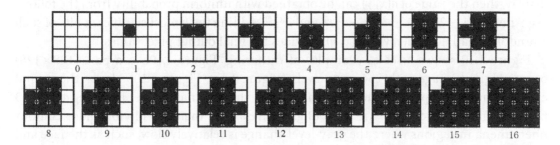

FIGURE 1.9   Divide a mask into 4×4 grids to output 17 gray levels.

which are 0/4, 1/4, 2/4, 3/4, and 4/4 (or written as 0, 1, 2, 3, and 4). However, if a pixel is represented by four bits, the pixel can have 16 gray levels. From this point of view, when the half-tone output uses the same storage unit, if the number of output levels increases, the number of output units will decrease.

To maintain the sharpness of the details in the image, it is necessary to have more lines per inch; at the same time, to represent these details, it also needs to have more brightness levels. This requires the printer to be able to print a large number of very small dots. Dividing a template into 8×8 grids can print 65 gray scales. For printing at 125 lines per inch, this corresponds to 8×125 = 1,000 dpi. In most applications, this is the lower limit of the printed image. Color printing requires smaller dots, and high-quality printing often requires 2,400–3,000 dpi.

When outputting images on different media, the required resolutions are often different. For example, when an image is displayed on the screen, the number of rows per inch generally corresponds to the number of grids per inch. When displaying images in newspapers, a resolution of at least 85 lines per inch is often used; for magazines or books, a resolution of at least 133 lines or 175 lines per inch is often used.

1.1.4.3 Dithering Technology

Half-tone output technology improves the resolution of the image amplitude by reducing the spatial resolution of the image or sacrificing the number of spatial points of the image to increase the number of gray levels of the image. It can be seen from the above discussion that if one wants to output an image with more gray levels, the spatial resolution of the image will be greatly reduced; if one wants to maintain a certain spatial resolution, the output gray level will be relatively small. That is, if one wants to preserve the spatial details, the number of gray levels cannot be too much. However, when the gray level of an image is relatively small, the visual quality of the image will be relatively poor, such as the appearance of false contours. To improve the quality of the image, *dithering* technology is often used, which improves the display quality of the quantized coarse image by adjusting or changing the amplitude value of the image.

Dithering can be achieved by adding a random small noise $d(x, y)$ to the original image $f(x, y)$. Since the value of $d(x, y)$ has no regular relationship with $f(x, y)$, it can help eliminate false contours in the image caused by insufficient quantization.

A specific method of dithering is as follows. Let b be the number of bits in the image display, then the value of $d(x, y)$ can be obtained with uniform probability from the following 5 numbers: $-2^{(6-b)}$, $-2^{(5-b)}$, 0, $-2^{(5-b)}$, and $2^{(6-b)}$. Adding the b most significant bits of such a random small noise $d(x, y)$ to $f(x, y)$ provides the final output pixel values.

Figure 1.10 shows a set of examples of dithering. Figure 1.10a is a part (128×128) of an original image with 256 gray levels (Figure 1.1a); Figure 1.10b shows the output effect of half-tone printing at the same size as the original image, by using the 3×3 half-tone mask. Since there are only 10 gray levels now, there are obvious false contour phenomena in regions where the gray-level change is relatively slow, such as the face and shoulders (the original continuously changing gray levels seem to have sharply changed gray levels now). Figure 1.10c is the result of adjusting the original image using dithering

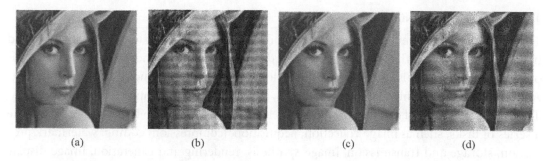

FIGURE 1.10 Example for dithering.

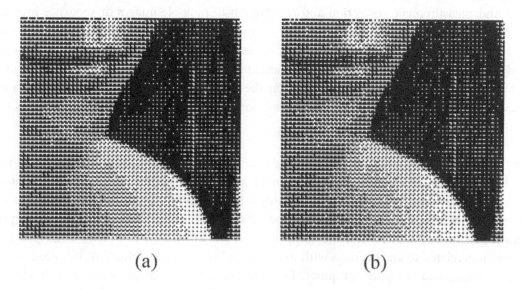

FIGURE 1.11 Comparison of half-tone image and dithering half-tone image.

technology, and the superimposed dithering value is evenly distributed in the interval [−8, 8]; Figure 1.10d shows the output effect of half-tone printing of the same size image after the dithering technology is used for improvement. The false contour phenomenon has been amended.

Figure 1.11a and b, respectively, show the partial images (42×42) corresponding to the half-tone image of Figure 1.10b and the dithering half-tone image of Figure 1.10d because each pixel in the original image is represented by a matrix of 3×3 units, so the image at this time includes 126×126 units. It can be seen from the figure that the relatively regular false contour becomes irregular due to dithering, and therefore it is not easy to observe.

It can be seen from the above example that the use of dithering technology can eliminate some false contour phenomena that are generated in the image at the smooth gray level region due to the use of too few gray levels. According to the dithering principle, the larger the superimposed dither value, the more obvious the effect of eliminating false contours. However, the superimposition of the dither value also brings noise to the image, and the larger the dither value, the greater the influence of noise.

1.2 IMAGE TECHNOLOGY

The utilization of images has a long history, and the use of computers to process, analyze, and interpret digital images has a history of several decades, so many technologies have been developed. *Image technology* is a general term for various image-related technologies in a broad sense. At present, people mainly study digital images, and mainly apply computer image technology. This includes the use of computers and other electronic equipment to carry out and complete a series of tasks, such as image collection, acquisition, (compression) coding, watermark protection, storage and transmission, image synthesis, rendering and generation, image display and output, image transformation, enhancement, restoration and reconstruction of images, image segmentation, object detection, representation and description of images, feature extraction and measurement, correction and registration of multiple images or sequence images, 3-D scenery reconstruction and restoration, image database establishment, indexing and extraction, image classification, representation and recognition, image model establishment and matching, image and scene interpretation and understanding, and decision-making and behavior planning based on them. In addition, the image technology can also include the hardware design and production technology for accomplishing the above-mentioned functions.

1.2.1 Image Engineering

The above-mentioned technologies can be unified together and called *image engineering* (IE) technology. IE is a new interdisciplinary subject that systematically studies various image theories, technologies, and applications (Zhang 1996). From the perspective of its research methods, it can learn from many disciplines, such as mathematics, physics, physiology, psychology, electronics, and computer science. From the perspective of its research scope, it is related to and overlaps with many disciplines, such as pattern recognition, computer vision, and computer graphics. In addition, the research progress of IE is closely related to theories and technologies such as artificial intelligence, neural networks, genetic algorithms, fuzzy logic, and machine learning. Its development and application are related to and indivisible with medicine, remote sensing, communication, document processing, industrial automation, and intelligent transportation, and so on.

If considering the characteristics of various IE technologies, they can be divided into three levels that are both connected and differentiated (as shown in Figure 1.12): *image processing* (IP) technology (Zhang 2017a), *Image analysis* (IA) technology (Zhang 2017b), and *Image understanding* (IU) technology (Zhang 2017c).

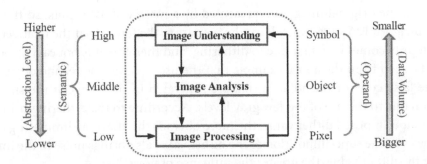

FIGURE 1.12   Schematic diagram of three levels of image engineering.

IP emphasizes the transformation between images. Although people often use IP to refer to various image technologies, the more narrowly defined IP mainly refers to various processing of images to improve the visual effect of the image and lay the foundation for automatic recognition or to compress and encode the image to reduce the storage required space or transmission time to meet the requirements of a given transmission path.

IA is mainly used to detect and measure objects of interest in the image to obtain their objective information to establish a description of the image. If IP is a process from image to image, then IA is a process from image to data. Here, the data can be the result of the measurement of the object feature, or a symbolic representation based on the measurement. They describe the characteristics and properties of the object in the image.

IU is focused on further studying the nature of the objects in the image and their inter-relationships based on IA and obtaining an understanding of the meaning of the image content and the interpretation of the original objective scene. If IA is mainly based on the observer-centered study of the objective world (mainly studying observable things), then IU is to a certain extent centered on the objective world, and with the help of knowledge, experience, etc., to grasp and interpret the whole objective world (including things that are not directly observed).

In summary, IP, IA, and IU have their own characteristics in terms of abstraction and data volume, and their operation objects and semantic levels are different. See Figure 1.12 for their interrelationships. IP is a relatively low-level operation, which is mainly processed at the pixel level of the image, and the amount of processed data is very large. IA enters the middle level. Segmentation and feature extraction transform the original image described by pixels into a more concise description of the object. IU is mainly a high-level operation. The object of the operation is basically the symbols abstracted from the description, and its treating processes and methods have many similarities with human thinking and reasoning. In addition, it can be seen from Figure 1.12 that the amount of data gradually decreases as the degree of abstraction increases. In particular, the original image data is gradually transformed into a more organized and more abstract representation through a series of operating procedures. In this process, semantics are continuously introduced, the objects of operation are changed, and the amount of data is compressed. On the other hand, high-level operations have a guiding effect on low-level operations and can improve the efficiency of low-level operations.

1.2.2 Classification of Image Technology

Beginning in 1996, the author carried out year-by-year statistics on the IE literature (more than 16,000 articles in total) for 15 important domestic academic journals and has analyzed and reviewed its development. This survey task has been conducted for 26 consecutive years. The review series formed by yearly overview reflects the evolution of IE to a certain extent and shows the development trends of IE. Some summary references can be found in (Zhang 1996, 2002, 2009b, 2015, 2018a, b).

The review series also carried out *image technology classification* (currently includes 23 sub-categories). Image technology in IP has six subcategories, IA has five subcategories, and IU has five subcategories. Other subcategories belong to technology applications. The classification of the three levels is shown in Table 1.4.

TABLE 1.4   The Current Image Technology in the Three Levels of Image Processing, Analysis, and Understanding

Three Layers	Image Technology Categories and Names
Image Processing	Image acquisition (including various imaging methods, image capturing, representation and storage, camera calibration, etc.)
	Image reconstruction (including image reconstruction from projection, indirect imaging, etc.)
	Image enhancement/image restoration (including transformation, filtering, restoration, repair, replacement, correction, visual quality evaluation, etc.)
	Image/video coding and compression (including algorithm research, implementation and improvement of related international standards, etc.)
	Image information security (including digital watermarking, information hiding, image authentication and forensics, etc.)
	Image multi-resolution processing (including super-resolution reconstruction, image decomposition and interpolation, resolution conversion, etc.)
Image Analysis	Image segmentation and primitive detection (including edges, corners, control points, points of interest, etc.)
	Object representation, object description, feature measurement (including binary image morphology analysis, etc.)
	Object feature extraction and analysis (including color, texture, shape, space, structure, motion, saliency, attributes, etc.)
	Object detection and object recognition (including object 2-D positioning, tracking, extraction, identification and classification, etc.)
	Human body biological feature extraction and verification (including detection, positioning and recognition of human body, face and organs, etc.)
Image Understanding	Image matching and fusion (including registration of sequence and stereo image, mosaic, etc.)
	Scene restoration (including 3-D scene representation, modeling, reconstruction, etc.)
	Image perception and interpretation (including semantic description, scene model, machine learning, cognitive reasoning, etc.)
	Content-based image/video retrieval (including corresponding labeling, classification, etc.)
	Spatial-temporal techniques (including high-dimensional motion analysis, object 3-D posture detection, spatial-temporal tracking, behavior judgment and behavior understanding, etc.)

1.2.3 IP System

This book is focused on IP technology. To solve the problems in actual image applications, it is necessary to combine various IP technologies to build an application system. The composition of a basic *image processing system* can be represented in Figure 1.13. The seven modules in Figure 1.13 have specific functions, namely image acquisition (imaging), image generation (synthesis), IP, image display, image printing, image communication and image storage. Among them, image acquisition and image generation constitute the input of the system, and the output of the system includes image display and image printing. It should be pointed out that not every actual IP system must or only include all these modules. For some special IP systems, some modules may be omitted, but other modules may also be included.

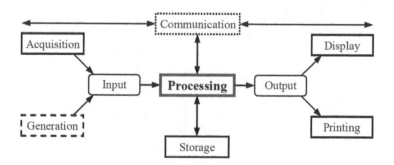

FIGURE 1.13   Schematic diagram of the structure of the image processing system.

In Figure 1.13, each module may use many different technologies, but this book focuses on IP technologies in its narrow sense (i.e., the parts in the processing module), so for other modules, except for the simple introduction above, they will not be included in the following because they are out of the scope of this book. For an in-depth introduction to related topics, interested readers can refer to other books, such as (Pratt 2007; Zhang 2009a; Sonka et al. 2014; Zhang 2017a; Gonzalez and Woods 2018; Zhang 2021).

1.3 CHARACTERISTICS OF THIS BOOK

There are many books about image technology, so what are the special characteristics of this book? Let's have the discussion from the three aspects of writing motivation, material selection and contents, as well as structure and arrangement.

1.3.1 Writing Motivation

IE covers a wide range of fields and contains many technologies. It is a huge project to fully understand and master image technology step by step. However, in many image applications and related scientific research and development work, it is often necessary to use specific and specialized image technology to complete the task as soon as possible. Many textbooks introduce a lot of image technology little by little from shallow to deep, but it takes a long time for readers to reach a certain height and depth through learning one after another. Although some monographs have in-depth introduction to specific image technology, they require readers to have a better foundation at the beginning, so they are not suitable for readers who are initially exposed to image technology and have a special task to perform.

Refer to the schematic diagram in Figure 1.14. A complete introduction to IE should include three parts (similar to any discipline and field), or three layers (corresponding to the three parts from bottom to top in the figure): first layer: essential concepts and basic principles; second layer: specific methods and practical techniques; third layer: research frontiers and latest development. In general, various textbooks mainly focus on the first layer (as shown by the lower-middle triangle in Figure 1.14) and cover mostly essential concepts and basic principles. If one starts with the essential concepts and learns basic principles little by little, the foundation will be relatively solid, but it will take a long time to reach the second layer. It will be difficult for people in different working fields who only

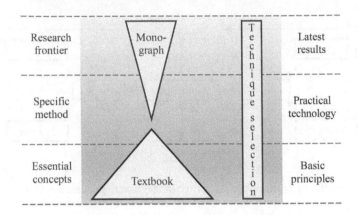

FIGURE 1.14   A complete introduction to the three layers of image processing.

need certain skills, and many other concepts and principles are not used. The monographs mainly focus on the third layer (as shown by the upper-middle triangle in Figure 1.14) and mainly focus on the research frontiers and latest development, which can be used as a reference for the cutting-edge innovative scientific research, but they have higher requirements for the reader's relevant foundation and need to have a more professional foreshadowing, and some technologies and methods may not be mature enough to solve the current real world problems in practical applications.

This book attempts to combine the strengths of the textbook and monograph, and fill the gap between them, to meet the needs of readers who do not have the foundation of comprehensive image technology but need to use image techniques to solve specific tasks. To this end, according to the classification of image technology, we first select some of the more recently applied techniques to meet the needs of readers with specific applications; and then provide the introduction of each type of technology step by step, starting with the basic principles, so that readers with less fundamental knowledge can learn. We call it a selection of techniques, and for these selected techniques, three layers are penetrated, as shown in the rectangle on the right of Figure 1.14. When introducing these techniques, it not only starts overviewing the essential concepts and basic principles, providing enough introduction and explanation of current specific methods and practical techniques but also involves some discussion on research frontier trends and latest results in conjunction with the development of technical methods.

1.3.2 Material Selection and Contents

This book focuses on (narrowly) IP (refer to Zhang 2017a) and selects seven types of technical fields and directions that are currently receiving widespread attention and are commonly used in many applications for introduction. They are as follows: (i) Image de-noising, (ii) Image de-blurring, (iii) Image repairing, (iv) Image de-fogging, (v) Image reconstruction from projection, (vi) Image watermarking, and (vii) Image super-resolution. Related terms appearing in the book can be found in (Zhang 2021).

Each chapter focuses on one type of technology. The following summarizes the contents of these seven chapters separately:

Chapter 2 introduces image denoising technology. Based on the analysis of common noise types and characteristics, it first summarizes some typical methods based on image filtering to eliminate noise and then discusses the selective filtering framework that can specifically eliminate different types of noise. It also introduces the switching median filtering methods and their improvements that have received a lot of research recently. Finally, some recent developments and further research are included.

Chapter 3 introduces image deblurring technology. After explaining the traditional image deblurring technology, the estimation of motion blur kernel with the help of a neural network and the deblurring method for low-resolution images are discussed. Finally, some recent developments and further research are included.

Chapter 4 introduces image inpainting technology. First, the origin of the name is explained, and then an algorithm combining sparse expression, a weighted sparse non-negative matrix factorization algorithm and a context-driven hybrid method are introduced. Some recent developments have been introduced. Finally, some recent developments and further research are included.

Chapter 5 introduces the image defogging technology. First, it introduces the typical dark channel priori defogging algorithm and discusses some improvement techniques for its shortcomings. It also introduces the algorithm that focuses on reducing the distortion and the subjective and objective evaluation of the dehazing effect. Some recent developments have been introduced. Finally, some recent developments and further research are included.

Chapter 6 introduces techniques for image reconstruction from projections. First introduced different projection reconstruction methods, analyzed the principle of reconstructing images from projection, and then introduced methods such as inverse Fourier transform reconstruction, inverse projection reconstruction, and algebraic reconstruction in turn. Some recent developments have been introduced. Finally, some recent developments and further research are included.

Chapter 7 introduces image watermarking technology. After introducing the watermark embedding and detection process, the watermarking technology in the discrete cosine transform domain and the watermarking technology in the discrete wavelet transform domain are introduced respectively. Some recent developments have been introduced. Finally, some recent developments and further research are included.

Chapter 8 introduces super-resolution technology. After introducing the super-resolution restoration based on a single image and the super-resolution reconstruction based on multiple images, the super-resolution technique based on learning and the reconstruction technique based on local constrained linear coding are introduced. Some recent developments have been introduced. Finally, some recent developments and further research are included.

This book assumes that the reader has a certain background in science and engineering, and has some understanding of linear algebra, matrices, signal processing, statistics, and probability. It would be better if there was certain knowledge of some basic image concepts, such as pixels, image representation, image display, image transformation, image filtering, and so on. It will be helpful to have some basic elementary information of signal processing because 2-D image can be seen as an augmentation of 1-D signal, and IP is an extension of signal processing. This book is dominated by image technology to solve practical problems, and the work experience and basic skills of practitioners in related industries are also very useful.

This book does not give too much consideration to the content from a comprehensive and systematic point of view, rather, it only focuses on several specific technologies and provides information from the shallower to the deeper. Although it is not written as a pure textbook, it can be used as a supplement to the textbook, especially for in-depth introductions to specific directions. This book is not a monograph in the traditional sense. It does not only emphasize advanced and real-time features but mainly introduces some of the more mature technology methods in the near future (and also considers some of the latest scientific research results). This book attempts to cover the vertical range from introductory textbooks to research monographs in selected technical directions to meet the specific needs of readers (Figure 1.14).

1.3.3 Structure and Arrangement

The styles of the following chapters of this book are relatively consistent. At the beginning of each chapter, in addition to the introduction of the basic concepts and overall content, some application fields and occasions of the corresponding technologies are listed, which are reflected in the idea of application services; there is also an overview of each section to grasp the context of the whole chapter.

There are some similarities in the arrangement and structure of the body content of each chapter. Each chapter has multiple sections, which can be divided into the following three parts from beginning to end (corresponding to the three levels in Figure 1.14).

1. Principle and technology overview

    The first section at the beginning of each chapter has the contents as in typical textbooks. It introduces the principle, history, use, method overview and development of the image technology. The goal is to give more comprehensive and basic information (a lot of examples and demonstrations can be found in Zhang (2011)), most of which come from professional textbooks (refer to (Zhang 2017a)).

2. Description of specific technical methods

    The next few sections in the middle of each chapter have the contents combined from textbooks and monographs. They introduce several related typical technologies, which are described in detail in terms of methods. The goal is to give some ideas that can effectively and efficiently solve the problems faced by this type of image technology and provide solutions for practical applications. These sections can have a certain progressive relationship or a relatively independent parallel relationship. Many contents are mainly extracted from the literature in journals or conference papers. Most of them are followed up and researched, but they have not been written into professional textbooks or books.

TABLE 1.5 The Classification Table of the Corresponding Sections of the Text of Each Chapter in This Book

#	Technology	Principle	Typical Technique	Progress/Trends
Chapter 2	Image denoising	Section 2.1	Sections 2.2 ~ 2.4	Section 2.5
Chapter 3	Image deblurring	Section 3.1	Sections 3.2 ~ 3.4	Section 3.5
Chapter 4	Image repairing	Section 4.1	Sections 4.2 ~ 4.4	Section 4.5
Chapter 5	Image defogging	Section 5.1	Sections 5.2 ~ 5.5	Section 5.6
Chapter 6	Image reconstruction from projection	Section 6.1	Sections 6.2 ~ 6.6	Section 6.7
Chapter 7	Image watermarking	Section 7.1	Sections 7.2 ~ 7.4	Section 7.5
Chapter 8	Image super-resolution	Section 8.1	Sections 8.2 ~ 8.4	Section 8.5

3. Introduction to recent developments and directions

The last section of each chapter is more research-oriented. It is based on the analysis and review of relevant new documents in some important journals or conference proceedings in recent years. The goal is to provide some of the latest relevant information on focusing techniques and to help understand the progress and trends in the corresponding technology.

The arrangement of the main text in sections of each chapter is shown in Table 1.5.

From the perspective of understanding the technical overview, one can only look at the sections of the principle introduction. If one wants to solve practical problems, one needs to learn some typical techniques. To master the technology more deeply, one can also refer to the recent progress/trends and look at more references.

REFERENCES

Bow, S. T. 2002. *Pattern Recognition and Image Preprocessing*, 2nd Ed. New York: Marcel Dekker, Inc.

Gonzalez, R. C., R. E. Woods. 2018. *Digital Image Processing*, 4th Ed. UK, Cambridge: Pearson.

Lau, D. L., and G. R. Arce. 2001. Digital halftoning. In: Mitra S. K., and Sicuranza G. L., Eds. *Nonlinear Image Processing*, Chapter 13. Cambridge, MD: Academic Press.

Pratt, W. K. 2007. *Digital Image Processing: PIKS Scientific Inside*, 4th Ed. Hoboken, NJ: Wiley Interscience.

Sonka, M., V. Hlavac, and R. Boyle. 2014. *Image Processing, Analysis, and Machine Vision*, 4th Ed, Singapore: Cengage Learning.

Zhang, Y.-J. 1996. Image engineering and bibliography in China. In *Technical Digest of International Symposium on Information Science and Technology*, pp. 158–160.

Zhang, Y.-J. 2002. Image engineering and related publications. *International Journal of Image and Graphics*, 2(3): 441–452.

Zhang, Y.-J. 2009a. *Image Engineering: Processing, Analysis, and Understanding*. Singapore: Cengage Learning.

Zhang, Y.-J. 2009b. A study of image engineering. In: Khosrow-Pour M., Ed. *Encyclopedia of Information Science and Technology*, 2nd Ed., Vol. VII: Chapter 575 (pp. 3608–3615).

Zhang, Y.-J. 2011. A net courseware for "Image Processing". *Proceedings of the 6th ICCGI*, pp. 143–147.

Zhang, Y.-J. 2015. Statistics on image engineering literatures. In: Khosrow-Pour M., Ed. *Encyclopedia of Information Science and Technology*, 3rd Ed., Chapter 595 (pp. 6030–6040).

Zhang, Y.-J. 2017a. *Image Engineering, Vol.1: Image Processing.* Germany: De Gruyter.

Zhang, Y.-J. 2017b. *Image Engineering, Vol.2: Image Analysis.* Germany: De Gruyter.

Zhang, Y.-J. 2017c. *Image Engineering, Vol.3: Image Understanding.* Germany: De Gruyter.

Zhang, Y.-J. 2018a. Development of image engineering in the last 20 years. In: Khosrow-Pour M., Ed. *Encyclopedia of Information Science and Technology,* 4th Ed., Chapter 113 (pp. 1319–1330).

Zhang, Y.-J. 2018b. An overview of image engineering in recent years. *Proceedings of the 21st IEEE International Conference on Computational Science and Engineering,* pp. 119–122.

Zhang, Y.-J. 2021. *Handbook of Image Engineering.* Singapore: Springer Nature.

## CHAPTER 2

Image De-Noising

NOISE IS A TERM borrowed directly from signal processing. Noise in the image is a very common image degradation, which is often produced during the image recording process, and can also be generated during the image processing or transmission process (Zhang 2017). Noise can come from the collection environment, collection equipment, measurement errors, counting errors, and so on. Noise is a relatively broad concept. There are many types of noise, each with its own characteristics. Noise can be defined and described not only in terms of intensity from a physical point of view but also in terms of human susceptibility from a physiological point of view. Image noise is often thought to be annoying because it affects the viewing and acceptance of content of interest.

There are many types of noise, and noise elimination is very common in image applications, such as:

1. The snowflakes on the television will affect people's visual experience and reduce the viewer's ability to understand the content of the program.

2. The noise in the image reduces the quality of the image and hinders the acceptance of the information in the image.

3. The influence of haze on outdoor scenes can also be regarded as a kind of noise that reduces visibility. For images collected on a haze day, in order to fully understand and obtain information about the scene, it is often necessary to eliminate the haze noise first.

Noise can be eliminated using image enhancement technology or using image restoration technology. Although different enhancement techniques can be used according to the general understanding of noise characteristics, if one has a better grasp of a specific noise model, it is possible to obtain better results by using image restoration techniques.

The contents of each section of this chapter are arranged as follows.

Section 2.1 discusses a number of common sources and types of noise, including thermal noise, shot noise, flicker noise, and colored noise, and then analyzes the characteristics of Gaussian noise, impulse noise, uniform noise, and Rayleigh noise.

DOI: 10.1201/9781003241416-2

Section 2.2 introduces the principle of noise elimination technology based on image filtering, as well as discusses spatial noise filters (including average, order, and hybrid filters) and frequency domain noise filters (including band-pass, band-stop, and notch filtering), respectively.

Section 2.3 introduces a selective filter that combines different types of filters. When the image is affected by both Gaussian noise and impulse noise, based on the detection of the positions of different noises in the image, the corresponding filters can be selected to eliminate different noises.

Section 2.4 discusses a type of switching median filter specifically used to eliminate impulse noise. It focuses on the noise detection steps that distinguish the pixels affected by noise from the pixels not affected by noise based on the noise model. On this basis, only the pixels affected/corrupted by noise are processed, and a good de-noising effect can be achieved.

Section 2.5 provides a brief introduction to some technique developments and promising research directions in the last year.

2.1 NOISE TYPES AND CHARACTERISTICS

There are many sources and types of noise, and they all have different characteristics. From the perspective of research and application, a certain classification of noise is needed.

2.1.1 Different Noises

The noise in the image can be defined as the undesired part of the image or the unwanted part of the image. Noise has a certain degree of randomness, like snowflake dots on a TV screen; however, noise may also have certain regularity, such as when the noise source has a certain period. When the TV image produces independent bright spots due to the interference of the motor of the refrigerator or the interference of the engine of the passing motorcycle, the noise has both random and regular characteristics. In general, noise will cause uncertain degradation of image quality.

For the signal, *noise* is a kind of external interference. However, noise itself is also a kind of signal; it only carries information about the noise source. If the noise has nothing to do with the signal, it is impossible to predict the characteristics of the noise based on the characteristics of the signal. But on the other hand, if the noise is independent, the noise can be considered separately when there is no required signal at all. Some kinds of noise are essentially related to the signal, but the relationship is often very complicated at this time. In many cases, noise is seen as an uncertain, random phenomenon, and the methods of probability theory and statistics are mainly used to deal with it. It should be noted that the required signal itself, such as thermal microwave or infrared radiation used for ground measurement, may also have randomness. From the preceding discussion, we can see that the noise in the image does not need to be opposed to the signal; instead, it can be closely related to the signal. If the signal is removed, the noise may also change.

The problem of noise is often not completely regarded as a purely scientific problem or a purely mathematical problem. Since noise mainly affects humans felling, it is important to consider at least human response in the definition and measurement of noise. For example, one person's noise may be the signal of another person, and the reverse is also true. The effect of noise disturbing people's attention and receiving ability is first related to its own characteristics, but it is also related to people's physical and psychological factors. For example, when watching TV, black noise (i.e., black dots on the screen) has far less impact than white noise (such as snowflakes).

In many cases, the (random/regular) characteristics of noise are not very important, what is important is its intensity, or people are mostly concerned with its intensity. The commonly used term *signal-to-noise ratio* (SNR) refers to the ratio of signal strength to noise strength. The SNR is an important quality indicator of an amplifier or communication system. The typical SNR is defined by the energy ratio (or voltage-squared ratio):

$$SNR = 10\log_{10}\left(\frac{V_s^2}{V_n^2}\right) \tag{2.1}$$

where V_s is the signal voltage and V_n is the noise voltage. But in some specific applications, there are also some variations. For example, in TV applications, the signal voltage V_s uses peak-to-peak value and the noise voltage V_n uses root mean square (RMS) as the unit. The value obtained at this time is 9.03 dB higher than the value obtained in both root-mean-square units.

The SNR, defined as follows, is used for control when synthesizing images (Kitchen and Rosenfeld 1981):

$$SNR = \left(\frac{C_{ob}}{\sigma}\right)^2 \tag{2.2}$$

where C_{ob} is the gray-scale contrast between the object and the background, and σ is the noise mean square difference.

There are many reasons for the formation of noises, and their nature is also very different, such as:

1. Thermal noise

   Thermal noise is related to the absolute temperature of the object. The reason for this is that the molecules in any substance are always in motion driven by temperature, so the conductive carriers are thermally disturbed to produce noise. This kind of heat-induced noise is uniformly distributed from zero frequency to a very high-frequency range. It is generally believed that it can produce a spectrum with the same energy at different wavelengths (or anywhere in the spectrum, the energy within the same frequency interval is the same). This kind of noise is also called *Gaussian noise* (its spatial amplitude conforms to the Gaussian distribution) or *white noise* (its frequency covers the entire frequency spectrum).

2. Shot noise

   Shot noise is a kind of noise caused by non-uniform current flow. This non-uniformity is particularly noticeable when electrons are emitted from the hot cathode of a vacuum tube or the emitter of a semiconductor triode. For example, the current in the iconoscope changes in response to the random movement of the electrons as well as to the change of the image signal. In this way, there is actually an AC component in the DC component that should be stable. The emitted noise is also often called "roof rain" noise. It is also a Gaussian distributed noise, which can be quantified by the principles of statistics and probability.

3. Flicker noise

Flicker noise is also the result of the randomness of electronic motion. The flow of electrons or charges is not a continuous, perfect process. Their randomness will produce an AC component (random AC) that is difficult to quantify and measure. In the resistance composed of carbon, this randomness will be far greater than the value that can be estimated by general statistics, and it will be reflected in the image display as flickering and dimming. Flicker noise generally has a frequency spectrum that is inversely proportional to the frequency ($1/f$), so it is also called $1/f$ noise, which is usually obvious at low frequencies below 1,000 Hz. Some people call it pink noise. *Pink noise* has the same energy in the logarithmic frequency interval (e.g., the energy of pink noise is the same between 1 and 10 Hz and between 10 and 100 Hz).

4. Colored noise

Colored noise refers to broadband noise with a non-white spectrum. Typical examples are noise generated by moving cars, computer fans, electric drills, and so on. In addition, white noise will also be "colored" after passing through a certain channel and become colored noise. Figure 2.1 shows an example of two common colored noises: pink noise on the left and *brown noise* on the right. Compared with white noise, low-frequency components in colored noise occupy a larger proportion.

The above-mentioned noises are relatively common, but there are other kinds of noises, and different noises may also appear in an imaging process at the same time. Take the entire process of using CCD imaging as an example, where there are many kinds of noises: photon noise, thermal noise, on-chip electronic noise, amplification noise, quantization noise, and so on. Here, *photon noise* refers to the noise caused by the fluctuation of the number of photons in the range of continuous natural light reaching a pixel, and it is related to the characteristics of the light source, light path, and imaging environment. Thermal noise is

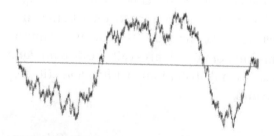 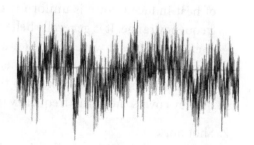

FIGURE 2.1 Example of pink noise and brown noise.

closely related to the working temperature of the CCD. As the working temperature of the CCD increases, more electrons are released from the silicon material of the CCD, and these electrons and the photoelectrons excited by the photon reaching the pixel cannot be distinguished by the brightness of quantizer. *On-chip electronic noise* is also called readout noise, which is proportional to the pixel readout rate of the CCD. The higher the readout rate, the more obvious the readout noise. *Amplified noise* refers to the noise caused by the amplifier. In general, the higher the gain, the greater the noise generated. The *quantization noise* corresponds to the error caused when the analog signal is converted into a digital signal. This is because no matter how many quantization bit values are used, the analog voltage value caused by the photoelectron in a single pixel cannot be exhausted.

2.1.2 Noise Characteristics and Description

Owing to the influence of noise, the gray scale of image pixels will change. Noise is often random, and the effect of random noise on a particular image is uncertain. In many cases, people can at most have some knowledge of statistical characteristics of this process, so noise is often described as a statistical process. Noise is often superimposed on the original image, which is called additive noise at this time; however, some noise is multiplied with the original image, which is called multiplicative noise at this time. If the gray level of the noise itself is regarded as a random variable, its distribution can be described by the *probability density function* (PDF). Several important noise probability density functions are introduced below.

2.1.2.1 Gaussian Noise

Gaussian noise is very common. The PDF of a Gaussian random variable z can be represented as:

$$p(z) = \frac{1}{\sqrt{2\pi}\,\sigma} \exp\left[-\frac{(z-\mu)^2}{2\sigma^2}\right] \tag{2.3}$$

where z represents the gray level, μ is the mean value of z, and σ is the standard deviation of z. An example of the Gaussian probability density function is shown in Figure 2.2. The gray value of Gaussian noise with Gaussian distribution characteristics is mostly

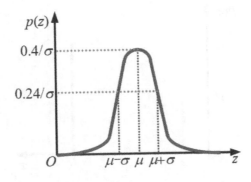

FIGURE 2.2   The probability density function of Gaussian noise.

concentrated near the mean value, and the function value decreases as the distance from the mean value increases.

Typical examples of Gaussian noise are the noise of electronic equipment or the noise of sensors (due to poor lighting or high temperature). The Gaussian noise model is relatively easy to handle mathematically, and many noises with a distribution close to the Gaussian distribution are also handled approximately by the Gaussian noise model. Gaussian distribution is also called normal distribution.

2.1.2.2 Impulse (Salt and Pepper) Noise

The PDF of random variables corresponding to *impulse noise* can be represented as:

$$p(z)=\begin{cases} P_a & \text{if} & z=a \\ P_b & \text{if} & z=b \\ 0 & \text{otherwise} \end{cases} \tag{2.4}$$

where P_a and P_b are the noise densities. An example of the probability density function of impulse noise is shown in Figure 2.3. Its distribution is equivalent to two delta pulses at $z = a$ and $z = b$.

In general, the noise pulse can be positive or negative. Because the impact of pulse is often greater than the intensity of the signal in the image, impulse noise is generally quantified into the ultimate gray scale in the image (displayed as white or black). In practice, it is generally assumed that both a and b are "saturated" values, that is, they take the maximum and minimum gray levels allowed by the image. If $b > a$, the pixel with gray level b is displayed as a white point in the image, and the pixel with gray level a is displayed as a black point in the image. If P_a or P_b is 0, impulse noise is called unipolar noise. If both P_a and P_b are not 0, especially when the two values are very close, impulse noise is like salt and pepper grains randomly scattered on the image. For this reason, bipolar impulse noise is also called *salt and pepper noise*. In the image display, negative pulses are displayed as black (pepper noise) and positive pulses are displayed as white (salt noise). For 8-bit images, there are $a = 0$ (black) and $b = 255$ (white). Error exchange, shot noise, and spike noise can all be described by the probability density function of impulse noise.

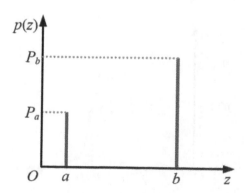

FIGURE 2.3 The probability density function of impulse noise.

2.1.2.3 Uniform Noise

The PDF of the random variable corresponding to *uniform noise* can be represented as (a and b are the upper and lower limits of the random variable value):

$$p(z) = \begin{cases} 1/(b-a) & \text{if} \quad a \leq z \leq b \\ 0 & \text{otherwise} \end{cases} \qquad (2.5)$$

The mean and variance of uniform noise are respectively:

$$\mu = (a+b)/2 \qquad (2.6)$$

$$\sigma^2 = (b-a)^2/12 \qquad (2.7)$$

An example of the probability density function of uniform noise is shown in Figure 2.4. The gray value of uniform noise is evenly distributed within the defined range, that is, statistically, the probability of all values appearing is equal.

Uniform noise density is often used as the basis of many random number generators. For example, it can be used to generate Gaussian noise.

2.1.2.4 Rayleigh Noise

The PDF of the random variable corresponding to *Rayleigh noise* can be expressed as (a and b are constants):

$$p(z) = \begin{cases} \dfrac{2}{b}(z-a)e^{-(z-a)^2/b} & \text{if} \quad z \geq a \\ 0 & \text{if} \quad z < a \end{cases} \qquad (2.8)$$

The mean and variance of Rayleigh noise are respectively:

$$\mu = a + \sqrt{\pi b/4} \qquad (2.9)$$

$$\sigma^2 = b(4-\pi)^2/4 \qquad (2.10)$$

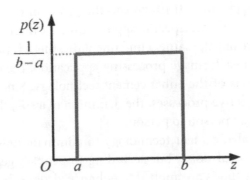

FIGURE 2.4 The probability density function of a uniform noise.

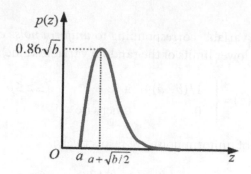

FIGURE 2.5   The probability density function of Rayleigh noise.

An example of the probability density function of Rayleigh noise is shown in Figure 2.5. The distribution of Rayleigh noise has a certain offset from the origin (determined by a) and the overall shape is toward the right (right tail).

In addition to the above-mentioned noise probability density functions, noise probability density functions such as exponent function and gamma function are also used when describing noise. Some noises need to use multiple noise probability density functions depending on the situation. For example, the common speckle noise in ultrasound tomography imaging systems is an example. When the number of scatters per unit is greater than 10, the speckle noise obeys the Rayleigh distribution with a SNR of 1.92; when the number of scatters per unit is very small, the speckle noise obeys the K distribution, which is also called the Rice distribution or generalized Rayleigh distribution (Rayleigh distribution is a special case). The Rice probability density function is an envelope form of a sine wave plus a narrow-band Gaussian distribution.

2.2 IMAGE FILTERING AND DE-NOISING

Image filtering and de-noising refers to the use of *image enhancement* techniques to eliminate noise (Zhang 2017). Image enhancement technology is the most basic and most commonly used image processing technology, and it is also often used as a pre-processing technique before using other image technologies. The purpose of image enhancement is to transform the processed image into an image with "better" visual quality and more "useful" for the particular application through specific processing of the image. Because the purpose and requirements of each specific application are different, the meanings of "better" and "useful" here are not the same. Fundamentally, there is no universal standard for image enhancement. For each image processing application, the observer is the ultimate judge of the pros and cons of the enhancement technology. Since visual inspection and evaluation are quite subjective processes, the definition of a so-called "good image" is not fixed and often varies from person to person.

When using image enhancement technology to eliminate noise, it does not pay special attention to the cause of noise, but according to people's general understanding of image quality, various methods are applied to enhance visual effects for image processing to reduce the impact of noise on image visual quality.

Noise elimination based on image enhancement mainly adopts filtering modes, which can be performed in the spatial domain or in the frequency domain; it can also be performed automatically or interactively.

2.2.1 Spatial Noise Filter

Enhancement de-noising can be achieved by means of image filtering in the spatial domain. A filter that filters out noise directly in the image domain is called a *spatial noise filter*. Common spatial noise filters include mean filters, order statistical filters, and filters that combine them.

2.2.1.1 Mean Filter

The *mean filter* performs action by calculating the mean value and is a large class of spatial noise filters. The mean filters are mostly linear, but there are also non-linear ones. Several typical ones are as follows:

1. Arithmetic mean filter

    Given an $m \times n$ mask (also called window), the arithmetic mean of the image region W centered at (x, y) in the image $f(x, y)$ covered by W is:

$$f_a(x,y) = \frac{1}{mn} \sum_{(p,q) \in W} f(p,q) \tag{2.11}$$

When the collected noise image is represented by $g(x, y)$, the de-noising image $f_e(x, y)$ obtained by the *arithmetic mean filter* is:

$$f_e(x,y) = \frac{1}{mn} \sum_{(p,q) \in W} g(p,q) \tag{2.12}$$

It should be noted that this filter also blurs the image while removing some noise.

2. Geometric mean filter

    According to the definition of geometric mean, the de-noising image $f_e(x, y)$ obtained by *geometric mean filter* is:

$$f_e(x,y) = \left[\prod_{(p,q) \in W} g(p,q) \right]^{\frac{1}{mn}} \tag{2.13}$$

The geometric mean filter has the same smoothing effect on the image as the arithmetic mean filter, but it can keep more original details in the de-noising image than the arithmetic mean filter.

3. Harmonic mean filter

    According to the definition of the harmonic mean, the de-noising image $f_e(x, y)$ obtained by the *harmonic mean filter* is:

$$f_e(x,y) = \frac{mn}{\displaystyle\sum_{(p,q)\in W} \frac{1}{g(p,q)}} \qquad (2.14)$$

The harmonic mean filter has a better filtering effect on Gaussian noise. It has asymmetric effects on the two parts of salt and pepper noise, and it is more suitable for filtering salt noise than for filtering pepper noise. Refer to Figure 2.6, where Figure 2.6a is an image superimposed with 20% pepper noise, Figure 2.6b is the result obtained with a harmonic mean filter; Figure 2.6c is an image superimposed with 20% salt noise, Figure 2.6d is the result obtained with the harmonic mean filter. It can be observed that the filtering effect of the harmonic mean filter on salt noise is much better than that on pepper noise.

4. Inverse harmonic mean filter

This is a more general mean filter, and the de-noising image $f_e(x, y)$ obtained from it is:

$$f_e(x,y) = \frac{\displaystyle\sum_{(p,q)\in W} g(p,q)^{k+1}}{\displaystyle\sum_{(p,q)\in W} g(p,q)^{k}} \qquad (2.15)$$

where k is the order of the filter. The *inverse harmonic mean filter* has a better filtering effect on salt and pepper noise, but it cannot filter both pepper noise and salt noise at the same time. When k is a positive number, the filter can filter out pepper noise; when k is a negative number, the filter can filter out salt noise. In addition, when k is 0, the inverse harmonic mean filter degenerates into an arithmetic mean filter; when k is −1, the inverse harmonic mean filter degenerates into a harmonic mean filter.

A comparison of the effects of filtering Gaussian noise with the above four kinds of linear mean filters is shown in Figure 2.7. Among them, Figure 2.7a is an image superimposed with Gaussian noise with a mean value of zero and a variance of 256.

(a)   (b)   (c)   (d)

FIGURE 2.6 The different effects of the harmonic mean filter to eliminate pepper noise and salt noise.

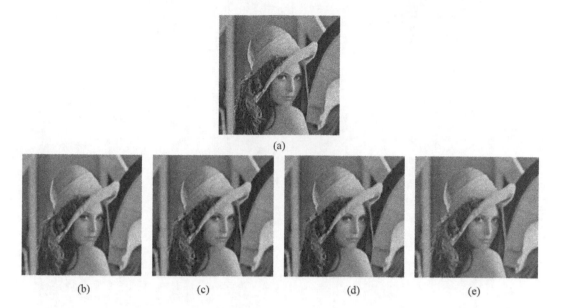

(a)

(b)   (c)   (d)   (e)

FIGURE 2.7   The effects of various mean filters to eliminate Gaussian noise.

Figures 2.7b–e show the results obtained by using arithmetic mean filter, geometric mean filter, harmonic mean filter and inverse harmonic mean filter in order, and there is little difference between them.

See Figure 2.8 for a comparison of the effects of the above four linear mean filters in filtering impulse noise. Among them, Figure 2.8a is an image superimposed with 20% impulse noise. Figures 2.8b–e are the results obtained by using arithmetic mean filter, geometric mean filter, harmonic mean filter and inverse harmonic mean filter in order. It can be seen from this figure that, contrary to the arithmetic mean filter, the other three filters may enhance the effect of impulse noise.

Comparing Figures 2.7 and 2.8, the effect of the mean filter in filtering out Gaussian noise is better than that in filtering out impulse noise.

5. Non-linear mean filter

Given N numbers x_i, $i = 1, 2, …, N$, their non-linear mean can be expressed as:

$$g = f(x_1, x_2, …, x_N) = h^{-1}\left(\frac{\sum_{i=1}^{N} w_i h(x_i)}{\sum_{i=1}^{N} w_i}\right) \tag{2.16}$$

where $h(x)$ is generally a non-linear single-valued analytic function; w_i is the weight. The nature of the non-linear mean depends on the function $h(x)$ and the weight w_i. If $h(x) = x$, it gets the arithmetic mean. If $h(x) = 1/x$, the harmonic mean value is obtained. If $h(x) = \ln(x)$, it gets the geometric mean.

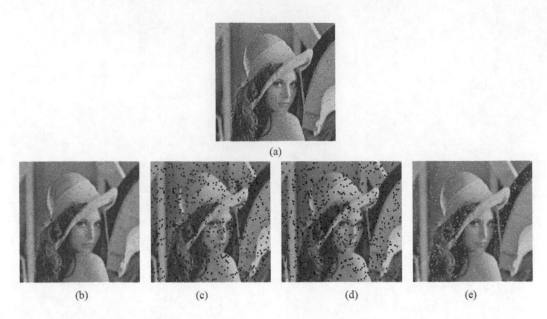

FIGURE 2.8 The effects of various mean filters to eliminate impulse noise.

If the length of a 1-D *non-linear mean filter* is odd, that is, $N = 2n + 1$ (n is an integer), then

$$g_l = f(x_{l-n}, \ldots, x_l, \ldots, x_{l+n}) \qquad l \in \mathbf{I} \tag{2.17}$$

When the length is an even number or the filter is 2-D, similar definitions can be obtained.

2.2.1.2 Order Statistical Filter

The *order statistical filter* achieves the filtering effect by sorting the gray value and is another large type of spatial noise filter, which belongs to the non-linear filter. Several typical ones are as follows:

1. Median filter

   It uses the median value of the pixels in the region covered by the mask as the filtering result:

$$f_e(x, y) = \underset{(p,q) \in W}{\text{median}}\{g(p, q)\} \tag{2.18}$$

   The *median filter* is more effective in eliminating impulse noise. For color images, a *vector median filter* can be used.

2. Maximum value filter and minimum value filter

   The median of a sequence is the value of the middle element in the sequence. According to specific applications, any value in the sequence can also be taken as the filtering result. If the maximum value of the sequence is taken, one gets the *maximum value filter*:

$$f_e(x,y) = \max_{(p,q)\in W}\{g(p,q)\} \qquad (2.19)$$

The maximum value filter is more effective in eliminating pepper noise. If the minimum value of the sequence is taken, one gets the *minimum value filter*:

$$f_e(x,y) = \min_{(p,q)\in W}\{g(p,q)\} \qquad (2.20)$$

The minimum value filter is more effective to eliminate salt noise.

3. Mid-point filter

It uses the average value of the maximum pixel value and minimum pixel value in the region covered by the mask as the filtering result:

$$f_e(x,y) = \frac{1}{2}\left[\max_{(p,q)\in W}\{g(p,q)\} + \min_{(p,q)\in W}\{g(p,q)\}\right] \qquad (2.21)$$

The *mid-point filter* selects the average value of the outputs of the maximum value filter and the minimum value filter, which can be considered as a combination of order statistical calculation and average calculation. The mid-point filter is more effective to eliminate Gaussian noise and uniform random distribution noise.

Figure 2.9 shows a set of results obtained by using various order statistical filters to eliminate Gaussian noise. Among them, Figure 2.9a is an image superimposed with Gaussian noise with a mean value of zero and a variance of 256. Figures 2.9b −e are the results obtained by using the median filter, the maximum value filter, the minimum value filter, and the mid-point filter in sequence. In comparison, the median filter has the best effect,

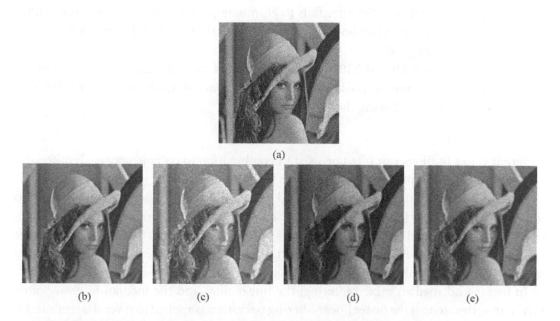

(a)

(b)   (c)   (d)   (e)

FIGURE 2.9 The effects of various orders of statistical filters to eliminate Gaussian noise.

FIGURE 2.10 The effects of various orders of statistical filters to eliminate impulse noise.

and the maximum value filter and the minimum value filter give brighter and darker results, respectively.

Figure 2.10 shows a set of results obtained by using various order statistical filters to eliminate impulse noise. Among them, Figure 2.10a is an image with 20% salt and pepper noise superimposed, and Figure 2.10b–e are results obtained by using median filter, maximum value filter, minimum value filter, and mid-point filter in sequence. It can be seen that the median filter gives the best results, the maximum value filter fails to eliminate salt noise, and the minimum value filter fails to eliminate pepper noise. The mid-point filter has a little suppression effect on both pepper noise and salt noise, but the elimination effect cannot be counted as good.

Comparing Figures 2.9 and 2.10, the filtering effect of the order statistical filter is not as good as filtering the Gaussian noise, except for the median filter, which is better at filtering the impulse noise than filtering the Gaussian noise.

2.2.1.3 Hybrid Filter

Different types of filters can often be used in combination to complement each other and obtain better results and performance than a single type of filter.

When a relatively large-sized mask is used, a large amount of calculation is required to implement non-linear filtering. One way to solve this problem is to mix fast filters (especially linear filters) and order statistical filters (non-linear filters) so that the resulting filter is close to the desired effect in terms of effect, but great improvements have been made in terms of computational complexity.

In linear and median mixed filtering, the linear filter and the median filter are often mixed in series, so that the faster linear filtering operation is applied to several larger masks, and the median value output from these linear filters is the final output of the hybrid filter.

Consider a 1-D signal $f(i)$. The *linear-median hybrid filtering* composed of sub-structures $H_1, H_2, \ldots, H_M$ (M is an odd number) can be written as:

$$g(i) = \text{median}\{H_1[f(i)], H_2[f(i)], \ldots, H_M[f(i)]\} \tag{2.22}$$

where $H_1, H_2, \ldots, H_M$ are linear filters. As an example, consider the following structure:

$$g(i) = median\{H_L[f(i)], H_C[f(i)], H_R[f(i)]\} \tag{2.23}$$

Among them, the filters H_L, H_C, and H_R are all low-pass filters, and the subscripts L, C, and R represent left, center, and right, indicating the corresponding filter position relative to the current output value, as shown in Figure 2.11.

The simplest structure includes the same mean filters H_L and H_R as well as direct pass filter $H_C[f(i)] = f(i)$. At this time, the entire filter can be represented as:

$$g(i) = \text{median}\left[\frac{1}{k}\sum_{j=1}^{k} f(i-j), f(i), \frac{1}{k}\sum_{j-1}^{k} f(i+j)\right] \tag{2.24}$$

This filter has a very similar filtering effect to the standard median filter, but the calculation is much faster. If the iterative run-length summation is used, its computational complexity has nothing to do with the mask/window size and is a constant.

In actual 2-D image applications, the number of elements in the filter mask is often taken as 5. For example, the following filter

$$g(x,y) = \text{median}\left\{\frac{1}{2}[f(x,y-2)+f(x,y-1)], \frac{1}{2}[f(x,y+1)+f(x,y+2)], f(x,y)\right.$$
$$\left.\frac{1}{2}[f(x+2,y)+f(x+1,y)], \frac{1}{2}[f(x-1,y)+f(x-2,y)]\right\} \tag{2.25}$$

corresponds to each mask shown in Figure 2.12a. Figure 2.12b and c show the other two groups of typical masks.

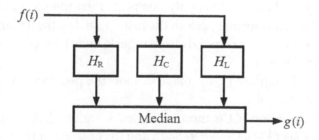

FIGURE 2.11   Using sub-filters to achieve basic linear and median hybrid filtering.

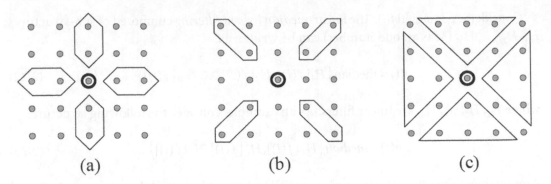

FIGURE 2.12   Masks for linear and median mixed filtering.

2.2.1.4 Mode Filter

The mode value represents the most likely value in a distribution. The mean, median, and mode values are all relative to the region covered by the mask. Similar to the mean filter or median filter, the *mode filter* takes the most-frequency value in the mask as the output of the filter.

Using the mode filter can not only eliminate noise (especially impulse noise) but also sharpen the edge of the object. This is because, in the neighborhood close to the edge, the mode filter will move the mode closer to the center of the edge, thereby making the edge sharper. This can be explained as follows: the pixels on the background side of any edge mainly have background gray values, so the output of the mode filter is the gray value of the background; while the pixels on the foreground side of any edge mainly have foreground gray values, so the output of the mode filter is the gray value of the foreground. In this way, at a certain point on the edge, the main peak of the local grayscale distribution changes from the background to the foreground or from the foreground to the background, thereby tending to enhance the edge. This is different from averaging filter, which blurs the edges. Averaging filtering will produce an edge profile with a mixture of background and foreground gray levels, which will reduce the local contrast between these two regions.

The grayscale distribution in a region can be represented by the histogram of the region, and the mean, median, and mode are all closely related to the histogram. The mean value of the histogram of a region also gives the mean gray value of the region. The median value of the histogram of a region also gives the median gray value of the region. The mode value of the histogram of a region is the gray value with the largest statistical value. If the histogram is symmetrical and there is only one peak, then the mean, median, and mode are all the same. If there is only one peak in the histogram, but the left and right are asymmetric, then the mode value corresponds to that peak, and the median is always closer to the mode value than the mean.

Figure 2.13 gives a histogram of an image to show the positional relationship between the mean, median, and mode.

In Figure 2.13, the position of the mode value is $7 = \arg\{\max[H(z)]\}$, and the position of the median value is 6 (as $1+3+4+5+6 = 9+8+2$), and the position of the mean value is $5.69 = (1\times1+2\times3+3\times4+4\times5+5\times6+6\times7+7\times9+8\times8+9\times2)/(1+2+3+4+5+6+7+8+9) = 256/45$). It can be

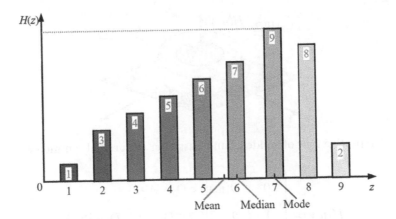

FIGURE 2.13 A histogram showing the positional relationship between the mean, median, and mode.

seen that the position of the median value is closer to the position of the mode value than the position of the mean value.

Direct detection of the mode value may be inaccurate due to the influence of noise. If the median value has been determined, the median position can be used to further determine the mode position. The method of truncating median filtering can be used here. First, according to the median value, cut the longer part of the tail to make it the same length as the un-truncated part, then calculate the median value of the remaining part, and then cut it off as above so that the iteration will gradually approach the mode position. Here the relationship that the median position is closer to the mode position than the mean position is used.

2.2.2 Frequency Domain Periodic Noise Filter

Periodic noise refers to the regular repetition of noise in the image. This kind of noise is often caused by electrical interference when collecting images, and it varies with the spatial position. Because periodic noise has a specific frequency, frequency domain filtering is often used to eliminate it. Commonly used filters include band-pass filters, band-stop filters, notch filters, and so on. When eliminating noise, in some cases, manual interaction can be used to achieve better results.

2.2.2.1 Band-Pass Filter

The *band-pass filter* is a filter that allows signals in a certain frequency range to pass but prevents signals in other frequency ranges from passing.

In practice, the band-pass filter that allows signals in a circular ring with the origin of the surrounding frequency as the center to pass through is radially symmetric. The perspective diagram of the transfer function $H(u, v)$ of a radially symmetric ideal band-pass filter is shown in Figure 2.14, which can be written as (W is the width of the ring zone, D_0 is the frequency of the center of the ring zone):

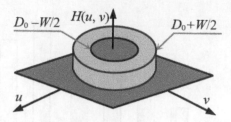

FIGURE 2.14   Perspective view of an ideal band-pass filter with radial symmetry.

$$H(u,v) = \begin{cases} 0 & D(u,v) < D_0 - W/2 \\ 1 & D_0 - W/2 \leq D(u,v) \leq D_0 + W/2 \\ 0 & D(u,v) > D_0 + W/2 \end{cases} \qquad (2.26)$$

The transfer function of an n-th order radially symmetric Butterworth band-pass filter is:

$$H(u,v) = \frac{\left[D(u,v)W \right]^{2n}}{\left[D^2(u,v) - D_0^2 \right]^{2n} + \left[D(u,v)W \right]^{2n}} \qquad (2.27)$$

2.2.2.2 Band-Stop Filter

The *band-stop filter* is a filter that prevents signals in a certain frequency range from passing and allows signals in other frequency ranges to pass.

In practice, the band-stop filter that prevents the signals in a circular ring with the origin of the surrounding frequency as the center from passing through is radially symmetric. The perspective diagram of the transfer function $H(u, v)$ of a radially symmetric ideal band-stop filter is shown in Figure 2.15, which can be written as (W is the width of the ring zone, D_0 is the frequency of the center of the ring zone):

$$H(u,v) = \begin{cases} 1 & D(u,v) < D_0 - W/2 \\ 0 & D_0 - W/2 \leq D(u,v) \leq D_0 + W/2 \\ 1 & D(u,v) > D_0 + W/2 \end{cases} \qquad (2.28)$$

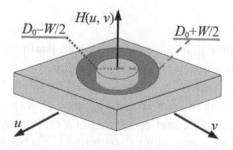

FIGURE 2.15   Perspective view of an ideal band-stop filter with radial symmetry.

The transfer function of an *n-th* order radially symmetric Butterworth band-stop filter is:

$$H(u,v) = \frac{\left[D^2(u,v) - D_0^2\right]^{2n}}{\left[D^2(u,v) - D_0^2\right]^{2n} + \left[D(u,v)W\right]^{2n}} \tag{2.29}$$

The band-pass filter and the band-stop filter are complementary. So if $H_R(u, v)$ is set as the transfer function of the band-stop filter, the corresponding band-pass filter $H_P(u, v)$ only needs to flip $H_R(u, v)$:

$$H_P(u,v) = -\left[H_R(u,v) - 1\right] = 1 - H_R(u,v) \tag{2.30}$$

It can be seen from the above equation that if a band-pass filter is used to extract the frequency components in a certain frequency band and then subtract them from the image, the effect of eliminating or reducing the components in a certain frequency range in the image can also be obtained.

2.2.2.3 Notch Filter

A *notch filter* can block or pass frequencies in a range centered on a certain frequency, so it is still a band-stop filter or band-pass filter in essence, and they can be called notch band-stop filter and notch band-pass filter, respectively.

The transfer function $H(u, v)$ of an ideal notch band-stop filter used to eliminate all frequencies in the region, with (u_0, v_0) as the center and D_0 as the radius, can be written as:

$$H(u,v) = \begin{cases} 0 & \text{if } D(u,v) \leq D_0 \\ 1 & \text{if } D(u,v) > D_0 \end{cases} \tag{2.31}$$

where

$$D(u,v) = \left[(u - u_0)^2 + (v - v_0)^2\right]^{1/2} \tag{2.32}$$

Because the Fourier transform is symmetry, in order to eliminate the frequency in a given region that is not centered on the origin of the coordinate system, the notch band-stop filter must work symmetrically, that is, $H(u, v)$ needs to be rewritten as :

$$H(u,v) = \begin{cases} 0 & \text{if } D_1(u,v) \leq D_0 \text{ or } D_2(u,v) \leq D_0 \\ 1 & \text{otherwise} \end{cases} \tag{2.33}$$

where

$$D_1(u,v) = \left[(u - u_0)^2 + (v - v_0)^2\right]^{1/2} \tag{2.34}$$

$$D_2(u,v) = \left[(u + u_0)^2 + (v + v_0)^2\right]^{1/2} \tag{2.35}$$

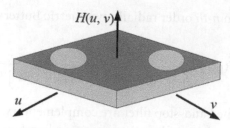

FIGURE 2.16   Perspective view of the ideal notch band-stop filter.

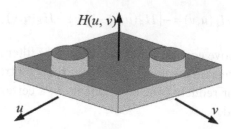

FIGURE 2.17   Perspective view of the ideal notch band-pass filter.

A perspective schematic diagram of a typical ideal notch band-stop filter $H(u, v)$ is shown in Figure 2.16. The two lower circular regions are regions where the signal frequency cannot pass.

Similar to the complementary relationship between the band-pass filter and the band-stop filter, the notch band-pass filter and the notch band-stop filter are also complementary.

A perspective schematic diagram of a typical ideal notch band-pass filter $H(u, v)$ is shown in Figure 2.17. The two higher circular regions are regions where the signal frequency can pass.

The transfer function of the n-th order Butterworth notch band-stop filter used in practice is:

$$H(u,v) = \frac{1}{1 + \left[\dfrac{D_0^2}{D_1(u,v)D_2(u,v)}\right]^n} \tag{2.36}$$

When $u_0 = v_0 = 0$, the above-mentioned notch band-stop filter becomes a high-pass filter. When $u_0 = v_0 = 0$, the above-mentioned notch band-pass filter will become a low-pass filter due to the complementary relationship between the band-pass filter and the band-stop filter.

2.2.2.4 Interactive Filtering

The use of the aforementioned various filters to eliminate periodic noise requires prior knowledge of the frequency of the noise so that it is possible to design the filter to automatically eliminate noise. In practice, if the frequency of periodic noise is not known in advance, the spectral amplitude map $G(u, v)$ of the degraded image can be displayed. Since the noise of a single frequency will produce two bright spots far away from the origin of the coordinate on the spectrum amplitude map, it is easy to rely on visual observation to interactively determine the position of the pulse component in the frequency domain and use a band-stop filter to eliminate them at this position. This kind of human–computer interaction can improve the flexibility and efficiency of the filtering process.

In practice, the periodic noise often has multiple frequency components, for which the main frequency needs to be extracted. This requires placing a band-pass filter $H(u, v)$ at the position corresponding to each bright spot in the frequency domain. If we can construct a $H(u, v)$ that allows only components related to the interference pattern to pass, then the Fourier transform of this pattern is:

$$P(u,v) = H(u,v)G(u,v) \tag{2.37}$$

To build such a $H(u, v)$, many judgments are needed to determine whether each bright spot is an interference bright spot. So this work often needs to be done interactively by observing the spectrum display of $G(u, v)$. When a filter is determined, the periodic noise can be obtained by the following equation:

$$p(x,y) = \mathcal{F}^{-1}\{H(u,v)\,G(u,v)\} \tag{2.38}$$

If the $p(x, y)$ can be completely determined, then subtracting $p(x, y)$ from $g(x, y)$ can provide $f(x, y)$. In practice, only a certain approximation of this pattern can be obtained. To reduce the influence of the components that are not considered in the estimation of $p(x, y)$, the weighted $p(x, y)$ can be subtracted from $g(x, y)$ to obtain an approximation of $f(x, y)$:

$$f_e(x,y) = g(x,y) - w(x,y)\,p(x,y) \tag{2.39}$$

In the above equation, $w(x, y)$ is called the weight function. By changing it, the optimal noise elimination result can be obtained in a certain sense.

An example of using interactive methods to eliminate sinusoidal interference patterns (a type of periodic noise) is shown in Figure 2.18. Figure 2.18a is an image covered by a sinusoidal interference pattern. Figure 2.18b is its Fourier spectrum amplitude map, on which there is a pair of more obvious (pulse) white dots (at the intersection of bright lines). One can place two band-stop filters at these two white points in an interactive way, as shown in Figure 2.18c, to filter out the pulse. Then the inverse Fourier transform is used to get the de-noising result shown in Figure 2.18d.

2.3 SELECTIVE FILTER

The linear filter can effectively eliminate Gaussian noise and uniformly distributed noise, but the effect of eliminating salt and pepper noise is very poor. The median filter can effectively eliminate impulse noises such as salt and pepper noise and will not cause too much blur to the image; however, the effect of eliminating Gaussian noise is not very good. When the image is affected by different noises at the same time, the method of selective filtering

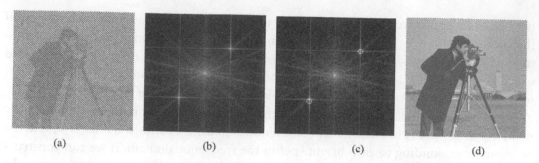

FIGURE 2.18   Interactive de-noising example.

can be adopted, and different filters are selected to filter the image at positions affected by different noises, so as to take advantage of the respective characteristics of different filters and achieve a good overall effect. The following introduces a *selective filter* as an example (Li et al. 2006).

This filter can be used to eliminate Gaussian noise and impulse (salt and pepper) noise. Its block diagram and workflow are shown in Figure 2.19. It includes four modules, namely, salt and pepper noise detection, filter selection, salt and pepper noise elimination, and Gaussian noise elimination. For the input noise image, salt and pepper noise detection is first performed to detect the pixels affected by the salt and pepper noise. For these pixels, a median filter can be used to eliminate noise, and for the remaining pixels, a mean filter can be used to filter out the noise. Finally, the two parts of the results are combined to get results that have both Gaussian noise and salt and pepper noise being filtered out.

The gray value of pixels affected by salt and pepper noise will take the two extreme values of the image grayscale range. Therefore, the pixels affected by salt and pepper noise can be judged and detected according to the following two criteria.

1. Grayscale range criterion: Set the image grayscale range as $[L_{min}, L_{max}]$, and if the grayscale value of a pixel is outside the range of $[L_{min} + T_g, L_{max} - T_g]$, it is likely to be affected by salt and pepper noise, where T_g is the grayscale threshold for detecting salt and pepper noise.

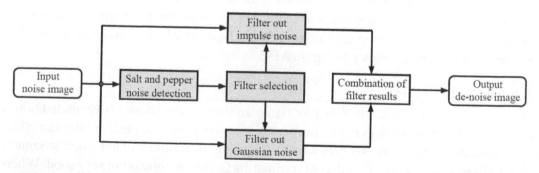

FIGURE 2.19   Block diagram of the selective filter.

2. Local difference criterion: Here, the correlation of the gray value between adjacent pixels in the image is used. Considering the 8-neighborhood of a pixel, if there are more neighboring pixels having a greater difference than the gray value of this pixel, then this pixel is more likely to be a pixel affected by salt and pepper noise. Specifically, two thresholds can be designed, T_v and T_n. T_v is used to determine whether the difference in gray values between neighboring pixels is large enough, and T_n is used to determine whether the number of pixels with large enough gray values is big enough. If the difference between the gray value of a pixel to be detected and the gray value of the pixels in its neighborhood is greater than T_v and the number of these pixels is greater than T_n, this pixel is likely affected by salt and pepper noise.

Suppose the neighborhood of the pixel at (x, y) is $N(x, y)$, and the pixel belonging to this neighborhood is $f(s, t)$. The above criterion can be expressed as (#[•] represents the number, so the denominator represents the number of pixels in the neighborhood, while T_n represents the percentage threshold):

$$\frac{\#\left[\left|f(x,y)-f(s,t)\right|>T_v\right]}{\#\left[N(x,y)\right]}>T_n \tag{2.40}$$

Two criteria are needed here because if only the first criterion is used, normal pixels with original gray values in the range of $[L_{\min} + T_g, L_{\max} - T_g]$ may be misjudged as pixels affected by salt and pepper noise; if only the second criterion is used, many normal edge pixels may be misjudged as pixels affected by salt and pepper noise. To avoid these two problems, two criteria need to be combined. Pixels that meet the two criteria at the same time are more likely to be affected by salt and pepper noise.

When the image is affected by both salt and pepper noise and Gaussian noise, the image can be divided into two sets after detecting the pixel set affected by the salt and pepper noise as described above. One set is only affected by Gaussian noise, while the other set is affected by both Gaussian noise and salt and pepper noise. The influence of Gaussian noise on these pixels affected by salt and pepper noise can be ignored since the gray scale of the pixels affected by salt and pepper noise takes the two extreme values of the gray scale of the image. To eliminate salt and pepper noise in pixels affected by salt and pepper noise, the surrounding pixels not affected by salt and pepper noise can be used for interpolation. An adaptive Wiener filter (see Sub-section 3.2.2) can be used to eliminate Gaussian noise from pixels that are not affected by salt and pepper noise. Finally, the two results are combined to provide the output de-noise image.

Figure 2.20 shows a set of example images using the selective filter. Among them, Figure 2.20a is the original image, Figure 2.20b is the image affected by the mixed noise (the mean value of Gaussian noise is 0, the variance is 162; the noise density of salt and pepper noise is 20%), and Figure 2.20c is the image obtained after removing noise with a combined filter. Here $T_g = 15$, $T_v = 15$, $T_n = 80\%$.

(a)   (b)   (c)

FIGURE 2.20 Example of selective filtering.

Experiments show that utilizing the effect of using combined filters based on selective filtering is better than using a single filter for eliminating mixed noises of varied mixing ratios.

2.4 SWITCHING MEDIAN FILTER

The impact of salt and pepper noise on images has its own characteristics. On the one hand, the spatial distribution of salt and pepper noise is discrete, meaning it does not affect all pixels; on the other hand, the amplitude of salt and pepper noise is quite considerable. The pixels that are affected by this noise are either very close to white or very close to black, which greatly changes the original grayscale of the pixel. According to these characteristics of salt and pepper noise, there are some methods to detect or judge the pixels affected by the salt and pepper noise before processing the image affected only by this noise. If the pixel is not affected by this noise, it does not need to be processed at all. If it is affected by this noise, it will be processed in a targeted manner.

A filter designed to eliminate salt and pepper noise based on this idea and based on a median filter is the *switching median filter*. The following introduces the basic method first and then discusses some improvement measures.

2.4.1 The Principle of Switching Median Filter

The first step in switching to median filtering to eliminate *impulse noise* is to identify the noise pixels, and then filter these pixels to eliminate the noise. The first step is not only the basis of subsequent noise elimination but also has a certain degree of difficulty. The first step is mainly discussed below.

2.4.1.1 Noise Model

The PDF of random variables corresponding to impulse noise given by Equation (2.4) is a common situation. There can be four kinds of PDFs corresponding to impulse noise, and they can be called as four *noise models*. In the following, they are introduced in order from special to general (still using the convention in Sub-section 2.1.2).

1. Model 1

In this model, image pixels are affected (corrupted, damaged, polluted, and contaminated) by two extreme values (for 8-bit grayscale images, 0 and 255 respectively). In Model 1, the probabilities of the two extreme values are the same, that is, the noise density $P = P_a = P_b$. If the pixel $f(x, y)$ at position (x, y) is affected by noise and becomes $g(x, y)$, then the probability density function of Model 1 is

$$p^{(1)}(z) = \begin{cases} P/2 & z = 0 \\ 1 - P & z = g(x, y) \\ P/2 & z = 255 \end{cases} \qquad (2.41)$$

2. Model 2

In this model, the image pixels are still affected by two extreme values (for 8-bit grayscale images, 0 and 255, respectively). Different from Model 1, Model 2 does not assume that the two extreme values have the same probability, and that the corrupted pixel may be affected by pepper noise or salt noise, that is, the noise density is the sum of pepper noise density and salt noise density, $P = P_a + P_b$ (and $P_a \neq P_b$). If the pixel $f(x, y)$ at position (x, y) is affected by noise and becomes $g(x, y)$, then the probability density function of Model 2 is

$$p^{(2)}(z) = \begin{cases} P_a/2 & z = 0 \\ 1 - P & z = g(x, y) \\ P_b/2 & z = 255 \end{cases} \qquad (2.42)$$

3. Model 3

In this model, image pixels are no longer affected by two fixed extreme values (for 8-bit grayscale images, 0 and 255, respectively), but by two extreme value ranges. Assuming that the probability of these two numerical ranges is the same, and their width is both W. For example, when $W = 6$, these two ranges are $[0, 5]$ and $[250, 255]$, respectively. In this way, if the pixel $f(x, y)$ at position (x, y) is affected by noise and becomes $g(x, y)$, then the probability density function of Model 3 is

$$p^{(3)}(z) = \begin{cases} P/2W & 0 \leq z < W \\ 1 - P & z = g(x, y) \\ P/2W & 255 - W < z \leq 255 \end{cases} \qquad (2.43)$$

4. Model 4

In this model, as in Model 3, it is considered that image pixels are no longer affected by two fixed extreme values (for 8-bit grayscale images, 0 and 255 respectively), but by two extreme value ranges. It is similar to the extension from Model 1 to Model 2, which no longer sets the probability of these two numerical ranges to be the same (but still set the sum of the probabilities of these two numerical ranges to 1, as in Model 2, and $P_a \neq P_b$), and still sets their widths to W. In this way, if the pixel $f(x, y)$ at position (x, y) is affected by noise and becomes $g(x, y)$, the probability density function of Model 4 is

$$p^{(4)}(z) = \begin{cases} P_a/2W & 0 \leq z < W \\ 1 - P & z = g(x, y) \\ P_b/2W & 255 - W < z \leq 255 \end{cases} \tag{2.44}$$

It can be seen that Model 4 is the most general model.

2.4.1.2 Noise Detection

To detect pixels affected by impulse noise, a method called *"boundary discriminant noise detection (BDND)"* can be used (Ng and Ma 2006). This method uses local histograms to adaptively determine the decision boundary between noise-free pixels and noisy pixels. Specifically, it checks whether each pixel in the noise image is corrupted, and outputs a binary (mask) image corresponding to the noise image, where 0 represents the corresponding pixel un-corrupted (noise-free), and 1 represents the corresponding pixel corrupted. To make such a judgment, a neighborhood centered on each pixel is selected; and according to the calculation of the neighborhood pixels, all pixels are divided into three clusters, which are low-gray pixel cluster, middle-gray pixel cluster, and high-gray pixel cluster. Here, two thresholds, T_a and T_b, are used to separate pixels affected by pepper noise from un-corrupted pixels as well as to separate pixels affected by salt noise from uncorrupted pixels. Specifically, consider the pixel $g(x, y)$, if $0 < g(x, y) < T_a$, then classify $g(x, y)$ into the low-gray pixel cluster; if $T_b < g(x, y) < 255$, then classify $g(x, y)$ into the high-gray pixel cluster; if $T_a < g(x, y) < T_b$, classify $g(x, y)$ into the middle-gray pixel cluster. The result of the classification can be written as

$$C[g(x, y)] = \begin{cases} \text{pepper noise} & g(x, y) \leq T_a \\ \text{noise free} & T_a < g(x, y) \leq T_b \\ \text{salt noise} & g(x, y) > T_b \end{cases} \tag{2.45}$$

It is clear that if $g(x, y)$ is classified into middle-gray pixel cluster, that is, its gray value is not an extreme value, it should be treated as if it is un-corrupted; if $g(x, y)$ is classified into low-gray pixel cluster or high gray pixel cluster, it is likely to be a pixel corrupted by (pepper or salt) noise. Here it is assumed that the original image is not a severely underexposed or severely overexposed image, that is, the overall distribution of various gray levels is relatively balanced. Under such conditions, impulse noise will cause higher peaks at both ends of the histogram of pixel neighborhood, with two valleys visible between these two peaks and the histogram bins of the original image. The part between the corresponding peaks and valleys constitutes the aforementioned three clusters.

According to the above analysis, the steps of noise detection can be summarized as follows:

1. For each pixel $g(x, y)$ in the noisy image, take it as the center, select a larger window as the neighborhood of the pixel.

2. The pixels in the window are sorted into a gray value vector V_g according to the gray level, and the median value m of the sequence is determined.

3. Calculate the difference vector V_d of V_g, that is, the vector composed of the gray-level difference of two adjacent pixels in the sequence.

4. Determine the pixels corresponding to the maximum values of the two intervals [0, m] and [m, 255] in V_g, and use the gray values of these two pixels as the thresholds T_a and T_b for clustering.

5. According to the determined thresholds T_a and T_b, the pixels in the center of the window are divided into three categories according to Equation (2.45).

6. If the pixel in the center of the window belongs to the middle-gray pixel cluster, it is considered to be noise-free.

7. If the pixel in the center of the window belongs to the low-gray pixel cluster or the high-gray pixel cluster, repeat the calculation and judgment according to step (2) to step (5) using a smaller window.

It can be observed that pixels that are deemed to belong to the low-gray pixel cluster or the high-gray pixel cluster based on the boundary require two calculations. Use a larger window for the first time, and a smaller window for the second time to realize the judgment from coarse to fine. The size of these two windows can be selected based on experience; for example, the larger window is selected as 21×21, and the smaller window is selected as 3×3.

2.4.1.3 Noise Adaptive Filtering

After the noisy pixels are detected, they need to be filtered to eliminate the noise. In this case, a *noise adaptive filter* (Eng and Ma 2001) can be used. The filter starts from the minimum filter window size. If the noise density in the window is relatively large, the window is expanded to continue the calculation. If N_u represents the number of noise-free pixels in the window, S_a represents the number of all pixels in the window, W_l represents the current size of the window side length, and W_m represents the maximum size of the window side length, then the iterative selection step of the window size is:

1. Initialize $W_l = 3$.

2. Calculate in the current window.

3. If $(N_u < S_a)$ OR $(N_u = 0)$, $W_l = W_l + 2$.

4. If $W_l \leq W_m$, return to step (2); otherwise, the iteration ends.

TABLE 2.1 Selection of the Largest Window Size

Noise Density	Maximum Allowable Window Size
$0\% < P < 20\%$	3×3
$20\% < P < 40\%$	5×5
$P > 40\%$	7×7

Before iterative selection, it is needed to determine the maximum allowable window size to avoid excessive blurring of the image. This size is related to the noise density. Here, it can be determined based on the number of 1 in the vector V_d calculated for the first time, that is, dividing the element of 1 in the window by the size of the window as the noise density, and then making the choice experimentally according to Table 2.1.

Finally, calculate the median in the $W_l \times W_l$ filter window:

$$g_e(x,y) = \underset{(s,t)\in W}{\text{median}}\big\{g(x-s,y-t)\big\} \tag{2.46}$$

where

$$W = \big\{(s,t)\,|-(W_l-1)/2 \leq s,t \leq (W_l-1)/2\big\} \tag{2.47}$$

Here, the center pixel can be excluded from the ranking operation because the pixels that enter the filter are all noisy pixels, resulting in less distortion.

2.4.2 Switch-Based Adaptive Weighted Mean Filter

The aforementioned boundary discrimination noise detection method needs to be performed on each pixel in the image. In the first iterative calculation, a larger window with a size of 21×21 is used, so a larger amount of calculation is required. To overcome this problem, a *switch-based adaptive weighted mean (SAWM)* filter can be used. It combines a directional difference noise detector with an adaptive weighted mean filter to restore the contaminated image (Zhang and Xiong 2009).

2.4.2.1 Directional Differential Noise Detector

Suppose the square window centered on the noise image pixel $g(x,y)$ is $W(x,y)$, and the side length of the window is L, then $W(x,y) = \{(x+s, y+t)\,|-(L-1)/2 \leq s, t \leq (L-1)/2\}$. If the pixels in the window are sorted (according to increase or decrease order), the noise pixels are mainly concentrated at the beginning and end of the sequence. If g_k is used to represent the k-th pixel in the sequence, the noise candidate pixels in the window can be written as

$$N(x,y) = \big\{(x+s,y+t)\,|(x+s,y+t)\in W(x,y) \wedge \big(g_{x+s,y+t} \leq g_r \vee g_{x+s,y+t} \geq g_{L\times L-r+1}\big)\big\} \tag{2.48}$$

where r is an integer selected according to the type of noise, and satisfies $1 \leq r \leq (L^2-1)/2$.

In the image, the pixels along the edge direction have similar pixel values. To use this feature to distinguish the edge from the impulse noise, the detection window can

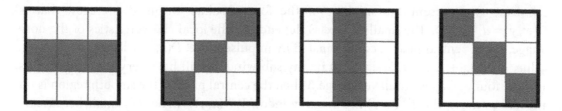

FIGURE 2.21　The decomposition of the 3×3 detection window.

be decomposed into four direction sub-windows. The decomposition result of side length $L = 3$ can be seen in Figure 2.21.

For larger windows, simulations have shown that decomposition in more directions can only increase little noise detection accuracy, but the computational cost increases more. Therefore, it is more appropriate to consider only four directions in practice. The four sub-windows used to eliminate noise can be written as:

$$W^{(1)}(x,y)=\left\{(x,y+s)|(x,y+s)\in W(x,y)\wedge(x,y+s)\notin N(x,y)\right\} \tag{2.49}$$

$$W^{(2)}(x,y)=\left\{(x+s,y-s)|(x+s,y-s)\in W(x,y)\wedge(x+s,y-s)\notin N(x,y)\right\} \tag{2.50}$$

$$W^{(3)}(x,y)=\left\{(x+s,y)|(x+s,y)\in W(x,y)\wedge(x+s,y)\notin N(x,y)\right\} \tag{2.51}$$

$$W^{(4)}(x,y)=\left\{(x+s,y+s)|(x+s,y+s)\in W(x,y)\wedge(x+s,y+s)\notin N(x,y)\right\} \tag{2.52}$$

For any sub-window $W^{(k)}(x, y)$, where $1 \le k \le 4$, the absolute weighted mean of the difference between the center pixel and the neighboring pixels is

$$\overline{d}^{(k)}(x,y)=\begin{cases}\dfrac{\displaystyle\sum_{(x+s,y+t)\in W^{(k)}(x,y)}w(x+s,y+t)d(x+s,y+t)}{\displaystyle\sum_{(x+s,y+t)\in W^{(k)}(x,y)}w(x+s,y+t)} & W^{(k)}(x,y)\neq\varnothing \\[6pt] g_{L\times L-r+1}-g_r & W^{(k)}(x,y)=\varnothing\end{cases} \tag{2.53}$$

where $\varnothing$ represents the empty set, $d(x + s, y + t)$ represents the difference between $d(x + s, y + t)$ and $g(x, y)$, $w(x + s, y + t)$ is the weight of $g(x + s, y + t)$. Suppose that $w(x + s, y + t)$ decreases as the absolute value of $d(x + s, y + t)$ increases to weaken the influence of the absolute weighted average of large differences. Simulation experiments show that $w(x + s, y + t)$ can be selected as follows

$$w(x+s,y+s)=\frac{1}{1+\left|d(x+s,y+s)\right|^2} \tag{2.54}$$

Let $D(x, y)$ represent the smallest of the four absolute weighted averages, that is, $D(x,y)=\overline{d}^{(k)}(x,y)$. The smallest $D(x, y)$ depends on the local characteristics of the noise image. If the central pixel is contaminated by impulse noise, $D(x, y)$ will take a very large value, and $g(x + s, y + t)$ and $g(x, y)$ in any sub-window will have very large differences, and the four averages are all very large. When the central pixel in the smooth region is not affected by noise, the $\overline{d}^{(k)}(x,y)$ in any sub-window $W^{(k)}(x, y)$ will be very small, because the pixels in $W^{(k)}(x, y)$ have similar gray values, so the value of $D(x, y)$ will be small. Similarly, if the center pixel is a pixel that is not affected by noise, the value of $D(x, y)$ will also be small, because the characteristics of the edge ensure that one of the four mean values will be small.

The above analysis shows that $D(x, y)$ can be used as a measure for detecting impulse noise. By comparing $D(x, y)$ with a predetermined threshold T, if $D(x, y) \geq T$, the pixel at (x, y) should be a noisy pixel. At this time, use a binary label $b(x, y) = 1$ to mark it; if $D(x, y) < T$, the pixel at (x, y) should be a noise-free pixel, and use a binary label $b(x, y) = 0$ to mark it. Experiments show that choosing $0 < T < 10$ can get a better detection effect.

2.4.2.2 Adaptive Weighted Mean Filter

The previously detected impulse noise can be eliminated by an adaptive weighted mean filter. For noisy pixels detected at (x, y), a filter window of size $L_g \times L_g$ can be used. Let $N_{(x,y)}$ be the number of noise-free pixels in the filter window centered on (x, y), the size of the filter window will be adaptively adjusted according to $N_{(x,y)}$. Starting from $L_g = 3$, the window is iteratively extended one pixel at a time in four directions until $N_{(x,y)} \geq 2$. Compared with the BDND filter which iteratively expands the window to $N_{(x,y)} \geq (1/2)(L_g \times L_g)$, the SAWM filter obtains a smaller filtering window, higher computational efficiency, and better detail retention capability.

If $U_{(x,y)}$ is used to represent the coordinate set of noise-free pixels in the filter window centered on (x, y), that is, $U_{(x,y)} = \{(x+s, y+t)|b(x+s, y+t) = 0 \wedge -(Lg-1)/2 \leq s, t \leq (Lg-1)/2\}$. Then, the weighted mean of the noise-free pixels in the filter window is

$$g'(x,y) = \frac{\displaystyle\sum_{(x+s,y+s)\in U(x,y)} V(x+s,y+s)g(x+s,y+s)}{\displaystyle\sum_{(x+s,y+s)\in U(x,y)} V(x+s,y+s)} \tag{2.55}$$

where $V(x + s, y + t)$ is the weight of $g(x + s, y + t)$. The calculation of these weights is based on the *degree of compatibility* (DOC) between two pixels, and the compatibility between two pixels can be determined according to the following formula:

$$v(x+s,y+t;x+p,y+q) = \exp\left[-\frac{|g(x+s,y+s)-g(x+p,y+q)|}{\dfrac{1}{N_{(x,y)}}\sqrt{\displaystyle\sum_{(x+p,y+q)\in U(x,y)}[g(x+s,y+s)-g(x+p,y+q)]^2}}\right] \tag{2.56}$$

From Equation (2.56), it can be seen that $v(x+s, y+t; x+p, y+q)$ will increase in following the decrease of absolute difference between $g(x+s, y+t)$ and $g(x+p, y+q)$. Furthermore, if there are more noise-free pixels whose gray value is close to $g(x+s, y+t)$, then a larger $V(x+s, y+t)$ should be used to strengthen the contribution of $g(x+s, y+t)$ to the filtered output. Therefore, $V(x+s, y+t)$ is determined as the sum of compatibility between $g(x+s, y+t)$ and its neighboring pixels:

$$V(x+s,y+t)= \sum_{(x+p,y+q)\in U(x,y)} v(x+s, y+s; x+p, y+q) \tag{2.57}$$

Finally, the output of the switch-based adaptive weighted mean filter is

$$g(x,y)=b(x,y)\cdot g'(x,y)+[1-b(x,y)]\cdot g(x,y) \tag{2.58}$$

2.4.3 Further Improvements

Some further improvements are as follows (Duan and Zhang 2010).

2.4.3.1 New Classification Criteria

Switch-based adaptive weighted mean filtering is a statistic-based method. According to the noise detection steps in Sub-section 2.4.1, in order to judge whether the pixels in the noisy image are noisy (corrupted) or noise-free (un-corrupted), a search strategy from coarse to fine is used. Start with a larger 21×21 window, which is reasonable from a statistical point of view. However, in the next refining stage, only a window of 3×3 was used. This order of magnitude is seriously lacking in statistical significance, and the obtained decision boundary may not be very reliable. For example, Figure 2.22 shows that two windows of 7×7 are extracted from the Lena image contaminated by 20% salt and pepper noise, and their detection will cause mis-classification. Among them, the detection of Figure 2.22a will produce a false alarm result, and the detection of Figure 2.22b will produce a mis-detection result.

12	7	9	9	5	255	39
9	7	5	7	4	5	30
4	5	9	8	4	9	39
4	5	5	4	4	0	255
3	255	4	4	4	16	255
11	6	5	255	7	15	255
0	4	8	9	255	78	118

(a)

119	124	119	118	125	255	115
122	116	118	0	0	255	118
121	117	123	255	118	115	115
255	123	255	255	255	120	255
122	120	255	255	119	116	120
116	120	0	119	118	120	119
121	125	125	255	119	122	0

(b)

FIGURE 2.22   Two examples of mis-classification using the BDND method.

To overcome the problem of mis-classification, the *classification criterion* of Equation (2.55) is changed to

$$C[g(x,y)] = \begin{cases} \text{pepper noise} & g(x,y) \leq \min(T_a, W) \\ \text{salt noise} & g(x,y) \geq \max(T_b, 255-W) \\ \text{noise free} & \text{otherwise} \end{cases} \tag{2.59}$$

Here, the prior knowledge of noise characteristics is embedded in the classifier, and the decision boundary calculated from the local histogram will have the opportunity to be adjusted. The noise-free pixels whose intensity is not within the range of the "noise" interval will not have the chance to enter the second iteration of the calculation.

2.4.3.2 New Windows

To improve the reliability of the decision boundary, it is not a wise choice to simply expand the window size in the second iteration because this operation may expand the window too large and reduce the computational efficiency. Here, the method of accurately quantifying the intensity difference between the current pixel and its neighboring pixels in the four representative directions in the previous sub-section can be used. However, considering the accuracy and calculation efficiency, the four window sizes were selected as 7×7 and the windows are redesigned, as shown in Figure 2.23.

Using these windows as the mask for convolution with the noisy image, four convolution results can be obtained for each pixel. The absolute value of the convolution result can be used as a measure of the intensity uniformity H in the neighborhood of the current pixel. This calculation strategy can be represented as:

$$H^{(k)}(x,y) = \left| g(x,y) \otimes W_c^{(k)}(x,y) \right| \qquad k = 1,2,3,4 \tag{2.60}$$

where $W_c^{(k)}(x,y)$ represents the k-th convolution mask.

0	0	0	0	0	0	0
0	0	0	0	0	0	0
0	0	0	0	0	0	0
-1	-1	-1	6	-1	-1	-1
0	0	0	0	0	0	0
0	0	0	0	0	0	0
0	0	0	0	0	0	0

0	0	0	-1	0	0	0
0	0	0	-1	0	0	0
0	0	0	-1	0	0	0
0	0	0	6	0	0	0
0	0	0	-1	0	0	0
0	0	0	-1	0	0	0
0	0	0	-1	0	0	0

0	0	0	0	0	0	-1
0	0	0	0	0	-1	0
0	0	0	0	-1	0	0
0	0	0	6	0	0	0
0	0	-1	0	0	0	0
0	-1	0	0	0	0	0
-1	0	0	0	0	0	0

-1	0	0	0	0	0	0
0	-1	0	0	0	0	0
0	0	-1	0	0	0	0
0	0	0	6	0	0	0
0	0	0	0	-1	0	0
0	0	0	0	0	-1	0
0	0	0	0	0	0	-1

FIGURE 2.23 Four windows with size 7×7.

2.4.3.3 New Decision-Making Rules

In Sub-section 2.4.2, only the smallest absolute weighted average of the four windows is used. Because the intensity uniformity information exists in all four windows, this decision rule does not utilize all the detection information. In addition, by comparing the minimum value only with a given threshold to determine whether the current pixel is damaged, it will be biased toward the detection of isolated impulse noise pixels. If the noise density is relatively high, a specific type of impulse noise ("salt noise" or "pepper noise") will often stick together in a specific direction to form clusters. In these cases, the aforementioned decision rules will fail. To overcome this problem, the maximum and minimum values of the absolute weighted averages in the four windows can be used simultaneously to provide more reliable decision-making. The calculation of the maximum and minimum values is as follows:

$$D^{(max)}(x,y) = \max\left\{H^{(1)}(x,y), H^{(2)}(x,y), H^{(3)}(x,y), H^{(4)}(x,y)\right\} \tag{2.61}$$

$$D^{(min)}(x,y) = \min\left\{H^{(1)}(x,y), H^{(2)}(x,y), H^{(3)}(x,y), H^{(4)}(x,y)\right\} \tag{2.62}$$

The final classification criterion is as follows: If $D^{(min)}(x, y) > T_l$ or $D^{(max)}(x, y) - D^{(min)}(x, y) > T_h$, then the pixel $g(x, y)$ will be judged as damaged; otherwise, the pixel $g(x, y)$ will be noise-free. Here, T_l and T_h are two predefined thresholds.

The logic of the final *classification criterion* is as follows:

1. If the current pixel corresponds to isolated pixel with impulse noise, each of the four convolution values must be large.

2. If there is very little noise in the neighborhood of the current pixel, all four convolution values must be small, and the difference between these values is not so obvious.

3. If the current pixel is not corrupted but is classified as a corrupted category, the difference between the four convolution values should be below a certain level because the impulse noise is evenly distributed on a given image.

2.4.3.4 Comparison of Detection Results

The previously discussed three methods have been compared with some selected public images and superimposed impulse noise in simulation experiments.

For each test image, select the noise density of 10%, 20%, 30%, 40%, 50%, 60%, 70%, 80%, 90%, superimpose each noise density 20 times, and perform 20 times of detection. Then the average value of 20 results is taken as the final result. The evaluation measures used are the number of mis-detected pixels (noise is not detected) and the number of false alarms (noise-free is judged to be noisy). They can be obtained by comparing the detected value with the true value.

Tables 2.2 and 2.3 respectively show the detection results obtained by superimposing the noise density of 20%, 40%, 60%, 80%, and 90% on the Lena image and the Baboon image.

TABLE 2.2   The Noise Detection Results in Lena Image by Three Methods

	Mis-detection			False alarm		
Noise Density (%)	BDND	SAWM	Improved	BDND	SAWM	Improved
20	0	0	0	2	0	0
40	0	0	0	5	0	0
60	0	0	0	6	0	0
80	21	0	0	10	0	0
90	190	0	0	5	0	0

TABLE 2.3   The Noise Detection Results in Baboon Image by Three Methods

	Mis-Detection			False Alarm		
Noise Density (%)	BDND	SAWM	Improved	BDND	SAWM	Improved
20	0	6	0	30	51	4
40	0	9	0	29	2	3
60	0	8	0	24	1	1
80	6	5	0	21	1	1
90	272	2	0	16	0	1

2.5 SOME RECENT DEVELOPMENTS AND FURTHER RESEARCHES

In the following sub-sections, some technical developments and promising research directions in the last few years are briefly overviewed.

2.5.1 Non-switching Random Impulse Noise Cancellation

Impulse noise can be divided into two categories: *fixed-valued impulse noise* (FVIN) and *random-valued impulse noise* (RVIN). Relative to FVIN noise, the brightness value of RVIN noise pixels can be any value within the allowable range of the brightness value of the image pixel point. This value is often not much different from the brightness value of the pixel point in the neighborhood, and it is difficult to distinguish. Therefore, the detection and removal of RVIN noise are more challenging.

The noise reduction model of non-switching RVIN constructed using *deep convolutional neural network* (DCNN) is more advantageous than the mainstream switching RVIN in terms of noise reduction effect and execution efficiency, but in practical applications, the performance of this type of training-based (data-driven) noise reduction model is limited by whether it can accurately determine the severity of noise interference from the noise reduction image (i.e., the existence of data dependency issues).

To solve this problem, a fast RVIN *noise ratio estimation* (NRE) model based on shallow convolutional neural networks has been proposed (Xu et al. 2020). The noise ratio is used as a predictive index to measure the degree of image interference caused by noise. After training on a large number of training sets, the NRE prediction model is obtained. Combining the proposed NRE prediction model with the *de-noising convolutional neural networks* (DnCNN), the constructed non-switching noise reduction algorithm can adaptively call the corresponding pretrained depth noise reduction model for a specific interval

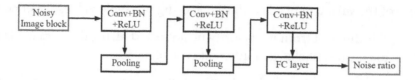

FIGURE 2.24   The network structure of the constructed NRE noise ratio estimation model.

(the range of the noise ratio value in the training image set is limited to a narrow range), depending on the severity of the noise interference from the RVIN noise of the image to be reduced, so as to efficiently complete high-quality noise reduction effects.

The network structure used is shown in Figure 2.24. The input of the NRE noise ratio prediction model constructed is an $n \times n$ noise block, which passes through multiple convolutional layers (each convolutional layer uses $3 \times 3 \times 16$ convolution kernel to generate an intermediate feature map) and uses the ReLU activation function to extract features and combines pooling and fully connected layers (FC) to reduce the dimensionality to obtain the final noise ratio value.

2.5.2 De-Noise Feature Extraction

In medical disease diagnosis, de-noise is a basic procedure. A method is designed for noise exclusion and effective diseases identification in MRI brain images (Sreelakshmi and Inthiyaz 2021). The performance is improved by the combined use of *adaptive median filter* (AMF), *convolution neural networks* (CNN), *gradient boosting* (GB) and *machine learning* (ML) mechanisms, as shown by the flowchart in Figure 2.25.

For input image, de-noising is performed based on the adaptive median filter and convolutional neural network mechanisms. If the output images have more noise than a threshold value, then they are automatically assigned to the AMF-CNN block. If this noise density is less than the threshold value, then the process has been moved to the GB-ML block. In the GB-ML block, disease classification and regression are performed using a tree structure. A statistical deep learning function can help the filtering process at the extraction stage.

The feature selection includes the following steps:

1. Read the input image, note that median$[A(x) + B(x)] \neq$ median$[A(x)]$ + median$[B(x)]$.

2. Spatial processing is used to confine which pixel of an image has been effected the different types of noises.

3. It classifies the pixels as per noise and differentiates each pixel in the image from its neighboring surround pixels.

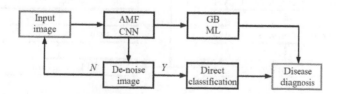

FIGURE 2.25   Flowchart of AMF-CNN with GB-ML.

4. The size of the surround pixel is adjustable using threshold values as per comparison.

5. If the pixel is different from its majority neighbors, structural alignment is necessary for these pixels. It is labeled as a different type of noises.

6. These noise pixels are then replaced with median pixels that are passed for the noise-removing function.

7. Compute convolutional neural networks for effective de-noising.

2.5.3 Strong Noisy Image De-Noising

To improve the quality of image de-noising (specific Gaussian noise and random Gaussian noise) in a strong noise environment, an algorithm based on a symmetric extended convolution residual network has been proposed (Gai and Bao 2020). In a strong noise environment, there is relatively little effective information available inside the image. Therefore, in the network training process, it is necessary to more fully excavate and use the effective information of the image to extract and learn image features.

The overall flow of the algorithm is shown in Figure 2.26, with 10 layers in total. In the design, the following factors are considered in turn:

1. The Leaky ReLU function is used, which can better retain the effective information of the image during the network training process and obtain the best de-noising effect.

2. *Batch normalization* (BN) is used, which can be used to solve the transfer of covariates within the network, overcome the shortcomings of deep neural networks that

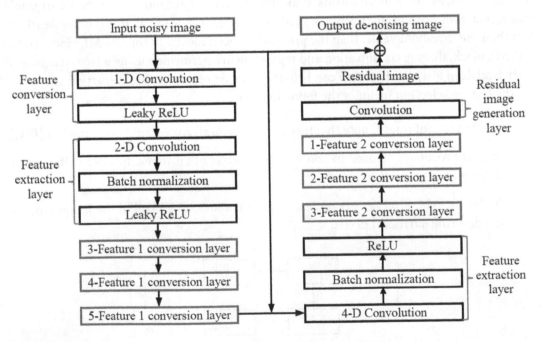

FIGURE 2.26   Flowchart of the strong noisy image de-noising method.

are difficult to train, and effectively prevent gradient dispersion. It can also speed up the convergence speed during the training process and improve the model accuracy, reducing the sensitivity of model initialization.

3. The expanded convolution technology is adopted to increase the receptive field of the network without increasing the computational burden of the network, so as to balance the size of the receptive field of the neural network and the depth of the network. Make the network obtain and make full use of the image. More effective context information in the de-noising image can be used to restore the damaged pixels in the de-noising image and complete the image de-noising task.

4. The residual learning strategy is adopted, which makes the deep convolutional neural network easy to train and can improve the accuracy of image classification and target detection.

2.5.4 Classify Noise Filtering Results in Seismic Images

Seismic imaging is the main technology used for subsurface hydrocarbon prospection. The raw seismic data is heavily contaminated with noise and unwanted reflections that need to be removed before further processing. Therefore, the noise attenuation is done at an early stage and often while acquiring the data. Remote sensing images are often affected by noise in the process of digitization and transmission processes. De-noising is an indispensable way of improving image quality (Wu et al. 2020).

To give confidence in the de-noising process, *quality control* (QC) is required. It can ensure that a costly data re-acquisition is not needed. A supervised learning approach to build an automatic QC system is proposed (Mejri and Bekara 2020). The QC system is an attribute-based classifier that is trained to classify three types of filtering (optimal = good filtering; harsh = over filtering, the signal is distorted; mild = under filtering, noise remains in the data). The attributes are computed from the data and represented geo-physically for the statistical measures of the quality of the filtering.

Experimental results show that some attributes show a good level of visual separation between the different types of filtering, particularly the harsh one. The clusters of attributes for the mild and the optimal filtering are close as they reflect the observation made earlier about the subtle differences between the two types of filtering.

In this system, *multi-layer perceptron* (MLP) is used for classification. Based on the fundamental assumption that without regularization, an optimal MLP structure tends to over fit as its depth is increased, a secure MLP-building strategy is adopted to build the multi-layer perceptron model with the least validation cross-entropy error.

Figure 2.27 depicts the flowchart of the one-vs-all binary classification process. The training and the validation sets were split into K subsets of equal size using the bootstrap aggregation strategy. The training and validation subsets were converted to $N = 3$ binary sets. Then, the binary MLP generator is used to predict binary decision subspaces. The predicted class members are then fed forward to a voting system, which decides on the class based on the majority vote, resulting in more accurate classification results.

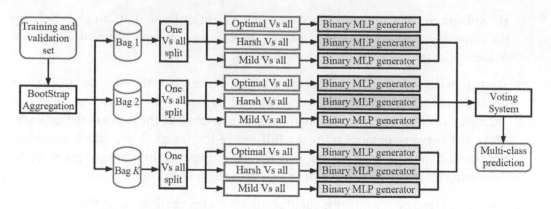

FIGURE 2.27   Multi-class MLP generator decision strategy.

REFERENCES

Duan, F., and Y.-J. Zhang. 2010. A highly effective impulse noise detection algorithm for switching median filters. *IEEE Signal Processing Letters*, 17(7): 647–650.

Eng, H.-L., and K.-K. Ma. 2001. Noise adaptive soft-switching median filter. IEEE Transaction on Image Processing, 10(2): 242–251.

Gai, S., and Z.-Y. Bao. 2020. High noise image denoising algorithm based on deep learning. *Acta Automatica Sinica*, 46(12): 2672–2680.

Kitchen, L., and A. Rosenfeld. 1981. Edge evaluation using local edge coherence. *IEEE-SMC*, 11(9): 597–605.

Li, R., Y.-J. Zhang, and H. C. Tan. 2006. A hybrid filter training and design method for adaptive noise cancellation. *Journal of Electronics & Information Technology*, 28(7): 1165–1168.

Mejri, M., and M. Bekara. 2020. Application of machine learning for the automation of the quality control of noise filtering processes in seismic data imaging. *Geosciences*, 10(12): 475.

Ng, P.-E., and K.-K. Ma. 2006. A switching median filter with boundary discriminative noise detection for extremely corrupted images. *IEEE Transaction on Image Processing*, 15(6): 1506–1516.

Sreelakshmi, D., and S. Inthiyaz. 2021. Fast and denoise feature extraction based ADMF–CNN with GBML framework for MRI brain image. *International Journal of Speech Technology* 24(3): 1–16.

Wu, C. Z., X. Chen, and S. Zhan. 2020. Remote sensing image denoising using residual encoder-decoder networks with edge enhancement. *Journal of Remote Sensing* 24(1): 27–36.

Xu, S. P., Z. Y. Lin, and C. X. Li, et al. 2020. A shallow CNN-based noise ratio estimation model. *Journal of Image and Graphics* 25(7): 1344–1355.

Zhang, X.-M., and Y.-L. Xiong. 2009. Impulse noise removal using directional difference based noise detector and adaptive weighted mean filter. *IEEE Signal Processing Letters*, 16(4): 295–298.

Zhang, Y.-J. 2017. *Image Engineering, Vol.1: Image Processing*. Germany: De Gruyter.

## CHAPTER 3

Image De-Blurring

I*MAGE BLUR* IS A COMMON process or result of image degradation. It is often generated during the image acquisition process and can also be caused by some image processing operations (Zhang 2017). General image blur will limit the spectrum width of the object to a certain extent, which will decrease the sharpness of the image, reduce the resolution, and lose useful information.

There are many reasons for blurring images. Among the more typical image blurs are motion blur caused by the movement between the camera and the scenery, distortion blur caused by atmospheric turbulence or haze, out-of-focus blur caused by the limited depth of field of the lens, aberration blur caused by defects in the optical system, and diffraction blur caused by diffracted light aperture, and so on. From the perspective of image sharpness, some people refer to the image quality degradation caused by noise as a kind of blurring.

Image de-blurring refers to remove the blur in the image, and image restoration techniques are often used for this purpose. There are many ways to de-blur the image. Restoration can be classified into two categories based on whether or not the physical constraints of the image are considered: unconstrained restoration and constrained restoration. It can be divided into two categories based on whether or not external intervention is required in the restoration: automatic restoration and interactive restoration. It can be divided into two categories based on the number of images used: single image de-blurring and multiple image de-blurring. It can be divided into two categories based on whether the prior knowledge of the cause of blurring is used to model and solve the problem: blind de-blurring and un-blind de-blurring.

Before the 1990s, image de-blurring technology was mainly based on spatial local filtering method. The advantage of this type of method is that the calculation speed is fast, but its de-blurring effect is relatively poor. From then until the beginning of the 21st century, image de-blurring technology based on sparse transformation has received more attention and research, and the image quality after de-blurring by such methods is higher. In the past 10 years, image de-blurring technology has begun to combine non-local similarity methods and neural network methods.

DOI: 10.1201/9781003241416-3

The contents of each section of this chapter will be arranged as follows.

Section 3.1 first discusses the general image degradation model. Then it analyzes the characteristics of image blur as a kind of degradation and discusses several common image blur types and main estimation methods of the blur function.

Section 3.2 first introduces the method of de-blurring using image restoration technology. The inverse filtering technology of unconstrained restoration and the Wiener filtering and least square filtering technology of constrained restoration are introduced, respectively. The method of interactive restoration is also discussed.

Section 3.3 discusses the estimation problem of motion blur kernel. The method of fast blind de-convolution and the method based on the convolutional neural network (CNN) using an end-to-end learning model are respectively introduced.

Section 3.4 discusses the use of different strategies to achieve de-blurring of low-resolution images. A method based on generative adversarial networks (GAN) is introduced emphatically. Its network structure and loss function are analyzed, and it is extended to multiple types of GANs.

Section 3.5 provides a brief introduction to some technique developments and promising research directions in the last year.

3.1 OVERVIEW OF IMAGE DE-BLURRING

Image blur is a process of image degradation, which leads to a decrease in image clarity and affects object recognition. The quality of *blurred images* can be improved by image restoration technology (called de-blurring), that is, to model the process of image degradation, and reconstruct or restore the original clear image based on the corresponding degradation model and related knowledge.

3.1.1 General Image Degradation Model

There are many cases of *image degradation*, and the corresponding models are different. A commonly used linear degradation model is shown in Figure 3.1, which is a simple *general image degradation model* (Zhang 2017). In this model, the image degradation process is modeled as a (linear) system H acting on the input image $f(x, y)$, that is, the *point spread function* (PSF), whose Fourier transform is the *transfer function*. Its combined effect with an additive noise $n(x, y)$ leads to a degraded image $g(x, y)$. Restoring an image according to this model is a process of obtaining a certain approximation to $f(x, y)$ based on a given $g(x, y)$ and H representing the degradation.

The input and output in Figure 3.1 have the following relationship:

$$g(x, y) = H[f(x, y)] + n(x, y) \tag{3.1}$$

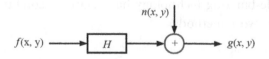

FIGURE 3.1 Simple general image linear degradation model.

If the *degenerate system H* satisfies the following four properties (here suppose $n(x, y) = 0$), the restoration will be relatively simple.

1. Linear: If k_1 and k_2 are constants, $f_1(x, y)$ and $f_2(x, y)$ are two input images, then

$$H\left[k_1 f_1(x,y) + k_2 f_2(x,y)\right] = k_1 H\left[f_1(x,y)\right] + k_2 H\left[f_2(x,y)\right] \tag{3.2}$$

2. Additivity: If $k_1 = k_2 = 1$ in Equation (3.2), it can become

$$H\left[f_1(x,y) + f_2(x,y)\right] = H\left[f_1(x,y)\right] + H\left[f_2(x,y)\right] \tag{3.3}$$

The above equation indicates that the response of a linear system to the sum of two input images is equal to the sum of its responses to the two input images.

3. Consistency: If $f_2(x, y) = 0$ in Equation (3.2), it can become

$$H\left[k_1 f_1(x,y)\right] = k_1 H\left[f_1(x,y)\right] \tag{3.4}$$

The above equation indicates that the response of a linear system to the product of a constant and any input is equal to the product of the constant and the response of the linear system to the input.

4. Position (space) invariance: If for any $f(x, y)$ and constants a and b, there is

$$H\left[f(x-a, y-b)\right] = g(x-a, y-b) \tag{3.5}$$

The above equation indicates that the response of the linear system at any position in the image is only related to the input value at that position and has nothing to do with the position itself.

If a linear degenerate system also satisfies the three properties of (2) ~ (4) above, that is, it satisfies additivity, consistency, and position (space) invariance, then Equation (3.1) can be written as ($\otimes$ represents convolution)

$$g(x,y) = h(x,y) \otimes f(x,y) + n(x,y) \tag{3.6}$$

In the equation, $h(x, y)$ is the *impulse response* of the degenerate system. Using the corresponding matrix representation, Equation (3.6) can be written as

$$g = hf + n \tag{3.7}$$

According to the convolution theorem, the frequency domain representation corresponding to Equation (3.6) is represented as ($G(u, v)$, $H(u, v)$, $F(u, v)$, and $N(u, v)$ are the Fourier transforms of $g(x, y)$, $h(x, y)$, $f(x, y)$, and $n(x, y)$, respectively):

$$G(u,v) = H(u,v)F(u,v) + N(u,v) \tag{3.8}$$

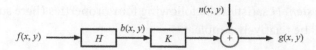

FIGURE 3.2   An image degradation model considering nonlinear degradation.

The above-mentioned degradation model with invariant linear space is the most common model. In some cases, nonlinear degradation (such as the D-logE curve of film) needs to be considered. At this time, there is a model that can be represented in Figure 3.2 (Zhang 2017). It is believed that the nonlinear degradation can be decomposed into a combination of a linear degradation part H and a pure nonlinear degradation part K. In this way, the input and output in Figure 3.2 have the following relationship:

$$g(x,y) = K\{H[f(x,y)]\} + n(x,y) = K[b(x,y)] + n(x,y) \tag{3.9}$$

From a formal point of view, Equation (3.9) is somewhat similar to Equation (3.1). Compared to Equation (3.1), $b(x, y)$ in Equation (3.9) is the result of linear degenerate system H acting on $f(x, y)$, and K can be regarded as a pure nonlinear degenerate system.

3.1.2 Blurring Degradation

Image blur is a common image degradation situation or process, which can also be represented by the model shown in Figure 3.1, where the blur is generated by the system H, which is also called the *blur kernel* at this time. In Figure 3.1, the input image is affected by both blur and noise. As a result, the degraded image $g(x, y)$ becomes a noisy blurred image.

If the blur kernel is known, only the clear image needs to be solved. This problem can be called *non-blind de-blurring*. If both the blur kernel and the clear image need to be solved, this problem is called *blind de-blurring*. For the blind de-blurring problem, if the blur kernel can be obtained, the problem can be transformed into a non-blind de-blurring problem.

Solving the blind de-blurring problem directly is an ill-conditioned (underdetermined) problem because the solution is not unique. In the actual solving process, it is necessary to introduce prior knowledge about the blur kernel or clear image (including the heuristic knowledge of enhancing the edge and the knowledge of constructing the prior probability distribution model). According to the mathematical method to solve the underdetermined problem, one can consider constructing a regularized cost function based on the prior information of the image to transform the problem into a variational problem, in which the variational integral depends on the data and smoothing constraints at the same time. For example, for the problem of estimating function f from a set of values $y_1, y_2, …, y_n$ at points $x_1, x_2, …, x_n$, the regularization method is to minimize the functional

$$H(f) = \sum_{i=1}^{N} [f(x_i) - y_i]^2 + k\Phi(f) \tag{3.10}$$

In the equation, $\Phi(f)$ is a smoothing functional, and k is a positive parameter, which is called a *regularization number*.

The blur caused by different reasons will have different effects on the image quality (different changes in the image), and the blur kernels corresponding to different types of blur can also be very different.

The necessary condition for *motion blur* is that there is relative motion between the camera and the object during the imaging process. This motion can originate from camera motion (global motion), object motion (local motion), or both. In practice, if the imaging time is long and/or the motion is relatively violent, resulting in the length of the trajectory of the motion reaching the pixel level during the imaging process, visible motion blur will be formed on the captured image. Motion blur is embodied in the image that the scenery stretches along the direction of motion and produces double shadows, so it is also called *motion smear*. The image acquisition system (with a narrow field of view) that uses a telescope lens is very sensitive to this type of image degradation.

The *out-of-focus blur* is related to the *depth of field* of the camera lens. The depth of field of the lens corresponds to the distance between the closest object and the farthest object that can be clearly imaged in the scene. When the camera lens is focused at a certain distance, the scene at that distance is the clearest, and the scene deviating from this distance will gradually blur with the degree of deviation. In general, within a certain range (depth of field) before and after this distance, the blur does not reach the pixel level, and the resulting blur cannot be noticed; the scene beyond this range will show the blur effect on the collected image. This blur is generally isotropic, which limits the resolution sharpness of image. Therefore, if it does not focus on the object one wants to observe (missing focus), the object in the image may not be clear enough.

Figure 3.3a shows an original clear image and its two corresponding images with motion blur (Figure 3.3b) and out-of-focus blur (Figure 3.3c). The upper left corner of Figure 3.3b and c shows the blur kernel (image) that produces the corresponding blur. It can be seen that the blur kernel of motion blur is a straight line reflecting the motion trajectory (it will be a curve for complex motion), and the blur kernel of out-of-focus blur is a disc. Motion blur is directional, while out-of-focus blur is more consistent in all directions. The difference in the blur kernel here corresponds to the blurring of the scene in Figure 3.3b and c.

In addition, atmospheric turbulence blur contains some of the characteristics of the above two kinds of blur in a certain sense. Atmospheric turbulence is an important form of motion in the atmosphere. It is a state of motion in which air particles change irregularly

(a)   (b)   (c)

FIGURE 3.3 Examples of motion blur and out-of-focus blur.

or randomly. This motion obeys a certain statistical law. Atmospheric turbulence can cause the image to be blurred and un-cleared, and even distorted. The turbulent distorted image contains the diffraction limit information of the imaging system and the object. Atmospheric turbulence causes the refractive index of the atmosphere to change randomly with time and space. The direction and phase of light propagation in the turbulence will be jittered, causing the imaging focal plane to produce random fluctuations in the intensity of the image point, resulting in phenomena such as intensity distribution diffusion, peak reduction, image blur, and position shift.

3.1.3 Blur Kernel Estimation

According to the image degradation model, to restore the blurred image (de-blurring), it is necessary to determine the blur function, that is, estimate the blur kernel. In practice, the blur function is often difficult to be completely determined from the image, but it can be estimated with the help of some prior knowledge. In the case that the blur function cannot be obtained directly, performing image restoration to eliminate blur is also called *blind de-convolution*.

The estimation methods for blur functions can be divided into three categories:

1. Estimation with the help of image observation.

2. Estimation by using point source image experiment.

3. Estimation with the help of modeling degradation.

3.1.3.1 Using the Image Observation to Estimate the Blur Function

Consider the case where the image is affected by linear space invariant degradation. If only a degraded image $g(x, y)$ is given without any knowledge about the image degradation function, only the information contained in this image can be used to estimate the degradation function.

When the degradation is caused by the blur process, a (sub) region with a typical structure in the image can be selected. To reduce the influence of noise, the region should preferably contain obvious edges or high-contrast borders between the object and the background. If the grayscale contrast between the object and the background is C_{ob}, and the mean square error of the noise is σ, then the signal-to-noise ratio can be defined as (Kitchen and Rosenfeld 1981).

$$SNR = \left(\frac{C_{ob}}{\sigma} \right)^2 \tag{3.11}$$

Here, it is required to choose a region with a large signal-to-noise ratio.

Suppose the region in the selected blurred image is $g_s(x, y)$, $g_s(x, y)$ needs to be processed to obtain $f_s(x, y)$, where $f_s(x, y)$ is the estimation of the original image $f(x, y)$ at the position corresponding to $g_s(x, y)$. If the signal-to-noise ratio of the selected region is large enough to ignore the influence of noise, then according to Equation (3.8), it will have

$$H_s(u,v) = \frac{G_s(u,v)}{F_s(u,v)} \qquad (3.12)$$

In the equation, $G_s(u, v)$ and $F_s(u, v)$ are the Fourier transform of $g_s(x, y)$ and $f_s(x, y)$, respectively, and $H_s(u, v)$ is the blur function of the corresponding region.

If it is assumed that the blur is invariant in linear space, then $H(x, y)$ can be inferred from $H_s(x, y)$ in theory. Of course, this method is quite crude and requires more troublesome manual operation.

3.1.3.2 Using the Point Source Image Experiment to Estimate the Blur Function

If the type of equipment that collects the blurred image $g(x, y)$ is known and one has similar equipment on hand, it is possible to make a more accurate estimation of the blur. First, use the equipment on hand to make different system settings or parameter selections and try to obtain an image close to the given blurred image. Next, according to the same system settings or parameter selection, a small spot (approximately one pulse) is imaged to obtain the *impulse response* of the blur process (the characteristics of the linear space invariant system are completely determined by its impulse response).

An image can be regarded as a collection of multiple point source images. For example, if the point source image is regarded as the approximation of the unit impulse function $(F[\delta (x, y)] = 1)$, then there is $G(u, v) = H(u, v)F(u, v) \approx H(u, v)$. In other words, the *transfer function* $H(u, v)$ of the blur system at this time can be approximated by the Fourier transform of the blurred image.

In practical applications, it is hoped that the small light spot should be as bright as possible, and the contrast with the background should be as large as possible so that the influence of noise can be reduced to a minimum or even negligible. Because the Fourier transform of a pulse is a constant (here set to C), according to Equation (3.8), one can write

$$H(u,v) = \frac{G(u,v)}{C} \qquad (3.13)$$

In the equation, $G(u, v)$ is the Fourier transform of the blurred image $g(x, y)$, and $H(u, v)$ is the blur function.

3.1.3.3 Using Blur Modeling to Estimate the Blur Function

If a model of the blur process can be established, it is possible to obtain an analytical blur function to restore the blurred image according to Equation (3.8). In practice, only for some special blur forms, the blur function used for restoration can be obtained analytically. The following are two special cases.

1. The image (out-of-focus) blur caused by the inaccurate focus of the thin lens can be described by the following function:

$$H(u,v) = \frac{J_1(dr)}{dr} \qquad (3.14)$$

In the equation, J_1 is a first-order Bessel function, $r^2 = u^2 + v^2$, and d is the amount of model translation (note that this model changes with position). This function can be used as a blur function for de-blurring the image.

2. In a darker scene, the camera needs a longer exposure time. If there is relative movement between the camera and the object, the captured images are often (motion) blurry. Consider the case where the relative motion is a uniform linear motion (generating a *uniform linear motion blur*). Suppose an image $f(x, y)$ is collected for a scenery moving at a uniform speed on a plane, and $x_0(t)$ and $y_0(t)$ are, respectively, the motion component of the moving object in the x and y directions, T is the length of the acquisition time. Ignoring other factors, the collected blurred image $g(x, y)$ can be represented as

$$g(x,y) = \int_0^T f\left[x - x_0(t), y - y_0(t)\right] dt \tag{3.15}$$

Its Fourier transform can be represented as

$$G(u,v) = \int_{-\infty}^{\infty} \int_{-\infty}^{\infty} g(x,y) \exp\left[-j2\pi(ux+vy)\right] dx\, dy = F(u,v) \int_0^T \exp\left\{-j2\pi\left[ux_0(t)+vy_0(t)\right]\right\} dt \tag{3.16}$$

By defining

$$H(u,v) = \int_0^T \exp\left\{-j2\pi[ux_0(t)+vy_0(t)]\right\} dt \tag{3.17}$$

as a motion blur degradation function, when the motion components $x_0(t)$ and $y_0(t)$ can be determined or estimated, the blur can be eliminated (see the next section for an example).

3.2 IMAGE RESTORATION AND DE-BLURRING

Research on de-blurring has a history of many years, and people have proposed a variety of classic methods, which have been widely used in practice. The following paragraph briefly introduces the methods based on image restoration technology to eliminate blur.

Image restoration is a large category of technology in image processing. *Image restoration* is closely related to image enhancement. The similarity between image restoration and image enhancement is that they can both improve the visual quality of the input image. The difference between them is that image enhancement technology generally only uses the characteristics of the human visual system to obtain good-looking visual results, while image restoration considers that the image (quality) is degraded or deteriorated under certain circumstances/conditions (i.e., the image quality has been reduced and distorted), and now it is necessary to reconstruct or restore the original image based on the corresponding degradation model and knowledge. In other words, the image restoration technology is to model the image degradation process and restore it according to the determined image degradation model to obtain the original desired effect.

Under the conditions of a given model, image restoration techniques can be divided into two categories: unconstrained and constrained. The method of unconstrained restoration only regards the image as a digital matrix, without considering the physical constraints that the image should be subjected to after restoration, and mainly deals with it from a mathematical point of view. The constrained restoration method also considers that the restored image should be subject to certain physical constraints, such as being relatively smooth in space and the image gray value is always positive.

By the way, although noise is random, it often has certain statistical laws. If a certain model of noise can be established, or the process of image degradation affected by noise can be modeled, then image restoration technology can also be used to denoise the image based on the noise degradation model.

Based on the basic image degradation model established in the previous section, the following summarizes three typical methods, namely, inverse filter restoration, Wiener filter restoration, and constrained least squares restoration (Zhang 2017). In addition, it also introduces, with examples, how to use human–computer interaction methods to improve the flexibility and efficiency of image restoration.

3.2.1 Inverse Filtering

Inverse filtering is a simple and direct, unconstrained restoration method.

3.2.1.1 Unconstrained Restoration

The *unconstrained restoration* method treats the image as only a digital matrix and restores the image from a mathematical point of view without considering the physical constraints that the image should be subjected to after restoration.

Starting from the general image degradation model given in Figure 3.1, it can be obtained from Equation (3.7):

$$n = g - hf \tag{3.18}$$

Without any prior knowledge of n, image restoration can be described as looking for an estimate f_e of the original image f so that hf_e is closest to the degraded image g in the sense of minimum mean square error, that is, the norm of n is to be minimized:

$$\|n\|^2 = n^T n = \|g - hf_e\|^2 = (g - hf_e)^T (g - hf_e) \tag{3.19}$$

According to the above equation, the restoration problem can be regarded as to determine the minimum value of the following equation for f_e:

$$L(f_e) = \|g - hf_e\|^2 \tag{3.20}$$

Here it is only needed to differentiate L to f_e and set the result to 0, when h^{-1} exists, then the unconstrained restoration equation can be obtained:

$$f_e = (h^T h)^{-1} h^T g = h^{-1} (h^T)^{-1} h^T g = h^{-1} g \tag{3.21}$$

3.2.1.2 Inverse Filtering Principle

According to Equation (3.21), the estimated f_e of the original image f can be obtained by (left) multiplying the degraded image with the inverse representation matrix of the degraded system. If Equation (3.21) is transformed into the frequency domain, the estimation of the Fourier transform of the original image is:

$$F_e(u,v) = \frac{G(u,v)}{H(u,v)} \tag{3.22}$$

That is, if the Fourier transform of the degraded image is divided by the degraded system function, an estimate of the Fourier transform of the original image can be obtained. If $H(u, v)$ is regarded as a filter function, dividing $G(u, v)$ by $H(u, v)$ is an inverse filtering process (here $H(u, v)$ is an ideal inverse filter). The restored image can be obtained by applying the inverse Fourier transform of the result of Equation (3.22):

$$f_e(x,y) = \mathcal{F}^{-1}\left[F_e(u,v)\right] = \mathcal{F}^{-1}\left[\frac{G(u,v)}{H(u,v)}\right] \tag{3.23}$$

It can be seen from Equation (3.23) that the key to restoring the image at this time is to design an appropriate filter function $H(u, v)$. In practice, only for some special degraded forms, the filter function used for restoration can be obtained analytically. Two examples are the image blur caused by the inaccurate focus of a thin lens that can be described by Equation (3.14) and the uniform linear motion blur caused by the relative movement between the camera and the object that can be described by Equations (3.15)–(3.17), see the last section.

Another example is the image blur caused by atmospheric disturbance. At this time, the temperature inconsistency at different locations will cause the light passing through the air to shift. This can be described by the following function:

$$H(u,v) = \exp\left(-k \cdot r^{5/3}\right) \tag{3.24}$$

In the equation, k is a constant that depends on the type of disturbance, and the power of 5/3 is often approximated by 1.

3.2.1.3 Restoration Transfer Function

As mentioned above, the image restoration problem can be solved by inverse filtering. But in the previous discussion, the noise item $N(u, v)$ is not considered, as in Equation (3.8). In reality, noise is inevitable. After considering the noise, the inverse filtering form of the corresponding Equation (3.22) is

$$F_e(u,v) = F(u,v) + \frac{N(u,v)}{H(u,v)} \tag{3.25}$$

Two problems can be seen from Equation (3.25). First, because $N(u, v)$ is random, even if the degradation function $H(u, v)$ is known, the original image cannot always be restored accurately. Second, if $H(u, v)$ takes 0 or a very small value on the UV plane, $N(u, v)/H(u, v)$ will make the restoration result and the expected result have a big gap (the calculation of $H(u, v)$ will also encounter problems). In practice, the $H(u, v)$ decreases rapidly as the distance between (u, v) and the origin increases, while the noise $N(u, v)$ changes slowly in general. In this case, the restoration can only be performed in a range closer to the origin (close to the center of the frequency domain), at this time $H(u, v)$ is larger than $N(u, v)$. In other words, in general, the inverse filter is not exactly $1/H(u, v)$, but a restricted function of u and v, which can be denoted as $M(u, v)$. $M(u, v)$ is often called the *restoration transfer function*, so the combined image degradation and restoration model can be represented in Figure 3.4.

How to determine the restoration transfer function? A common method is to take $M(u, v)$ as the following function:

$$M(u,v)= \begin{cases} 1/H(u,v) & u^2+v^2 \le w_0^2 \\ 1 & u^2+v^2 > w_0^2 \end{cases} \tag{3.26}$$

In the equation, the selection principle of w_0 is to remove the point where $H(u, v)$ is 0. The disadvantage of this method is that the ringing effect of the restoration result is more obvious.

Another improved method is to take $M(u, v)$ as

$$M(u,v)= \begin{cases} k & H(u,v) \le d \\ 1/H(u,v) & \text{otherwise} \end{cases} \tag{3.27}$$

where both k and d are constants less than 1, and it is better to choose a smaller d.

Figure 3.5 gives an example of comparing the above two restoration transfer functions. Figure 3.5a is a simulated degraded image obtained by blurring an ideal image with a low-pass filter. According to the restoration transfer function of Equations (3.26) and (3.27), the restoration results obtained by inverse filtering are shown in Figure 3.5b and c, respectively. Compared to these two figures, the ringing effect in Figure 3.5c is relatively small.

In practice, the transfer function $H(u, v)$ of the degraded system can be approximated by the Fourier transform of the degraded image. An image can be regarded as a collection of multiple point source images. If the point source image is regarded as the approximation of the unit pulse function $(F[\delta(x, y)] = 1)$, then $G(u, v) = H(u, v)F(u, v) \approx H(u, v)$.

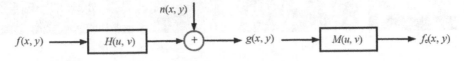

FIGURE 3.4   Image degradation and restoration model.

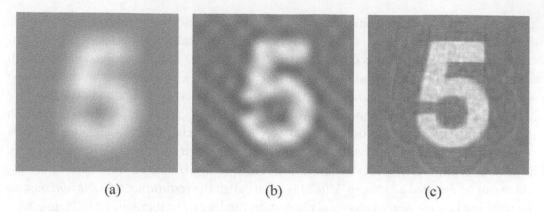

FIGURE 3.5 Comparison of the effects of different restoration transfer functions.

The motion blur caused by the movement between the camera and the scenery can be eliminated by inverse filtering technology. Figure 3.6 shows an example of eliminating the blur caused by a fixed camera shooting a uniform linear motion scenery. Figure 3.6a shows a frame of 256×256 image blurred due to the relatively uniform linear motion between the camera and the subject. Here, the distance that the subject moves horizontally during shooting is 1/8 of the size of the image in this direction, that is, 32 pixels. Figure 3.6b is the result of estimating the moving distance as 32, and the image is well restored. Figure 3.6c and d are the results obtained by taking the moving distances as 24 and 40, respectively. Since these two estimations of the movement speed (also the moving distance) are not accurate, the restoration effects are not good.

3.2.1.4 Fast Decomposition Calculation

If the degradation source can be modeled by a first-order operator (filter), the inverse filter can be realized without Fourier transform (Goshtasby 2005). First-order operators refer to operators that can be decomposed into a combination of 1-D operators. For example, the following first-order operator R can be decomposed into

$$R = \begin{bmatrix} ac & a & ad \\ c & 1 & d \\ bc & b & bd \end{bmatrix} = \begin{bmatrix} a \\ 1 \\ b \end{bmatrix} \begin{bmatrix} c & 1 & d \end{bmatrix} = st^T \tag{3.28}$$

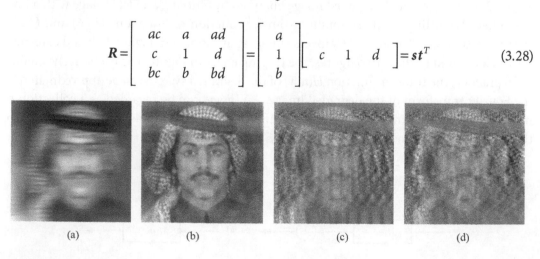

(a)   (b)   (c)   (d)

FIGURE 3.6 Eliminate the blur caused by uniform linear motion.

Convolving an image with the filter R is equivalent to convolving the image with the filter s and then convolving with the filter t. Similarly, performing inverse filtering with filter R on an image is equivalent to performing inverse filtering with filter t first and then performing inverse filtering with filter s. Only the inverse filter calculation for the filter s will be discussed below, and the inverse filtering calculation for the filter t can be achieved by inverse filtering the transposition of the image with the transposition of the filter t and then transposing the result.

Assuming that f is an image of $M \times N$, the convolution of the image and the filter r can be written as follows:

$$g(j) = \mathcal{F}^{-1}\{\mathcal{F}[f(j)] \cdot \mathcal{F}(r)\} \qquad j = 0,1,\ldots,N-1 \qquad (3.29)$$

In the equation, $f(j)$ and $g(j)$ are the j-th column of the image before filtering and the image after filtering, respectively. The dot "•" represents point-to-point multiplication, and F and F⁻¹ represent Fourier transform and inverse Fourier transform, respectively. Now, given the filtered (blurred) image g and filter s, the image before blur can be calculated as follows:

$$f(j) = \mathcal{F}^{-1}\left\{\frac{\mathcal{F}|g(j)|}{\mathcal{F}(s)}\right\} \qquad (3.30)$$

In the equation, division is also point-to-point. This operation is only possible when the Fourier transform coefficients of s are not zero.

For first-order filters, the calculation of the inverse filter does not require the use of Fourier transform. If the image g is obtained by convolving the image f of $M \times N$ with the filter s, then

$$g(x,y) = \sum_{i=-1}^{1} s(i)f(x,y+i), \qquad x = 0,1,\ldots,M-1; \qquad y = 0,1,\ldots,N-1 \qquad (3.31)$$

In the equation, $g(x, y)$ is the xy-th item of the convolution image, $s(-1) = a$, $s(0) = 1$, $s(1) = b$. In Equation (3.31), suppose that for $x = 0, 1, \ldots, M-1$, $f(x, -1)$ and $f(x, N)$ are both 0. Equation (3.31) can also be written as $g = hf$ in matrix form, where

$$h = \begin{bmatrix} 1 & b & & & & & \\ a & 1 & b & & & & \\ & a & 1 & \vdots & & & \\ & & a & \vdots & b & & \\ & & & \vdots & 1 & b & \\ & & & & a & 1 \end{bmatrix}_{M \times M} \qquad (3.32)$$

Note that given the filter s, the matrix h is completely determinable. Taking into account the special form of the matrix h, the original image f can be determined row by row or column by column. Let $f(j)$ and $g(j)$ be the j-th column of f and g respectively, $f(j)$ can be obtained by solving the following equation

$$hf(j) = g(j) \tag{3.33}$$

To solve Equation (3.33), replace h with bD, here

$$D = \begin{bmatrix} \alpha & 1 & & & & \\ \beta & \alpha & 1 & & & \\ & \beta & \alpha & \vdots & & \\ & & \beta & \vdots & 1 & \\ & & & \vdots & \alpha & 1 \\ & & & & \beta & \alpha \end{bmatrix} = \begin{bmatrix} 1 & & & & \\ k_0 & 1 & & & \\ & k_1 & 1 & & \\ & & k_2 & \vdots & \\ & & & \vdots & \alpha \\ & & & & k_{M-2} & \alpha \end{bmatrix}$$

$$\begin{bmatrix} l_0 & 1 & & & & \\ & l_1 & 1 & & & \\ & & l_2 & \vdots & & \\ & & & \vdots & 1 & \\ & & & & l_{M-2} & 1 \\ & & & & & l_{M-1} \end{bmatrix} = KL \tag{3.34}$$

In the equation, $\alpha = 1/b$, $\beta = a/b$, $l_0 = a$, $k_{i-1} = \beta/l_{i-1}$, and $l_i = a - k_{i-1}$, for $i = 1, 2, \ldots, M-1$. It has been proved that the KL decomposition of matrix D only exists when a, $b < 0.5$. Now rewrite Equation (3.33) as

$$bKLf(j) = g(j) \tag{3.35}$$

Let vector E satisfy $KE = g(j)$ and substitute it into Equation (3.35), then according to $bLf(j) = E$, $f(j)$ can be calculated. Calculating each element of the matrix f row by row requires only 4 multiplications. Therefore, the multiplication required to calculate the inverse filter (using a 3×3 first-order filter) is in the order of $O(N^2)$. Compared to the $O(N^2\log_2 N)$ order of multiplication required to calculate the inverse filtering of an $N \times N$ image by using the fast Fourier algorithm, for a larger N, the amount of calculation saved is still relatively large.

3.2.2 Wiener Filtering

Wiener filtering is a method of constrained restoration, which is different from unconstrained restoration methods such as inverse filtering. The method of constrained restoration also considers that the restored image should be subject to certain physical constraints, such as being relatively smooth in space, the gray value is positive, and so on. Therefore, it needs to realize the joint optimization of image restoration and physical constraints.

3.2.2.1 Constrained Restoration

Also starting from Equation (3.7), constrained restoration considers selecting a linear operator Q (transformation matrix) of f_e so that $\|Qf_e\|^2$ is the smallest. This problem can be solved by the Lagrangian multiplier method. Let l be the Lagrangian multiplier, find f_e that minimizes the following criterion function:

$$L(f_e) = \|Qf_e\|^2 + l(\|g - Hf_e\|^2 - \|n\|^2) \tag{3.36}$$

Similar to solving Equation (3.20), the constrained restoration equation can be obtained (let $s = 1/l$):

$$f_e = [H^T H + sQ^T Q]^{-1} H^T g \tag{3.37}$$

3.2.2.2 Wiener Filter

The *Wiener filter* is a minimum mean square error filter. It can be derived directly from Equation (3.37). In the frequency domain, the general representation of the Wiener filter is:

$$F_e(u,v) = H_W(u,v)G(u,v) = \frac{H^*(u,v)}{|H(u,v)|^2 + s[S_n(u,v)/S_f(u,v)]} G(u,v) \tag{3.38}$$

In the equation, s is a parameter (see below), and $S_f(u, v)$ and $S_n(u, v)$ are the Fourier transform of the correlation matrix elements of the original image and noise, respectively.

There are several variants of Equation (3.38):

1. If $s = 1$, $H_W(u, v)$ is the standard Wiener filter.

2. If s is a variable, it is called a *parametric Wiener filter*.

3. When there is no noise, $S_n(u, v) = 0$, the Wiener filter degenerates into the ideal inverse filter of the previous sub-section.

Because s must be adjusted to satisfy Equation (3.37), when $s = 1$, the optimal solution that satisfies Equation (3.37) cannot be obtained by using Equation (3.38), but it is optimal in the sense of minimization of $E\{[f(x, y) - f_e(x, y)]^2\}$. Here, both $f(\bullet)$ and $f_e(\bullet)$ are regarded as random variables, and a statistical criterion is thus obtained.

In practice, $S_n(u, v)$ and $S_f(u, v)$ are often unknown. At this time, Equation (3.38) can be approximated by the following equation (where K is a predetermined constant):

$$F_e(u,v) \approx \frac{H^*(u,v)}{|H(u,v)|^2 + K} G(u,v) \tag{3.39}$$

Figure 3.7 shows a comparison example of inverse filter de-blurring and Wiener filter de-blurring in two degradation situations. Figure 3.7a shows a column of images that first convolve a normal image with a smooth function $h(x, y) = \exp\left[\sqrt{(x^2 + y^2)}/240\right]$ to produce a

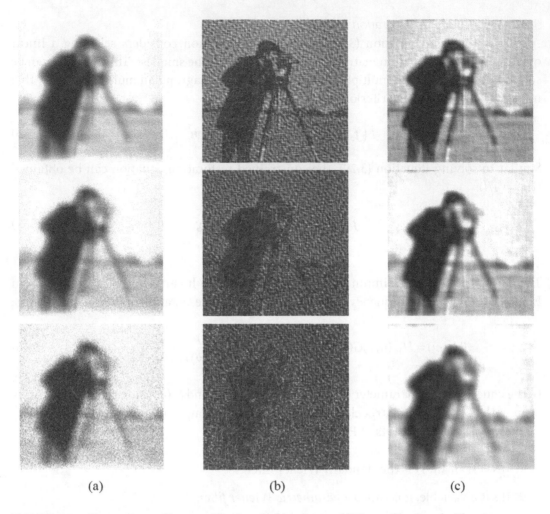

FIGURE 3.7   Comparison of inverse filtering de-blurring and Wiener filtering de-blurring.

blur effect (similar to the atmospheric disturbance effect in remote sensing imaging), and then superimpose the Gaussian random noises of zero mean value, whose variances are 8, 16, and 32, respectively. This set of images (degraded images) are to be restored. Figure 3.7b shows a column of the results obtained by using the inverse filtering method to restore. Figure 3.7c shows a column of the results obtained by using the Wiener filtering method to restore. It can be seen from Figure 3.7b and c that when the image is deblurred, if the image is still affected by noise, the effect of Wiener filtering is better than that of inverse filtering, and the stronger the noise, the more obvious this advantage.

In addition, the Wiener filter given by Equation (3.38) can be further generalized to obtain a *geometric mean filter*:

$$H_W(u,v) = \left[\frac{H^*(u,v)}{|H(u,v)|^2} \right]^t \left[\frac{H^*(u,v)}{|H(u,v)|^2 + s\left[S_n(u,v)/S_f(u,v) \right]} \right]^{1-t} \tag{3.40}$$

In Equation (3.40), s and t are both positive real numbers. This geometric mean filter consists of two parts, the exponents are t and $1-t$. Equation (3.40) becomes an inverse filter and a parametric Wiener filter at $t=1$ and $t=0$, respectively; and if $s=1$ at $t=0$, it becomes a standard Wiener filter. In addition, $t=1/2$ can also be taken here, at this time, Equation (3.40) becomes the product of two representations with the same power (satisfying the definition of geometric mean, the name of the filter is derived from this). When $s=1$, $t<1/2$, the geometric mean filter is closer to the inverse filter; if $t>1/2$, the geometric mean filter is closer to the Wiener filter.

3.2.3 Constrained Least Squares Restoration

The method of Wiener filtering is a statistical method. The optimal criterion it uses is based on the respective correlation matrices of the image and noise, so the result obtained is only optimal in the average sense. The *constrained least squares restoration* method is another constrained restoration method. It only needs knowledge about the noise mean and variance to get the optimal result for each given image.

In the frequency domain, the formula for constrained least squares recovery is

$$F_e(u,v) = \left[\frac{H^*(u,v)}{|H(u,v)|^2 + s|L(u,v)|^2} \right] G(u,v) \qquad u,v = 0,1,\ldots,M-1 \qquad (3.41)$$

In this equation, $L(u, v)$ represents the 2-D Fourier transform corresponding to the function that extends the Laplacian (calculating the sum of the second-order partial derivatives along the X and Y directions) to the image size. The form of Equation (3.41) is somewhat similar to the form of the Wiener filter. The main difference is that there is no need for knowledge of other statistical parameters except for the estimation of noise mean and variance.

Figure 3.8 shows a comparison example of Wiener filtering and constrained least square filtering in two degraded situations. Figure 3.8a is the degraded image obtained by blurring the Cameraman image with a filter of a defocus radius of $R=3$. Figure 3.8b is the result of restoring Figure 3.8a with Wiener filtering, Figure 3.8c is the result of restoring Figure 3.8a with the constrained least square filter. Figure 3.8d is a degraded image with random noise of a variance of 4 superimposed on Figure 3.8a, Figure 3.8e is the result of restoring Figure 3.8d with Wiener filter, Figure 3.8f is the result of restoring Fig. 3.8d with a constrained least square filter. It can be seen from these figures that when there is both blur and noise, the effect of constrained least square filtering is slightly better than Wiener filtering; when there is only blur but no noise, the effects of the two methods are the same.

3.2.4 Interactive Restoration

Interactive restoration uses the combination of man and machine to control the restoration process to obtain some special effects.

In practice, sometimes the image will be covered by a 2-D sinusoidal interference pattern (also called correlated noise). Let $S(x, y)$ represent the sinusoidal interference pattern with amplitude A and frequency components (u_0, v_0), namely

$$S(x, y) = A\sin(u_0 x + v_0 y) \qquad (3.42)$$

FIGURE 3.8 Comparison of Wiener filter de-blurring and constrained least square filter de-blurring.

Its Fourier transform is

$$N(u,v) = \frac{-jA}{2}\left[\delta\left(u - \frac{u_0}{2\pi}, v - \frac{v_0}{2\pi}\right) - \delta\left(u + \frac{u_0}{2\pi}, v + \frac{v_0}{2\pi}\right)\right] \quad (3.43)$$

The above equation has only imaginary components, which represents a pair of coordinates $(u_0/2\pi, v_0/2\pi)$ and $(-u_0/2\pi, -v_0/2\pi)$ located on the frequency plane, and the intensities of pulse are $-A/2$ and $A/2$, respectively. Because the degradation here is only caused by noise, there is

$$G(u,v) = F(u,v) + N(u,v) \quad (3.44)$$

If the amplitude image of $G(u, v)$ is displayed, the two noise pulses will become two bright spots when A is large enough and their coordinates are far from the origin. In this way, the positions of the pulse component can be determined in the frequency domain by visual observation and the band-stop filter (see Sub-section 2.2.2) can be used to eliminate them at these positions to remove the influence of the sinusoidal interference pattern.

In practice, the situation is often more complicated. For example, the image obtained by an electro-optical scanner is often covered by a 2-D periodic structure pattern because the sensor is disturbed by small signal amplification in the electronic circuit. In this case, there are often multiple sine components. If the above method is used, it is possible to remove too much image information, so the following method is required. First, the main frequency of the interference pattern must be extracted. This requires placing a band-pass filter $H(u, v)$ at the position corresponding to each bright spot in the frequency domain. If one can construct a $H(u, v)$ that allows only components related to the interference pattern to pass, then the Fourier transform of this structural pattern is

$$P(u,v) = H(u,v)G(u,v) \tag{3.45}$$

To build such a $H(u, v)$, many judgments are needed to determine whether each bright spot is an interference bright spot. So this work often needs to be done interactively by observing the spectrum display of $G(u, v)$. When a filter is determined, the structural mode corresponding to the spatial domain can be obtained by the following equation:

$$p(x,y) = \mathcal{F}^{-1}\{H(u,v)\, G(u,v)\} \tag{3.46}$$

If the $p(x, y)$ can be accurately determined, then subtract $p(x, y)$ from $g(x, y)$ can give $f(x, y)$. In practice, only a certain approximation of this pattern can be obtained. To reduce the influence of components that are not considered in the estimation of $p(x, y)$, the weighted $p(x, y)$ can be subtracted from $g(x, y)$ to obtain an approximation of $f(x, y)$:

$$f_a(x,y) = g(x,y) - w(x,y)\, p(x,y) \tag{3.47}$$

where $w(x, y)$ is called the weight function, and the optimal result in a certain sense can be obtained by adjusting it. A specific method is to choose $w(x, y)$ so that the variance of $f_a(x, y)$ is the smallest in the specific neighborhood of each point (x, y). Suppose the neighborhood of the point (x, y) is $(2X+1) \times (2Y+1)$, then the neighborhood mean and variance are respectively

$$\overline{f_a}(x,y) = \frac{1}{(2X+1)(2Y+1)} \sum_{m=-X}^{X} \sum_{n=-Y}^{Y} f_a(x+m, y+n) \tag{3.48}$$

$$\sigma^2(x,y) = \frac{1}{(2X+1)(2Y+1)} \sum_{m=-X}^{X} \sum_{n=-Y}^{Y} \left[f_a(x+m, y+n) - \overline{f_a}(x,y) \right]^2 \tag{3.49}$$

Substituting Equation (3.47) into Equation (3.49), and assuming that $w(x, y)$ is a constant in the neighborhood, then Equation (3.49) becomes

$$\sigma^2(x,y) = \frac{1}{(2X+1)(2Y+1)} \sum_{m=-X}^{X} \sum_{n=-Y}^{Y} \{[g(x+m,y+n)$$

$$-w(x+m,y+n)p(x+m,y+n)] - [\bar{g}(x,y) - \overline{w(x,y)p(x,y)}]\}^2$$

$$= \frac{1}{(2X+1)(2Y+1)} \sum_{m=-X}^{X} \sum_{n=-Y}^{Y} \{[g(x+m,y+n)$$

$$-w(x,y)\,p(x+m,y+n)] - [\bar{g}(x,y) - w(x,y)\,\bar{p}(x,y)]\}^2 \qquad (3.50)$$

Take the derivative of Equation (3.50) with respect to $w(x, y)$ and make the result to 0 to obtain $w(x, y)$ that minimizes $\sigma^2(x, y)$ as

$$w(x,y) = \frac{\overline{g(x,y)\,p(x,y)} - \bar{g}(x,y)\,\bar{p}(x,y)}{\overline{p^2}(x,y) - \bar{p}^2(x,y)} \qquad (3.51)$$

Calculate $w(x, y)$ from Equation (3.51) and substitute it into Equation (3.47) to get the restored result (an approximation of the original image).

Figure 3.9 shows an example of using interactive restoration to eliminate sinusoidal interference patterns. Figure 3.9a is an image after a normal image is covered by a sinusoidal interference pattern as defined by Equation (3.42). Figure 3.9b is its Fourier spectrum amplitude map, on which there is a pair of more obvious (pulse) white dots (the intersection of bright lines). People can place two band-stop filters at the two white points in an interactive way to filter out the pulses, as shown in Figure 3.9c, and then by taking the inverse Fourier transform, one can get Figure 3.9d. As shown in the restoration result, the sinusoidal interference pattern is eliminated here. Note that the radius of the band-stop filter should be relatively small for better restoration. The centers of the two band-stop filters used in Figure 3.9e are the same as those in Figure 3.9c, but their radius is 5 times larger. The restoration results obtained are shown in Figure 3.9f. There is a more obvious ringing effect in this figure.

3.3 ESTIMATING MOTION BLUR KERNEL

Image blur is a degradation process. According to the theory of image restoration, it is necessary to reconstruct or restore the original image using the corresponding degradation model and knowledge. According to the model in Figure 3.1, to achieve image de-blurring, the key is to determine the blur degradation function, that is, the *blur kernel*. Two methods of estimating the motion blur kernel are introduced below.

3.3.1 Fast Blind De-Convolution

According to Equation (3.6), if blurring is regarded as a convolution process, then de-blurring should be a de-convolution process.

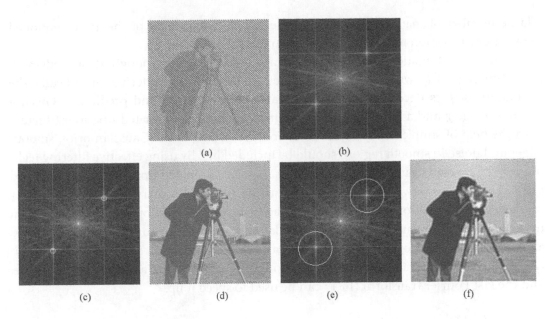

FIGURE 3.9 Interactive restoration example.

3.3.1.1 Basic Idea

According to Equation (3.7), it is an ill-conditioned problem to realize *blind de-convolution* (here, *blind de-blurring*), that is, there is only one blurred image, but the blur kernel and the original clear image must be determined at the same time. In other words, various combinations of h and f can satisfy Equation (3.7) when only g is known. To this end, it is not only necessary to introduce prior knowledge but also to estimate h and f iteratively and optimally (Cho and Lee 2009):

$$f_e = \arg\min_f \left\{ \|\, g - hf \,\| + R_f(f) \right\} \tag{3.52}$$

$$h_e = \arg\min_h \left\{ \|\, g - hf \,\| + R_h(h) \right\} \tag{3.53}$$

In the equations, $\|\, g - hf \,\|$ is the data fitting item (commonly using L_2 norm), and R_f and R_h are regular items (e.g., both can use total variation).

The purpose of using iterative optimization is to gradually refine the motion blur kernel h. Once h is obtained, non-blind de-blurring can be further used, that is, f is obtained by using h and g to achieve non-blind deconvolution. Here, the f_e obtained in the iterative process does not directly affect the final result of de-blurring, but only indirectly affects the refinement of the motion blur kernel h.

In the foregoing iterative optimization, two important steps in the estimation of f_e are used to achieve an accurate estimation of the blur kernel: sharp edge restoration and noise removal in the smooth region. The former can help accurately estimate the blur kernel, while the latter can eliminate the influence of noise on the estimation of the blur kernel. The direct use of Equation (3.52) often requires the use of computationally complex nonlinear optimization methods, and the use of Equation (3.53) to estimate the blur kernel involves a large number of matrix operations, so the calculation amount of the aforementioned iterative optimization method will be very large.

To calculate Equation (3.52), it is assumed that there are enough strong edges in the estimation of f_e, which can be performed with the help of filtering. Specifically, the estimation of f_e is decomposed into two parts: deconvolution and prediction. Given a blurred image g and a blur kernel h, the blur in g must be eliminated first to estimate f_e with the help of simple and fast deconvolution. According to the Gaussian prior, smooth edges and noise in smooth regions should be included in f. By using effective filtering techniques, strong edges can be restored and noise can be eliminated from f to obtain a refined estimate f_0. In this way, f_0 provides a higher quality f_e for preliminary kernel estimation.

To calculate Equation (3.53), a similar strategy can be used. In optimization, it is often necessary to perform multiple gradient calculations on the energy function, which requires a lot of matrix operations. To speed up the calculation of Equation (3.53), the characteristics of the matrix operation corresponding to the convolution operation can be used here, and the fast Fourier transform (FFT) can be used to speed it up.

3.3.1.2 Blind De-Convolution Process

The process of implementing blind de-convolution is shown in Figure 3.10 (Cho and Lee 2009). To refine f_e and h progressively, three steps need to be iteratively calculated: prediction (including bilateral filtering, impulsive filtering, and gradient amplitude thresholding), kernel estimation, and deconvolution. Put the prediction here at the beginning of the loop is to provide the initial f_e value for kernel estimation.

In the prediction step, two gradient maps of f ($G_x = \partial f / \partial x$ and $G_y = \partial f / \partial y$) need to be calculated to eliminate the noise in the smooth region and predict the significant edges in f. Except at the beginning of the iteration, the input to the prediction step is the estimate of f obtained in the deconvolution step in the previous iteration. In the kernel estimation step, the predicted gradient image and the gradient image of g need to be used. In the deconvolution step, h and g need to be used to obtain an estimate of f, which will be used in the prediction step of the next iteration.

To make the estimation of h and f more effective and efficient, the scheme from coarse to fine can be adopted. At the roughest level, a down-sampled version of g can be used to initialize the process of the prediction step. After the final estimate of f is roughly obtained, it is up-sampled by bilinear interpolation and then used in the next finer level of prediction step. Such a coarse-to-fine scheme can still achieve better results when the blur is large and when only using image filtering to predict may not be sufficient to capture sharp edges.

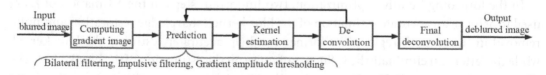

FIGURE 3.10   Blind deconvolution process.

In the process of iteratively updating h and f from coarse to fine, grayscale versions of g and f can be used. After obtaining the final h at the finest scale (input image size), perform final deconvolution with h for each color channel to obtain a de-blurring result.

3.3.1.3 Calculation Details

Some technical details to implement the above three steps are as follows:

1. *Prediction*

    In the prediction step, only strong edges in the gradient image can be retained, while other regions have zero gradients. In fact, in the kernel estimation step, only strong edges have an impact on kernel optimization, because no matter what the kernel function is, the convolution with zero gradient is always zero.

    The prediction steps include bilateral filtering, impact filtering, and gradient amplitude thresholding, as shown in Figure 3.11. First, use bilateral filtering (Tomasi and Manduchi 1998) on the current estimate of f to suppress possible noise and small details. Then use the impact filter to restore the strong edge of f. The result of impact filtering contains not only high-contrast edges but also enhanced noise. The noise can be eliminated by thresholding the gradient magnitude.

    The strong edges in f can be recovered using the impact filter. Impact filter is an effective tool to enhance image features and can recover clear edges from blurred step signals (Osher and Rudin 1990). The iterative equation of the impact filter is as follows:

$$f_{t+1} = f_t - \mathrm{sign}\left(\Delta f_t\right)\|\nabla f_t\|\,\mathrm{d}t \tag{3.54}$$

where f_t is the image at time t, Δf_t and ∇f_t are the Laplacian and gradient of f_t, respectively, and $\mathrm{d}t$ is the time step of each iteration.

2. *Kernel Estimation*

    To use the predicted gradient map to estimate the motion blur kernel, the following energy functions need to be minimized (the asterisk represents the wildcard subscript symbol):

$$E_h(h) = \sum_{\left(G_*,\,g_*\right)} w_* \left\|hG_* - g_*\right\|^2 + k\|h\|^2 \tag{3.55}$$

where $(G_*,\ g_*)$ belongs to the set $\{(G_x,\ \partial_x h),\ (G_y,\ \partial_y h),\ (\partial_x G_x,\ \partial_{xx} h),\ (\partial_y G_y,\ \partial_{yy} h),\ and$ $(\partial_x G_x + \partial_y G_y)/2,\ G_{xy} h)\}$, w_* represents the weight added to each partial derivative, and k is the weight of Tikhonov's regularization (Yuan et al. 2007). Each $(hG_* - g_*)$ constitutes an image, and the image I can be defined $\|I\|^2 = \Sigma_{(x,\,y)} I(x,\,y)^2$, where $(x,\,y)$ is one pixel location in I.

    The pixel value is not used in the energy function of Equation (3.55), only the derivative is used. Equation (3.55) can be written in matrix form:

$$E_h(h) = \|Ah - b\|^2 + k\|h\|^2 = (Ah - b)^T (Ah - b) + kh^T h \tag{3.56}$$

where A is a matrix containing 5 G_*s, and b is a matrix containing 5 g_*s. To minimizeEquation (3.56), the gradient of $E_h(h)$ can be used

$$\frac{\partial E_h(h)}{\partial h} = 2A^T Ah + 2kh - 2A^T b \tag{3.57}$$

This equation needs to be calculated many times in the minimization process.

Owing to the large size of A, the calculation of Equation (3.57) will be time-consuming. If the dimensions of f and h are $n \times n$ and $m \times m$, respectively, then the dimension of A will be $5n^2 \times m^2$. However, this calculation can be accelerated by FFT. Specifically, 12 FFTs need to be calculated for each iteration. To reduce the number of FFTs, the calculations of Ab and A^TAh can be directly connected in series, which can reduce the calculation of 10 FFTs (Cho and Lee 2009).

3. *De-Convolution*

In the de-convolution step, f is estimated from the given kernel h and the input blur image g. The energy function used is:

$$E_f(f) = \sum_{\partial_*} w_* \left\| h \, \partial f - \partial g \right\|^2 + l \left\| \nabla f \right\|^2 \tag{3.58}$$

In this equation, ∂_* belongs to the set $\{\partial_0, \partial_x, \partial_y, \partial_{xx}, \partial_{xy}, \partial_{yy}\}$, which represents partial derivative operations in different directions and orders (usually till second order); w_* represents the weight added to each partial derivative; l represents the weight of the regular item, which can be 0.1. The first item of the energy function is based on a blur model (Shan et al. 2008), which uses derivatives to reduce ring artifacts. The regular item selects f with a smooth gradient (Levin et al. 2007). In the frequency domain, only two FFTs are needed to quickly optimize with pixel-by-pixel division.

3.3.2 CNN-Based Method

In recent years, the restoration of blurred images based on *convolutional neural networks* (CNN) has received widespread attention. The blind de-convolution method introduced in the previous sub-section can be regarded as a filtering-based method, which mainly relies on recovering the clear edge information of the image in a process of blur kernel estimation from large scale to small scale, from coarse to fine.

The following introduces a method of using CNN to extract clear edge information from blurred images (Xu et al. 2018). It still includes two steps: suppression of irrelevant details and noise, and enhancement of sharp edges. It uses the learned clear image edges to remove blur and no longer requires the heuristic operations of the previous sub-section (such as coarse-to-fine multiscale blur kernel estimation and edge selection using thresholds). Therefore, this method can simplify the estimation of the blur kernel and reduce the calculation amount of the algorithm. In other words, it can reduce the computational complexity and running time of the entire blur kernel estimation process.

3.3.2.1 Principle and Process

This CNN-based method uses an end-to-end learning model, which can establish a mapping function from blur image input to corresponding clear edge output. The model framework and flowchart are shown in Figure 3.11.

This is a network with six layers. Given an input blurred image, first calculate its gradient images G_x and G_y in the horizontal and vertical directions, respectively. Then, the results are used as the input of the network (Figure 3.11 only draws the calculation process for the horizontal gradient, the calculation process for the vertical gradient is also the same). The first three layers of the network correspond to the first step of suppressing noise and details. They are equivalent to filtering operations in the gradient domain to maintain the main structure of the image and eliminate some redundant image details. The last three layers of the network correspond to the second step of enhancing clear edges. They are equivalent to an impact filter to further enhance the main structure of the extracted image and obtain clear edges.

The above process can be illustrated using Figure 3.12, where the left column corresponds to the input image, the middle column corresponds to the middle feature layer, and the right column corresponds to the output result. In each column, the upper image is the edge image,

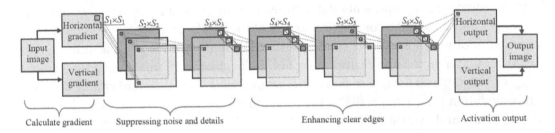

FIGURE 3.11 The framework and flowchart of using a convolutional neural network to estimate the degradation function.

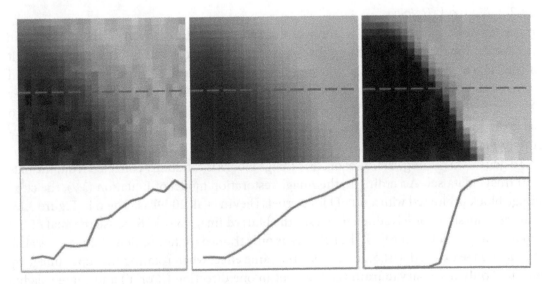

FIGURE 3.12 Schematic diagram of the clear edge recovery process.

and the lower image is the gray value curve corresponding to the section (dash) line of the upper image. It can be seen that the first three layers of the network remove/smooth the noise and details from the input image (the gray value curve is smoothed), and the last three layers of the network enhance the edges of the smooth image (the gray value curve is steeper).

3.3.2.2 Network Structure

Figure 3.11 uses a CNN to recover clear edges from blurred inputs. Using the modeling Equation (3.7) for the blur process, the network can be defined as follows:

$$T^0(G_x) = G_x \qquad (3.59)$$

$$T_n^l(G_x) = P\left[\sum_m T_m^{l-1} \otimes w_{m,n}^l + b_n^l\right] \qquad l=1,2,3,4,5 \qquad (3.60)$$

$$T_o(G_x) = Q\left[\sum_m T_m^5 \otimes w_m^6 + b^6\right] \qquad (3.61)$$

In these equations, T_n^l represents the n-th feature image of the l-th layer, w^l and b^l are the weight and bias of the convolution kernel of the l-th layer, respectively, and the subscripts m, n of w^l represents the connection relationship from the m-th feature image of the current layer to the n-th feature image of the next layer. In this model, the size of w^l is $c_{l-1} \times s_l \times s_l \times c_l$, and the size of b^l is $c_l \times 1$, where c_l and s_l are the number and size of the l-th convolution kernel, respectively. The function $P(\bullet)$ represents the modified linear unit (ReLU) (Nair and Hinton 2010). The gradient of the image is normalized to $[-2, 2]$, so $Q(\bullet) = 2\tanh(\bullet)$ is used as the final *activation function* to limit the output response of the filter. The final output image $T_o(G_x)$ of the network corresponds to the predicted edge image.

3.3.2.3 Network Training

In the network training, the first three layers and the last three layers of the network are trained separately. To train the first three layers of the network, the bilinear filtering result of the clear image is used as the training true value to reduce the influence of noise and unnecessary details. To train the last three layers of the network, the L_0 sparse prior filter (Xu et al. 2013) is used to extract the main structure from the clear image. After the two parts of the network are trained separately, connect them in series to get the network structure in Figure 3.11 (Xu et al. 2018).

To generate training data, a set of clear image blocks is randomly collected from the natural image data set. According to the image restoration model of Equation (3.7), the clear image block is blurred with a set of blur kernels (Levin et al. 2009) as shown in Figure 3.13, and 1% Gaussian noise is added to obtain the blurred image block. Because the goal of the model is to predict clear edges, the network is only trained in the gradient domain. Because the clear edge extraction should produce the same effect when rotating the input image by 90°, it is only necessary to train the gradient in one direction (X or Y) and share weights between the trained network and the other direction (Y or X).

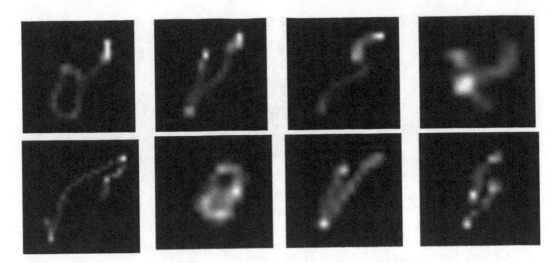

FIGURE 3.13   A set of blur kernels is used to generate blurred images.

According to Figure 3.11, the output of the third layer of the network consists of c_3 feature images, which can be represented by $\{T_m^3; m = 1, 2, \ldots, c_3\}$. The weighted average of these feature images is used as the output of the first three layers of the network (a_m is a coefficient that can be learned):

$$O_3(\boldsymbol{G}_x) = \sum_{m=1}^{c_3} a_m T_m^3 \tag{3.62}$$

To train the last three layers of the network, write their output as:

$$T_n^4(\boldsymbol{G}_x) = P\left[g_n * O_3(\boldsymbol{G}_x) + b_n^4 \right] \tag{3.63}$$

$$T_n^5(\boldsymbol{G}_x) = P\left[\sum_m T_m^4 * w_{m,n}^5 + b_n^5 \right] \tag{3.64}$$

$$T_o^6(\boldsymbol{G}_x) = Q\left[\sum_m T_m^5 * w_m^6 + b^6 \right] \tag{3.65}$$

where g_n is the convolution kernel that can be learned, and the size is $s_4 \times s_4$. After training the two sub-networks of the first three layers and the last three layers, they can be connected by recalculating the convolution kernel of the 4-th layer:

$$w_{m,n}^4 = a_m g_n \qquad m = 1, 2, \ldots, c_3 \qquad n = 1, 2, \ldots, c_4 \tag{3.66}$$

This connection process can increase the capacity of the network (the original number of free parameters is $m+n$, and after connection is mn), then it can better help the estimation of clear edges.

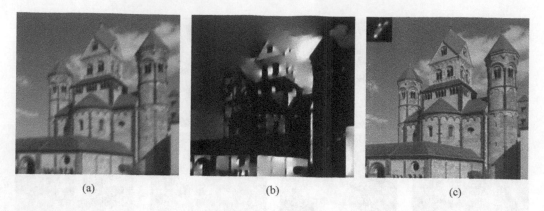

      (a)   (b)   (c)

FIGURE 3.14   The result of de-blurring using the convolutional network.

3.3.2.4 Fuzzy Kernel and Clear Image Estimation

After the main edge $T_o(G_x)$ is obtained from the blur input image, the *blur kernel* can be estimated by solving the two optimization problems of Equation (3.53) and Equation (3.54), respectively.

After the blur kernel is determined, the final clear image can be estimated by a variety of non-blind de-convolution methods. For example, the super Laplacian prior of the $L_{0.8}$ norm can be used to restore a clear image, and its mathematical expression is:

$$f_e = \arg\min_f \|g - hf\| + l\|G\|_{0.8} \tag{3.67}$$

This optimization problem can be solved by the iterative reweighted least squares method (Levin et al. 2007).

Figure 3.14 shows the experimental results of a real image with blurring. Figure 3.14a is the original blurred image, Figure 3.14b is the edge image output by the network, and Figure 3.14c is the de-blurring result of the convolutional network. Since the clear edges can be effectively recovered from the blurred image, the blur kernel can be better estimated, and a fairly clear de-blurring effect can be obtained. The network settings here are: blur kernel size $s_1 = 9$; $s_2 = 1$; $s_3 = 3$; $s_4 = 5$; $s_5 = 1$; $s_6 = 3$; the number of blur kernel $c_n = 128$, where $n = 1, 2, 3, 4, 5$. Because the input and output of the network are both the gradient of the grayscale image, both c_0 and c_6 are set to 1.

Figure 3.15 shows the experimental results of a real image, where Figure 3.15a is the original blurred image, Figure 3.15b is the edge image output by the network, and Figure 3.15c is the de-blurring result of the convolutional network. Figure 3.15d shows the result of de-blurring using the blind de-convolution method in the previous section. It can be seen from the figure that the result obtained by using the convolutional network is clearer than the result obtained by using the blind de-convolution, and the ringing effect is also smaller.

3.4 LOW-RESOLUTION IMAGE DE-BLURRING

De-blurring of low-resolution images is also an ill problem because it is necessary to improve the resolution of the image and remove the blur in the image. Under normal circumstances, the use of *blind de-convolution* method for de-blurring often assumes that

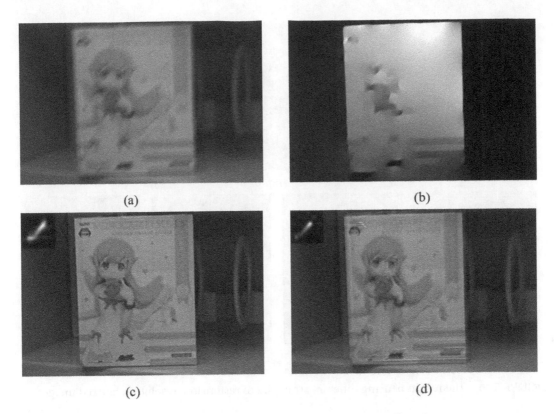

FIGURE 3.15   Convolutional network and blind deconvolution de-blurring effect comparison.

the input image has a higher resolution and contains main edges that can be extracted so that the unknown blur kernel can be recovered according to this assumption. If the input image has a low resolution and lacks clear details, the blur kernel and clear image cannot be restored accurately. To improve the resolution of the image, some people use *super-resolution* technology (see Chapter 8). However, super-resolution technology requires clear input, and if used for de-blurring, it often requires a known form of blur kernel. When the low-resolution input image contains complex forms of motion blur, the existing super-resolution methods often produce results with large structural distortions. If one simply performs super-resolution and blind de-convolution one after another, in addition to ringing effects and other problems, the error in the blur kernel estimation will be amplified by the subsequent super-resolution operation, and the undesirable effects caused by the super-resolution will also be diffused by the following de-blurring methods.

Figure 3.16 gives a set of experimental images to explain the above problems. Figure 3.16a is a low-resolution blurred image, Figure 3.16b is the result obtained by the super-resolution method, and Figure 3.16c is the result obtained by using the blind de-convolution method, Figure 3.16d is the result obtained by first using the super-resolution method and then followed by the blind de-convolution method, and Figure 3.16e is the result obtained by first using the blind deconvolution method and then followed by the super-resolution method. Figure 3.16f is the result obtained by using the GAN method (see below), and Figure 3.16g is the grand truth image. It can be seen from Figure 3.16b that the resolution of the image is

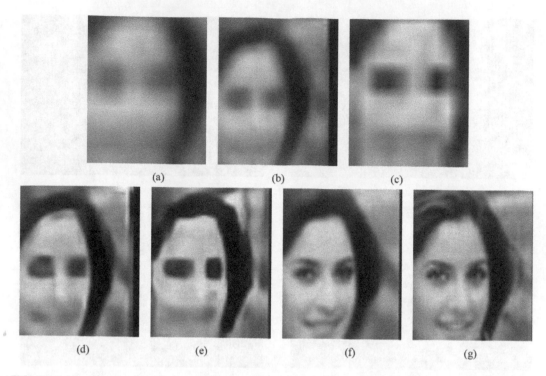

FIGURE 3.16   The results of using different strategies to restore low-resolution blurred images.

somewhat improved compared to the original image, but the blur is still obvious (because most super-resolution algorithms only assume a parameterized blur kernel and cannot explain complex motion blur). It can be seen from Figure 3.16c that the blur degree of the image is slightly lower than that of the original image, but the resolution is still relatively low, and it contains a lot of ringing effects and noise. It can be seen from Figure 3.16d and e that the adverse effects of the first step are more obvious after the second step, and the image quality is not too high.

The following introduces a low-resolution image de-blurring method based on a GAN approach, and Figure 3.16f is one of the results it obtained. This method combines the improvement of image resolution with de-blurring and directly starts from the low-resolution blurred input image to restore the high-resolution clear image (Xu et al. 2017).

3.4.1 Network Structure

The *generative adversarial network* (GAN) can learn a generative model through the adversarial process. It trains a generator network and a discriminator network at the same time. These two networks are against each other. Given a discriminator D, the generator G learns to generate samples that can fool the discriminator; given a generator G, the discriminator learns to distinguish between real data (clear images) and samples output from the generator (blurred images). In the network training process, the generator and the discriminator need to be optimized in turn.

3.4.1.1 Loss Function

The network training process is an optimization process. Mathematically speaking, the loss function (training cost function) to be optimized can be expressed as:

$$\max_{d} \min_{g} \left\{ E_{f \sim P_{\text{data}}(f)} \left[\log D_d(f) \right] + E_{n \sim P_n(n)} \left[\log \left(1 - D_d \left[G_g(n) \right] \right) \right] \right\} \tag{3.68}$$

where n is random noise; f represents actual data; g and d are the parameters of G and D, respectively. By training the discriminator, it is necessary to assign a large probability value to the actual data (the first item), and then assign a small probability value to the sample generated by the generator (the second item).

GANs can be used to learn discriminators and effective discriminating features. In the model below, the generator takes low-resolution blurred images instead of random noise as input and generates high-resolution clear images. The discriminator is trained to distinguish between the blurred image synthesized by the generator and the real, clear image.

3.4.1.2 Generator Network

The architecture of the deep CNN used is shown in Table 3.1, where C represents the convolution layer, U represents the de-convolution layer, and 2X represents up-sampling.

Similar models have been proven to be very effective for image de-blurring (Hardis et al. 2015). The generator of the network here also contains two up-sampling layers, using a fractional step size convolution layer (Radford et al. 2015), which is usually also called a de-convolution layer. Each de-convolution layer consists of a learnable convolution kernel. Compared with a single bi-cubic interpolation kernel function (Dong et al. 2016), these learned convolution kernels can work together to achieve better interpolation effects. The generator network first up-samples the low-resolution blurred image through the de-convolution layer and then uses the convolution operation to generate a clear image. Specifically, after each layer, the *batch normalization* (BN) function (Ioffe and Szegedy 2015) and the *rectifier linear unit* (ReLU) are used as the activation function. A hyperbolic tangent function is used as the activation function in the last layer.

3.4.1.3 Discriminator Network

The discriminator used is a 5-layer CNN, and its architecture is shown in Table 3.2, where C represents the convolution layer and FC represents the fully connected layer.

The input of the discriminator network is an image, and the output is the probability that the input image is clear. In this discriminator network, except for the sigmoid function used in the last layer, the *leaky rectifier linear unit* (leaky ReLU) (Mass et al. 2013) is used

TABLE 3.1 The Architecture of the Generator Network

Layer Type	U	C	U	C	C	C	C	C	C	C	C	C
# of convolution kernels	64	64	64	64	64	64	64	64	64	64	64	3
Convolution kernel size	6	5	6	5	5	5	5	5	5	5	5	5
Step size	2X	1	2X	1	1	1	1	1	1	1	1	1

TABLE 3.2   The Architecture of the Discriminator Network

Layer Type	C	C	C	C	FC
# of convolution kernels	64	64	64	64	1
Convolution kernel size	4	4	4	4	—
Step size	2	2	2	2	—

as the activation function (Radford et al. 2015). In addition, the BN function (Ioffe and Szegedy 2015) is used after each convolutional layer except the first convolutional layer to speed up training.

3.4.2 Loss Function Design and Effects

The design of the loss function should consider both the discriminator and generator comprehensively. Different loss functions will cause different image de-blurring results. Several loss functions are considered and combined to provide better results.

3.4.2.1 Various Loss Functions

The following four loss functions are considered.

1. Semantic-Level Loss Function

    The discriminator can be regarded as a semantic prior and the GAN is used to learn the prior. At this time, one of the most direct training methods is to use the loss function in Equation (3.68). If let $\{f_i, i = 1, 2, ..., N\}$ represent a high-resolution clear image, and let $\{g_i, i = 1, 2, ..., N\}$ represent a corresponding low-resolution blurred image, then the loss function of the training generator can be represented as:

$$\min_g \left\{ \frac{1}{N} \sum_{i=1}^{N} \log\left\{1 - D_d\left[G_g(g_i)\right]\right\} \right\} \qquad (3.69)$$

2. Pixel-Level Loss Function

    To optimize the design of the loss function, a simple and further constraint is to require the output of the generator to be as close to the grand truth as possible, namely

$$\min_g \left\{ \frac{1}{N} \sum_{i=1}^{N} \left\| G_g(g_i) - f_i \right\|^2 \right\} \qquad (3.70)$$

    The above loss item penalizes the pixel-level difference between the output of the generator and the grand truth image, which can help the generator output higher quality results.

3. Joint Loss Function

    One can combine the above two loss functions to get

$$\min_g \left\{ \frac{1}{N} \sum_{i=1}^{N} \left\| G_g(g_i) - f_i \right\|^2 + k \log\left\{1 - D_d\left[G_g(g_i)\right]\right\} \right\} \qquad (3.71)$$

    where the scalar k is a balanced weight.

4. Feature Matching Loss Function

To further improve the image quality, a feature matching loss function can be added:

$$\min_g \left\{ \frac{1}{N} \sum_{i=1}^{N} \left\| R_d^l [G_g(g_i)] - R_d^l(f_i) \right\|^2 \right\} \tag{3.72}$$

where $R_d^l(f)$ represents the characteristic response of input f in the l-th layer of the discriminator network. The loss function causes the restored image and the real image to have similar feature responses in the middle layer of the discriminator network, and these features are more likely to reflect the structural information of the image. The feature here is dynamically extracted from the discriminator network, so it has a strong discriminatory effect on specific types of real data and generated data. In this way, with the help of feature matching items, the result obtained has more realistic image characteristics.

3.4.2.2 Combined Final Loss Function

The finally combined loss function is described as follows.

By combining the feature matching loss item, the training of the generator and the discriminator requires to solve the following optimization problems:

$$\max_d \min_g \left\{ \frac{1}{N} \sum_{i=1}^{N} \left\| G_g(g_i) - f_i \right\|^2 + k_1 \left\| R_d^l [G_g(g_i)] - R_d^l(f_i) \right\|^2 \right.$$

$$\left. + k_2 \left\{ \log D_d(f_i) + \log \{1 - D_d[G_g(g_i)]\} \right\} \right\} \tag{3.73}$$

where k_1 and k_2 are used to balance the weight of each item.

Because it is hoped that the distance between the real image and the generated image should be greater than the distance between the two real images, the loss function can be further adjusted to convert the training of the generator and the discriminator into solving the following optimization problems:

$$\min_g \left\{ \frac{1}{N} \sum_{i=1}^{N} \left\| G_g(g_i) - f_i \right\|^2 + k_1 \left\| R_d^l [G_g(g_i)] - R_d^l(f_i) \right\|^2 + k_2 \left\{ \log \{1 - D_d[G_g(g_i)]\} \right\} \right\} \tag{3.74}$$

$$\min_d \left\{ \sum_{i=1}^{N} \frac{1}{N} - \log D_d[G_g(f_i)] - \log \{1 - D_d[G_g(g_i)]\} + \right.$$

$$\left. k_3 \left[\left\| R_d^l(f_i) - R_d^l(f_i) \right\|^2 - \left\| R_d^l[G_g(g_i)] - R_d^l(f_i) \right\|^2 + e \right]_+ \right\} \tag{3.75}$$

In the equation, $[\cdot]_+$ represents the modified linear activation function, and e is the desired distance between the real image and the generated image in the feature space. The loss function Equation (3.74) of generator G is composed of Equations (3.69), (3.70), and (3.71), which respectively promote the generator's output and real data to be similar in semantic, pixel, and structure. The loss function Equation (3.75) of the discriminator D makes a real sample f be closer to another real sample f' instead of the generated sample $G_g(g)$. Note that when updating G using Equation (3.74) and updating D using Equation (3.75), the choice of convolutional layer l can be different. By default, the second convolutional layer of D is used in Equation (3.74) to maintain the main structural features of the input; and the third convolutional layer of G is used in Equation (3.75) to better represent higher layers of semantic information.

3.4.2.3 Comparison of Loss Functions

Figure 3.17 gives a set of experimental images obtained with the above-discussed loss functions, where Figure 3.17a is a low-resolution blurred image, and Figure 3.17b is the result obtained with the semantic-level loss function, Figure 3.17c is the result obtained with the pixel-level loss function, Figure 3.17d is the result obtained with the joint loss function, and Figure 3.17e is the result obtained with the joint loss function combining the feature matching loss item. Figure 3.17f is the grand truth image.

In Figure 3.17, the PSNR of Figure 3.17b is 18.68dB, the PSNR of Figure 3.17c is 24.31dB, the PSNR of Figure 3.17d is 22.65dB, and the PSNR of Figure 3.17e is 24.16dB.

Some further discussions on the results are in the following.

Figure 3.17b shows the generated result with semantic-level loss function is relatively clear overall, but there are some low-quality regions around the face and eyes.

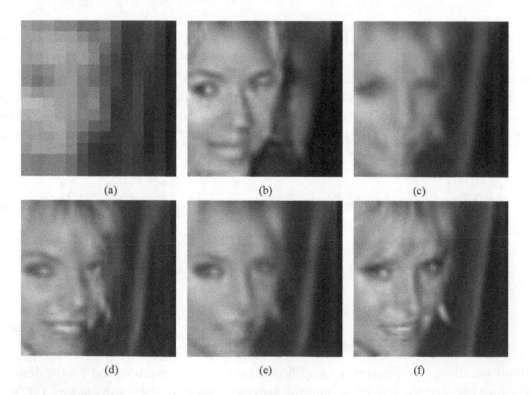

FIGURE 3.17 The effect of using different loss functions.

Figure 3.17c shows the pixel-level loss function can encourage the network to generate a visually better image, but the image will be over-smoothed to a certain extent.

Figure 3.17d shows the PSNR of the restored image with the joint loss function is significantly lower than the result of using only the pixel-level loss function, but the visual perception is closer to the real image (still contains structural distortion and noise in some smooth regions).

Figure 3.17e shows the use of a joint loss function combined with feature matching loss items can help the network generate clearer and higher image quality results.

3.4.3 Multi-Class GAN

The network method introduced above is designed for the same type of image, which can be called a *single-class generative adversarial network* (SCGAN). If one wants to apply to different image categories, it is needed to train new corresponding networks.

3.4.3.1 Basic Principle

In practical applications, different types of images are often involved. To this end, a single model can be used to design a *multi-class generative adversarial network* (MCGAN). Such a network has only one generator, but multiple discriminators. Assuming there are K discriminators, it can be expressed as $\{D_d^j, j = 1, 2, \ldots, K\}$. Using these K discriminators, it is possible to achieve joint de-blurring and super-resolution for K low-resolution blurred images of different categories.

If $D_{dj}(f)$ is used to represent the probability that f is classified as a real image in class j (C_j). Then the loss functions of Equations (3.69) and (3.72) become

$$\frac{1}{N} \sum_{i=1}^{N} \log \left\{ 1 - \sum_{j=1}^{k} D_{dj} \left[G_g(g_i) \right] \delta(g_i \in C_j) \right\} \tag{3.76}$$

$$\frac{1}{N} \sum_{i=1}^{N} \sum_{j=1}^{K} \left\| R_{dj}^l \left[G_g(g_i) \right] - R_{dj}^l(f_i) \right\|^2 \delta(g_i \in C_j) \tag{3.77}$$

In the equation, $R_{dj}^l(f)$ represents the feature image of the l-th layer of the discriminator $D_{dj}(f)$, and $\delta(l_e)$ takes the value 1 when the expression l_e is true and takes the value 0 when it is false.

The training process of the generator in the multi-class generative confrontation network can be seen in Figure 3.18. In the figure, there is a generator and two discriminators (which can be used to classify two types of real and generated images). There are two types of degraded images. If there are K types of degraded images, K discriminators are needed.

The training of multi-class GANs needs to alternate between the update generator and the update discriminator, where the loss function of the training generator should combine the three functions of Equations (3.70), (3.76), and (3.77). Given a fixed generator, all discriminators $\{D_{dk}\}$ are updated simultaneously by Equation (3.64). After such training, the generator obtained through learning can be used to restore any type of input image among the K types of images.

Degraded image → Generator G → $G(y)$ → Discriminator D_1 → Semantic-level loss

$G(y)$ → Pixel-level loss → Discriminator D_2 → Semantic-level loss

Grand truth → Pixel-level loss

Grand truth → Feature matching

FIGURE 3.18 The training process of the generator in the multi-class generative adversarial network.

3.4.3.2 Experimental Effect

As an example of de-blurring multiple types of images, consider two types of images: text images and face images. The text images come from the database of the literature (Hardis et al. 2015). The face images are obtained based on the database of the literature (Liu et al. 2015) and convolution with the blur kernel of the literature (Hardis et al. 2015). All images are added by Gaussian noise with the standard deviation uniformly sampled in [0, 7/255].

Figures 3.19 and 3.20 show the result of de-blurring the synthesized low-resolution text image and low-resolution face image, respectively. Figures 3.19a and 3.20a are blurred images, respectively. Figures 3.19b and 3.20b are the results of MCGAN, respectively; and Figures 3.19c and 3.20c are the results of SCGAN, respectively. Figures 3.19d and 3.20d are grand truths, respectively. It can be seen from Figures 3.19 and 3.20 that the result of MCAGAN is only slightly lower in quality than the result of SCGAN, but MCAGAN can remove the blur of two types of images.

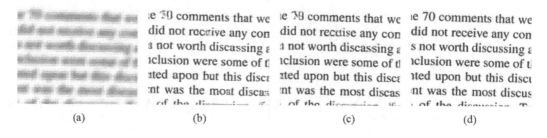

(a)　　　　(b)　　　　(c)　　　　(d)

FIGURE 3.19 The result of de-blurring the synthesized low-resolution text image.

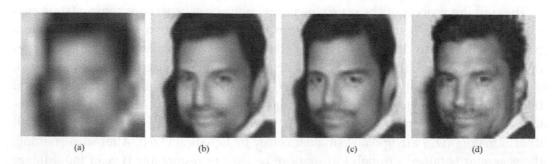

(a)　　　　(b)　　　　(c)　　　　(d)

FIGURE 3.20 The result of de-blurring the synthesized low-resolution face image.

(a) (b) (c)

FIGURE 3.21   The result of de-blurring the real low-resolution text image.

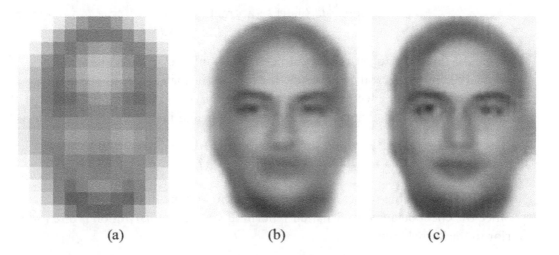

(a) (b) (c)

FIGURE 3.22   The result of de-blurring the real low-resolution face image.

Figures 3.21 and 3.22 separately show the results of de-blurring real low-resolution text images and face images. Figures 3.21a and 3.22a are blurred images, respectively; Figures 3.21b and 3.22b are the results of MCGAN, respectively; Figures 3.21c and 3.22c are the results of SCGAN, respectively. The conclusions about the results of MCAGAN and the results of SCGAN obtained from the previous Figures 3.19 and 3.20 are still basically valid, that is, MCAGAN can remove the blur of the two types of images by itself, and the result has only a small amount of quality degradation than the result of SCGAN.

3.5 SOME RECENT DEVELOPMENTS AND FURTHER RESEARCH

In the following, some technique developments and promising research directions in the last few years are briefly overviewed.

3.5.1 Various De-Blurring Approaches

3.5.1.1 Hybrid Regularization

Solving highly ill-conditioned de-blurring problems is often carried out by extracting the known statistical prior information of the original image for regularization. Two common regularizations are low-rank regularization and total variational regularization.

1. Low-Rank Regularization

    Generally, natural images are dominated by principal components, so for natural images f, there is a low-rank matrix f_1 to make $\|f - f_1\|$ relatively small, and the way to obtain f_1 is to directly perform singular value decomposition (SVD) on f, and then take the part corresponding to the larger singular value. Therefore, the mathematical expression for solving *low-rank regularization* is

$$\min_f \left\{ \frac{1}{2} \|B(f) - e\|2 + \lambda \times \text{rank}(f) \right\} \tag{3.78}$$

    where $\lambda > 0$ is the regularization parameter. Low rank is essentially the sparseness of the matrix in the spectral domain, and the rank of the matrix can also be regarded as the zero norm in the spectral domain. Consider the convex approximation model of Equation (3.78), its mathematical expression is (Sun and Li 2020):

$$\min_f \left\{ \frac{1}{2} \|B(f) - e\|^2 + \lambda \|f\|_* \right\} \tag{3.79}$$

    where $\|f\|$ means the kernel norm of f, that is, the sum of all the singular values of f. Since the effect obtained by Schatten-p norm ($0 < p < 1$) regularization is often superior to the kernel norm, it is

$$\min_f \left\{ \frac{1}{2} \|B(f) - e\|^2 + \lambda \sum_i S_i(f)^p \right\} \tag{3.80}$$

    The kernel norm is a relatively rough approximation of the rank norm, while the Schatten-p norm is closer to the rank norm. When $p = 1/2$, Equation (3.80) has a fast algorithm.

2. Total Variation Regularization

    Total variational regularization considers the minimization in the sense of $D(X)$ sparseness. The convex total variational regularization model can be expressed as

$$\min_f \left\{ \frac{1}{2} \|B(f) - e\|^2 + \eta \|D(f)\|_1 \right\} \tag{3.81}$$

    where $\eta > 0$ is the regularization parameter. Consider the model of p-norm-induced sparsity, namely $\|D(f)\|_p$, $0 < p < 1$ regularization (Qiu et al. 2021):

$$\min_{f}\left\{\frac{1}{2}\|B(f)-e\|^2+\eta\|D(f)\|_p^p\right\}$$ (3.82)

1. Hybrid Regularization

Total variation regularization and low-rank regularization are based on two different basic characteristics of the image: one is the smoothness of the image, that is, the horizontal and vertical differences $D(X)$ of the image are very sparse; the other is the low-rank nature of the image, that is, the image can often be approximated well by a low-rank matrix. The early work of image de-blurring is to use a single property, and the combined use was proposed recently (He et al. 2016). Due to the combined use of two different features, the effect of hybrid regularization is better than that of a single feature regularization. The following hybrid regularization model (only convex functions are used) is proposed:

$$\min_{f}\left\{\frac{1}{2}\|B(f)-e\|^2+\lambda\|f\|+\eta\|D(f)\|_1\right\}$$ (3.83)

Since both the approximate point operators of $L_{1/2}$ norm and Schatten-1/2 kernel norm have fast algorithms, so the $L_{1/2}$ norm and Schatten-1/2 kernel norm are used instead of the L norm and kernel norm in Equation (3.83). The following regularization problem is considered (Sun and Li 2020):

$$\min_{f}\left\{\frac{1}{2}\|B(f)-e\|^2+\lambda\sum_{i}\sqrt{S_i(f)}+\eta\|D(f)\|_{1/2}^{1/2}\right\}$$ (3.84)

where $\eta>0$ and $\lambda>0$ are regularization parameters.

3.5.1.2 Motion De-Blurring Based on DenseNets

Regarding de-blurring as a special problem of image generation, a fast de-blurring method based on neural network is proposed (Wu et al. 2020). The generator network adopts the recently proposed *densely connected convolution network* (DenseNets) structure, which can make full use of network parameters and reduce the number of network layers to a certain extent. Perceptual loss is used in the loss function to ensure the sensory consistency between the generated image and the clear image.

There are mainly three types of dense blocks in this network, and their structures are shown in Figure 3.23. Figure 3.23a can be called Convolution dense block, Figure 3.23b

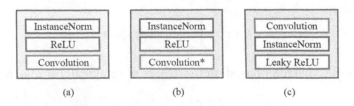

FIGURE 3.23 Three types of dense blocks.

can be called Convolution transpose (*) dense block, and Figure 3.23c can be called Convolution leaky dense block. These blocks include three modules: (for normalization) InstanceNorm, (for convolution) Convolution or Convolution transpose, and (for activation) Rectified linear unit (ReLU) or Leaky rectified linear unit (leaky ReLU).

The generator network first down-samples the image with two convolutional layers (using Convolution dense block) to obtain 256 feature maps, then uses dense blocks for feature extraction, and finally uses a Convolution dense block and two Convolution transpose dense blocks to restore the channel and size of the original image. In addition, a residual connection is added between the input and the output, so that the generated image retains the color information of the original image as much as possible, which will make the network training faster and the effect better.

The discriminator network is composed of five convolutional layers. The first convolutional layer uses a Convolution leaky dense block (no normalization and activation are required). The next three convolutional layers use a complete Convolution leaky dense block. Sigmoid activation is added after Convolution leaky dense block (no need for normalization and activation) to calculate the probability of true and false images.

3.5.1.3 Motion De-Blurring Using Deep Learning-Based Intelligent Systems

In the context of 3-D reconstruction of the human body, a BF-WGAN algorithm, which combines the *bilateral filtering* (BF) de-noising theory with the *Wasserstein generative adversarial network* (WGAN), to remove motion-blurred images by an intelligent decision-making way (Zhang et al. 2021). The BF-WGAN algorithm contains two parts.

1. Bilateral Filter De-Noising Algorithm

   The bilateral filter de-noising algorithm is used to remove the noise and retain the details of the blurred image. This algorithm has three steps:

   i. Compute the Gaussian weight region filter based on the spatial distances:

$$r(x) = k_d^{-1}(x) \int_{-\infty}^{\infty} \int_{-\infty}^{\infty} f(p)w(p,x)\,dp = k_d^{-1}(x) \int_{-\infty}^{\infty} \int_{-\infty}^{\infty} f(p)\exp\left[-\frac{1}{2}\left(\frac{d(p,x)}{\sigma_d}\right)^2\right]dp \quad (3.85)$$

   where $f(x)$ and $f(p)$ represent the input image and output image, respectively; p is in the neighborhood centered on x; $w(p, x)$ is the Gaussian weight based on spatial distance, which is used to measure the spatial distance between the center x and the point p; $d(p, x) = d(p − x) = ||p − x||$; σ_d is the standard deviation, and $k_d(x)$ is the normalization factor:

$$k_d(x) = \int_{-\infty}^{\infty} \int_{-\infty}^{\infty} w(p,x)\,dp \quad (3.86)$$

   ii. Obtain the edge filter based on the degree of (grayscale) similarity:

$$r(x) = k_g^{-1}(x) \int_{-\infty}^{\infty} \int_{-\infty}^{\infty} f(p)S[f(p), f(x)]\,dp \quad (3.87)$$

where $S[f(p), f(x)]$ is the weight based on the degree of similarity between pixels:

$$S[f(p), f(x)] = \exp\left[\frac{1}{2}\left(\frac{T[f(p), f(x)]}{\sigma_T}\right)^2\right] \quad (3.88)$$

where $T[f(p), f(x)] = T[f(p) - f(x)] = \|f(p) - f(x)\|$, σ_T is the standard deviation, $k_g(x)$ is the normalization factor:

$$k_g(x) = \int_{-\infty}^{\infty}\int_{-\infty}^{\infty} S[f(p), f(x)]\,dp \quad (3.89)$$

iii. Create the bilateral filter by combining the Gaussian weight region filter with the edge filter:

$$r(x) = k^{-1}(x)\int_{-\infty}^{\infty}\int_{-\infty}^{\infty} f(p)w(p, x)S[f(p), f(x)]\,dp \quad (3.90)$$

where $k(x)$ is the normalization factor:

$$k(x) = \int_{-\infty}^{\infty}\int_{-\infty}^{\infty} w(p, x)S[f(p), f(x)]\,dp \quad (3.91)$$

After the local sub-region Q is defined, the discretized form of Equation (3.90) can be represented by:

$$r(x) = k^{-1}(x)\sum_{Q} f(p)w(p, x)S[f(p), f(x)] \quad (3.92)$$

The advantage of the bilateral filter theory is that it not only considers the spatial distance between pixels but also considers the degree of (scale) similarity between pixels, which ensures that the pixel values near the edge are preserved.

2. WGAN De-blurring Algorithm

The blurred image and corresponding sharp image are input into the WGAN. This algorithm distinguishes the motion-blurred image from the corresponding sharp image according to the WGAN loss and perceptual loss functions, which allows the finer texture-related details to be restored and the high-precision contours of the image to be revealed.

The WGAN between generator G and discriminator D is the minimax value using Kantorovich-Rubinstein duality:

$$\min_{G}\max_{D\in L}\left\{\mathop{E}_{x\sim P_d}[D(x)] - \mathop{E}_{x\sim Pm}[D(x')]\right\} \quad (3.93)$$

where x represents the original sharp image and E represents the expectation; L is the set of 1-Lipschitz functions. P_d is the data distribution, and P_m is the model distribution, defined by $\sim\!x' = G(z)$, in which the input z represents the blurred image. $D(x)$ represents the probability that x is a real image.

Finally, it should be noted that the BF-WGAN algorithm has fewer parameters compared to multiscale CNN, which heavily speeds up the inference.

3.5.2 Treating Blurred Images in Applications

In many image applications, image de-blurring is a step in pre-processing, the de-blurred images are further used toward the goal. For these applications, to obtain the final good results, it is more important to extract the required suitable information from the blurred image so as to realize the final target.

The following are two examples.

3.5.2.1 Vehicle Logo Recognition

In the recognition of vehicle logo from the real blurred images, it is possible to first de-blurring the original image and then using the de-burred image for recognition. However, such a process is a bit cumbersome, and the time complexity would be greatly increased, which is a great test for the real-time performance of, for example, the vehicle logo recognition in application scenarios.

The vehicle logo image mainly contains edge information and texture information. Combining the *anti-texture blur feature* and the *anti-edge blur feature* is a feasible method to solve the problem of vehicle logo recognition from a blurred image. In other words, it can be considered to directly extract anti-blur features from the original blurred vehicle logo image for recognition (He et al. 2020). The basic flow chart is shown in Figure 3.24. The pyramid structure for vehicle logo image is first constructed. Then, two kinds of anti-blur features are extracted. By fusing the two features, logo recognition can be performed.

1. Anti-Texture Blur Feature Extraction

   With the help of local phase quantization (LPQ), a feature vector that resists texture blur can be obtained. Consider that the blurred image $g(x, y)$ is the result of the convolution of the original image $f(x, y)$ and the point spread function $h(x, y)$. In the Fourier transform domain, this can be expressed as

$$G(u,v) = F(u,v) \cdot H(u,v) \tag{3.94}$$

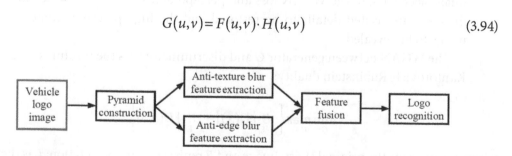

FIGURE 3.24   Flowchart of blurred vehicle logo image recognition.

where, $G(u, v)$, $F(u, v)$, $H(u, v)$ represent the results of the Fourier transform of the blurred image, the original image and the point spread function, respectively. If the subscripts "a" is used for amplitude and "p" is used for phase, then

$$G_a(u,v) = F_a(u,v) \cdot H_a(u,v) \tag{3.95}$$

$$G_p(u,v) = F_p(u,v) + H_p(u,v) \tag{3.96}$$

If the point spread function satisfies the center symmetry (the point spread functions of blurred imaging such as defocus blur and motion blur are all center symmetric), then the phase $H_a(u, v)$ of $H(u, v)$ in the frequency domain coordinates (u, v) satisfies

$$H_a(u,v) = \begin{cases} 0 & H_a(u,v) \geq 0 \\ \pi & H_a(u,v) < 0 \end{cases} \tag{3.97}$$

Therefore, at the frequency domain point where $H(u, v) \geq 0$, the phases of the original vehicle logo image and the blurred vehicle logo image satisfy

$$G_p(u,v) = F_p(u,v) \qquad H(u,v) \geq 0 \tag{3.98}$$

According to the phase consistency between the original vehicle logo image and the blurred vehicle logo image, the short-time Fourier transform (STFT) is used to calculate the spectral information in the local region of the image. The Fourier transform result at the frequency w is:

$$P(w,x) = \sum_{y \in N_x} f(x-y) \exp(-j2\pi w^T y) \tag{3.99}$$

where, N_x represents the $N \times N$ neighborhood of x, and y is the pixel point in the neighborhood of pixel x.

Choose four frequency points $w_1 = [e, 0]^T$, $w_2 = [0, e]^T$, $w_3 = [e, e]^T$, $w_4 = [e, -e]^T$ to calculate Fourier transform coefficients, where e is a real number that is small enough to satisfy Equation (3.96), it gets:

$$P_x(w,x) = \begin{bmatrix} P(w_1,x) & P(w_2,x) & P(w_3,x) & P(w_4,x) \end{bmatrix} \tag{3.100}$$

Further, the phase information is recorded by performing quantization and encoding processing on the Fourier transform coefficient vector of the pixel x at four frequency points. First, separate the real part $\mathrm{Re}\{P_x\}$ and the imaginary part $\mathrm{Im}\{P_x\}$ in P_x to get the vector:

$$Q = \begin{bmatrix} \mathrm{Re}\{P_x\} & \mathrm{Im}\{P_x\} \end{bmatrix} \tag{3.101}$$

Finally, the vector Q is quantized into 0–1 mode of binary code vector B through function mapping, which constitutes the quantized feature of the phase information in the recorded Fourier coefficients, where the elements in B can be expressed as:

$$\mathbf{B}_i = \begin{cases} 1 & Q_i \geq 0 \\ 0 & Q_i < 0 \end{cases} \qquad (3.102)$$

2. Anti-Edge Blur Feature Extraction

Histogram of gradient (HOG) is a feature that can represent the gradient information of the edge in the image. When the image is blurred, the original weaker gradient region will tend to be flat as the blur degree of the image becomes larger, and the discriminative ability of the HOG feature weakens. While the original strong gradient region can maintain a certain intensity, HOG features also have a certain ability to discriminate. In other words, strong gradients are more resistant to influence caused by blur than weak gradients. If the component corresponding to the weak gradient information in the HOG feature can be reduced or eliminated, and only the component corresponding to the strong gradient information can be retained or relatively enhanced, the anti-blur ability of the obtained HOG feature can be improved.

According to this idea, a simple method is to use the average value of the global gradient histogram of the image as the threshold to remove the feature components below the threshold and retain only the feature components above the threshold to obtain features with anti-edge blur ability.

If the edge information of each part of the image is relatively more changeable (vehicle logo images include various geometric patterns), due to the large feature difference between the parts, using the mean of the global gradient histogram as the threshold will cause the loss of local feature information. At this time, the threshold can be selected according to the gradient mean value of the local region. The image is divided into blocks, and the gradients in each direction in the block are determined according to the following equation:

$$H_{ij} = \begin{cases} H_{ij} & H_{ij} \geq \mathrm{mean}(H_i) \\ 0 & H_{ij} < \mathrm{mean}(H_i) \end{cases} \qquad (3.103)$$

In the equation, $\mathrm{mean}(H_i)$ represents the mean value of the gradient histogram of the i-th block of the image, and H_{ij} represents the gradient value of the gradient histogram in the j-th direction of the i-th block.

3. Fusion of Blur Features

The image's anti-texture blur features and anti-edge blur features can be combined with the vector fusion method based on *canonical correlation analysis* (CCA). Specifically, it includes the following steps:

i. Mark the two feature vectors as x and y, respectively. For the given n vehicle logo training samples, two sample space matrices A and B are obtained, and the two projection vectors P_x and P_y are used to map x and y to another coordinate system.

ii. Calculate the overall covariance matrix S_{xx} and S_{yy} of A and B, respectively, and the cross covariance matrix S_{xy}.

iii. Perform singular value decomposition of the covariance matrices in step (ii) to obtain the singular values $\lambda_1, \lambda_2,..., \lambda_m$ of the matrix H and the corresponding left and right singular vectors u_i and v_i ($i = 1, 2, 3,..., m$)

$$H = S_{xx}^{-1/2} S_{xy} S_{yy}^{-1/2} \tag{3.104}$$

$$H = \sum_{i=1}^{m} \lambda_i u_i v_i^T \tag{3.105}$$

From which, the maximum singular value λ and the corresponding left and right singular vectors u and v can be obtained.

iv. Calculate the projection vectors P_x and P_y:

$$P_x = S_{xx}^{-1/2} u \tag{3.106}$$

$$P_y = S_{yy}^{-1/2} v \tag{3.107}$$

v. Map the original concatenated feature vector to the new space to obtain the fused feature vector:

$$Q = \begin{bmatrix} P_x^T & A \\ P_y^T & B \end{bmatrix} \tag{3.108}$$

Here, through the mapping of the transformation matrix, the correlation coefficients of the two sets of feature vectors can be maximized. This process effectively reduces the redundancy between features, and the extracted feature vectors are more descriptive, which is conducive to subsequent classification and recognition.

3.5.2.2 Adversarial Attack Detection

Artificial intelligence (AI) systems have had wider applications in our society. However, it can malfunction due to intentionally manipulated data coming through normal channels. For example, it has been shown that the AI systems no longer recognize images correctly when a small amount of well-designed noise, called *adversarial noise*, is added to the images. The adversarial noise is a carefully designed small perturbation that can lead the neural network to make a wrong decision when added to the original input to the network. The combination of the adversarial noise with the original image is called an *adversarial example*. Using such adversarial examples to intentionally malfunction the AI system is called an AI *deception attack*, which poses a major threat to the real world.

The seriousness of such a deception attack lies in the fact that the deception attack can be made without breaking into the system through abnormal routes. Thus, it is necessary to detect adversarial examples, to detect deception attack, to defend the systems. For example, a real-time adversarial attack detection with *deep image prior* (DIP) initialized as a high-level representation based blurring network that is trained only with normal images has been proposed, which detects adversarial noise without knowing what kind of adversarial noise the attacker uses and does not require adversarial examples to train the *convolutional neural network* (CNN) (Sutanto and Lee 2020).

The overall flowchart of the method can be seen in Figure 3.25. The main idea is to compare the outputs of the target CNN with two different inputs: the test image that contains the adversarial noise and the image reconstructed by the DIP. Using the test image as the target to be reconstructed by the DIP, the DIP will slowly reconstruct the noise input to the DIP into the test image. During the reconstruction process, high-frequency components that do not include adversarial noise are first reconstructed and the adversarial noise is reconstructed later, which is due to the noise resistance characteristics of the DIP. Therefore, if the reconstruction process is interrupted before the adversarial noise is reconstructed, the reconstructed image will show a different effect than the original test image on the target CNN. Thus, by measuring the correlation between the two outputs of the target CNN, it is possible to determine whether the input contains adversarial noise or not.

In the implementation, an auto-encoder architecture with skip connections for both the blurring network and the DIP network is used. Early stopping for the blurring network is made if the validation loss did not improve for certain continuous epochs to avoid over-training. With the DIP, an early stopping to recover only the image and not the adversarial noise is performed. As the parameters of the blurring network are copied into the DIP, the DIP with only a few iterations is already reconstructed.

The blurry image can be trained to blur the image in the direction of the correct classification result. The blurring will eliminate the high-frequency components, and therefore, remove the adversarial noise to some extent. However, when eliminating the high-frequency components, the components which are helpful for correct classification will also be eliminated. Therefore, to prevent this undesired side-effect, a high-level representation guiding term in the loss function is added so that the image will be blurred in the direction that its high-level responses are similar to those of non-blurred noise-free images.

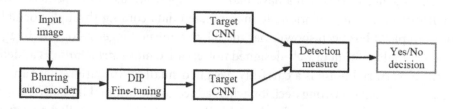

FIGURE 3.25 The overall flowchart of adversarial attack detection.

REFERENCES

Cho, S., and S. Lee. 2009. Fast motion deblurring. *ACM Transactions on Graphics* 28(5): 145.1–145.8.

Dong, C., C. Loy, and X. Tang. 2016. Accelerating the super-resolution convolutional neural network. *Proc. of ECCV*, 1–16.

Goshtasby, A. A. 2005. *2-D and 3-D Image Registration – for Medical, Remote Sensing, and Industrial Applications.* Hoboken, NJ: Wiley-Interscience.

Hardis, M., J. Kotera, P. Zemcik, et al. 2015. Convolutional neural networks for direct text deblurring. *Proc. of BMVC*, 1–13.

He, M. X., Y. Yu, J. T. Xu, et al. 2020. Vehicle logo recognition based on anti-blur feature extraction. *Journal of Image and Graphics* 25(3): 605–617.

He, W., H. Zhang, L. Zhang, et al. 2016. Total-variation-regularized low-rank matrix factorization for hyperspectral image restoration. *IEEE Transactions on Geoscience and Remote Sensing* 54(1): 178–188.

Ioffe, S., and C. Szegedy. 2015. Batch normalization: Accelerating deep network training by reducing internal covariate shift. *JMLR.org*

Kitchen, L., and A. Rosenfeld. 1981. Edge evaluation using local edge coherence. *IEEE-SMC*, 11(9): 597–605.

Levin, A., R. Fergus, F. Durand, et al. 2007. Image and depth from a conventional camera with a coded aperture. *ACM Transactions on Graphics* 26(3): 70.1–70.9.

Levin, A., Y. Weiss, F. Durand, et al. 2009. Understanding and evaluating blind deconvolution algorithms. *Proc. of CVPR*, 1964–1971.

Liu, Z., P. Luo, X. Wang, et al. 2015. Deep learning face attributes in the Wild. *Proc. of ICCV*, 3730–3738.

Mass, A. L., A. Y. Hannun, and A. Y. Ng. 2013. Rectifier nonlinearities improve neural network acoustic models. *Proc. of ICML*, 1–6.

Nair, V. and G. E. Hinton. 2010. Rectified linear units improve restricted Boltzmann machines. *Proc. of ICML*, 807–814.

Osher, S. and L. I. Rudin. 1990. Feature-oriented image enhancement using shock filters. *SINUM* 27(4): 919–940.

Qiu, D., M. R. Bai, M. K. Ng, et al. 2021. Robust low-rank tensor completion via transformed tensor nuclear norm with total variation regularization. *Neurocomputing*, 435: 197–215.

Radford, A., L. Metz, and S. Chintala. 2015. Unsupervised representation learning with deep convolutional generative adversarial networks. *Computer Science.*

Shan, Q., J. Jia, and A. Agarwala. 2008. High-quality motion deblurring from a single image. *ACM Transactions on Graphics* 27(3): 73.1–73.8.

Sun, T., and D.-S. Li. 2020. Nonconvex low-rank and total-variation regularized model and algorithm for image deblurring. *Chinese Journal of Computers* 43(4): 643–652.

Sutanto, R. E., and S. Lee. 2020. Real-time adversarial attack detection with deep image prior initialized as a high-level representation based blurring network. *Electronics* 10.1: 52.

Tomasi, C. and R. Manduchi. 1998. Bilateral filtering for gray and color images. *Proceedings of ICCV*, 839–846.

Wu, D., H. T. Zhao, and S. B. Zheng. 2020. Motion deblurring method based on DenseNets. *Journal of Image and Graphics* 25(5): 890–899.

Xu, L., S. Zheng, and J. Jia. 2013. Unnatural L_0 sparse representation for natural image deblurring. *Proceedings of CVPR*, 1107–1114.

Xu, X. Y., D. Q. Sun, J. S. Pan, et al. 2017. Learning to super-resolve blurry face and text images. *Proc. of ICCV*, 251–260.

Xu, X. Y., J. S. Pan, Y.-J. Zhang, et al. 2018. Motion blur kernel estimation via deep learning. *IEEE Transactions on Image Processing*, 27(1): 194–205.

Yuan, L., J. Sun, L. Quan, et al. 2007. Image deblurring with blurred/noisy image pairs. *ACM Transactions on Graphics*, 26(3): 1.1–1.10.

Zhang, J., K. Yu, Z. Wen, et al. 2021. 3D Reconstruction for motion blurred images using deep learning-based intelligent systems. *Computers, Materials and Continua*, 66(2): 2087–2104.

Zhang, Y.-J. 2017. *Image Engineering, Vol.1: Image Processing*. Germany: De Gruyter.

## CHAPTER 4

Image Repairing

IN THE VARIOUS PROCESSES of image acquisition, storage, transmission, and processing, it may happen that some regions of the image are defective or missing, the gray level of adjacent pixels inside and outside the missing part changes sharply, and the image looks incomplete. Processing such an image, filling in the missing parts, and restoring the original appearance of the image have a wide range of applications in many fields. For example:

1. In the restoration of old photos, remove scratches, creases, stains, defects, and so on.

2. In the production of film and television stunts and special effects, remove unwanted objects (or even replace the background).

3. Remove the scratches (horizontal and vertical lines) and spots on the old film and supplement the missing frames.

4. In the protection of cultural relics and cultural heritages, improve the visual quality of calligraphy, painting, and artwork.

5. Error concealment in video communication.

6. In the video viewing, remove the interference of subtitle icons and so on.

7. Carry out super-resolution analysis on the image, enlarge the image, and avoid the mosaic phenomenon.

8. When shooting a street view video, the main landscape (such as buildings) in the picture is often affected by obstructions (such as trees, street signs, street lamps, etc.) and becomes incomplete. At this time, it is needed to remove the obstructions in the video and repair the void region after removal to maintain the integrity and consistency of the landscape concerned.

In recent years, solving this kind of problem has received extensive attention and research, and the methods adopted are mostly based on the principle that is similar to image

DOI: 10.1201/9781003241416-4

restoration. The common name used for this task is often called image inpainting. Image inpainting normally refers to the techniques used to recover the damaged image and to fill the regions, which are missing in original image in a visually plausible way. However, with the deeper research and wider application, it is better to name it with a more comprehensive and appropriate name: *image repairing* (Zhang 2015). Its main feature is to use the information of the intact part of the original image to recover the information of the defective part and restore the original appearance of the image. People have long been repairing cracks and other damage to art works. The word inpainting was also first proposed by the museum art repair staff in the early days. Repairing with the help of manual interaction is very common in practice, such as special effects processing or repairing work performed by experienced personnel in photo studios with the help of tools such as Photoshop. The following paragraphs, in this chapter, mainly consider some techniques for automatically repairing images.

The contents of each section of this chapter are arranged as follows.

Section 4.1 first identifies and analyzes image repairing, discusses its relationship with image restoration, and points out that it can be further divided into image inpainting and image completion. Then, the general principle of image repairing is introduced, and the characteristics and relationships between image inpainting for small-size repair and image completion for large-size image repair are respectively analyzed.

Section 4.2 introduces the image repairing methods combined with sparse representation, introduces the basic principle and basic algorithm of sparse representation, and discusses several ways to improve the basic algorithm.

Section 4.3 introduces a weighted sparse image repairing method based on non-negative matrix factorization. The key steps are discussed in detail, including the decomposition formula, the filling algorithm, and the realization and effects obtained with the EM method.

Section 4.4 discusses hybrid repairing methods that combine diffusion-based methods and example-based methods. It can not only overcome the blur problem but also reduce the amount of calculation. In addition to the overall process, various modules and implementation steps are described in detail.

Section 4.5 provides a brief introduction to some technique developments and promising research directions in the last year.

4.1 IMAGE REPAIRING OVERVIEW

First, discuss why "image repairing" is used to describe this kind of problem and task more comprehensively, then introduce the basic principles of image repairing, and then introduce the different characteristics of the two types of image repairing methods and also some commonly used methods.

4.1.1 Discrimination and Analysis of Image Repairing

There are many situations in which the image is damaged, or there are many reasons or sources that lead to the deterioration of the image quality. For example, (i) part of the image content is missing when collecting the image of an occluded scenery or scanning a damaged old picture; (ii) the blank left after removing a specific region (irrelevant scenery) in image processing; (iii) overlaying text or being affected by the image interference (photo tearing or scratches) caused by the gray or color change of the corresponding region; (iv) when transmitting data (on the network), some pixels are lost due to network failure.

4.1.1.1 Discrimination

Judging from different examples of image damage, there are some similarities but also differences with traditional image restoration techniques to solve the image degradation situation. The similarity stems from the damage of these images, which can be regarded as a special case of image degradation. The image quality has deteriorated, and certain information is lost. In principle, the damage process is relatively definite, so it is possible to establish damage models and recover them in a targeted manner. The difference is that these damages are often local in time and space, and the integrity and regularity are not strong.

For example, taking an image affected by noise interference or blurring as an example, the image pixels that are generally contaminated by noise still contain useful information in the image, and the original low-frequency information is still in the blurred image due to the loss of high-frequency information. On the other hand, in the foregoing example of image damage, the information in the image failure region is often completely lost, and it is difficult to obtain any valuable image information from these regions. As a result, traditional image restoration techniques cannot be directly promoted or applied to the image repairing techniques discussed here. On the other hand, because there is not enough information to ensure that the damaged part can uniquely be restored correctly. Therefore, some people try to estimate the solution of this problem with the help of analysis from the perspective of visual psychology and put forward various hypotheses.

It can also be seen from the above discussion that the appearances of image deterioration caused by image damage are also very different. From the perspective of the affected pixels, there are often changes in both the pixel grayscale/color and the pixel position. In other words, to restore the original appearance of the damaged image, both position information and grayscale/color information need to be considered.

In general, the region where the image is damaged or degraded in quality can be large or small. When the size and scale of such regions are significantly different, the image repairing techniques used are often different. In general, the region with a smaller restoration scale is called *image inpainting*, such as the interpolation of oil paintings in the museum at the early days, and the smoothing of scratches on expired or old films in the later days. If the region with a larger restoration scale often needs to be filled, for example, a patch needs to be added after the clothes are worn out, which can be called *image completion*. Therefore, it is more comprehensive and appropriate to consider these two situations, namely inpainting and completion, and to collectively call them as *image repairing*. When inpainting small-scale defects, pixels are often used as the basic operation unit; while completing large-scale defects is considered, image blocks or patches (sets of pixels) are often used as the basic operation unit.

Fundamentally, image repairing is based on the incomplete image and prior knowledge of the original image, and by adopting corresponding methods to correct the aforementioned region defect problem, so as to achieve the purpose of restoring the original appearance of the image. Judging from the currently used technologies, the technologies used for inpainting and completion have their own characteristics. The inpainting mostly uses the local structure information of the image rather than the texture information of the region and is carried out in a diffusion method; while the completion often requires the consideration of the global information of an image and fills the region with the help of texture information. In terms of function, the former is mostly used for image restoration and the latter is mostly used for scenery removal. Of course, there are no strict boundaries between them in terms of scale, or the boundaries are relative and fuzzy.

4.1.1.2 Image Repairing Example

An example of each is given below. The set of images in Figure 4.1 is an example of image inpainting that removes overlaid text. From left to right, the original image, the image with superimposed text (the image needs to be repaired), and the inpainting result image are given in sequence. The image on the far right is the difference image between the original image and the inpainting result image (the histogram equalization has been used for a clear display), where the PSNR between the two images is about 20 dB. In this example, the strokes to be repaired are line-shaped, and the size of the defect is relatively small in a certain direction, and the repairing can be done directly with the help of the neighboring information of the defect.

The set of images in Figure 4.2 gives an example of image completion that removes (unnecessary) scenery. From left to right, the original image, the image marked with the

FIGURE 4.1   Image repairing example: Remove text.

FIGURE 4.2   Image completion example: Remove scenery.

range of the scenery to be removed (the image needs to be complemented), and the completion result are given in sequence. The scale of the scene here is relatively large (it has a larger depth or area compared to the text stroke), but the visual effect of the completion is still relatively satisfactory (see Sub-section 4.1.2 for the specific method). In this example, the region to be repaired has a certain depth, or the defect has a certain scale in all directions, and the repairing effect is often not guaranteed by directly relying on the adjacent information of the defect site, and a larger range of surrounding information needs to be considered.

It should be noted that in applications such as image scratch removal and text removal, the goal is to restore the original image as much as possible (without leaving traces). At this time, indicators such as signal-to-noise ratio can often be used to measure the quality of the image restoration. In the region filling of the image after the (part of) scenery is removed, damaged, missed, and so on, the goal is to make the filled image visually look like a real image after the filling. This situation often requires human eyes to observe the result to judge the quality of the image restoration.

4.1.2 Principle of Image Repairing

It should be pointed out that if there is no prior knowledge about the missing part of the image or the reason for the missing information, the repairing of the image is an ill-posed problem and the solution is uncertain. The difficulty or complexity of image repairing (especially completion and filling) comes from three aspects (Chan and Shen 2005).

1. Domain complexity: The region to be repaired varies with the application domain. For example, in the removal of overlay text, the repairing region is composed of different characters; in the scenery removal, the repairing region may be of any shape.

2. Image complexity: the performance of image properties is different at diverse scales. For example, at small scales, there are many details/structures, but at large scales, it can be approximated by a smooth function.

3. Pattern complexity: visually meaningful patterns (objects with high-level meaning) must be considered.

Here are two examples, as shown in the two pairs of graphs in Figure 4.3. The pair of graphs in Figure 4.3a indicate that the small gray blocks in the center should be filled. If viewed from the left part, it is more reasonable to fill it with a black block; but from the overall view on the right, it is more reasonable to fill it with a white block. The pair of pictures in Figure 4.3b shows that the vertical bars missing in the center should be filled. From the aspect ratio on the left, the vertical bars should be the background, and the task should be to distinguish the two characters "E" and "3." From the aspect ratio on the right, the vertical bar should be in the foreground, and the task should be to restore the partially occluded letter "B."

In practice, it is often necessary to build a certain model and make a certain estimation for repairing an image, which is the same for inpainting and completion. As a special case

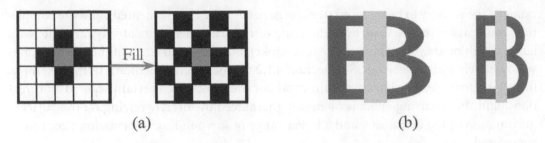

(a)   (b)

FIGURE 4.3   Example of pattern complexity. (a) indicate that the small gray blocks in the center should be filled; (b) shows that the vertical bars missing in the center should be filled.

of image degradation, image defect has its own characteristics. After the original image is affected by the defect, some regions of it may be completely lost, but other regions may not change at all.

For an original image $f(x, y)$, let the spatial region of its distribution be denoted by F; if the missing part or the part to be repaired is $d(x, y)$, the spatial region is denoted by D; then the image to be repaired is $g(x, y)$, the spatial region of its distribution is also F, but some parts of them remain intact and some parts are completely missing. The so-called repair is to use the original spatial region, that is, the information in F–D to estimate and restore the missing information in D. It can be considered as the art of restoring lost parts of the image and reconstructing them based on the background information, i.e., it is the process of reconstructing lost or deteriorated parts of images using information from surrounding regions.

Refer to Figure 4.4, where the left image is the original image $f(x, y)$ and the right image is the image to be repaired $g(x, y)$, where the region D represents the part to be repaired (the original information is completely lost), and the region F–D represents the part of the original image that can be used to repair the region D, also called the *source region*, and the region D is also called the *target region*.

FIGURE 4.4   Schematic diagram of various areas in image repair.

Referring to the degradation model in image restoration (see Section 3.1), the image repairing model can be expressed as

$$\left[g(x,y)\right]_{F-D} = \left\{H\left[f(x,y)\right] + n(x,y)\right\}_{F-D} \tag{4.1}$$

The left side of the above equation is the part of the degraded image that has not been degraded. The goal of image repairing is to estimate and restore $\{f(x,y)\}_D$ using Equation (4.1). From the perspective of the repair effect, on the one hand, the gray scale, color, and texture in the region D after the repairing should be similar or consistent with the gray scale, color, and texture around D; on the other hand, the structural information around D should be extended to the interior of D (such as the fractured edge and contour line should be connected) so that the inside and outside of the boundary of D should be coordinated and corresponding.

If the noise points in the image are regarded as the target region, the image de-noising problem can also be treated as an image repairing problem, that is, the pixels that are not affected by the noise are used to restore the grayscale of the pixels affected by the noise. If the repairing of the image that is affected by text superposition or scratches, is regarded as the repairing of the curved target region, and if the repairing of the scenery-removed image is regarded as the repairing of the planar target region, then the repairing of the image affected by noise can also be considered as a repair to the point-shaped target region. The above discussion mainly focuses on impulse noise because impulse noise is very strong, superimposed on the image, which will cause the gray values of the affected pixels to become extreme values, and the original pixel information is completely covered by noise. If it is Gaussian noise, then the pixels that are superimposed with the noise often still contain certain original grayscale information, and the pixels in the target region in the image repairing generally no longer contain the original image information (the information is removed).

4.1.3 Image Inpainting for Small-Scale Repairing

First, discuss the repair technology that is used to remove scratches or small-scale (including small size in one dimension, e.g., linear or curved regions such as strokes, ropes, text, etc.) target regions. The methods commonly used here are mostly based on partial differential equations or total variation models, and the two can be derived equivalently with the help of the principle of variation. This type of image repairing method achieves the purpose of repairing the image by diffusing it in the target region pixel by pixel. The following section only introduces the total variation model and its variants, and a more detailed discussion of the methods can be found in the literature (Chan and Shen 2005).

4.1.3.1 Total Variation Model

The intuitive idea of solving small-scale repairing is to diffuse the information around the target region into the interior of the target region, and the specific diffusion information and expansion direction need to be determined. A typical method is to extend and diffuse from the source region to the target region along the line of equal intensity (line of equal gray value) (Bertalmio et al. 2001), which helps to maintain the structural characteristics of the image itself. In the case of specific diffusion, the *total variation* (TV) model can be used to restore the missing information in the image. A further improvement is the *curvature-driven diffusion* (CDD) equation proposed for the continuity principle that is not valid in the *total variation model* (Chan and Shen 2001). The advantage of this type of method is that the linear structure in the image can be maintained well, but the disadvantage is that the image details may not be maintained. The main reason here is that blur will be introduced during the diffusion process, especially when repairing a large portion of the target region, so it is not suitable for repairing a large-size region.

The total variation model is a basic and typical image repairing model. The total variation algorithm is a non-isotropic diffusion algorithm that can be used for de-noising while maintaining the continuity and sharpness of the edges.

Define the cost function of diffusion as

$$R[f] = \iint_F |\nabla f(x, y)| \, \mathrm{d}x \, \mathrm{d}y \tag{4.2}$$

where ∇f is the gradient of f. Considering the case of Gaussian noise, in order to remove the noise, the above equation is also subject to the following constraints:

$$\frac{1}{\|F - D\|} \iint_{F-D} |f - g|^2 \, \mathrm{d}x \, \mathrm{d}y = \sigma^2 \tag{4.3}$$

In the equation, $\|F{-}D\|$ is the area of the region $F{-}D$, and σ is the noise mean square error. The function of Equation (4.2) is to make the region to be repaired and its boundary part as smooth as possible, while the function of Equation (4.3) is to make the repairing process more robust to noise.

Using Lagrangian factor λ, the constrained problem formed by combining Equations (4.2) and (4.3) can be transformed into an unconstrained problem:

$$E[f] = \iint_F |\nabla f(x, y)| \, \mathrm{d}x \, \mathrm{d}y + \frac{\lambda}{2} \iint_{F-D} |f - g|^2 \, \mathrm{d}x \, \mathrm{d}y \tag{4.4}$$

If the extended Lagrangian factor λ_D is introduced:

$$\lambda_D(r) = \begin{cases} 0 & r \in D \\ \lambda & r \in (F - D) \end{cases} \tag{4.5}$$

then, Functional (4.4) becomes

$$J[f] = \iint_F |\nabla f(x, y)| \, \mathrm{d}x \, \mathrm{d}y + \frac{\lambda_D}{2} \iint_F |f - g|^2 \, \mathrm{d}x \, \mathrm{d}y \tag{4.6}$$

According to the variational principle, the corresponding energy gradient descent equation is obtained as

$$\frac{\partial f}{\partial t} = \nabla \cdot \left[\frac{\nabla f}{|\nabla f|} \right] + \lambda_D (f - g) \tag{4.7}$$

In the equation, ∇ represents divergence.

Equation (4.7) is a nonlinear reaction diffusion equation, and the diffusion coefficient is $1/|\nabla f|$. In the interior of the region D to be repaired, λ_D is zero, and Equation (4.7) degenerates into a pure diffusion equation; while around the region D to be repaired, the second term of Equation (4.7) makes the solution of the equation tend to the original image. The original image can be obtained by solving the partial differential Equation (4.7).

4.1.3.2 Mixed Model

In the total variation model introduced above, the diffusion only proceeds in the orthogonal direction of the gradient (i.e., the edge direction), not in the direction of the gradient. When the diffusion is performed near the contour of the region, this feature of the total variation model can maintain the edge; but in the smooth position inside the region, the edge direction will be more random, and the total variation model may produce false contours affected by noise.

If the gradient term in the cost function in the total variation model is changed to the gradient square term, then

$$R[f] = \iint_F |\nabla f(x, y)|^2 \, dx \, dy \tag{4.8}$$

In addition, consider the constraint conditions of Equation (4.3) and transform it into an unconstrained problem, and then the extended Lagrangian factor of Equation (4.5) can be used to obtain the functional

$$J[f] = \iint_F |\nabla f(x, y)|^2 \, dx \, dy + \frac{\lambda_D}{2} \iint_F |f - g|^2 \, dx \, dy \tag{4.9}$$

In this way, a harmonic model is obtained. The *harmonic model* is an isotropic diffusion without distinguishing between the edge direction and the gradient direction, so it can reduce the problem of false contours caused by noise, but it may cause a certain amount of blur on the edge.

A hybrid model that takes the weighted sum of the two models using the gradient term in the cost function is

$$R_h[f] = \iint_F h|\nabla f(x, y)| + \frac{(1 - h)}{2} |\nabla f(x, y)|^2 \, dx \, dy \tag{4.10}$$

In the equation, $h \in [0, 1]$ is the weighting parameter. The functional of the mixed model is

$$J_h[f] = \iint_F h|\nabla f(x,y)| + \frac{(1-h)}{2}|\nabla f(x,y)|^2 \, \mathrm{d}x\mathrm{d}y + \frac{\lambda_D}{2}\iint_F |f-g|^2 \, \mathrm{d}x\mathrm{d}y \tag{4.11}$$

Comparing Equations (4.2) and (4.11), it is known when $h=1$, Equation (4.11) becomes a total variational model.

Another hybrid model that combines the two models is the *p-harmonic model* (Zhang et al. 2007), where the gradient term in the cost function is

$$R_p[f] = \iint_F |\nabla f(x,y)|^p \, \mathrm{d}x\mathrm{d}y \tag{4.12}$$

In the equation, $p \in [1, 2]$ is the control parameter. The functional of the *p*-harmonic model is

$$J_p[f] = \iint_F |\nabla f(x,y)|^p \, \mathrm{d}x\mathrm{d}y + \frac{\lambda_D}{2}\iint_F |f-g|^2 \, \mathrm{d}x\mathrm{d}y \tag{4.13}$$

Comparing Equations (4.6) and (4.13), it can be seen that $p=1$ corresponds to a total variation model; comparing Equations (4.9) and (4.13), it can be seen that $p=2$ corresponds to a harmonic model, and when $1<p<2$, a good balance is achieved between these models.

4.1.4 Image Completion for Large-Scale Repairing

The method introduced in Sub-section 4.1.3 is more effective for repairing the missing region on a small scale, but some problems will occur when the missing region is on a large scale. On the one hand, the above method is to diffuse the information around the missing region into the missing region. For large-scale missing regions, diffusion will cause a certain blur, and the degree of blur increases with the increase in the size of the missing region (the possibility of error propagation accumulation will increase). On the other hand, the above method does not consider the texture characteristics inside the missing region and directly moves the texture characteristics around the missing region into the missing region. Due to the large scale of the missing region, the texture characteristics of the inside and outside may be quite different, resulting in unsatisfactory repairing results. To solve the problem in large-size region repairing, other methods are needed. One method is introduced as follows.

4.1.4.1 Basic Idea

At present, the basic ideas for realizing large-size repairing include the following two.

1. Decompose the image into structural parts and texture parts. For the structurally strong parts, the diffusion method in Sub-section 4.1.3 can still be used for region filling, and for the parts with obvious texture, the technology of texture synthesis is

used for region filling. This can be seen as a hybrid approach, trying to take different approaches to different regions. Since natural images are mostly composed of texture and structural parts, first repairing the structural parts can obtain better results. On this basis, the texture part can use some surrounding structure information obtained by diffusion, but when the target region is relatively large, there is still a certain risk of using the synthesized texture to fill in. Moreover, it is difficult to select the size of the texture mask and the order of texture synthesis.

2. Select some sample (example) blocks in the undegraded part of the image, use these sample blocks to replace the image blocks at the boundary of the region to be filled (the undegraded parts of these blocks have similar characteristics to the selected sample blocks), and gradually fill the interior of the region to be filled in progress. This method can be called an *sample-based image completion* method and is also often referred to as an example-based image completion method. This type of method directly uses the information in the source region to fill the target region. This idea was inspired by the texture filling. For the image block in the target region, find the most similar image block in the source region (or combine several image blocks into a new image block) and directly replace it by filling. It seems that sample-based methods can often achieve better results in filling texture content than diffusion methods based on partial differential equations, especially when the scale of the target region is relatively large.

4.1.4.2 Basic Method Based on Sample

The sample-based image completion method uses the original spatial region to estimate and fill in the missing information in the part to be repaired (Criminisi et al. 2003). To this end, a gray value (0 can be used to indicate that it has not been filled) and a confidence value are assigned to the pixels in each target region. The confidence value reflects the degree of confidence in the gray value of the pixel, and it will no longer be changed after the pixel is filled. In addition, during the filling process, a temporary priority value is assigned to the image blocks on the filling front to determine the order in which the image blocks are filled. In the basic sample-based method, the entire filling process is iterative and consists of the following three steps.

1. Calculate the priority of image blocks

    For large-scale target regions, the work of filling image blocks is carried out from the outside to the inside. A priority value is calculated for each image block on the filling front, and then the filling order of the image blocks is determined according to the priority value. Taking into account the need to maintain structural information, this value is relatively large for image blocks on continuous edges and surrounded by high-confidence pixels. In other words, generally fill in regions with strong continuous edges (people are more sensitive to edge information) and regions with more known information (this is more likely to be correct) first.

The priority value of the image block $P(p)$ centered on the boundary point p can be calculated as follows:

$$P(p) = C(p) \cdot D(p) \tag{4.14}$$

In the equation, the first term $C(p)$ is also called the confidence item, which represents the proportion of intact pixels in the current image block; the second term $D(p)$ is also called the data item, which is equal to the inner product of the iso-illuminance line (the line with equal gray values) and the unit normal vector. The more intact pixels are in the image block, the greater the value of the first term $C(p)$; the more consistent the normal direction of the current image block is with the iso-illuminance line, the greater the value of the second term $D(p)$, which makes the algorithm preferentially repairing along the direction of the iso-illuminance line so that the repaired image can well maintain the structural information of the target region. Initially, $C(p)=0$ and $D(p)=1$.

2. Propagating image block information

When the priority values of all the image blocks on the front line are calculated, the image block with the highest priority can be determined, and then the image block data selected from the source region can be used to fill it. When selecting the image block to be filled in the source region, the sum of the square differences of the filled pixels in the two image blocks should be minimized. If the image block contains texture and structure information, the result of this filling can spread the texture and structure properties from the source region to the target region.

3. Update the confidence value

When an image block is filled with new pixel values, the confidence value in it is also updated with the confidence value of the image block where the new pixel is located. This simple update rule can help measure the relative confidence between image blocks on the fill front.

The above three steps can be illustrated with the help of a series of schematic diagrams in Figure 4.5. Figure 4.5a shows an original image, where T represents the region to be filled (target region), two S (S_1 and S_2) represent regions (in the source region) that can be used for filling task, two B represent the boundary between the target region to be filled and the source region (including the two segments B_1 and B_2). Figure 4.5b shows the currently to be filled image block R_p centered on the pixel p on B (part of R_p is in the target region, and the other part is in the source region). Figure 4.5c shows two candidate image blocks found in the regions that can be used for filling, one of which R_u is at the junction of the two regions that can be used for filling, which is very close to the image block to be filled; the other R_v is completely inside the first region that can be used for filling and has a large (structural) gap with the image block to be filled. Figure 4.5d shows the result of partially filling the region to be filled by copying the closest candidate image block (here R_u) to R_p (here, only one candidate image block is used, so it is also called a single sample). The above filling process is performed sequentially on all image blocks in T and finally the region to be filled (in the target region) can be filled with the content (in the source region) used for filling.

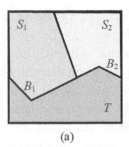 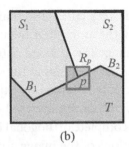 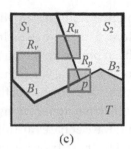 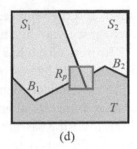

(a)   (b)   (c)   (d)

FIGURE 4.5   Schematic diagram of filling process based on sample; (a) shows an original image; (b) shows the currently to be filled image block R_p centered on the pixel p on B (part of R_p is in the target region, and the other part is in the source region); (c) shows two candidate image blocks found in the regions that can be used for filling; (d) shows the result of partially filling the region to be filled by copying the closest candidate image block.

In the filling process, the sequential selection of image blocks can adopt the order of "peeling the onion," that is, repairing the target region according to the order from the outside to the inside and from the contour to the interior. If the boundary point of the target region is the center of the image block, the pixels of the image block in the source region are known, and the pixels in the target region are unknown and need to be repaired. For this reason, it can also be considered to assign weights to the image block to be repaired. The more known pixels it contains, the larger the corresponding weight, and the higher is in the repairing order.

4.2 ALGORITHMS COMBINED WITH SPARSE REPRESENTATION

The sample-based method introduced in the previous Sub-section 4.1.4 often requires a lot of calculations because each image block in the region D to be filled requires an exhaustive search in the region F–D (when looking for a matching block, the global search method is generally used), so it is time-consuming. In addition, this search has a greater possibility of false matches. To solve these problems, an algorithm combined with sparse representation was introduced.

4.2.1 Principle of Sparse Representation

One way to reduce the amount of calculation based on the sample method is to use the concept of sparse representation, that is, to integrate sparse representation technology into the image repairing process.

4.2.1.1 Sparse Representation

The *sparse representation* of the signal means that the signal has a sparse representation in a redundant dictionary. In this way, the image repairing problem can be regarded as restoring incomplete image signals, where the image is decomposed into a collection of patches (regions), each patch corresponds to a signal, and the sparse representation of each patch is used to fill in the incomplete part. Specifically, given an image, it can be expanded with a set of over-complete bases, which can be selected adaptively and flexibly according to the nature and characteristics of the image itself. Since the number of base functions is small, and the representation result obtained is very concise so that sparse representation of the image can be obtained, thereby reducing the amount of calculation.

Theoretically, it has been proved that if an image is expanded onto a set of linearly independent complete orthogonal bases, when the image belongs to the space formed by the set of linearly independent bases, then the coefficients obtained by expanding the image are unique. In practical engineering applications, the commonly used discrete Fourier bases, discrete cosine bases, and wavelet bases are all complete orthogonal bases. The transformation coefficients obtained by these transformations of the image are unique, and the coefficients obtained also have a certain degree of sparseness.

To obtain an even sparse image representation, over-complete redundant bases can be used instead of general complete orthogonal bases. If x is used to represent the coordinates of the pixel $f(x, y)$, the vector $f \in \mathbf{R}^N$ composed of all pixels of an image can be written as

$$f = zx \tag{4.15}$$

In the formula, z is called an over-complete dictionary, which is an $N \times K$-dimensional matrix, where $K \gg N$, $x \in \mathbf{R}^K$ can be regarded as the coefficient of the linear expansion of the image f on the over-complete dictionary z. When $\|x\|_0 \ll N$, that is, when the number of non-zero elements in the x set is much smaller than N, the above representation can be said to be a sparse representation.

4.2.1.2 Sparse Coefficient

For image repairing with the help of sparse representation, a regularization method based on *least absolute shrinkage and selection operator* (Lasso) can be considered. In which, the L_1 norm is used to punish the common least squares regularized loss function to obtain the sparsity of the coefficients. Given a normalized dictionary $z = [z^1, z^2, ..., z^N]$ and an input signal $x = [x_1, x_2, ..., x_K]^T$, the Lasso algorithm needs to estimate the coefficient β of a signal on the given dictionary:

$$\hat{\beta} = \arg\min\left\{\|x - z\beta\|_2^2 + \lambda\|\beta\|_1\right\} \tag{4.16}$$

Among them, the first item in braces represents the error of signal reconstruction, and the second item is a measure of the sparsity of the fitting coefficient vector, so λ is a weighting coefficient that controls the balance between reconstruction error and sparsity. The model on which this equation is based is $x = z\beta$, and β is sparse, that is, only a few of β are non-zero.

When some signal components are damaged, the above model can be improved to:

$$x = z\,\beta + e \tag{4.17}$$

Among them, e represents the error, that is, e_i is non-zero only if x_i is damaged. The index set of the damaged signal component can be denoted as I, $I = \{i|e_i \neq 0\}$. If $x\backslash_I$ is used to represent the vector obtained by removing the component of its index in I from x, that is, $x\backslash_I$ is composed of all the undamaged components in x; $z\backslash_I$ is used to represent the corresponding dictionary matrix that is obtained through removal of all the columns whose index in I from z, then the sparsity coefficient β can be estimated as follows:

$$\hat{\beta} = \arg\min\left\{ \left\| x_{\backslash I} - z_{\backslash I}\beta \right\|_2^2 + \lambda \left\| \beta \right\|_1 \right\} \tag{4.18}$$

Next, the damaged signal can be restored with the help of Equation (4.18):

$$\hat{x}_i = \begin{cases} x_i & i \notin I \\ \left(z\hat{\beta} \right)_i & i \in I \end{cases} \tag{4.19}$$

Combining Equations (4.18) and (4.19), the damaged signal can be restored. It should be pointed out here that the original sparsity is defined by the L_0 norm ($\|x\|_0$ represents the number of non-zero elements in the vector x), but this will cause the optimization problem to become an NP problem. However, it has been proved that in the case of sufficient sparseness, using L_1 norm as a penalty term instead of L_0 norm as a penalty term, the solutions obtained by the two are equivalent. Therefore, the L_1 norm is used in Equation (4.18) to transform an NP problem into a non-NP problem.

4.2.2 Basic Sparse Representation Algorithm

The image repairing algorithm using sparse representation corresponding to the sample-based image repairing algorithm in Sub-section 4.1.4 still uses the method of calculating the weights of edge pixels in the image to determine the priority of the image block, thereby deciding the repairing order of the image blocks in target region (Shen et al. 2009).

4.2.2.1 Algorithm Steps

The algorithm first builds a set of suitable bases. This is because to use the sparse representation of the image, it is necessary to calculate the sparse coefficient vector of the image. From the perspective of image filling, the target region to be filled must be visually consistent with the source region as much as possible, that is, the texture, structure and even the noise level between the two should be as close as possible. To achieve this goal, one can directly sample in the image source region or directly use a complete image block as the base. By the way, the basic sample-based image repairing algorithm introduced in the previous Sub-section 4.1.4 can also be regarded as a special case of the sparse representation algorithm, which is the special case of using only one basis to fill the image at a time.

Now consider filling the image block R_p centered on the pixel p. Assuming that the size of the image block is $n \times n$, the k-dimensional vector composed of pixels in the image block is f_p ($k = n \times n$). Because p is located on the boundary between the source region and the target region, some pixels in the image block R_p centered on p belong to the source region and the remaining pixels belong to the target region. If I represents the set of all pixels i in the image block R_p, S represents the set of pixels belonging to the source region in the image block R_p, and T represents the set of pixels belonging to the target region in the image block R_p, then set $I = $ set $S + $ set T. Let Z be a set of bases formed by several image blocks selected from the source region of the image, then Z^S is an over-complete base. Now one can calculate the coefficient vector x of f_p defined on S and expanded on Z^S, and then update the pixels belonging to part T in f_p according to the obtained coefficient x. This can be represented with reference to Equations (4.18) and (4.19) as

$$\hat{x} = \arg\min_{x} \left\{ \left\| f_p^S - Z^S \cdot x \right\|_2^2 + \lambda \|x\|_1 \right\} \tag{4.20}$$

$$\hat{f}_p^i = \begin{cases} f_p^i & i \notin I \\ (Z \cdot \hat{x})^i & i \in I \end{cases} \tag{4.21}$$

After calculating the coefficient vector according to Equation (4.20), the current image block can be updated according to Equation (4.21). This process needs to be performed on all image blocks in the target region.

Figure 4.6 shows a comparison of image repairing using this sparse representation algorithm and the algorithm in Sub-section 4.1.4. Figure 4.6a is the original image; Figure 4.6b is the image with the target region marked (i.e., it needs to delete the animal on the right side of the image); Figure 4.6c is the result of the algorithm in Sub-section 4.1.4, while deleting unnecessary scenery, other unnecessary content has been introduced; Figure 4.6d is the result of using the sparse representation algorithm here. The algorithm in Sub-section 4.1.4 always selects the most similar image block to fill the current position every time, so it is a greedy method, and it may introduce some content from the source region into the target region, resulting in undesirable targets or artifacts in the repaired region; while the algorithm using sparse representation selects multiple bases to combine and to reconstruct the image each time, and the possibility of introducing unnecessary content is less.

4.2.2.2 Algorithm Key Points
The main points of image repairing with sparse representation include:

1. Filling order

   The key to the sample-based image repairing algorithm is to determine the order of filling so that to restore the texture and structure in a balanced manner. Given an input image, it is needed to select the target region to be removed and filled. Here, use δD to denote the boundary or contour of the target region.

   The image grows from the boundary of the region to the interior. The selection of filling order should be able to effectively retain structural information. In each iteration, the priority $P(p)$ of each pixel p on the boundary δD is calculated, and the pixel with the largest priority is selected as p_m. The patch at the center of p_m is the one to be considered in the current iteration. Because the center of the patch is on the boundary, some pixels in the patch are in the target region. The patch can be regarded as an incomplete signal. The pixels corresponding to the source region are the existing

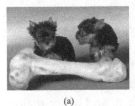 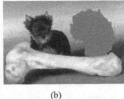 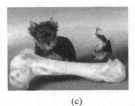 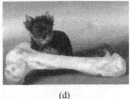

(a)   (b)   (c)   (d)

FIGURE 4.6 Using the sparse representation algorithm to compare with the algorithm in Sub-section 4.1.4; (a) is the original image; (b) is the image with the target region marked; (c) is the result of the algorithm in Sub-section 4.1.4; (d) is the result of using the sparse representation algorithm.

components and the pixels corresponding to the target region are missing components. After restoring the current patch, the target region is updated. Then calculate the next pixel with the highest priority, and select the patch to be considered in the next iteration. Go on like this.

2. Signal restoration

Now consider the pixels selected as p_m. Let k-D vector $\boldsymbol{\Psi}_{pm}$ denote the patch with the center at p_m, and its height and width are both n, then $k = n \times n$. Regarding $\boldsymbol{\Psi}_{pm}$ as the $\boldsymbol{x}$ to be restored, and I as the index set belonging to the target region components in $\boldsymbol{x}$, the sparse representation of the current patch can be restored using Equations (4.18) and (4.19):

$$\hat{\boldsymbol{\beta}} = \arg\min\left\{\left\|\boldsymbol{\Psi}_{pm \backslash I} - \boldsymbol{x}_{\backslash I}\boldsymbol{\beta}\right\|_2^2 + \lambda\|\boldsymbol{\beta}\|_1\right\} \tag{4.22}$$

$$\hat{\boldsymbol{\Psi}}_{pm}^i = \begin{cases} \boldsymbol{\Psi}_{pm}^i & i \notin I \\ \left(\boldsymbol{x}\hat{\boldsymbol{\beta}}\right)_i & i \in I \end{cases} \tag{4.23}$$

3. Dictionary construction

To calculate the sparse representation of the signal, it is necessary to construct a dictionary to solve the Lasso regularization problem. This problem can be solved by using techniques such as matching pursuit or kernel singular value decomposition (K-SVD).

The filled target region should be consistent with the source region so that the entire image can look reasonable and credible. Here, not only must the texture be consistent, but also the noise level must be close. Therefore, all the patches in the source region must be used to construct the dictionary.

4.2.3 Improvements to the Sparse Representation Algorithm

The aforementioned sparse representation algorithm has some rooms that can be improved, and three targeted measures are introduced below (Chen and Zhang 2010).

1. Improvements to the filling order

The previous method mainly considers the iso-illuminance factor when selecting the image block for priority filling so that the filling is carried out along the edge and boundary of the object, so that the structural information of the image in the target region can be better maintained. However, in regions where the edges of some objects are not noticeable, such as when repairing blue sky, lake surface, and other regions, where the iso-illuminance line is not obvious, the effect of the above method may not be ideal at this time. For this reason, one can consider choosing a different image block filling order according to the characteristics of the region: where the edge is obvious in the image, the factor of the iso-illuminance line is mainly considered, and fill in along a specific direction; while for the position where the edge is not obvious in the image, the "peeling the onion" sequence is considered, and the filling is carried out layer by layer from the outside to the inside. This avoids the accumulation of errors caused by filling in a single direction and makes the filled target region more consistent and continuous with the surrounding source region.

Figure 4.7 shows a set of improved effects for filling order, where Figure 4.7a is the original image; Figure 4.7b is the image with the target region marked (that is, the building on the beach is hoped to be removed from the image) Figure 4.7c is the filling result of the aforementioned basic sparse representation algorithm. There is an island-like part on the sea level, as shown inside the box; Figure 4.7d is the result of improving the filling sequence, No artifact appears, indicating that the improvement is effective.

Figure 4.8 shows another set of improved effects for filling order, where Figure 4.8a is the original image; Figure 4.8b is the image with the target region marked (that is, the giraffe on the right is hoped to be removed from the image) Figure 4.8c is the filling result of the aforementioned basic sparse representation algorithm. There is an extra house-like part on the grass, as shown in the box. Figure 4.8d is the result of improving the filling order, showing the improvement is effective.

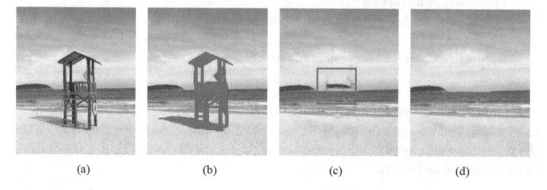

(a) (b) (c) (d)

FIGURE 4.7 One example of improvement effect for filling order; (a) is the original image; (b) is the image with the target region marked; (c) is the filling result of using the basic sparse representation algorithm; (d) is the result of improving the filling sequence.

FIGURE 4.8   Another example of improvement effect for filling order; (a) is the original image; (b) is the image with the target region marked; (c) is the filling result of using the basic sparse representation algorithm; (d) is the result of improving the filling order.

The following is a detailed explanation of the above problems with reference to Figure 4.9. Figure 4.9a is an intermediate result of the filling process of Figure 4.7. Part of the image block has been filled, and the remaining part still belongs to the target region. Image Block 1 in Figure 4.9b is selected by the basic algorithm, which is the image block to be filled. Image Block 2 was selected to fill Image Block 1 in consideration of iso-illuminance factors. This introduces artifacts in the target region and spreads in the target region, and finally this leads to the problem in Figure 4.7c. Image Block 3 in Figure 4.9c is the next image block to be filled that is selected by the improved method, and the improved method also selects Image Block 4 to repair Image Block 3, thus avoiding the introduction of a false image block, and finally getting the result of Figure 4.7d.

2. Improvement to filling error

When filling the image block on the boundary between the source region and the target region, the part of the image block belonging to the source region should be used to search for the source region in the image. At this time, it may happen that the closest image block searched out is very close to the source region part of the image block that needs to be filled, but the other part of the closest image block is very different from the target region part of the image block that needs to be filled. In this case, if one chooses the closest image block, it will not only cause a large error in the filling of the image block to be filled but also may cause the error to gradually accumulate and diffuse in the target region, affecting the filling effect of other image blocks in the target region. The improvement idea is to consider the first few closest image blocks at the same time. The algorithm based on sparse representation uses a set of bases composed of multiple image blocks. However, when Equation (4.20) is used, the corresponding coefficients of the image blocks arranged in the front are often much larger than the corresponding coefficients of some subsequent image blocks. At this time, it is the first image block that plays a major role. For this reason, consider removing the

(a)   (b)   (c)

FIGURE 4.9   Comparison of different filling order; (a) is an intermediate result of the filling process of Figure 4.7; (b) shows the selected blocks by the basic algorithm; (c) shown the introduced artifacts in the target region and spreads in the target region.

limit of L_1 norm in Equation (4.20) from the optimized representation, and adding another limit on the number of image blocks, which can be written as

$$\hat{x} = \arg\min_{x}\left\{\left\|f_p^S - Z^S \cdot x\right\|_2^2\right\} \quad \|x\|_0 < t \tag{4.24}$$

where t is a threshold that limits the number of image blocks. The coefficient calculated according to Equation (4.24) will reduce the weight of the closest image block when the first few image blocks are relatively close, thereby reducing the problem of filling with only one image block. From this point of view, t should be larger, but too large t will cause the filling result to be blurred, so it should be as small as possible while meeting the error requirements. An ideal situation is that the first few closest image blocks are relatively similar to each other, and the coefficients calculated from this situation will also be relatively close. At this time, the effect of blurring will be relatively small.

3. Improvements for the current image block

The gray value variance information in the image block to be filled currently reflects the characteristics of the image block. If the gray value variance of the part of the image block belonging to the source region is very small, the gray value of the image block is relatively smooth. When filling the part of the image block belonging to the target region, consider adding the average gray value of current image block to a certain ratio, that is, the part of the image block belonging to the source region also contributes to the filling of the part of the image block belonging to the target region. If the gray value variance of the part of the image block belonging to the source region is large, the gray value contrast of the image block will be relatively large.

When filling the part of the image block belonging to the target region, it is necessary to consider reducing the contribution from the source region.

4.3 WEIGHTED SPARSE NON-NEGATIVE MATRIX FACTORIZATION

A key step in the sample-based repairing process is to use the candidate patches in the source region to synthesize the desired texture. The methods that can be used include selecting the best single patch, but the problem is that there may be a risk of complete failure if it makes a mistake. On the other hand, a group of similar candidate patches can also be selected for averaging, but this will introduce undesirable blur.

The method introduced in the previous Sub-section 4.2.2 (Shen et al. 2009) can obtain clear recovery results with fewer greedy calculations. However, in reality, the closest candidate plays a decisive role in most cases compared to the rest (the role of the rest is ignored), although some of them are actually very similar to the closest candidate. At this point, the useful information of the remaining patches is discarded, even though the dictionary itself is over-complete. From this perspective, this method is greedy, leading to undesirable targets in the repaired region.

The method introduced in the previous Sub-section 4.2.3 (Chen and Zhang 2010) solves this problem in the original image domain. The weights of all the candidate patches are the same, although they are not the same as the closest candidate. To more appropriately use the information of the next closest candidate patch, this problem can be transferred to the transform domain to solve it. One method is to perform image repairing under the framework of sequence low-rank matrix restoration and completion. Specifically, assuming that the image patch to be repaired and the several similar candidate patches in the front are random samples from the same source, they are used to construct an incomplete data matrix. For this matrix completeness problem, an improved *weighted sparse non-negative matrix factorization* (WSNMF) method can be used to solve the problem (Wang and Zhang 2011).

4.3.1 Weighted Non-Negative Matrix Factorization

The purpose of *low rank approximation* (LRA) is to find a compact representation. The derivation of the low-rank approximation can be seen as decomposing the original data matrix into two or three low-rank factor matrices. By adding non-negative constraints, a new paradigm of low-rank approximation was born: *non-negative matrix factorization* (NMF). Due to its pure additive nature, non-negative matrix factorization has the ability to represent in parts.

In the case of an incomplete data matrix (some items in the matrix are not observed or missing), it is necessary to predict the missing elements to obtain a low-rank representation to complete the matrix. By introducing a binary weight matrix with values of 0 and 1 to distinguish between observed and unobserved values, the problem of matrix completeness can be solved by the *weighted non-negative matrix factorization* (WNMF) method.

Generally speaking, given an M-D random matrix x with non-negative elements, its N observations are denoted as $x_j, j = 1, 2, ..., N$. Let the data matrix be $X = [x_1, x_2, ..., x_N] \in \mathbb{R} \geq 0^{M \times N}$, the non-negative matrix decomposition must determine the non-negative basis matrix $U \in R \geq 0^{M \times N}$ and the coefficient matrix $V \in R \geq 0^{M \times N}$, so that make $X \approx UV$. With the help of Frobenius norm, the following objective function can be minimized:

$$F_{NMF}(X, UV) = \frac{1}{2} \|X - UV\|_F^2 = \frac{1}{2} \sum_{ij} \left(X_{ij} - [UV]_{ij} \right)^2 \tag{4.25}$$

The weighted non-negative matrix factorization attempts to minimize the following objective function:

$$J_{WNMF}(X, UV) = \frac{1}{2} \sum_{ij} W_{ij} \left(X_{ij} - [UV]_{ij} \right)^2 \tag{4.26}$$

where W_{ij} is a non-negative weight.

The weighted non-negative matrix factorization can be solved by introducing the weight matrix and modifying the standard non-negative matrix factorization iterative update rule. Another method is to use the EM algorithm, in which the missing content can be replaced by the corresponding value of the E step estimated in the current model, and the unweighted non-negative matrix decomposition is used for the filling matrix of the M step.

4.3.2 Filling Algorithm

Given an input image F, set the target region to be removed and filled as D (the other parts are $F–D$), and use δD to denote the boundary or boundary of the target region. The M-D vector Ψ_p is used to represent the image patch of $k \times k$ with the center at pixel p, which is the basic processing unit in example/sample-based repairing. The entire repairing process includes continuously updating the boundary by sequentially advancing image patches into the target region according to a pre-defined sequence.

1. Filling order

    The order of filling the target region should encourage the filling of the patches on the high-confidence structure first. At each step, the priority $P(p)$ of the image patch Ψ_p centered on the pixel p on the boundary δD is calculated, and the patch Ψ_{pm} with the highest confidence is selected as the target of the current iteration. Here, the priority $P(p)$ of Ψ_p can be represented as

$$P(p) = C(p)D(p) \tag{4.27}$$

Among them, $C(p)$ is the confidence item, $D(p)$ is the data item, they are respectively

$$C(p) = \frac{\sum\limits_{q \in \Psi_p \cap (F-D)} C(q)}{|\Psi_p|} \tag{4.28}$$

$$D(p) = \frac{\nabla I_p \cdot n_p}{N_D} \tag{4.29}$$

where $|\mathbf{\Psi}_p|$ is the area of $\mathbf{\Psi}_p$, N_D is the normalization factor (when taking 255, $D(p)$ can be scaled to the inside of [0, 255]), and ∇I_p is the normalized vector of iso-illuminance line (in the filling direction), which represents the intensity of the iso-illuminance line entering the boundary δD, n_p is the unit normal vector at the pixel p on the boundary δD. During initialization, $C(p)$ can be taken as

$$C(p) = \begin{cases} 0 & p \in D \\ 1 & p \in F - D \end{cases} \tag{4.30}$$

It can be updated later according to the calculation process. Calculate in this way, and each time the target patch with the highest priority value $\mathbf{\Psi}_{pm}$ is selected as the target patch of the current iteration for filling.

By the way, to consider the texture pattern that is not perpendicular to the filling front line, a new term $E(p)$ can be added to the calculation of the priority $P(p)$ to represent the edge-ness of $\mathbf{\Psi}_p$ (Guillemot et al. 2013). The Equation (4.27) becomes:

$$P(p) = C(p)D(p)E(p) \quad \forall p \in \delta D \tag{4.31}$$

where

$$E(p) = \frac{\displaystyle\sum_{q \in \mathbf{\Psi}_P \cap (F-D)} B(q \in \{\text{Edge}\})}{|\mathbf{\Psi}_P \cap (F-D)|} \tag{4.32}$$

Among them, $B(\bullet)$ is a binary function. When the condition is satisfied, it is taken to be 1, otherwise, 0; the set {Edge} represents the set of edge pixels obtained by the edge detection operator.

1. The construction of the data matrix

Once the target patch $\mathbf{\Psi}_{pm}$ is found, it is filled with all the information that can be obtained from the source region. One method is to search for $N-1$ patches denoted as $\mathbf{\Psi}_{qj, j=2,3,\ldots,N}$ in the source region, they should be the most similar to $\mathbf{\Psi}_{pm}$. Here $\mathbf{\Psi}_{qj}$ is defined as:

$$\mathbf{\Psi}_{qj} = \arg\min_{\mathbf{\Psi}_q \in \mathbf{\Psi} \backslash \mathbf{\Psi}_{qk}, k=2,\cdots,j-1} d\left(\mathbf{\Psi}_{pm}, \mathbf{\Psi}_q\right) \tag{4.33}$$

Among them, the distance $d(\mathbf{\Psi}_a, \mathbf{\Psi}_b)$ between two patches is still measured by the *sum of squared differences* (SSD), and SSD is defined in the filled part of the two patches. Considering the computational cost, the source region in the image can be shrunk into a sub-source region defined in a window centered on the target pixel.

In this way, the data matrix can be constructed as follows:

$$X = \left[\mathbf{\Psi}_{pm}, \mathbf{\Psi}_{q2}, \ldots, \mathbf{\Psi}_{qj}, \ldots, \mathbf{\Psi}_{qN}\right] = [X_1, X_2, \ldots, X_N] \in \mathbb{R}_{\geq 0}^{M \times N} \tag{4.34}$$

The column vector is set to N observations of the same random vector. The $\boldsymbol{\Psi}_{pm}$ component corresponding to the unknown pixel falling in the target region is set to 0. Because the patch $\boldsymbol{\Psi}_{pm}$ is incomplete (some elements are missing), while $\boldsymbol{\Psi}_{qj,\,j=2,3,\ldots,N}$ is complete, so the data matrix X needs to be complete.

2. The construction of weight matrix

The following defines the weighting matrix $W = [W_1, W_2, \ldots, W_N] \in \mathbb{R}_{\geq 0}^{M \times N}$. Different weighting strategies should be adopted for the complete signal and the incomplete signal in X. Among them, for W_1, the binary weight is:

$$W_{i1} = \begin{cases} 1 & \text{if } X_{i1} \text{ inside source region} \\ 0 & \text{if } X_{i1} \text{ inside target region} \end{cases} \tag{4.35}$$

From the candidate patches $\boldsymbol{\Psi}_{q2}$ to $\boldsymbol{\Psi}_{qN}$, the similarity between them and the target patch gradually decreases, which also indicates that the confidence of these candidate patches is gradually decreasing. Therefore, the weight of the sequence $X_{j,\,j=2,3,\ldots,N}$ should be selected accordingly. One can choose a decreasing function of $d(\boldsymbol{\Psi}_a, \boldsymbol{\Psi}_b)$, such as $W(\boldsymbol{\Psi}_j) = \exp[-d(\boldsymbol{\Psi}_p, \boldsymbol{\Psi}_j)/h]$ or $W(\boldsymbol{\Psi}_j) = c/d(\boldsymbol{\Psi}_p, \boldsymbol{\Psi}_j)$. If the latter is chosen, there are

$$W_{ij} = \frac{\min\left[d\left(\boldsymbol{\Psi}_{pm}, \boldsymbol{\Psi}_{qj}\right)\right]}{d\left(\boldsymbol{\Psi}_{pm}, \boldsymbol{\Psi}_{qj}\right)} = \frac{d\left(\boldsymbol{\Psi}_{pm}, \boldsymbol{\Psi}_{q2}\right)}{d\left(\boldsymbol{\Psi}_{pm}, \boldsymbol{\Psi}_{qj}\right)} \quad i = 1, \ldots, M, \; j = 2, \ldots, N \tag{4.36}$$

Among them, the components from the same patch have equal weights. The weight obtained by Equation (4.36) is normalized.

4.3.3 WSNMF Based on EM process

After converting the original image repairing work into a matrix completeness problem, it can be solved by the *weighted non-negative matrix factorization* (WNMF) method. Further, adding the sparsity constraint to the coefficient matrix V can enhance the sharp/clear repairing result. This method is called *weighted sparse non-negative matrix factorization* (WSNMF), which is an improvement of weighted non-negative matrix factorization. The objective function to be minimized is:

$$J_{\text{WSNMF}}(X, UV) = \frac{1}{2} \sum_{ij} W_{ij} \left(X_{ij} - [UV]_{ij}\right)^2 + \lambda \sum_{ij} V_{ij} \tag{4.37}$$

Here, a low-rank matrix decomposition is used to predict the value of the loss (defect). The basic idea is to treat the problem as a maximum likelihood problem with missing values, but the optimization process needs to be adjusted to fit the new objective function. Using the EM method, in the E step, a filling matrix Y is calculated from the current model estimation, and in the M step, the unweighted *sparse non-negative matrix factorization* (SNMF) method is used to re-estimate the decomposition model for Y.

1. E step

   The update rules are as follows:

$$Y \leftarrow W \otimes X + (\mathbf{1}_{M \times N} - W) \otimes (UV) \qquad (4.38)$$

Among them, $\mathbf{1}_{M \times N} \in \mathbb{R}^{M \times N}$ is a matrix with all elements being 1, and $\otimes$ is the Hadamard product operator. Here the weighting matrix needs to be normalized so that its values are all between [0, 1]. At the beginning of the update iteration, the estimation of the missing pixel value in Y can take the mean value of the corresponding candidate patch.

2. M step

   In this step, a standard sparse non-negative matrix factorization is required for matrix Y. One available approach is the *stable and efficient non-negative sparse coding* (SENSC) algorithm (Li and Zhang 2009), which can provide a relatively low reconstruction error while preserving a certain sparsity. To speed up, one can use a technique called partial M steps that avoids the determining the optimal solution at the initial iteration stage.

As the EM iteration progresses, the current target $\varPsi_{pm}$ will be restored according to the learned low-rank matrix. Next, the boundary of the target region is updated, and the foregoing process is repeated until all pixels are filled.

Figure 4.10 shows a set of experimental images, Figure 4.10a is the original image, Figure 4.10b marks the target region on the original image, and Figure 4.10c is the result of using the single sample algorithm in Sub-section 4.1.4, Figure 4.10d is the result of using the sparse representation algorithm of Sub-section 4.2.2, and Figure 4.10e is the result of using the weighted sparse non-negative matrix factorization algorithm of this section. The lower half of Figure 4.10c–e respectively give partial enlarged views of the target region for more obvious comparison. It can be seen from Figure 4.10c that artifacts appear at the junction of the rock and the grass. It can be seen from Figure 4.10d that the rock pattern spreads into the grass at the junction of the rock and the grass. From Figure 4.10e, it can be seen that the above two problems have been solved well.

4.4 CONTEXT-DRIVEN HYBRID ALGORITHM

To overcome the ambiguity problem that is easy to produce based on the diffusion method and the problem that the sample-based method requires a lot of calculation, a hybrid method can be used. A typical hybrid algorithm has three main steps:

1. Decompose the original image into two parts, one part contains structural information such as strong edges and corners, and the other part contains texture information such as texture patterns.

2. Use the diffusion-based method for the structural part and use the sample-based method for the texture part to repair.

3. Combine the two parts of the repairing results to get the final repairing result.

FIGURE 4.10 Experimental comparison of different algorithms. (a) is the original image; (b) marks the target region on the original image; (c) is the result obtained by using the single sample algorithm in Sub-section 4.1.4; (d) is the result of using the sparse representation algorithm of Sub-section 4.2.2; (e) is the result of using the weighted sparse non-negative matrix factorization algorithm of Section 4.3.

The disadvantage of this method is that the hybrid method and the result are still used for regions with a strong structure or obvious texture, which will cause the degradation of visual quality. In addition, for images with obvious texture, the calculation time is still relatively long.

The following introduces a context-driven hybrid patching method that attempts to reduce the amount of calculation and maintain visual quality (Cai and Kim 2015). It mainly completes two tasks:

1. Determine the optimal order for repairing missing texture and structure targets.

2. Extract the best candidates for sub-images (source windows) containing the source patch.

4.4.1 Overall Flowchart

The overall flowchart of the *context-driven hybrid algorithm* is shown in Figure 4.11, which mainly includes three sequential steps. The first step is for the pre-processing, which is to

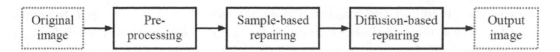

FIGURE 4.11 The overall flowchart of the hybrid algorithm.

extract the data related to the texture features from the image. The second step is the use of *sample-based repairing* techniques sequentially for the target region with dense texture (one can use any of the techniques described above or other technique). The last step is to use a *diffusion-based repairing* technique for all the remaining target regions together (one can also use any of the techniques described above or other technique). This method has no restrictions on which sample-based repairing algorithm and which diffusion-based repairing algorithm are used, so it is mainly a framework that combines two types of algorithms.

For a hybrid repairing algorithm, there are three orders for using diffusion-based repairing and sample-based repairing techniques: (i) Use diffusion-based repairing technique first; (ii) use sample-based repairing technique first; and (iii) use the two techniques alternately. Starting from the purpose of reducing the amount of calculation and maintaining visual quality, and most diffusion-based repairing techniques can combine multiple target regions into a set of partial differential equations, the first two orders should be more appropriate than the third order. In addition, since the diffusion-based repairing technique requires additional time to select the target region compared with sample-based repairing technique, the second order should save time than the first order because the subsequent use of diffusion-based repairing technique only requires the treating of the remaining target region after using the sample-based repairing technique. Of course, the premise here is that the amount of calculation based on the sample-based repairing technique itself must first be reduced, which will be discussed later in the sample-based repairing step.

4.4.2 Pre-Processing Step

The first step of pre-processing is to extract data related to texture features from the image. Specifically, three types of sub-images need to be extracted from the original image I: the mask I_{mask}, the strong edge image I_{se}, and the weak edge image I_{we}.

1. The mask image I_{mask} is used to mark the region that needs to be repaired, that is, the pixels belonging to region to be repaired are marked as 1 and the pixels belonging to other regions are marked as 0.

2. The strong edge image I_{se} can be obtained with the help of Canny operator. If the edge value of a pixel (representing the degree of edgeness) is greater than 0.9, the pixel is classified as belong to strong edge image, that is, it has strong texture characteristics.

3. The weak edge image I_{we} can also be obtained with the help of Canny operator. If the edge value of a pixel is detected to be greater than 0.3 but less than 0.9, the pixel is classified as belong to weak edge image, that is, it has weak texture characteristics.

Pre-processing is followed by initialization parameters. The original image I, the mask image I_{mask}, the strong edge image I_{se} and the weak edge image I_{we} are evenly divided into $n \times n$ basic blocks B_i, $i = 1, 2, \ldots, N$. For each B_i, initialize two parameters: $p(i)$ and $M(i)$.

The value of $p(i)$ can be calculated for B_i with the help of Equation (4.32). B_i with a large $p(i)$ value favors a large texture density, and B_i with a small $p(i)$ value favors a small texture density. Therefore, the value of $p(i)$ can be used to determine whether to add the corresponding block B_i to the search window.

$M(i)$ represents the Manhattan distance (measured by the number of blocks) from the position of B_i to the closest block on the boundary of the missing region containing B_i. If there are no unknown pixels in a B_i, its $M(i) = 0$; and if there are both unknown pixels and known pixels in a B_i, its $M(i) = 1$. A large $M(i)$ value indicates that B_i is more likely not to be selected as the target region, and a small $M(i)$ value indicates that B_i is more likely to be selected as the target region. It should be noted that the choice of target region also depends on the value of $p(i)$, as described in the following sample-based repairing step.

4.4.3 Sample-Based Repairing Step

This step can be divided into three sub-steps: (i) Re-evaluate the parameters; (ii) Update the parameters (include selecting the target, generating the source window and repairing); (iii) Conditional stop.

1. Re-evaluate the parameters

    Before the start of this step, the $p(\cdot)$ value of the block without unknown pixels in the current iteration has been set to 0. The step of re-evaluating the parameters uses the $p(\cdot)$ value of the surrounding blocks to estimate the $p(\cdot)$ value of the block. The value of $p(\cdot)$ can be calculated as follows:

$$p(i) = \begin{cases} p(i) & \text{if } p(i) \geq 0 \\ k \max_{B_j}[p(i)] & \text{if } p(i) = -1 \end{cases} \qquad (4.39)$$

where B_j represents all the neighboring blocks of B_i satisfying $M(j) = M(i) - 1$, and k is a control parameter with a value in $[0, 1]$. According to the $p(\cdot)$ values of all blocks, the average p_{avg}, the maximum p_{max} and the minimum p_{min} can be calculated. Furthermore, two parameters p_{smooth} and p_{sharp} are defined:

$$p_{smooth} = p_{min} + k_1 \left(p_{avg} - p_{min} \right) \qquad (4.40)$$

$$p_{sharp} = p_{avg} + k_2 \left(p_{max} - p_{avg} \right) \qquad (4.41)$$

Among them, k_1 and k_2 are the weights in $[0, 1]$, and the experimental values can be 0.5 and 0, respectively. According to the values of p_{smooth} and p_{sharp}, the interval $[p_{min}, p_{max}]$ can be divided into three sub-intervals: $R_{small} = [p_{min}, p_{smooth}]$, $R_{middle} = [p_{smooth}, p_{sharp}]$ and $R_{large} = [p_{sharp}, p_{max}]$.

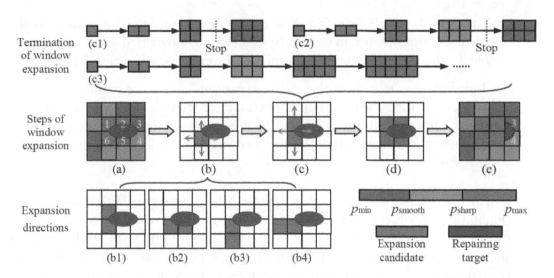

FIGURE 4.12 Schematic diagram of selecting the starting target patch and generating the source window by expanding the target patch.

2. Update the parameters

Among all target patches (basic blocks), the target patch with the largest $p(\cdot) \in R_{\text{large}}$ in the current iteration whose $M(\cdot)$ value corresponds to the layer number should be selected. For example, Figure 4.12a shows how to divide blocks into R_{smooth} (dark gray), R_{mix} (light gray), and R_{texture} (medium gray). Suppose that the values of $M(\cdot)$ from B_1 to B_6 are equal to the values of the layer number, and $p(6) \in R_{\text{large}}$ is the largest. Then, B_6 will be selected as the expanded starting target patch B_{start}. Next, iteratively expand B_{start} in four directions (see Figure 4.12b): top (Figure 4.12b1), right (Figure 4.12b2), bottom (Figure 4.12b3), and left (Figure 4.12b4).

The direction of each expansion must be selected according to the p value of the obtained window. If the maximum value of p is p_{exp}, the corresponding direction is selected as the direction of expansion. The iterative expansion process mainly has the following two situations.

A. The first case is shown in Figure 4.12c1 and c2. It stops when the expansion reaches $p_{\text{exp}} \in R_{\text{small}}$ because the expansion leads to the weakening of the texture feature.

B. The second case is shown in Figure 4.12c3. As long as $p_{\text{exp}} \in R_{\text{middle}} \cup R_{\text{large}}$, the expansion will continue.

In addition to the above two cases, there are three special cases in the continuation or termination of the control extension.

A. The first special case is that if the expansion stops too early, the resulting source window will be small, making the source information unnaturally covering the target block. Therefore, when the window size is smaller than a lower threshold, it needs to continue to expand.

B. The second special case is that if the expansion is too much in one direction, the imbalance information in the source window will be overused to repair the target block. Therefore, a minimum control over the expansion direction is required.

C. The third special case is that if the expansion causes the window to be too large, the window will contain unnecessary or redundant texture information relative to the target block. Therefore, it is necessary to control the number of expansion iterations so that the obtained window size is smaller than a higher threshold.

Once the source window is extracted with the help of expansion, the source information in the window can be used to perform example-based repair on the target block (the target block can contain multiple basic blocks with unknown pixels). Next, as shown in Figure 4.12e, update the image I, I_{mask}, I_{se}, I_{we}, and p values. Finally, repeat the loop in the previous Sub-step (2) until there is no block with an even big p value or no block with an M value equal to the other blocks in the layer.

3. Conditional stop

The iteration based on the sample-based repairing process stops when there are no target blocks that need to be modified (if there are still target blocks that need to be modified, return to Sub-step (1) and continue to proceed in three sub-steps in sequence), which means that there are no more target blocks whose p value is greater than the target block of p_{sharp}. The rest of the target blocks can be repaired using diffusion-based repairing methods.

4.4.4 Diffusion-Based Repairing Step

The remaining target blocks after the previous sample-based repairing process are blocks in a relatively smooth region. The diffusion-based repairing process is applied to the remaining target blocks in all these target region D, and a set of partial differential equations needs to be generated for these blocks. Note that since the value of each target pixel is estimated with the average value of the neighboring pixels of the pixel, there is no need to extract the window again in this step.

After using a sample-based repairing technique and a diffusion-based repairing technique in turn, the final hybrid repairing result can be obtained.

4.5 SOME RECENT DEVELOPMENTS AND FURTHER RESEARCH

In the following, some technique developments and promising research directions in the last years are briefly overviewed.

4.5.1 Categorization of Repairing Methods

Though image inpainting was originated from an ancient technique performed by artists to restore damaged paintings, the modern digital image repairing is only started in the beginning of this century (Jam et al. 2021), trying to imitate this process and perform the task automatically.

A large number of different techniques have been proposed since then. To the date, these techniques can be hierarchically classified as shown in Figure 4.13. In the first level, the image repairing techniques can be classified as traditional ones and (recently arising) DL (deep learning) ones. For traditional methods, the diffusion-based approaches and exemplar-based approaches have attracted many attentions. For the former, techniques using total variance (TV), partial deferential equation (PDE), and CDD are widely used. For the latter, both texture synthesis and structure synthesis techniques are commonly employed. In addition, techniques based on wavelet transform and sparse representation are also popular. These years, deep learning techniques develop rapidly and applied in the domain of image repairing. Currently, new techniques are mainly based on auto-encoder (AE), convolution neuron networks (CNN), and generative adversarial networks (GAN). With the increasing number of various techniques, more and more hybrid methods, both for traditional methods and/or for deep learning methods, are proposed.

4.5.2 AE and GAN in Image Repairing

Recently, several image repairing techniques based on AE and GAN have been proposed. Some techniques combining the advantages of two have also been introduced (Fan et al. 2020).

4.5.2.1 AE-Based Techniques

Auto-encoder (AE) is composed of two parts: encoder and decoder, and its basic structure diagram is shown in Figure 4.14. The encoder is composed of a convolutional network to achieve dimensionality reduction coding; the decoder is composed of a de-convolutional network, which uses the features extracted by the encoder to decode and reconstruct the image. In the encoding process, the image is compressed and mapped to the feature space. As the level deepens, the number of channels increases and the feature size decreases. The decoding process is the inverse process of encoding. The image is reconstructed from the deep features of multiple channels. The number of channels decreases and the image size increases.

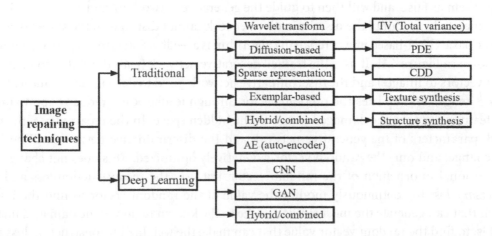

FIGURE 4.13   A hierarchical classification of image repairing techniques.

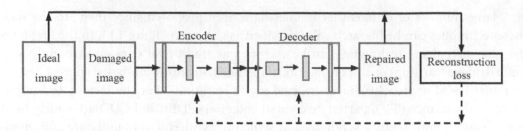

FIGURE 4.14 The structure diagram of AE network.

In the process of feature extraction, if the input image is damaged, there is information missing in the shallow features, but as the encoding deepens, the impact of the defect on the deep features gradually decreases, and the deep network can extract the main semantics of the image features. In the decoding process, the deep semantic features are fused and reconstructed step by step through the de-convolution network, and a relatively complete image can be output to achieve image restoration. The training phase of the AE network uses *reconstruction loss* to optimize its own parameters. After the training is completed, the defective image is input to the AE, and the output repaired image can be obtained. One example can be found in (Liu et al. 2018). The repairing process is a feedforward process.

In the AE coding and decoding process, the feature compression and extraction of each coding layer will cause the loss of some detailed features, and some detailed texture information may not be restored in the decoding and reconstruction stage. Therefore, the reconstructed image may show some excessive smoothness and blur.

4.5.2.2 GAN-Based Techniques

Generative adversarial network (GAN) consists of two networks: generative network G (generator) and discriminative network D (discriminator). The generative network is used to generate images, and the discriminative network is used to determine whether the generated images are true or false. If the generated image has unreasonable content, partial blurring and other problems that are inconsistent with the real image, the discriminative network will judge them as false, and will then to guide the generative network to continuously optimize the generated effect until the discriminative network cannot distinguish the authenticity.

The basic GAN-based image repairing algorithm is a feedback iterative repairing method, as shown in Figure 4.15. It uses the trained generative network (with the ability to map random vectors to images) and the discriminative network (used to determine the authenticity of the image), and updates the random vector through feedback to gradually approximate the feature vector of the damaged image in the hidden space. In the repair phase, the network parameters of the generative network and the discriminative network will no longer change, and only the random vector is iteratively optimized. This does not change the dimensional information of the random vector, but uses the reconstruction loss and the *adversary loss* to continuously modify the value of the random vector to find the image result that can generate the most similar image to the known region of the damaged image, that is, to find the random vector value that can make the weighted reconstruction loss and adversary loss smallest. One example can be found in (Dolhansky and Canton 2018).

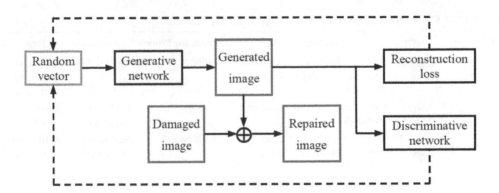

FIGURE 4.15   The structure diagram of GAN network.

4.5.2.3 Hybrid Techniques

The AE has a relatively strong ability to reconstruct damaged images, and the discriminator (D) in the GAN has a better ability to guide the generative network. Combining them will hopefully get better results. Most combined algorithms are called CE (context encoders) algorithms, such as (Gao and Grauman 2017; Iizuka et al. 2017; Yu et al. 2019; Nazeri et al. 2019).

The basic block diagram of CE algorithm is shown in Figure 4.16. The AE is used as the generative network in the GAN, and the authenticity of the generated image is judged through the discriminative network, and the parameters of the generative network are jointly optimized through the concurrent reducing *adversary loss* and *reconstruction loss*. In the training phase, the AE and the discriminative network are trained alternately. After the training is completed, the discriminator is no longer used, and the repair process depends on the feedforward process of the auto encoder.

4.5.2.4 Comparison

A comparison of the three types of technologies is shown in Table 4.1 (Fan, et al. 2020).

GAN-based repairing is a feedback process, and the number of iterations is generally more than 1,000. It relies too much on the ability of the GAN to generate images. When using small data sets for training, it is easy to produce problem of over-fitting and losing the diversity of the generated images. Both CE repairing and AE repairing belong to the feedforward process. There is no need to iterate and optimize the calculation again. The

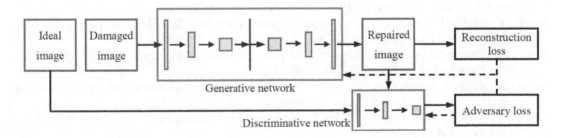

FIGURE 4.16   The flow chart of CE repairing algorithm.

TABLE 4.1   A Comparison of Three Types of Image Repairing Methods

Method	Input	Training Process	Repairing Process	Advantage	Drawback
GAN-based	Random vector	Alternate training of generative network and discriminative network	Feedback	Clear details	Poor repair result on small data sets
AE-based	Damaged image	Only training of the generative network	Feedforward	High repair similarity	Blurred repair result
CE method	Damaged image	Alternate training of generative network and discriminative network	Feedforward	Semantic repairing	Artifact in repair result

repairing is more efficient, but corresponding to GAN, the repairing of structural details often leads to blur, artifacts and other problems.

REFERENCES

Bertalmio, M., A. L. Bertozzi, and G. Sapiro. 2001. Navier–strokes, fluid dynamics, and image and video inpainting. *Proceedings of the CVPR*, 417–424.

Cai, L., and T. Kim. 2015. Context-driven hybrid image inpainting. *IET Image Processing* 9(10): 866–873.

Chan, T. F., and J. H. Shen. 2001. Non-texture inpainting by curvature-driven diffusions (CDD). *Journal of Visual Communication and Image Representation* 12(4): 436–449.

Chan, T. F., and J. H. Shen. 2005. *Image Processing and Analysis—Variational, PDE, Wavelet, and Stochastic Methods*. Philadelphia, PA: Siam.

Chen, Q. Q., and Y. -J. Zhang. 2010. An Improved Example-based Inpainting Method Using Sparse Representation. *Proceedings of the 15th NCIG*, 61–66.

Criminisi, A., P. Perez, and K. Toyama. 2003. Object removal by exemplar-based image inpainting. *Proceedings of the ICCV*, 721–728.

Dolhansky, B., and F. C. Canton. 2018. Eye in-painting with exemplar generative adversarial networks. *Proceedings of the CVPR*, 7902–7911.

Fan, C. Q., K. Ren, L. S. Meng, et al. 2020. Advances in digital image inpainting algorithms based on deep learning. *Journal of Signal Processing*, 36(1): 102–109.

Gao, R. H., and K. Grauman. 2017. On-demand learning for deep image restoration. *Proceedings of the ICCV*, 1086–1095.

Guillemot, C., M. Turkan, and O. Le Meur, et al. 2013. Object removal and loss concealment using neighbor embedding methods. *Signal Processing and Image Communication* 28(10): 1405–1419.

Jam, J., C. Kendrick, K. Walker, et al. 2021. A comprehensive review of past and present image inpainting methods. *Computer Vision and Image Understanding* 203: 103147.

Li, L., and Y.-J. Zhang 2009. SENSC: A stable and efficient algorithm for non-negative sparse coding. *Acta Automatica Sinica* 35(10), 1257–1271.

Liu, G., F. A. Reda, K. J. Shih, et al. 2018. Image inpainting for irregular holes using partial convolutions. *Proceedings of the ECCV*, 85–100.

Iizuka, S., E. Simo-Serra, and H. Ishikawa. 2017. Globally and locally consistent image completion. *ACM Transactions on Graphics (ToG)* 36(4): 107.

Nazeri, K., E. Ng, T. Joseph, et al. 2019. Edge connect: Generative image inpainting with adversarial edge learning. *arXiv preprint* arXiv: 1901.00212.

Shen, B., W. Hu, Y. M. Zhang, et al. 2009. Image inpainting via sparse representation. *Proceedings of the 34th ICASSP*, 697–700.

Wang, Y. X., and Y. J. Zhang. 2011. Image inpainting via weighted sparse non-negative matrix factorization. *Proceedings of the 18th ICIP*, 3470–3473.

Yu, J., Z. Lin, J. Yang, et al. 2019. Free-form image inpainting with gated convolution. *Proceedings of the ICCV*, 4471–4480.

Zhang, H. Y., B. WuB, Q. C. Peng, et al. 2007. Digital image inpainting based on p-harmonic energy minimization. *Chinese Journal of Electronics* 16(3): 525–530.

Zhang, Y.-J. 2015. Image inpainting as an evolving topic in image engineering. In *Encyclopedia of Information Science and Technology*, 3rd Ed. Hershey, PA: IGI Global, Chapter 122 (1283–1293).

## CHAPTER 5

Image De-Fogging

D URING THE IMAGE ACQUISITION or collection process, the image will be affected by various environmental factors (including bad weather conditions), and the quality will be degraded. Smog (including fog and haze) is a common natural phenomenon, which is caused by the scattering and absorption of light by tiny particles suspended in the atmosphere. The suspended particles in the atmosphere mainly include three types: air molecules, water vapor/droplets, and aerosols. The degree of image quality degradation caused by these particles is closely related to the type, composition, size, and shape of atmospheric particles. The radius and density of water droplets and aerosols are relatively large, and the scattering effect on light is relatively strong, and within a certain range, the scattering effect increases with the increase of the particle radius, which makes the degradation worse.

The influence of the scattering of tiny suspended particles on the imaging quality in smog weather includes:

1. Scattering attenuates the reflected light from the outdoor scene, reducing visibility, lowering the contrast of the acquired image, and blurring the image, which affects the visual experience of the observer and hinders the extraction of information.

2. Scattering interferes with the ambient light of the atmosphere and is mixed into the light received by the observer so that the scenery seen by the human eye is blurred, the sharpness of the image is reduced, and the scenery is difficult to distinguish.

3. Scattering will cause the color of the scene to be shifted and distorted, the color value distribution is relatively narrow, and the dynamic amplitude range is also narrow, which makes it difficult for the observer to distinguish the scene and the quality of the image is deteriorated.

The impact of smog on image quality may lead to serious consequences. For example, smog not only directly harms human health but also poses a threat to social security. Because if the camera cannot penetrate the thick particle layer and effectively take images, the role of the security monitoring system will be greatly reduced. For another example, on a foggy

DOI: 10.1201/9781003241416-5

day, lower visibility will seriously affect the driver's visual range during vehicle driving, greatly increasing the frequency of road traffic accidents.

Although fog and haze are often mentioned alternatively and are compared, yet they are different in visual perception and physical causes. From the perspective of visual perception, the images obtained in the two environments of fog and haze are different. Intuitively, the density distribution of fog in space is generally uneven, so the foggy image does not become more blurred as the depth of field increases. In addition, because the droplets are relatively large and can be discerned by the naked eye, it is difficult to see the original scenery in a foggy place. On the contrary, the concentration distribution of haze in the space is often relatively uniform, so the visibility decreases with the increase of the depth of field. Moreover, the particles of the haze are so small that it is difficult to distinguish with the naked eye, and it can also cause a certain degree of color distortion.

In terms of physical origin, because the size of the particles that make up the haze is only 0.01–1 μm, which is comparable to the wavelength of visible light (0.38–0.78 μm), both Rayleigh scattering and Mie scattering will occur (Miao and Li 2017). *Rayleigh scattering* occurs when the particle size is less than 1/10 of the wavelength of the light wave, and the scattering rate is inversely proportional to the fourth power of the light wavelength. *Mie scattering* occurs when the particle size is larger than the wavelength of the light wave, and the scattering rate is independent of the wavelength of the light, and the scattering direction is almost completely along the incident direction. Due to Mie scattering, the brightness at a distance will decrease; due to (multiple) Rayleigh scattering, most of the shortwave light reaching the imaging device is scattered. Because the human eye is more sensitive to the yellow-green light of about 0.55 μm, the far part and the sky part of the haze image mainly show yellow. In contrast, the size of the tiny water droplets that make up the fog is mostly 1–10 μm, which will only cause Mie scattering. Although the brightness will be reduced, the color will not be distorted.

When discussing the effect of removing smog on images, one often does not deliberately distinguish between fog and haze and uses image de-fogging as a general term. *Image de-fogging* generally refers to the use of specific image processing methods and means to reduce or eliminate the degrading effect of suspended particles in the air on the image, improve the visual effect of the image, increase the contrast, increase the sharpness, and reduce the blur, thereby improving the quality of the image to better and more effectively obtain the useful information in the image. In the following introduction and discussion in this chapter, fog is just used to uniformly represent fog and haze.

The contents of each section of this chapter are arranged as follows.

Section 5.1 summarizes and analyzes two major types of image de-fogging methods. Fog reduces image quality, so image processing technology must be used to improve it. This can be done either by image enhancement methods or by image restoration methods. Both methods have their own advantages and some problems, so they need to be selected according to the specific situation.

Section 5.2 introduces a typical method of de-fogging based on dark channel priors (DCP). The atmospheric scattering model and the DCP model on which the method is based are analyzed first, and then the specific technique steps and some problems exposed in practice are introduced.

Section 5.3 discusses the improvement techniques for some of the problems exposed by the above method based on the DCP, including the determination of the atmospheric light region, the correction of the atmospheric light value, the adaptation of the scale, the estimation of the atmospheric transmittance, and the de-fogging in dense foggy conditions.

Section 5.4 introduces a comprehensive algorithm aimed at ameliorating the distortion of the image after de-fogging. Its overall process, transmittance-space conversion, atmospheric scattering in transmittance space, sky region detection, and contrast enhancement are all analyzed.

Section 5.5 discusses how to evaluate the de-fogging effect. In addition to introducing some objective indicators to evaluate the de-fogging effect and the objective indicators considering visual perception, it also introduces an example of combined subjective and objective evaluation.

Section 5.6 provides a brief introduction to some technique developments and promising research directions in the last year.

5.1 SUMMARY OF IMAGE DE-FOGGING APPROACHES

Many methods to achieve image de-fogging have been proposed, and the research is still deepening, and new methods are still emerging.

The methods currently used for image de-fogging can be divided into two categories according to their mechanism of action: methods based on image enhancement and image restoration. They can also be regarded as non-model methods and degradation model-based methods, respectively. Here, the degradation model mainly refers to the physical model describing the laws of atmospheric scattering.

5.1.1 Methods Based on Image Enhancement

In general, the more obvious problem after the image degradation caused by the fog weather is that the contrast of the image has decreased. The method based on image enhancement directly starts with improving the contrast, trying to weaken or remove some influential or unwanted interference, and highlighting useful details to improve the visual quality of the image.

The method based on image enhancement does not consider the physical reasons for image degradation. Typical methods include histogram transformation (like histogram equalization), homomorphic filtering, gamma correction, wavelet transformation, and *retinal cortex (Retinex)* theory, and so on. (Miao and Li 2017).

Histogram equalization is an effective way to improve image contrast. It can expand the grayscale histogram originally gathered in a certain smaller grayscale interval to make it evenly distributed in the entire grayscale dynamic range, so as to achieve the purpose of contrast improvement in the image (Zhang 2017). If the fog scene is relatively simple and there is no large-scale change for depth of field in the image, histogram equalization can improve the contrast and enhance the visual effect of the image. However, the contrast-weakened regions in the actual fog image are often not evenly distributed and are more concentrated in the distant view that is more severely affected by the fog. Because the pixel gray values of these regions are relatively high, when their areas only account for a small proportion of the entire image, the desired effect is often not obtained (since the global histogram equalization method only performs macro operations on the entire image). One of the improved methods is to use the local histogram equalization method to enhance the local details of the image.

The method based on the retinal cortex (Retinex) theory mainly uses the characteristics of the human eyes for constant perception of colors (i.e., the color perception of objects is less affected by the non-uniformity of illumination) to improve the problem of reduced image contrast caused by differences in illumination. In the early days, people mostly used the theory of *single-scale retinal* (SSR) *cortex*, which decomposed the image into incident light components (i.e., the illuminance on the object determines the dynamic range of the image gray level) and reflected light components (the reflected part of the object collected by the imaging device). If the influence of the incident light component is reduced, the reflected light component can be increased to make the processed image closer to the reflected light component that retains the essence of the object. Recently, people have paid more attention to the use of *multi-scale retinal* (MSR) *cortex* theory to ensure high fidelity of the image and compression of the dynamic range of the image at the same time. For example, power transformation is used to compress the dynamic range of an image, nonlinear transformation is used to suppress the highlight region of the image, and an un-sharp mask filter is used to eliminate image blur, which can achieve better results.

The method of using homomorphic filtering is based on a similar idea (Zhang 2017). The image is also decomposed into incident light components and reflected light components, and their multiplicative relationship is converted to additive relationship by logarithmic transformation, and then high-pass filtering is performed to suppress low frequencies and enhance high frequencies.

The basic idea of image enhancement based on wavelet transform is similar to the abovementioned homomorphic filtering, except that the degraded image is converted into a multi-scale representation by means of wavelet transform, and non-low-frequency sub-blocks are enhanced according to their frequency characteristics. Because wavelet analysis has good local characteristics in both the spatial and frequency domains, it is beneficial to sharpen the details of the image and enhance the clarity of the image.

The method based on image enhancement is simple and fast and is suitable for the situation where the scene is relatively simple in structure, and can directly improve the contrast and color saturation of the blurred image. However, this kind of method may cause color distortion of the processed image or the long-range part of the processed image is not clear enough, but the close-range part will be too much contrasted due to excessive enhancement. Due to the inability to de-fog in a targeted manner, this type of method is also difficult to adjust the image in terms of visual indicators such as contrast, color, and brightness to a satisfactory range for human vision at the same time.

5.1.2 Methods Based on Image Restoration

Image restoration technology analyzes the degradation mechanism of fog images, uses prior knowledge or assumptions of image degradation, establishes a physical model of image degradation or estimates the properties of fog, so as to achieve targeted image de-fogging and scene restoration. This kind of method has more natural de-fogging effects and less distortion. It has become the mainstream method in the field of image de-fogging technology (some researchers also combine enhancement methods to adjust contrast and color after the image being essentially restored).

Image degradation in fog weather is closely related to atmospheric transmission and environmental illumination, so it should be an effective method to carry out atmospheric physical modeling based on this property. In practice, because there are many unknown parameters in the atmospheric physics model, using such a model to realize the fog-free image is essentially an indefinite equation-solving problem (see Section 5.2). Therefore, it is necessary to use various manners such as to take possible prior knowledge, to establish reasonable assumptions, and to obtain more information for converting the ill-posed task into the well-posed task in solving the model.

More information can come from the outside of the scene image or from the inside of the scene image. Methods using internal information can be divided into methods based on geometric priors and methods based on statistical priors.

In the method based on geometric priors, the transmission model from 3-D to 2-D imaging is generally used to calculate the depth of field information according to the imaging characteristics of the scene. The basic idea here is to consider that the posture or orientation of the target in the image has a close geometric constraint relationship with its depth of field, so as to obtain the geometric calculation formula of the depth of field for the pixels and help determine the image that takes into account the atmospheric transmission characteristics.

Among the methods based on statistical priors, the most representative one is the method based on *dark channel priors* (DCP) (see Section 5.2). This method first proves from a statistical point of view that the existence of an imaging object under natural scene conditions is similar to a black body and then uses the light absorption characteristics of the black body and the DCP to estimate the atmospheric transmission rate in the image, which can further solve the atmospheric physical model. Of course, this method will fail under certain conditions. Some improvements to it are introduced in Section 5.3.

A simpler way to use external information is to assume that some of the unknowns are limited to the scene or that the scene knowledge can be obtained from other channels. For example, the transmission rate in the atmospheric physical model is a key parameter that can reflect the depth information of the scene in the image. On the one hand, this relevant information can be added to the model with the help of user interaction input; on the other hand, it can also be extracted from a geographic information system and embedded in the model.

The depth of field information of the image can also be obtained through the difference between multiple images, and the depth of field can provide important clues for de-fogging.

At present, there are mainly three types of methods, using multiple images corresponding to different attributes of the fog:

1. Make use of the difference between multiple images in the same place at different times and weather conditions.

2. Use the difference between multiple images acquired under different polarization angles of the same scene.

3. Use the RGBN camera to obtain the difference between the normal color image and the near-infrared image.

The above methods all use multiple images, mainly because it is difficult to obtain depth information from a single image. However, in practice, the conditions for acquiring multiple images of the same scene are relatively harsh and are generally not suitable for real-time applications or dynamic scenes.

Since the collection of multiple images is often limited in practical applications, the work in recent years has mainly focused on the de-fogging of a single image. Among the existing methods, some utilize the prior information contained in a single image, and some establish a number of reasonable assumptions to achieve image de-fogging. The introductions later in this chapter are all centered on the de-fogging of a single image.

5.2 DCP DE-FOGGING ALGORITHM

The de-fogging algorithm based on DCP is a typical method that effectively utilizes image restoration ideas for image de-fogging, and has been widely concerned and applied.

The basic image de-fogging algorithm based on the DCP uses the atmospheric scattering model and then uses the DCP to determine the parameters of the model.

5.2.1 Atmospheric Scattering Model

The physical model describing the image degradation in the fog environment is (Narasimhan and Nayar 2003):

$$I(x) = I_\infty r(x)e^{-kd(x)} + I_\infty\left(1 - e^{-kd(x)}\right) \tag{5.1}$$

In the formula, x represents the spatial position ($x = [x\ y]^T$), $I(x)$ represents the fog image, I_∞ represents the intensity of the sky radiation (ambient light or global atmospheric light) at infinity, $r(x)$ represents the reflection rate, $e^{-kd(x)}$ represents the atmospheric transmittance, k represents the scattering coefficient (fog density influence coefficient), and $d(x)$ represents the scene depth (depth of field) at x. The model shows that there are two main factors for degradation: the absorption and scattering of the reflected light (which leads to direct attenuation of light) from the imaging object by the turbid medium in the air corresponding to the first item on the right side of Equation (5.1), and the multiple scattering interference caused by atmospheric particles in the air and ground reflected light during the scattering process to the imaging process corresponding to the second item on the

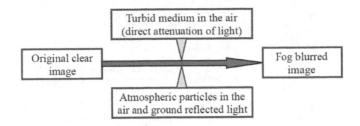

FIGURE 5.1　Fog image degradation model.

right side of Equation (5.1). The model can be represented in Figure 5.1, that is, the image that should have been clear is degraded by two factors.

The above model can be simplified to the following *atmospheric scattering model* (He 2011):

$$I(x) = J(x)t(x) + A[1 - t(x)]\tag{5.2}$$

In the formula, $J(x)$ represents the fog-free (no environmental interference) image or corresponding *scene radiation*; $t(x)$ is the *medium transmission* map, also called the *atmospheric transmittance*, and its value decays exponentially with the depth of field. For a homogeneous atmosphere, the atmospheric transmittance can be represented as

$$t(x) = e^{-kd(x)}, \quad 0 \le t(x) \le 1\tag{5.3}$$

In Equation (5.2), A represents the *global atmospheric light*, which is referred to as atmospheric light/sky light for short. It is generally assumed to be a global constant and has nothing to do with the local position x. The first term on the right side of Equation (5.2) corresponds to the attenuation of incident light, called *direct attenuation*, which describes the attenuation of the scene radiance in the atmosphere (the attenuation in propagation from the scene point to the observation point); the second term corresponds to the imaging of atmospheric scattering, called the *atmospheric scattering map* (also called atmospheric scattering function or atmospheric dissipation function), which represents the influence of atmospheric scattering on the light intensity of the observation point when imaging the scene, which causes the image blur, color distortion of the scenery, and other fog effects.

Various quantities in Equations (5.1)– (5.3) and the relationship between them are shown in Figure 5.2, where the small dots represent particles in the atmosphere, and after the radiation $J(x)$ in the distant scene is scattered by $J(x)[1 - t(x)]$, only $J(x)t(x)$ enters the camera, and $A[1 - t(x)]$ in the atmospheric light A is scattered and enters the camera. It should be noted that the various quantities related to the reflectivity $r(x)$ do not appear directly in the image entering the camera/observer due to attenuation or reflection.

According to Equation (5.2), the main work of image de-fogging is to estimate A and $t(x)$, so that the fog-free image $J(x)$ can be recovered:

$$J(x) = A - \frac{A - I(x)}{t(x)}\tag{5.4}$$

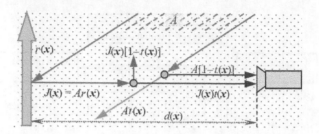

FIGURE 5.2   Details of the atmospheric scattering model.

To restore the fog-free image $J(x)$, it is necessary to obtain the global atmospheric light A and the atmospheric transmittance $t(x)$ separately, which is difficult to achieve in practice at the same time. In other words, this is a problem of solving an indeterminate equation.

5.2.2   DCP Model

Based on the statistical observation of a large number of fog-free images, it is found that (He et al. 2009): For some pixels in the non-sky part of the natural image, at least one of the color channels has a very low brightness value (toward 0). Based on this, the DCP model/hypothesis (also called the dark primary color prior theory [Yu and Zhang 2014]) can be obtained, that is, for any natural fog-free image $J(x)$, the dark channel image satisfies

$$J_{\text{dark}}(x) = \min_{y \in N(x)} \left[\min_{C \in \{R,G,B\}} J_C(y) \right] \to 0 \tag{5.5}$$

In the equation, $J_C(y)$ represents a certain R, G, B color channel of $J(y)$; $N(x)$ represents the neighborhood (radius is r) centered on pixel x, which can be denoted as $N_r(x)$. Assuming that the atmospheric transmittance value in the neighborhood of $N_r(x)$ is constant, denoted as $t^N(x)$, divide both sides of Equation (5.2) by A_C and perform the minimization operation (i.e., substituting the dark channel value), one can get:

$$\min_{y \in N(x)} \left[\min_{C \in \{R,G,B\}} \frac{I_C(y)}{A_C} \right] = \min_{y \in N(x)} \left[\min_{C \in \{R,G,B\}} \frac{J_C(y)}{A_C} \right] t^N(x) + \left[1 - t^N(x) \right] \tag{5.6}$$

If the *global atmospheric light A* is a known constant and $J_C(y) = 0$, the estimated value $t^N(x)$ of atmospheric transmittance in the neighborhood of $N_r(x)$ can be obtained:

$$t^N(x) = 1 - \min_{y \in N(x)} \left[\min_{C \in \{R,G,B\}} \frac{I_C(y)}{A_C} \right] \tag{5.7}$$

According to the DCP model, the brightness of the dark channel pixels of the fog-free image is usually very small, basically approaching 0, so the brightness value of the dark channel pixel in the foggy image is the concentration value of the fog. Therefore, the dark channel value of the image can be used to estimate the atmospheric light value A, and then the atmospheric transmittance can be obtained from Equation (5.7).

FIGURE 5.3   Example of the effect of the basic method of de-fogging.

The abovementioned method based on the DCP model provides a feasible route for solving the *atmospheric scattering model* and becomes a basic method to realize image de-fogging using image restoration technology.

An actual effect of image de-fogging using this method can be seen in the example in Figure 5.3, where the left image is the original image with fog, and the right image is the result after de-fogging. It can be seen that the de-fogging effect is very obvious.

5.2.3 Some Practical Problems

The abovementioned basic method of de-fogging based on the DCP will encounter a series of technical problems in practical applications. Several typical problems of this algorithm are listed below:

1. First, it is necessary to select a certain pixel to estimate the dark channel value in practice. In the basic method, select the first brightest 0.1% pixels in the dark channel map as the estimated point of atmospheric light in the original image (i.e., the value of A is the average value of the gray level of the first 0.1% of the bright pixels). However, this method does not guarantee the selection of the real highest brightness value, especially when there are light sources (like lamp) in the scene, which will often cause disturbing effect. At the same time, this approach will also cause the average brightness of the de-fogging image to be lower than that of the original image (see Sub-section 5.3.2).

2. Second, if Equation (5.7) is directly substituted into Equation (5.2) for inversion de-fogging, the image after actual de-fogging will often show obvious *halo* phenomenon or effect (i.e., blurry ghost images appear at the edge of the scene). This is also known

as halo artifacts, which directly affect the resolution and signal-to-noise ratio of the image. To solve this problem, the *soft matting* algorithm can be used to optimize the media transmission map (He et al. 2011), but the soft matting algorithm consumes a lot of memory, which causes the calculation speed to be slower and does not meet the requirements of real-time processing. A further improvement is to use *guided filtering* (see Sub-section 5.3.5) to replace the soft matting algorithm (He et al. 2013), but this is likely to cause the phenomenon that the de-fogging effect is not thorough enough.

3. In addition, the DCP model assumes that the atmospheric transmittance is constant in a local image block, but when the image block crosses the depth of field boundary in the scene, the *halo* phenomenon will also occur. One of the methods to alleviate the phenomenon of halo is to use image segmentation method to divide the image into blocks according to the depth of field, and assume that the depth of field in each block does not change so as to solve the atmospheric transmittance (Fang et al. 2010). However, the use of this segmenting operation will produce a blocking effect, and the atmospheric transmittance must be optimized and adjusted later.

4. Finally, the use of the DCP model often leads to the phenomenon of noise amplification. For this reason, it is necessary to use *bilateral filtering* (BF) for the foggy image and the de-fogging image to suppress the noise, such as in (Wang et al. 2013).

5.3 IMPROVEMENT IDEAS AND TECHNIQUES

To solve some of the specific problems encountered in the abovementioned basic method that is based on the DCP de-fogging, many improved ideas and methods have been proposed. These improvements are also enlightening and helpful for solving some other problems in image de-fogging. The following specifically introduces some typical improvement ideas and specific methods.

5.3.1 Determination of Global Atmospheric Light Region

The estimation of global atmospheric light plays a key role in achieving de-fogging. To estimate the atmospheric light, the basic method selects the first brightest 0.1% pixels in the dark channel image for statistical calculation. But in many cases, the brightest point in the image is not the place where the fog density is the highest. The basic method sometimes causes the estimated point to fall into the foreground region, and the accurate value of atmospheric light may not be obtained. These bright spots often originate from white objects or other artificial light sources in the scene, and their grayscale values are often higher than the true atmospheric light value.

To solve this problem, a variety of improvement methods have been proposed, two of which are introduced below.

5.3.1.1 Determine the Atmospheric Light Estimation Point Based on the Physical Meaning

According to Equation (5.1), the physical meaning of *global atmospheric light* is the background radiation at infinite depth of field. According to this description, it can be inferred that the estimated point of atmospheric light should meet the following conditions (Song et al. 2016):

1. As the ambient light source, atmospheric light should have high brightness.

2. The estimated point of atmospheric light should fall into the background region.

The estimated points of atmospheric light with higher brightness can be determined from one of these two conditions, and these points can be made to fall into the background region of the scene robustly.

For Condition (1), a luminance threshold value I_{th} can be set. The estimation method based on *retinal cortex* theory for image contrast (Jobson et al. 1997) is used to obtain the illuminance image from the original image brightness component I_{int}, and then the maximum value of the illuminance image is taken as the brightness threshold I_{th}.

$$I_{th} = \max\left\{\text{Gaussian}(x) \otimes I_{int}(x)\right\} \tag{5.8}$$

$$\text{Gaussian}(x) = \exp\left(-\frac{\|x\|_2^2}{\sigma^2}\right) \tag{5.9}$$

where σ is the scale of the convolutional Gaussian kernel function, which can be taken as $\sigma = 0.1 \min(H, W)$, and H and W are the height and width of the image, respectively.

For Condition (2), one can use the result of the morphological closing operation I_{close} on the binarized edge graph I_{canny} (the thresholding of the edge obtained by the Canny edge detection operator), and take the point where $I_{close}(x) = 0$, corresponding to the background region.

The constraint conditions obtained by Condition (1) and Condition (2) can be represented in the form of two masks:

$$\left\{ \begin{array}{l} \text{Mask}_1 = (I_{int} \geq I_{th}) \\ \text{Mask}_2 = (I_{close} = 0) \end{array} \right. \tag{5.10}$$

Using these two conditions to filter the dark channel map $D_C(x)$, the obtained non-zero point is the point most likely to become the estimation points of atmospheric light:

$$D_{Cp}(x) = \text{Mask}_1(x)\text{Mask}_2(x)D_C(x) \tag{5.11}$$

Consider the extreme situation. If $\text{Mask}_1(x) \cap \text{Mask}_2(x) = \varnothing$, that is, there is no high-brightness background region in the original image, then $D_{Cp}(x) = D_C(x)$ can be set, and the algorithm degenerates to use a dark channel map to estimate atmospheric light. Then, iteratively expand the radius from $D_{Cp}(x)$ to find the image block with the highest average brightness (block radius $r = r_{th} + n \cdot$ step, see Sub-section 5.3.4 for details), and use the average color in this block corresponding to the pixel in the original image as the estimated value of atmospheric light. Here, the local brightest block instead of the brightest single pixel is used to estimate the atmospheric light to further filter out the front spots that cannot be filtered by Mask$_1$ and Mask$_2$. The above steps can make the estimated point of atmospheric light fall into the background region more robustly.

5.3.1.2 Calculate the Densest Fog Region with the Help of a Quadtree

To avoid unreasonable estimation of the *global atmospheric light* value A, it is necessary to determine the region with the highest fog concentration in the image. The higher the fog density, the higher the pixel value; the smaller the difference between pixels, the larger the difference between the mean and the standard deviation (Yang et al. 2016). The following defines the difference in region *i* as S(*i*):

$$S(i) = |M(i) - C(i)| \tag{5.12}$$

where M(*i*) and C(*i*) are the mean and standard deviation of the region, respectively.

By using the quadtree structure of the image representation, the image can be recursively divided into four rectangular regions of the same size, and the difference S(*i*) of the four regions can be calculated respectively, where *i* = 1, 2, 3, 4. Select the region with the highest difference, continue the recursive decomposition and calculate the difference of its four sub-regions respectively. Repeat the above process until the size of the rectangular region meets the preset threshold. The finally selected region is the region with the highest fog density, denoted as R(x), and the value of atmospheric light can be estimated more accurately in this region.

5.3.2 Global Atmospheric Light Value Correction

To estimate the value of global atmospheric light, it is necessary not only to select the right region but also to estimate it reasonably. Inaccurate estimation of the atmospheric light value will cause the brightness of the de-fogging image to shift. It can be seen from Equation (5.2) that if I(x) and t(x) are known when the estimate of A becomes higher, the amplitude of the de-fogging image J(x) will become smaller and darker. Two methods for correcting the estimation of atmospheric light values are described below.

5.3.2.1 Global Atmospheric Light Value Weighted Correction

To obtain the value of *global atmospheric light* more robustly, after obtaining the region R(x) with the highest fog density, the value of the brightest pixel in R(x) is not directly taken but a weighted estimation is used for adjustment (Yang et al. 2016).

Divide all the pixels in R(x) into two parts: all the points with a gray value greater than the average value belong to the bright region, and all the points with a gray value less than the average value belong to the dark region. Let the number of pixels in the bright region and the dark region be N_b and N_d, respectively. Select a 3×3 block, and calculate the maximum values M_b and M_d of the dark channel values in the bright region and the dark region, respectively. Assuming that M_b and M_d are obtained at points $R(y)$ and $R(z)$, respectively, then the atmospheric light value A is

$$A = W_b R(y) + W_d R(z) \tag{5.13}$$

In the formula, $W_b = N_b/S_R$, $W_d = N_d/S_R$, and $W_b + W_d = 1$; here S_R is the size of $R(x)$ (i.e., $N_b + N_d$). In this way, when there are more pixels in the bright region, A is dominated by $R(y)$, while there are more pixels in the dark region, A is dominated by $R(z)$, but in any case, $R(y)$ and $R(z)$ all play a role together, restrict each other, and compensate for each other, so as to give a more reasonable atmospheric light value and help obtain a visually more natural de-fogging image.

To sum up, the specific steps for estimating the value of atmospheric light A are as follows:

1. Divide the image into four rectangular regions of the same size, and calculate the difference $S(i)$ of each region respectively.

2. Select the region with the largest difference, and repeat Step (1) until the preset threshold is met, so as to obtain the region with the highest fog density $R(x)$.

3. Dividing the pixels in the region $R(x)$ into dark and bright regions, respectively, and obtain the maximum values of the dark channel in the two regions.

4. Determine the position of the two maximum values in the image, and obtain the value A of atmospheric light by weighting.

5.3.2.2 Atmospheric Light Color Value Correction

When the background is blue sky, if the de-fogging image is solved directly by Equation (5.4), color distortion will occur. The following is a specific analysis of the causes of color distortion, and a solution to this problem is introduced (Song 2016).

According to Rayleigh's law, blue sky is formed due to the selectivity of *atmospheric scattering model* to wavelength, and the scattering coefficient has the following relationship with the wavelength of incident light (Narasimhan and Nayar 2003):

$$k(\lambda) \propto \frac{1}{\lambda^{\gamma}} \tag{5.14}$$

In the formula, the value of γ is related to the size of suspended particles in the atmosphere. Under normal circumstances, $0 < \gamma < 4$. In clear weather, $\gamma \to 4$, the short-wavelength blue light scattering coefficient is the largest, and the sky appears blue; in dense fog, $\gamma \to 0$, the scattering coefficient can be approximately regarded as independent of the wavelength, and the light scattering coefficients of all wavelengths are almost equal, and the sky is off-white. In other words, the blue sky is the color of atmospheric light after being scattered by the atmosphere, not the original color of atmospheric light. Therefore, when the estimated point falls into the blue sky region, in order to obtain the original color of the atmospheric light, the estimated value of the atmospheric light should be corrected. One way to correct the color of atmospheric light is to reduce the *saturation* of the color. The main steps are as follows:

1. Find the three components of the estimated value of A in the HSI space: hue A_H, saturation A_S, and brightness A_I.

2. Set the saturation threshold S_{th}. Its value should be as small as possible, but at the same time, it can maintain the color atmosphere of the original image (i.e., $S_{th} = 0$ cannot be directly taken). Similar to the solution process of the brightness threshold (such as Equation (5.3.1)), the minimum value of the saturation component of the fog image smoothed by Gaussian convolution ($\otimes$) is taken as S_{th}:

$$S_{th} = \min\{\text{Gaussian}(\boldsymbol{x}) \otimes I_{sat}(\boldsymbol{x})\} \tag{5.15}$$

3. Keep A_H and A_I unchanged, calculate

$$A_s' = \min(S_{th}, A_s) \tag{5.16}$$

Update A_S with A_s' and convert the three components from HSI space back to RGB space to obtain the corrected color value of atmospheric light.

5.3.3 Scale Adaptation

The DCP model assumes that the *atmospheric transmittance* is constant in the $N_r(\boldsymbol{x})$ neighborhood, and the value of r will have an impact on the de-fogging effect. Let's discuss the two cases where the r value is smaller and the r value is larger, respectively.

1. When r is small, there will be $0 < J_d(\boldsymbol{x}) < A$ in most regions corresponding to the foreground in the image, then $t(\boldsymbol{x}) > t^N(\boldsymbol{x})$, that is, the DCP estimated value of atmospheric transmittance will be less than its actual value. In addition, when A is a constant, it is known from Equation (5.4) that $t(\boldsymbol{x})$ is also a constant in $N_r(\boldsymbol{x})$, and $0 < t(\boldsymbol{x}) < 1$, that is, $\nabla J = \nabla I/t$, $\nabla J > \nabla I$. It can be seen that the essence of de-fogging is to increase the contrast by amplifying the amplitude changes of each color channel in the fog image. If the estimated value of $t(\boldsymbol{x})$ becomes smaller, the color change of the pixel in $N_r(\boldsymbol{x})$ will be over-enlarged, causing the restored image to produce over-saturation distortion. At the same time, it can be known from Equation (5.4) that when $I(\boldsymbol{x}) < A$, a smaller value of $t(\boldsymbol{x})$ will cause the amplitude of the de-fogging image $J(\boldsymbol{x})$ to become smaller and darker (because it is easier for the estimation point falling into the foreground region that does not match its physical meaning).

2. When r is large, most of the region corresponding to the foreground in the image will satisfy $J_d(\boldsymbol{x}) \longrightarrow 0$, at this time $t(\boldsymbol{x}) \approx t^N(\boldsymbol{x})$, the DCP estimated value of atmospheric transmittance will be closer to its actual value. However, a larger r may cause the dark channel solution block $N_r(\boldsymbol{x})$ to cross the edge of the depth of field and cause halo distortion in the restored image. Using guided filtering (see Sub-section 5.3.5) can reduce the halo phenomenon to a certain extent, but it cannot completely eliminate it.

From the above discussion, it can be seen that using only a single-scale (fixed r) DCP model and guided filtering cannot simultaneously take into account a good color restoration effect and a small halo distortion effect. One of the ways to solve this problem is to adopt a scale-adaptive strategy to find the appropriate dark channel solution scale r in different regions of the image, so as to increase the probability of $J_d(x) \to 0$; at the same time, the problem that the dark channel solution block $N_r(x)$ across the edge of the depth of field should be avoided.

The following introduces a scale-adaptive method, which adaptively obtains the pixel-level dark channel solution scale according to the color and edge characteristics of the image, so as to better meet the prior constraints of the dark channel and effectively suppress the halo phenomenon and color distortion (Song 2016). Specifically, different scales are used to compute the dark channel values for different regions in the image: in regions with low brightness or high saturation, use a smaller scale; while in regions with high brightness and low saturation, use a larger scale. In addition, in where the depth of field changes, use a smaller scale; in a smooth region, use a larger scale. The specific steps and details are as follows.

5.3.3.1 Initial Scale Based on the Color Characteristics

The purpose of selecting the scale is to make $J_d(x) \to 0$. In general, in the foreground with lower brightness or higher saturation, only a smaller scale can be used to make $J_d(x) \to 0$, while in the foreground with higher brightness and lower saturation, it is needed to use a larger scale that can make $J_d(x) \to 0$. However, for the sky background region, $J_d(x) \to 0$ cannot be obtained at any scale. Nevertheless, there is $I(x) \to A$ in the sky region, and $t^N(x) \longrightarrow 0$ can be obtained from Equation (5.7), which is exactly in line with the fact that the atmospheric transmittance tends to 0 at infinity. Therefore, no special treatment is required for the sky region, which can be regarded as a region with higher brightness and lower saturation, and a larger scale is used to compute the dark channel value.

First, several quantities related to pixel color characteristics are computed:

1. The minimum value $D_C(x)$ of the color channel in the fog image:

$$D_C(x) = \min_{C \in \{R,G,B\}} \left[I_C(x) \right] \tag{5.17}$$

2. The intensity component $I_{int}(x)$ at the minimum place in the fog image:

$$I_{int}(x) = \frac{I_R(x) + I_G(x) + I_B(x)}{3} \tag{5.18}$$

3. The saturation component $I_{sat}(x)$ at the minimum place in the fog image:

$$I_{sat}(x) = 1 - \frac{D_C(x)}{I_{int}(x)} \tag{5.19}$$

According to the color feature at the minimum place in the fog image, the pixel-level initial scale $r_0(x)$ can be obtained. From Equations (5.17)–(5.19), it can be seen that when $I_{int}(x)$

is smaller or $I_{sat}(x)$ is larger, a smaller scale should be used; when $I_{int}(x)$ is larger or $I_{sat}(x)$ is smaller, a larger scale should be used. Note that $D_C(x)$ is also smaller in the former case, and $D_C(x)$ is also larger in the latter case. Therefore, it can be considered that the scale is positively correlated with the minimum value of the channel. If $r_0(x) = k \cdot D_C(x)$ is used to represent the initial scale of the pixel level, in order to make the scale value an integer, $r_0(x)$ can be defined as

$$r_0(x) = \max\{1, \text{ round}[k \cdot D_C(x)]\} \tag{5.20}$$

5.3.3.2 Correct the Scale According to the Edge Features

Since the *halo* phenomenon occurs at a place with a sudden change in the depth of field, if a smaller scale is used near the edge, the atmospheric transmittance solution block $N_r(x)$ can be made to avoid crossing the depth of field boundary as much as possible, thereby reducing the halo phenomenon. Using a larger scale near the non-edge place can increase the probability of $J_d(x) \to 0$ to make the background of the restored image smoother, with less noise and distortion.

The steps for correcting the initial scale $r_0(x)$ by edge features are as follows:

1. Edge detection: use the Canny edge detection operator to perform edge detection on the brightness component $I_{int}(x)$ of the fog image, and threshold it to obtain the binarized edge image I_{canny}.

2. Foreground separation: Perform a morphological closing operation on I_{canny}, roughly distinguish the foreground and background of the image, and represent the result as I_{close}. The pixels with $I_{close} = 1$ cover the foreground region of the image.

3. Get the initial scale: set the edge pixel scale threshold r_{th}, filter the background with I_{close}, and get the foreground pixel initial scale $r_s(x)$:

$$r_s(x) = I_{close}(x)r_0(x) \tag{5.21}$$

   In the equation, the value of $r_0(x)$ is an integer in [0, 10], and the pixel where $r_s(x)$ is zero corresponds to the background region. The threshold r_{th} takes the non-zero value with the largest probability of occurrence in $r_s(x)$, which can increase the probability of $J_d(x) \to 0$ in the foreground region.

4. Using edge features to modify the scale: For any pixel x, if $0 < r_s(x) \leq r_{th}$, then the scale is not modified, that is: $r(x) = r_s(x)$; otherwise, if $r_s(x) = 0$ (i.e., x is located in the background region), or $r_s(x) > r_{th}$ (i.e., x is located in a higher intensity region), then the scale of x is modified. First, start from $r = r_{th} + \text{step}$ and gradually increase the scale, that is, take $r = [r_{th} + \text{step}, r_{th} + 2 \cdot \text{step}, \ldots, r_{th} + n \cdot \text{step}]$, until the edge point is included in the block with x as the center and $r(x)$ as the radius in the I_{canny} image. At this time, the $r_{th} + (n-1) \cdot \text{step}$ is the corrected scale at the point x. In such an incremental process, the solution block $N_r(x)$ should not cross the depth of field boundary, thereby reducing the possibility of halo phenomenon. The above parameters step and

n determine the adaptive range of the scale. Statistics show that step = 2 and $n = 5$ can be selected to limit the adaptive range of scale to $1 \sim r_{\text{th}} + n \cdot \text{step}$ $(1 \leq r_{\text{th}} < 10,$ $r_{\text{th}} + n \cdot \text{step} < 20)$. This range for the images of most natural scenes can achieve a good de-fogging effect. When $r_{\text{th}} + n \cdot \text{step} > 20$, the de-fogging effect is not improved much, but the calculation time will be longer.

If the point x is exactly on the edge, and $0 < r_s(x) \leq r_{\text{th}}$, then $r(x) = r_s(x)$ is taken; otherwise, $r(x) = r_{\text{th}}$ is taken. Therefore, r_{th} can be called the maximum scale of edge pixels. It can be seen that the smaller the value of r_{th}, the smaller the halo distortion of the restored image. However, if the saturation of the original image is low, a too small r_{th} value may make most regions of the image not meet $J_d(x) \longrightarrow 0$, which will oversaturate the color of the restored image and make the color unnatural.

If the (adaptive) scale at the point x is obtained, the following equation can be used to compute the dark channel value:

$$D_C(x) = \min_{y \in N_r(x)} \left[\min_{c \in \{R,G,B\}} I_C(y) \right] \tag{5.22}$$

5.3.4 Atmospheric Transmittance Estimation

The de-fogging method based on the DCP is to estimate the *atmospheric transmittance* in a local image block so that the atmospheric transmittance value obtained is constant within the block. However, in actual image processing, the atmospheric transmittance in the image block is not always constant, especially at the edge with large jumps in the depth, which will cause serious block effects in the *atmospheric transmittance map*, which will cause the restored image to produce a *halo* phenomenon. From a statistical point of view, when the image block is divided into larger blocks, the probability that the block contains dark pixels will also be higher, and the DCP are easier to meet; but when the size of the image block is too large, the assumption of constancy transmittance in the block will fail, resulting in color distortion.

5.3.4.1 Fuse Dark Channel Values to Estimate Atmospheric Transmittance

The appearance of a block effect indicates that the edge of the block contains some wrong high-frequency information. In other words, the low-frequency part of the atmospheric transmittance is closer to the actual transmittance, while the high-frequency part (corresponding to the edge of the block) of the atmospheric transmittance is quite different from the actual transmittance. It is conceivable that if the size of the block is reduced, or even to a single pixel, the blocking effect should not appear again, and all the details in the scene can be preserved, that is, the high-frequency part corresponds to the actual transmittance. However, the estimation of the low-frequency part will not be accurate enough, and the restored image will produce serious color distortion.

From the above analysis, it can be seen that the low-frequency part of the dark channel information of the larger block is close to the low-frequency part of the real transmittance, and the high-frequency part of the dark channel information of the smaller block is close

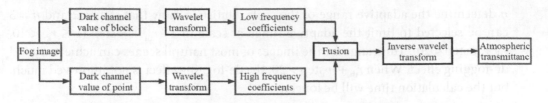

FIGURE 5.4 Fusion dark channel values of blocks and points to estimate atmospheric transmittance.

to the high-frequency part of the real transmittance. If these two parts for estimating the transmittance are combined, it should be able to get better results. Therefore, the transmittance can be estimated by referring to the flow chart in Figure 5.4 (Yang et al. 2016). First, take the larger block as a certain size block, and the smaller block as the point, and calculate the dark channel values of each block and the dark channel values of the point on the fog image. Then, with the help of wavelet transform, the low-frequency coefficients of the former and the high-frequency coefficients of the latter are respectively extracted and fused. Finally, perform the inverse wavelet transform to get a better estimate of atmospheric transmittance.

5.3.4.2 Refining Atmospheric Transmittance Based on Local Adaptive Wiener Filtering

The fusion of the dark channel values of blocks and points often inevitably introduces some wrong details. In this regard, a local adaptive Wiener filter (see Sub-section 3.2.2) can be used to refine the estimation of the transmittance so as to effectively remove the blocking effect and the halo phenomenon.

Assuming that the atmospheric light A is known because the wrong detailed information is introduced in the fusion process, the analysis of Equation (5.2) shows that the dark channel value $J_d(x)$ obtained after fusion can be regarded as the sum of the *atmospheric scattering map* $G(x) = A[1-t(x)]$ and the error detail information $n(x)$:

$$J_d(x) = G(x) + n(x) \tag{5.23}$$

It is assumed that $G(x)$ and $n(x)$ are independent of each other.

Given Equation (5.23), a local adaptive Wiener filter can be used to estimate $G(x)$ in the sampling block $N_r(x)$, denoted as $G^E(x)$:

$$G^E(x) = \mu_G(x) + \frac{\sigma_G^2(x) + \sigma_n^2}{\sigma_G^2(x)}[J_d(x) - \mu_d(x)] \tag{5.24}$$

where $\mu_G(x)$ and $\sigma_G^2(x)$ are the mean value and variance of $G(x)$ in the sampling block, respectively; $\mu_d(x)$ is the mean value of $J_d(x)$ in the sampling block; σ_n^2 is the variance of the detail information $n(x)$ (mean value is 0), assuming it is constant in the whole image, then it can be estimated as follows.

The variance of $J_d(x)$ in the sampling block $\sigma_d^2(x)$ is the sum of two parts:

$$\sigma_d^2(x) = \sigma_G^2(x) + \sigma_n^2 \tag{5.25}$$

In practice, atmospheric light is cross-correlated in the larger sampling block, and its variance $\sigma_G^2(x)$ is very small. Assuming $\sigma_G^2(x) \ll \sigma_n^2$, the global average of the variance of the dark channel value can be used as the estimation of the detail variance (superscript E stands for estimation)

$$\left(\sigma_n^2\right)^E = \frac{1}{M} \sum_{x=0}^{M-1} \sigma_d^2(x) \tag{5.26}$$

where M is the number of pixels in the whole image.

After estimating the mean and variance of $G(x)$ and the variance of the detailed information, the optimal estimate of the atmospheric light function $G^E(x)$ can be obtained by Equation (5.24), and the final atmospheric transmittance is

$$t(x) = 1 - p\frac{G^E(x)}{A} \tag{5.27}$$

In the equation, p is a constant (called the de-fogging depth parameter), and its function is to retain part of the fog in the result. This is because if the existence of the fog is completely removed, the overall effect of the de-fogging image will be unrealistic and lose the sense of depth (the sense of distance between the distant view and the close view). In general, the value of p ranges from 0.92 to 0.95; the larger value is used when the fog is thick, and the smaller value is used when the fog is thin.

5.3.5 Dense Foggy Image De-Fogging

When the basic method deals with scenes having high foggy density, the de-fogging image obtained will be darker. To this end, the concept of foggy density factor can be used to establish the relationship between *visibility* and *foggy density factor* with the help of atmospheric extinction coefficient when analyzing the factors affecting visibility in foggy days. The value of the foggy density factor can be estimated by estimating the visibility value, and then the guided filtering can be used to further estimate atmospheric light value to achieve fog removal (Long et al. 2016).

5.3.5.1 Algorithm Flowchart

Back to the physical model describing the image degradation in the fog environment, that is, Equation (5.1). Two main factors make the foggy image blurred: one is the absorption and scattering of the reflected light from the imaged object by the turbid medium in the air; the other is the multiple scattering interference on collected images, caused by the atmospheric particles in the air and the reflected light from the ground during the scattering process. They correspond to the first and second terms of Equation (5.1), respectively. Compared with the long-distance transmission of atmospheric light, the change of scene depth of the image acquired by the imaging device is small, especially under dense fog conditions. Therefore, the so-called *foggy density factor* G_k can be used instead of $e^{kd(x)}$.

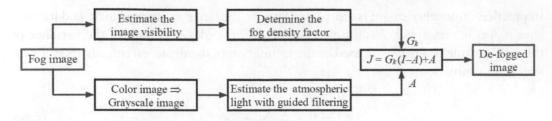

FIGURE 5.5   Dense foggy image de-fogging process.

Substituting G_k into Equation (5.2), the physical model of fog imaging and recovery can be represented as:

$$J(\boldsymbol{x}) = G_k(I(\boldsymbol{x}) - A) + A \tag{5.28}$$

Based on the model of Equation (5.28), it can be known that in order to obtain a clear original image, when the degraded image $I(\boldsymbol{x})$ is collected, the foggy density factor G_k and the atmospheric light value A must be estimated.

To this end, a de-fogging algorithm based on atmospheric extinction coefficient and guided filtering can be designed. The process is shown in Figure 5.5. For a dense foggy image to be de-fogged, first, estimate the visibility of the environment where the image is located and obtain the value of the foggy density factor G_k with the help of the established relationship between the visibility and the foggy density factor; at the same time, convert the foggy image to grayscale image, and then the atmospheric light value A is obtained by the guided filtering of the grayscale image, and finally, the image is de-fogged using Equation (5.28).

The following sections respectively introduce the estimation methods for the values of the foggy density factor G_k and the atmospheric light value A.

5.3.5.2 Fog Density Factor Estimation

Visibility (corresponding to transmittance) is a direct measure of foggy density. Large visibility means low foggy density, and vice versa. It can be seen that in the case of very low visibility, the foggy density will be very high. De-fogging an image with a large foggy density often makes the image even noisy after de-fogging. At this time, it is necessary to suppress image noise while de-fogging. Therefore, an incomplete de-fogging should relatively be a good selection. When the visibility rises to a relatively large distance, the foggy density is relatively low. At this time, the fog has less influence on the collected images. Therefore, different value ranges of the foggy density factor G_k can be given in different ranges corresponding to the visibility L:

$$G_k = \begin{cases} G_k = 8 & L < 50 \\ 1 \leq G_k \leq 8 & 50 \leq L \leq 1000 \\ G_k = 1 & L > 1000 \end{cases} \tag{5.29}$$

In foggy weather conditions, there are a large number of particles with a radius of 1–10 μm in the air. At this time, the visibility is $L \in [50, 1000]$ (unit in m). According to the foggy degradation model, an important cause of image degradation is the *Mie scattering* of light reflected on the imaged object by particles in the air, and the scattering characteristics of the particles are determined by the particle scale α, and $\alpha = 2\pi r/\lambda$, where r is the radius of the particle, and λ is the wavelength of the incident light. According to the wavelength range of visible light in the atmospheric light and the radius of the particles in the air, the characteristic scale range of the particles can be obtained: $\alpha \in [8, 157]$. Within this range, the atmospheric visibility L and the *atmospheric extinction coefficient e* have the following relationship (Long et al. 2016):

$$L \equiv -\frac{\ln T}{e} \tag{5.30}$$

In the equation, T is the visual contrast threshold, and L represents the maximum distance that a person with normal vision can see the outline of the target clearly under the current weather conditions. According to the regulations of the meteorological department on the human visual contrast threshold under dense foggy conditions, the human visual contrast threshold at this time is set to 0.05 (Long et al. 2016). Let the value of T in Equation (5.30) be 0.05 to get

$$L = 2.99/e \tag{5.31}$$

According to the scattering theory, without considering the absorption of light by fog particles, there is the following relationship between the atmospheric extinction coefficient e and the extinction efficiency factor Q_e, the fog particle density n, and the fog particle radius r:

$$e = \pi n r^2 Q_e \tag{5.32}$$

where the extinction efficiency factor Q_e varies with fog generally around $Q_e = 2$, so $Q_e = 2$ is taken below. According to Equations (5.31) and (5.32), it can be seen that the fog particle density n and the fog particle radius r are both factors that affect the atmospheric extinction coefficient e, which are also the factors that affect the visibility L. Moreover, the fog density is positively correlated with n or r, so the fog density factor G_L of visibility L can be defined as

$$G_L = G_a n_a r_a^2 \tag{5.33}$$

where the coefficient G_a is a constant for the given scale characteristic α. Combining Equations (5.31) and (5.32) into Equation (5.33), it can obtain:

$$G_L = \frac{2.99 G_a}{2\pi L} \tag{5.34}$$

It can be seen from Equation (5.34) that if the visibility is within 1,000 m as a foggy weather, when the visibility $L \in [50, 1000]$, the fog density factor G_L and the visibility L are in a direct proportional relationship. Taking 1,000 m as the reference standard at this time, it gets:

$$G_L = \frac{1000 G_{1000}}{L} \qquad (5.35)$$

In other words, when the distance of 1,000 m is used as the standard distance for fog, there is a proportional relationship between the fog density factor G_L and 1000/L. Since G_k is also a parameter describing the fog density factor, according to the value of the fog density factor in the visibility range defined by Equation (5.29), the relationship between the fog density factor G_k and the visibility L can be obtained:

$$G_k = \begin{cases} 8 & L < 50 \\ 0.36 \times 1000 / L + 0.64 & 50 \le L \le 1000 \\ 1 & L > 1000 \end{cases} \qquad (5.36)$$

5.3.5.3 Atmospheric Light Estimation Based on Guided Filtering

When restoring the foggy image, in addition to obtaining the value of the foggy density factor G_k, it is also necessary to estimate the value of atmospheric light. This can be achieved with the help of guided filtering with edge-preserving characteristics.

Guided filtering is a linear variable filtering. The basic idea of using it to estimate atmospheric light is as follows (He et al. 2013):

Let the input image be P, the guiding image be I, and the filtered output image be Q, then the following linear relationship exists in the k-th square image block W_k with a radius of r:

$$Q_i = a_k I_i + b_k \qquad \forall i \in W_k \qquad (5.37)$$

In the equation, a_k and b_k are local linear coefficients in the block, which are fixed values in a given block; i is the pixel index in the block. To achieve the best effect of guided filtering, the difference between the output image Q and the input image P must be minimized. At this time, the cost function $E(a_k, b_k)$ is required to satisfy:

$$E(a_k, b_k) = \min \sum_{i \in W_k} \left[(Q_i - P_i)^2 + \varepsilon a_k^2 \right] \qquad (5.38)$$

To obtain the minimum value of $E(a_k, b_k)$, the idea of least squares method can be used to solve the linear coefficients a_k and b_k:

$$a_k = \frac{\text{cov}_k(I, P)}{\text{var}_k(I) + \varepsilon} \qquad (5.39)$$

$$b_k = p'_k - a_k I'_k \qquad (5.40)$$

In the equation, ε is the regularization smoothing factor, $\text{cov}_k(I, P)$ is the covariance of the guiding image I and the input image P, $\text{var}_k(I)$ is the variance of I, p'_k is the mean value of p in the unit block W_k, I'_k is the mean value of I in the unit block W_k. After using the least square method to obtain the values of a_k and b_k that satisfy the minimum cost function, the image is filtered to obtain the atmospheric light value, that is, the atmospheric light A can be represented as:

$$A = F\left[\left(\frac{1}{|W|}\sum_{k \in W_i} a_k\right) P_i + \frac{1}{|W|}\sum_{k \in W_i} b_k\right] \tag{5.41}$$

In the equation, P_i is the pixel in the input image, W_i is the unit block centered on the pixel P_i, $|W|$ is the number of pixels in the unit block, and F is the filtering process for each pixel. This filtering method adopts the idea of least squares method and uses *box filter* and *integral image* technology to perform fast calculation. When performing filtering operations, its execution speed is independent of the size of the filter block.

5.4 INTEGRATED ALGORITHM FOR REDUCING DISTORTION

The purpose of image de-fogging is to improve the visual quality of the image, so in addition to improving the clarity of the de-fogging image, it is also necessary to avoid distortion caused by processing. The de-fogging algorithm introduced here also comprehensively improves the basic method (Li and Zhang 2017). Its characteristic is that while trying to improve the de-fogging effect of the algorithm, it also focuses on the means that can make the de-fogged image less distorted and more natural.

The following sections first give the flowchart of the improved algorithm and then introduce each step in turn.

5.4.1 Algorithm Flowchart

Back to the atmospheric scattering model describing the degradation of the fog image, that is, Equation (5.2). Image de-fogging is to first estimate A and $t(x)$ under the condition of only knowing $I(x)$, and finally get $J(x)$. Here, the recovery equation for $J(x)$ is represented as (He et al. 2011)

$$J(x) = \frac{I(x) - A}{\max[t(x), t_0]} + A \tag{5.42}$$

To prevent the denominator from appearing at 0, a lower threshold t_0 is added to the denominator.

The basic idea of comprehensive improvement is to calculate the *atmospheric scattering map* in the transmittance (T) space for de-fogging. The main steps are as follows:

1. Convert the image to T space.

2. Using guided filtering to obtain an atmospheric scattering map.

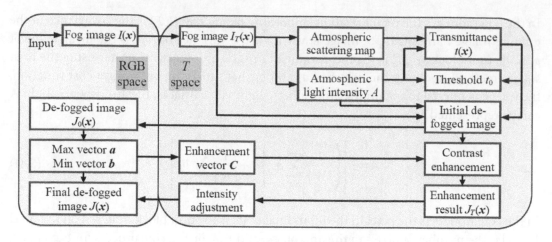

FIGURE 5.6 The flowchart of integrated improvement algorithm.

3. Determine the sky region.

4. Carry out contrast enhancement and intensity adjustment.

The entire algorithm flow chart is shown in Figure 5.6.

5.4.2 T Space Conversion

For color images, there is a certain correlation between the three RGB channels, or there is a coupling between the colors in the three channels. If the coupling between the channels can be weakened, the DCP model will be more easily satisfied. To this end, the spectral characteristics of ground objects and the human visual model can be used to calculate the *transmittance space*, that is, *T space*, with a lower degree of coupling (Shi et al. 2013). The conversion between *T* space and RGB space is:

$$T = MC \tag{5.43}$$

In the equation, $T = [T_1 - T_2 - T_3]^T$, representing the three channels in the transmittance space; $C = [R - G - B]^T$, representing the three channels in the original color space. The M obtained in this way is (here, each item is multiplied by 255 to make the [255; 255; 255] in the RGB space being converted to the T space and it is still [255; 255; 255]):

$$M = \begin{bmatrix} 0.0255 & -0.1275 & 1.0965 \\ -0.3315 & 1.5045 & -0.1785 \\ 0.5610 & 0.3825 & 0.0510 \end{bmatrix} \tag{5.44}$$

The image $I(x)$ in the RGB space is converted to the T space and then denoted as $I_T(x)$. Experiments have shown that the proportion of dark channel pixels in T space is higher (Shi et al. 2013). A comparison example of de-fogging in RGB color space and in T space

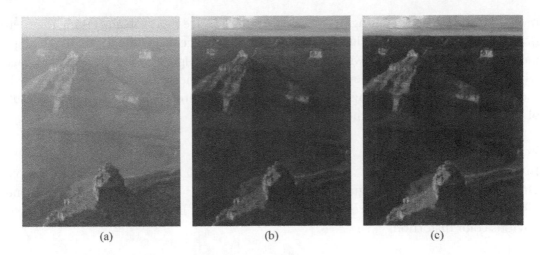

FIGURE 5.7 Comparison of de-fogging results in RGB space and T space; (a) is the original image with fog; (b) is the de-fogging result in RGB space; (c) shows the result of de-fogging in T space, and its color distortion is relatively small.

is shown in Figure 5.7. Figure 5.7a is the original image with fog, and Figure 5.7b is the de-fogging result in RGB space. Figure 5.7c shows the result of de-fogging in T space, and its color distortion is relatively small.

5.4.3 Atmospheric Scattering Map in Transmittance Space

According to the DCP model and the foggy image degradation model, the minimum value of the color channel in T space can be calculated:

$$D_T(x) = \min_{d \in (T_1, T_2, T_3)} \left[I_T^d(x) \right] \qquad (5.45)$$

The second term on the right side of Equation (5.2) is the atmospheric scattering map $G(x) = A[1 - t(x)]$. A blur version of $G(x)$, $G_m(x)$, is obtained after eliminating details in $D_T(x)$ with the help of guided filtering, so the calculation equation for $G(x)$ is:

$$G(x) = \max \left\{ \min \left[p \times G_m(x) DT(x) \right], 0 \right\} \qquad (5.46)$$

The p in Equation (5.46) has the same effect as the p in Equation (5.27), see Sub-section 5.3.4.

According to $G(x) = A[1 - t(x)]$, the transmittance $t(x)$ obtained from $G(x)$ is:

$$t(x) = 1 - 0.95 \times G / A \qquad (5.47)$$

Here, the average value of G and A is substituted into Equation (5.47) so that both the numerator and denominator have only one color channel.

According to Equations (5.46) and (5.47), when p is larger, $G(x)$ may be also larger, and $t(x)$ may be smaller. In Equation (5.42), since $I \leq A$ in general, the first term is negative. In this way, when t is smaller, the recovered J is also smaller, and over-saturated colors are more likely to appear, resulting in color distortion. To solve this problem, taking the coefficient $p = 0.75$, which can reduce color distortion and edge distortion more than using a larger p-value. Figure 5.8 shows a set of examples, where Figure 5.8a is the original image with fog; Figure 5.8b is the de-fogging result obtained when p is 0.9, the overall color is too saturated and the building has a yellowish tone. Figure 5.8c is the de-fogging result obtained when p is 0.75, and the color is more natural.

5.4.4 Sky Region Detection

In the basic method, simply setting the threshold t_0 as 0.1 may distort the sky region. One example is shown in Figure 5.9, where Figure 5.9a is an original foggy image, and Figure 5.9b is the de-fogging results obtained with $t_0 = 0.1$. Because t_0 is too small, there is obvious color distortion.

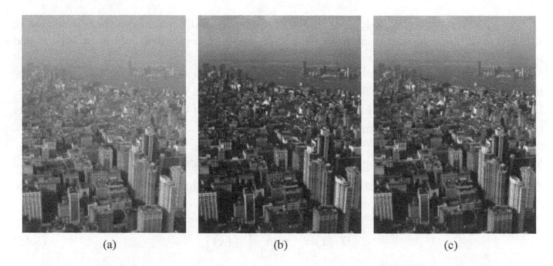

(a)　　　　　　　　(b)　　　　　　　　(c)

FIGURE 5.8　De-fogging results when p takes different values; (a) is the original image with fog; (b) is the de-fogging result obtained when p is 0.9, the overall color is too saturated and the building has a yellowish tone; (c) is the de-fogging result obtained when p is 0.75, and the color is more natural.

(a)　　　　(b)　　　　(c)　　　　(d)　　　　(e)

FIGURE 5.9　Sky region detection and effect; (a) is an original foggy image; (b) is the de-fogging results obtained with $t_0 = 0.1$; (c) is the experiment result with the coefficient $k = 1.5$; (d) is the experiment result when the neighborhood size of the dark channel is 120 and the edge neighborhood size is 60; (e) is the final de-fogging result.

If the dark channel is used to represent the depth $d(x)$, then Equation (5.3) can be used to calculate the atmospheric transmittance. Experiments show that when the coefficient k is 1.5, $t(x) \geq e^{-k} = e^{-1.5} = 0.2231$ is obtained, which can suppress the partial distortion of the sky region. The result is shown in Figure 5.9c. However, the coefficient k is selected based on experience, and the general meaning is not very strong.

Since there are generally fewer details in the sky region, the part of the image with brighter dark channels and fewer edges can be considered as the sky, and the brightest pixel value in this part is A. To this end, two thresholds can be designed (Chu et al. 2013): one is the dark channel threshold T_v, which can be set as 0.9×the maximum value of the dark channel; the other is the edge number threshold T_p, which can be set as the minimum value/0.9 of the number of edges in the neighborhood. In this way, only the part of image with the dark channel value≥threshold T_v and the number of edges in the neighborhood $\leq T_p$ is counted as the sky region.

Furthermore, a dynamic threshold t_0 (Fang and Liu 2013) can be used, and T_v can be appropriately relaxed to expand the sky region, so as to obtain a more accurate sky region and t_0. The specific method is to relax T_v to 0.88×max$[d(x)]$ for general images, and to 0.6×max$[d(x)]$ for images with more sky portion, and T_p remains unchanged. In this way, when the neighborhood size of the dark channel is 120 and the edge neighborhood size is 60, the sky region obtained is shown in Figure 5.9d, which is relatively complete. The brightest pixel value in the sky region gives the atmospheric light A. If the transmittance threshold value t_0 of the sky region proposed by (Fang et al. 2013) is calculated using the upper 0.99 quantile (standard normal distribution) of the sky region transmittance, $t_0 = 0.6643$ is obtained. The final de-fogging result is shown in Figure 5.9e.

5.4.5 Contrast Enhancement

Contrast enhancement can also be performed after de-fogging in T space (Shi et al. 2013). Let R, G, and B be the three channels of the de-fogging result image $J_0(x)$ in the RGB space, let $a = [\max(R), \max(G), \max(B)]^T$ be the maximum vector, $b = [\min(R), \min(G), \min(B)]^T$ be the minimum vector. The enhancement vector of T space can be calculated as follows (here the division is made with vector elements, that is, the division of arrays):

$$C = \frac{M(a-b)}{M\begin{bmatrix} 255 & 255 & 255 \end{bmatrix}^T} \tag{5.48}$$

where M is as in Equation (5.44).

In the T space, the enhancement result image $J_T(x)$ is obtained by dividing each component of the de-fogging result image $J_{T0}(x)$ by each component of the enhancement vector C. A comparison of the contrast enhancement effect is shown in Figure 5.10, where Figure 5.10a is the original foggy image; Figure 5.10b is the de-fogging result before the contrast enhancement, which is somewhat reddish; Figure 5.10c is the de-fogging result after the subsequent contrast enhancement, the reddish sky becomes bluer, clearer, and more natural, and the subjective visual quality of the image is improved.

FIGURE 5.10   Comparison of de-fogging results before and after contrast enhancement; (a) is the original foggy image; (b) is the de-fogging result before the contrast enhancement; (c) is the de-fogging result after the subsequent contrast enhancement.

It should be noted that the contrast enhancement will make the originally dark place darker, so attention should be paid to increasing the brightness of the dark place to restore these details. At this time, one can use the following intensity mapping curve $q = f(p)$ (Gan and Xiao 2013):

$$q = \frac{255}{\lg 256} \times \frac{\ln(p+1)}{\ln\left[2 + 8\left(\frac{p}{255}\right)^{\frac{\ln s}{\ln 0.5}}\right]} \tag{5.49}$$

where s is an adjustable parameter, and its value is inversely proportional to the intensity adjustment range (especially in the darker part of the image), generally five is acceptable. The above intensity adjustment needs to be performed separately for each channel.

Convert the result of intensity adjustment back to RGB space to get the final de-fogging image.

5.5 EVALUATION OF DE-FOGGING EFFECTS

With the proposal of many image de-fogging algorithms, in order to measure the effectiveness of different algorithms, to judge and select the appropriate algorithm for specific occasions, it is necessary to evaluate the effect of de-fogging.

The evaluation of the de-fogging effect is different from the general evaluation of the image quality or the evaluation of the image restoration effect. In practice, it is often difficult to obtain a real and clear image that has exactly the same as a foggy image scene, so there is often no ideal image (grand truth) as a reference for evaluation. In the evaluation, only the de-fogging image itself can be evaluated or compared with the foggy image. On the other hand, the subjective visual evaluation method is easily affected by the observer's personal factors, and the human visual perception itself is not a deterministic process. Therefore, subjective visual evaluation needs to be combined with objective visual evaluation, so as to make the judgment meaningful and useful.

The following first introduces some objective indicators used to evaluate the effect of de-fogging as well as some visual perception factors considering objective indicators, and then introduces an evaluation example that combines subjective and objective evaluation.

5.5.1 Objective Evaluation Index

Currently, there is no universally recognized objective index for evaluating image defogging algorithms or the quality of a de-fogged image.

In image processing, the existing objective image evaluation methods can be divided into three categories: full reference, semi-reference and no reference, according to the degree of demand for reference information. The first two categories require reference images. For the specific application of image de-fogging effect evaluation, it has been explained that the reference image is difficult to obtain, so the first two types of indicators are not very suitable.

5.5.1.1 No Reference Evaluation Index

Using objective evaluation methods without reference, commonly used evaluation indicators can be divided into four categories (Wu and Zhu 2015):

1. Pixel-based: Compare the corresponding pixels of the foggy image and the de-fogged image, and calculate the difference between their pixel values, so that the degree of distortion can be judged. For this purpose, indicators such as *peak signal-to-noise ratio* (PSNR) and *mean square error* (MSE) can be used.

2. Based on image composition: Compare the difference in the structure of the scene between the foggy image and the de-fogged image, and calculate the maintain ability of different components and details. In this regard, *structural similarity index measurement* (SSIM) is a commonly used indicator.

3. Based on image contrast: Compare the changes in local contrast between the foggy image and the de-fogged image, and analyze the improvement degree of the feature recognition of the scene. Although the method using this kind of index cannot correctly evaluate the de-fogging effect in excessively enhanced image, it is still widely used because it is more directly related to human visual perception.

4. Based on image fidelity: Compare the preservation of the color of the scene between the foggy image and the de-fogged image, and calculate the degree of color shift. This can be measured with the help of the similarity (correlation coefficient) of the image histogram.

5.5.1.2 Visible Edge Gradient

When people observe an image, they will first find and pay attention to the edges inside. It can be seen that the edge gradient method (Hautière et al. 2008) is a blind evaluation method commonly used in the field of de-fogging. It uses the *visibility level* (VL), also known as visibility, to evaluate the visual quality of de-fogged images. Visibility is related to the difference in intensity between the object and the background and is a relative concept. With the help of visibility, the problem of evaluating the performance of image contrast can be transformed into a problem of obtaining a *correlation contrast coefficient R. R* can be represented as

$$R = \frac{\Delta VL_J}{\Delta VL_I} = \frac{\Delta J}{\Delta I} \tag{5.50}$$

In the equation, VL_J and VL_I represent the VL of the object in the de-fogged image and the foggy image, respectively, and ΔJ and ΔI represent the gradient (gray level difference) of the visible edge pixels in the de-fogged image J and the foggy image I, respectively. It can be seen that R uses the correlation gradient between the de-fogged image and the foggy image to measure the degree of improvement in the VL caused by the de-fogging method (corresponding to the increase in contrast).

The relative contrast of the image can be calculated with the help of the de-fogged image and the foggy image. The following three evaluation indicators (for contrast) are defined here:

1. The proportion of visible edges added after de-fogging E

$$E = \frac{N_J - N_I}{N_J} \tag{5.51}$$

In the equation, N_J and N_I represent the number of visible edges in the de-fogged image and the foggy image, respectively. The larger the value of E, the more the number of visible edges in the de-fogged image increases.

2. The gradient mean G of the visible edge

$$G = \exp\left[\frac{1}{N_J} \sum_{q_i \in Q_J} \log G_i \right] \tag{5.52}$$

where Q_J is the set of visible edges in J, q_i is a specific visible edge in J, and G_i is the gradient ratio of ΔJ to ΔI at q_i. The greater the value of G, the greater the strength of the visible edges in the de-fogged image.

3. The percentage of saturated black pixels or white pixels S

$$S = \frac{N_s}{N} \tag{5.53}$$

In the equation, N_s is the number of saturated black or white pixels in J. In practice, it can be determined by calculating the sum of the number of pixels whose brightness value is 255 or 0 in the de-fogged image after changing the image into grayscale; N is the total number of pixels in the relative contrast map. The smaller the value of S, the higher the contrast of the de-fogged image.

Among the three indicators, the first two can reflect the improvement of the visual effect in the de-fogged image, the larger the better; the last one corresponds to the over-processing of the de-fogged image, and the smaller the better. But it should be noted that in practice, these three indicators often cannot get the optimal value at the same time. In addition, sometimes the optimal value does not necessarily correspond to the best visual effect.

5.5.1.3 Visual Perception Computing

When people observe an image, the perceived comfort and pleasure are not only related to the contrast in the image, but also related to the naturalness and richness of the color of the image. The three evaluation indicators discussed above are all calculated around the image contrast, which mainly reflects the contrast restoration ability of the de-fogging algorithm. However, the human visual system must also consider the color quality of the de-fogging image when judging the de-fogging effect of the algorithm. Here, the color naturalness and color richness perceived by human vision can be used to judge the color quality of the image. Combining contrast, naturalness, and richness, it is possible to evaluate *Contrast-Naturalness-Colorfulness* (CNC) by considering the perception of the human eye (Huang et al. 2006). It also specifically has three indicators: *Contrast Enhancement Index* (CEI), *Color Naturalness Index* (CNI), and *Color Colorfulness Index* (CCI).

The CEI is still based on the visible edge (see the parameter definition of Equation (5.51)), which can be written as:

$$CEI = \frac{N_I}{N_J} \tag{5.54}$$

The calculation of the CNI requires a series of steps: First, calculate the values of intensity L, hue H and saturation S of the image; retain the color with an intensity value of $20 \sim 80$ and a saturation value greater than 0.1; consider three ranges of hue value: U corresponds to [25, 70], V corresponds to [95, 135], W corresponds to [185, 260]; calculate the average saturation values S_{Ua}, S_{Va}, S_{Wa} and the numbers of pixels N_U, N_V, N_W for the three ranges, respectively; then calculate the local CNI value of the pixels in the three ranges:

$$CNI_U = \exp\left\{-0.5\left[(S_{Ua} - 0.76)/0.52\right]^2\right\} \tag{5.55}$$

$$CNI_V = \exp\left\{-0.5\left[(S_{Va} - 0.81)/0.53\right]^2\right\} \tag{5.56}$$

$$CNI_W = \exp\left\{-0.5\left[(S_{Wa} - 0.43)/0.22\right]^2\right\} \tag{5.57}$$

Finally, calculate the total CNI value:

$$CNI = (N_U \times CNI_U + N_V \times CNI_V + N_W \times CNI_W)/(N_U + N_V + N_W) \tag{5.58}$$

The CNI is an index that reflects whether the image scene measured by the human vision is real and natural. It is mainly used to judge the color naturalness of the de-fogged image J, and its value range is [0, 1]. The closer the CNI is to 1, the more natural the image is.

The CCI is an index that measures the vividness of colors. In the sRGB color space, the CCI of an image can be calculated by the following equation (Hasler and Suesstrunk 2003):

$$CCI = \sigma_{rgyb} + 0.3\mu_{rgyb} = \sqrt{\sigma_{rg}^2 + \sigma_{yb}^2} + 0.3\sqrt{\mu_{rg}^2 + \mu_{yb}^2} \tag{5.59}$$

where the subscripts rg and yb represent the components calculated according to the opposite color theory in the sRGB color space:

$$rg = R - G \tag{5.60}$$

$$yb = \frac{1}{2}(R+G) - B \tag{5.61}$$

The CCI is also used to judge the de-fogged image J. When the CCI is within a certain value range, the human vision has the most appropriate perception of the color of the image. Note that CCI is related to image content and is suitable for measuring the color richness of the same scene and the same scenery under different de-fogging effects.

Combining the CEI of the newly added visible edge ratio after de-fogging with the CNI and CCI can make a more comprehensive quantitative evaluation of the de-fogging effect. The overall process is shown in Figure 5.11 (Guo and Cai 2012).

The determination of the comprehensive evaluation function should consider the numerical change of each indicator under different fog conditions, so as to determine the respective weights of different indicators. To this end, it is possible to simulate different degrees of fog (from dense fog, heavy fog to mist, until no fog) and different degrees of de-fogging (from insufficient de-fogging, gradual clarity to proper de-fogging, and even excessive de-fogging), so as to calculate and count the value of each indicator to get the overall trend of each indicator.

Experiments show that the three indicators change their (curve) values with the degree of fog removal from small to large and then from large to small (although there are some oscillations). Among them, the values of indicators CEI and CCI rise steadily in fluctuations and then decline sharply until the excessive enhancement reaches a certain level

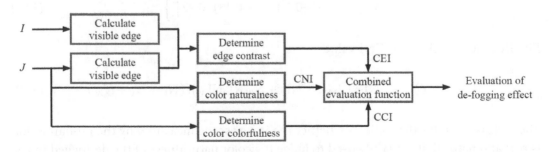

FIGURE 5.11 Comprehensive evaluation process based on visual perception.

(i.e., the best de-fogging effect is obtained before the curve reaches the peak). The value of the indicator CNI rises rapidly in fluctuations, and several local peaks will appear before reaching the best de-fogging effect and will begin to decline after reaching the best de-fogging effect. Because the color of the image may be more natural when there is a small amount of fog in reality, the most natural image is not necessarily the image with the best sharpening effect, but the clearest image must have a higher CNI value. On the whole, to make the curve peak of the comprehensive evaluation function close to the actual best de-fogging effect of the image, it is necessary to make the CEI and CCI curves in the range from reaching the best de-fogging effect until their peaks are offset by the decline of the CNI curve within this range as much as possible. Therefore, the complete evaluation function can be taken as the following form:

$$\mathrm{CNC} = \mathrm{CEI}^k \times \mathrm{CNI} + \mathrm{CCI}^h \times \mathrm{CNI} \tag{5.62}$$

In the equation, k and h are constants less than or equal to 1, used to adjust the weights of CEI and CCI relative to CNI.

5.5.2 Examples of Evaluations Combining Subjective and Objective Indices

The subjective evaluation index reflects the visual quality more directly, while the objective evaluation index is more convenient for quantitative calculation. It is a way of thinking to select objective evaluation indicators that are more in line with subjective quality (i.e., indicators that are closely related each other).

5.5.2.1 Evaluation Indicators and Calculations

Here the use of *SSIM* (Wang et al. 2004) is consider as an objective index to evaluate the image quality. The structural similarity takes advantage of the grayscale covariance and other information in the image, which has a certain descriptive effect on the structure in the image. Since the human eye is more sensitive to structural information, the structural similarity should reflect a certain subjective visual experience. The structural similarity measures the similarity between the structure of two (grayscale) images, and its value can be normalized to the interval [0, 1]. When the two images are the same, SSIM = 1. For color images, the image can be converted to CIELab space (Zhao et al. 2013), and the SSIM of the L channel can be calculated. This is because the SSIM of L channel is more representative than the SSIM of a channel or the SSIM of b channel.

To measure the correlation between the structural similarity and the subjective visual quality of the image, an approach of adding fog to image can be considered for the original image to obtain different fogged images as a reference, so as to calculate the structural similarity in various situations. Specifically, the algorithm of adding fog to the blue channel (Wang et al. 2014) can be used for adding fog to the result of de-fogging. There is a logarithmic relationship between the normalized blue channel $B(x)$ and the image depth of field, which can be represented as:

$$d(x) = -\log(1 - B(x)) \tag{5.63}$$

Use guided filtering to remove the details (blur) of $B(x)$ to get $B_d(x)$. According to Equations (5.3) and (5.63), the atmospheric transmittance has a linear relationship with the blue channel. The atmospheric transmittance can be written as:

$$t(x) = 1 - 0.95 \times B_d(x) \tag{5.64}$$

Select the brightest pixel value in the image as A, and then use Equation (5.2) to get the restored image I'.

An example of adding fog to image is shown in Figure 5.12, where Figure 5.12a is $I(x)$, Figure 5.12b is $J(x)$, Figure 5.12c is $B_d(x)$, and Figure 5.12d Is $I'(x)$.

Experiments using images with different degrees of fog show that the larger the SSIM value between the de-fogging result and the original image (i.e., they are more similar), also the larger the SSIM value between the fogging result and the original image. This shows that the larger the SSIM, the smaller the image distortion and the higher the subjective quality. The SSIM data points before and after fogging are marked in Figure 5.13, where the horizontal axis indicates the SSIM between the de-fogging image and the original image, while the vertical axis indicates the SSIM between the adding fog image and the original image. The series of red dots on the far right of Figure 5.13 indicate the SSIM obtained by adding fog to the original image, and its horizontal axis coordinate is 1 (the fog is completely removed).

As shown in Figure 5.13, the correlation coefficient between the SSIM of the de-fogging image and the SSIM of the adding fog image represented by the blue dot is as high as 0.8708. When the SSIM of the de-fogging image is larger, the growth of the SSIM of the adding fog image becomes slower. According to the red data points, if the SSIM of the de-fogging image continues to increase, the growth of the SSIM of the adding fog image will further slowdown or even decrease until reaching the red point. Although the subjective quality of the image may decrease when the SSIM is too high, but in the blue dot region, that is, in various actual de-fogging results, the larger the SSIM, the smaller the distortion, and the higher the subjective quality of the image. This shows that the structural similarity has a relative strong positive correlation with the subjective visual quality of the image.

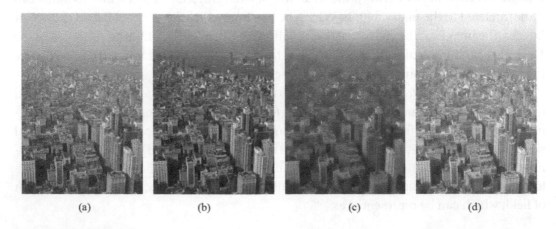

| (a) | (b) | (c) | (d) |

FIGURE 5.12 The effect of adding fog to image; (a) is $I(x)$; (b) is $J(x)$; (c) is $B_d(x)$; (d) is $I'(x)$.

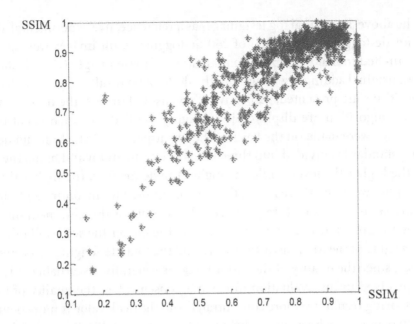

FIGURE 5.13   SSIM data points before and after fogging.

5.5.2.2 Experiments and Results

For the experiment, the images shown in the website and PPT were used as part of the test images (He et al. 2009). The size of these images is about 400×600. In addition, some fog images were taken when PM2.5 was about 300 to expand the data set (Figure 5.9a is an example). The size of these images is 2448×3264. A total of 50 test images were selected from these two parts. The content types of the test images are relatively scattered, including natural scenery and urban scenes, as well as images with high-light regions and images taken under backlight conditions.

For specific subjective and objective evaluation, five algorithms were selected to participate in the comparative experiment: Algorithm A (Gan and Xiao 2013) (see Sub-section 5.4.5), Algorithm B (Chu et al. 2013) (see Sub-section 5.4.4), Algorithm C (Shi et al. 2013) (See Sub-section 5.4.2), Algorithm D (combining Algorithm A and Algorithm B), and Algorithm E (Li and Zhang 2017) (see Section 5.4).

When calculating the atmospheric scatter map, the guided map and the input map of the guided filter are normalized to $D_T(x)$ in [0, 1], and the result is mapped back to the [0, 255] interval after filtering. Let W_r denote a square guided filter window with a radius of r. For a 400×600 image, take $W_r = 12$ and a regularization smoothing factor $\varepsilon = 0.04$; for an image of 2448×3264, take $W_r = 70$ and $\varepsilon = 0.04$. When calculating the sky region, for a 400×600 image, take $T_v = 0.88 \times \max[d(x)]$; for a 2448×3264 image, take $T_v = 0.6 \times \max[d(x)]$. For the 400×600 image, the size of the neighborhood of the dark channel is 30 and the size of the edge neighborhood is 15. For the 2448×3264 image, the size of the neighborhood of the dark channel is 120, and the size of the edge neighborhood is 60. When adding fog to the image, take $W_r = 5$ and $\varepsilon = 0.04$ for a 400×600 image; take $W_r = 30$ and $\varepsilon = 0.04$ for a 2448×3264 image.

Taking the above 50 original fog test images as a reference, five experimental algorithms were used for de-fogging, and a total of 250 de-fogging result images were obtained. 10 people were invited to make a subjective evaluation of these images (Li and Zhang 2017). Each time an original adding fog image and the de-fogging result image obtained by using the five algorithms are presented, respectively. To ensure fairness, the order in which the results of each algorithm are displayed is randomly shuffled. For each result image, the evaluation scores were made on the basis of the two aspects of distortion and de-fogging. Each scoring standard is divided into three levels of low, medium and high. The lower the distortion, the higher the level; while the higher the de-fogging, the higher the level. To widen the gap between the three levels, the weights of the low, medium, and high distortion items are set to 3, 2, and 1, respectively; the weights of the low, medium, and high de-fogging items are set to 1, 2, and 3 respectively. The higher the score of both items, the better. The weights of the total distortion score and the total de-fogging score are both 1.

In practice, since the quality of the result image is generally discernable, it is easier for the people involved in the evaluation to reach a consensus on the quality of the image. Finally, the scoring results are more concentrated and the peak value is more obvious. This shows that 10 people have been able to help find the statistical distribution of the score.

The distortion scores of the five algorithms involved in the comparison are shown in Figure 5.14, and the SSIM values of the five algorithms in the L channel are shown in Figure 5.15. It can be seen from these two figures that SSIM has a better recognition of the highest and lowest scores. The pink point with the highest SSIM value is also ranked first in the distortion score map, and the blue point with the lowest SSIM value is also ranked behind in the distortion score map. Among the five algorithms participating in the comparison, these two algorithms (the top-ranked algorithm E and the last-ranked algorithm A) have an average of 40% of the images with the same SSIM value and distortion score ranking.

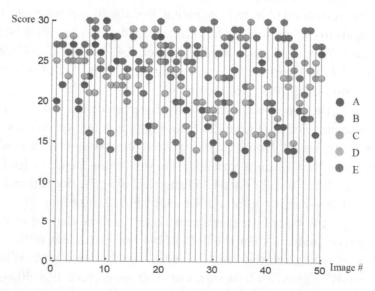

FIGURE 5.14   Comparison of the distortion scores of 5 algorithms.

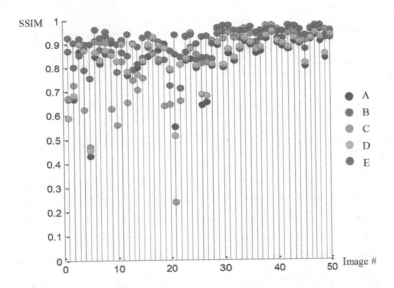

FIGURE 5.15 Comparison of the SSIM values of 5 algorithms in the *L* channel.

5.6 SOME RECENT DEVELOPMENTS AND FURTHER RESEARCH

In the following, some technique developments and promising research directions in the last years are briefly overviewed.

5.6.1 Nighttime Fog Removal

The characteristics of foggy images at night include uneven illumination, color distortion, and high noise. Directly using the daytime de-fogging method will lose the details of the over-bright regions in the image, and the effect would not be satisfied. Different from the uniform atmospheric light of the daytime image, the light sources of the night images are mainly visible artificial light sources, such as streetlights, car lights, building lights, etc., and the overall brightness is low. There are three key issues to consider when de-fogging at night:

1. Due to the characteristics of artificial light sources, the region close to the light source is sufficiently illuminated, but the region far from light source is insufficiently illuminated. Therefore, the atmospheric light is no longer uniform, and the image will have uneven illumination.

2. Various light sources may have different colors, and the color of light source would determine the naturalness of the color and the de-fogging effect.

3. Outdoor night images often have insufficient brightness and large noise; these would cause serious loss of image details.

5.6.1.1 A Photographic Negative Imaging Inspired Method

According to the observations on large amounts of the nighttime negative images (Shi et al. 2017), it is found that the nighttime negative images have some characteristics similar to blurred image with partial white colors, which make the negative image look like a foggy

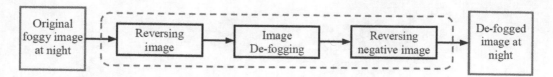

FIGURE 5.16   Flow chart of negative imaging inspired method.

image. Based on such an observation, the fog in image can be removed by the procedure shown in Figure 5.16.

In Figure 5.16, the image (negative image) reversed from the original foggy image at night is first obtained. Since this image has the similar characteristics as the foggy image during the day, the de-fogging methods based on the DCP (see Section 5.2) or its improvements (see Section 5.3) or other methods (such as in Section 5.4) can be used for de-fogging operation, and finally by reversing the negative image after de-fogging to obtain the final de-fogged image.

The idea of converting nighttime images into daytime images through preprocessing for de-fogging operation can also be achieved with the help of color transfer (Pei and Lee 2012). Specifically, the color transfer method is used to change the color characteristics of the original image by statistically correcting the input foggy image, to make the night foggy image have the color attributes (average hue and brightness) of the daytime image, and then use the de-fogging technique on the daytime image to achieve de-fogging. The process of this method can also be referred to Figure 5.16, but here the modules of "reversing image" and "reversing negative image" become "color transfer into new color space" and "color transfer back to original color space", respectively.

5.6.1.2 Combining Bright and DCP

The *dark channel priors* (DCP) can be combined with the *bright channel priors* (BCP). The flow chart is shown in Figure 5.17. First, the DCP theory is used to estimate the *global atmospheric light* value, and the brightest 10% pixels in the bright channel are selected and averaged as the global atmospheric light. Then use BCP to estimate the initial transmission map: When there is only one bright object (such as light source) in a local block in the scene, the initial transmission map will be wrong. To solve this problem, the DCP can be used as a supplement to make corrections to obtain a rough transmission map. Finally, the guided filter is used for refinement to obtain a de-fogged image.

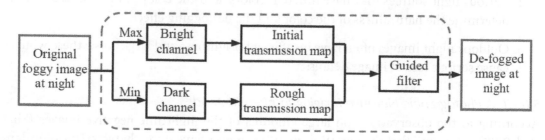

FIGURE 5.17   Flow chart of combining BCP and DCP.

This method does not fully consider the uneven illumination at night and the color of the light source when estimating the ambient light. Therefore, the estimation of the ambient light value is prone to problems, which may result in large noise and color distortion in the output image.

The above methods are mainly based on the DCP for de-fogging. Since there are no objects with low darkness near the light source at night, the dark channels in other regions may be caused by lack of light, so it is not easy to accurately estimate the transmittance. In addition, because the local maximum method is used to estimate the ambient light, the estimation of the ambient light may not be very accurate. Further improvements can consider multi-scale fusion (Ancuti et al. 2016), or hierarchical restoration (Yang and Wang 2018). In the latter approach, the image is divided into a structure layer (for main structure) and a texture layer (for image details), and the structure layer is restored, and then superimposed with the texture layer to form the final restored image.

After dividing the foggy image into the texture layer and the structure layer, another method (Tang et al. 2018) is to further divide the structure layer into the illuminating light component and the reflected light component according to the *retinal cortex* theory. Next it first estimates and optimizes the illuminating light component, and then the ratio of the structural layer illuminating light to the optimized illuminating light is used as the reflected light component to suppress strong light and noise, thereby obtaining a structural layer after strong light suppression. Next, the optimized illuminating light component is reversed as the estimated transmittance, and the structure layer is de-fogged. Finally, the texture layer is optimized and superimposed with the restored structure layer to form the final de-fogging image.

5.6.1.3 Deep Learning for Image De-Fogging

With the rapid development of deep learning and its wide application in the field of image processing, many new methods use deep learning to deal with the problem of image de-fogging.

There is a de-fogging method that uses the end-to-end haze density prediction network (HDP-Net) (Liao et al. 2018). The fog image degradation model here regards the fog image as the sum of the fog density prediction result as well as the texture layer and structure layer of the fog-free image. The function of HDP-Net is to estimate the fog density image from the foggy image at night and preserve the image details. Since the distribution and density of fog at night will be different in the image, a network architecture similar to fully convolutional networks (FCN) (Long et al. 2014) is used to construct a haze density prediction network. The number of layers of HDP-Net is based on the training image with a size of 128×128, the fully connected layer is transformed into one of 11 convolutional layers. Except for the last layer, each convolutional layer is followed by ReLU as a nonlinear activation function. Finally, de-convolve the output to get an image with the same size as the input image. CAFFE is used to implement the network designed for training. After 11 layers of multi-scale feature extraction, fusion and mapping operations, the effect of de-fogging can be achieved.

Another method introduces an iterative structure based on deep learning, which can not only remove haze/fog, but also remove *halo* (Kuanar et al. 2019). The specific steps are to first extract features from the fog image through extended convolution, and then use the end-to-end DehazeNet (Cai et al. 2016) to remove the haze/fog.

By the way, from the image degradation point of view, some other naturel atmosphere or weather environment interferences have the similar influences. Some techniques for rain removal (Song et al. 2020; Liu et al. 2020), snow removal (Huang et al. 2020), as well as sand-dust enhancement (Park and Eom 2021) have also been proposed.

5.6.2 More General Fog Removal Techniques

Most fog removal techniques are developed for general applications and can be adopted and adaptively modified for specific applications. There are different categorization schemes. For example, these techniques can be classified into three groups (Li et al. 2017b) from a point of view of fog model: (i) heuristic without model, (ii) prior with model, and (iii) learning with model. In the following, some common techniques for de-fogging are listed in two groups: non-learning and learning-based.

5.6.2.1 Non-Learning Image De-Fogging Techniques

Many non-learning de-fogging methods have been designed in the past ten years. A categorization of some typical non-learning de-fogging methods are listed in Table 5.1. More details on these methods, such as their effects and performances (computation speed, color distortion, blocking artifacts, halo artifacts, edge preservation, large haze gradient, gradient inversion artifacts, etc.) as well as their pros and cons can be found in (Singh and Kumar 2018; Babu and Venkatram 2020).

TABLE 5.1   A Categorization of Non-learning Image De-Fogging Methods

#	Class Name	Typical Technique
1	Depth estimation-based	Color attenuation prior (CAP) Dark channel priors (DCP) Optical model Visibility restoration
2	Enhancement based	Bi-histogram modification Quad trees Retinex
3	Filtering based	Anisotropic diffusor Bilateral filter Guided filter Median filtering
4	Fusion-based	Guided fusion High boost filtering Multiscale depth fusion
5	Meta-heuristic -based	Genetic algorithm Particle swarm optimization
6	Transform-based	Fast Fourier transform Fast Wavelet transform
7	Variational -based	Fusion-based Variational model Gradient residual minimization Variational model

5.6.2.2 Learning-Based Image De-Fogging Techniques

Generally, non-learning image de-fogging methods are confined to specific hand-crafted features. Recent researches have started focus on implementing machine learning and deep learning approaches for fast and reliable restoration of images in a well-organized manner.

A categorization of some typical machine learning-based image de-fogging methods are listed in Table 5.2 (Ngo et al. 2021).

A categorization of some typical deep learning-based image de-fogging methods are listed in Table 5.3 (Ngo et al. 2021).

TABLE 5.2   A Categorization of Machine Learning Image De-Fogging Methods

#	Class Name	Typical Technique
1	Probabilistic graphical model	Bayesian framework Inhomogeneous Laplacian-Markov random field Local consistent Markov random field
2	Regression analysis	Least squares regression Maximum likelihood estimates Random forest regression
3	Regularization	Adaptive regularization Information loss L_2 regularization Semantic-guided regularization Sparsity regularization Total variation regularization
4	Searching-based optimization and linear approximation	Fibonacci search Huber loss exploitation Nelder-Mead direct search
5	Others	Dictionary learning Independent component analysis k-means clustering Radial basis function

TABLE 5.3   A Categorization of Deep Learning-Based Image De-Fogging Methods

#	Class Name	Typical Technique
1	Convolutional neural network	DehazeNet and its variants Multi-scale convolutional neural network
2	Generative adversarial network	Compositional GAN and multiple level discrimination Encoder-decoder architecture Fully connected generator Heterogeneous GAN Physics-based GAN
3	Others	Data-and-prior-aggregated transmission network DCP loss for unsupervised learning Patch quality comparator and binary search Zero-shot learning

Some typical/example approaches are listed below:

1. AOD-Net (Li et al. 2017a).

2. DehazeNet (Cai et al. 2016), which can significantly estimate the transmission map by using the atmospheric scattering method with the help of a nonlinear activation function named bilateral rectified linear unit.

3. Gated Fusion Network (GFN) (Li and Guo 2018).

4. GMAN Generic Model-Agnostic CNN (Kang and Kim 2015).

5. Heterogeneous GAN (Park et al. 2020), which combines and takes the advantage of a cycle-consistent GAN (CycleGAN) and a conditional GAN (cGAN) via a fusion CNN.

6. Kernel regression (Xie et al. 2016), which uses restoration model to remove the effect of haze from the image.

7. Light weight Dual Task Network (LDTNet) (Li and Guo 2018).

8. Multiscale CNN (MSCNN) (Ren et al. 2016).

9. Patch quality comparator (Santra et al. 2018), which estimates the transmittance in local patches based on the quality of the de-fogging process, by generating several de-fogged patches with different transmittance values, performing patch quality comparison with CNN and binary search to determine the optimum transmittance value.

10. RYF-Net (Dudhane and Murala 2020), which is a variate of DehazeNet utilizing two DehazeNet-like CNNs for estimating two versions of the medium transmittance in RGB and YCbCr color spaces, respectively, and using a fusion network to fuse the two transmittance estimates to obtain a final transmittance.

11. Two-layer Gaussian regression (Fan et al. 2016), which can found the direct association among fog image and its depth knowledge by using both foggy image and fog-free image.

12. Unsupervised learning (Golts et al. 2019) which exploits the DCP to formulate the loss function.

Compared to non-learning image de-fogging method, these learning-based methods often have fast computational speed. However, the requirement of number of images with distinct scenes to train a specific model makes it harder to implement in real time.

REFERENCES

Ancuti, C., C. O. Ancuti, R. C. D. Vleeschouwe. 2016. Night-time dehazing by fusion. *Proceedings of the ICIP*, 2256–2260.

Babu, G. H., and N. Venkatram. 2020. A survey on analysis and implementation of state-of-the-art haze removal techniques. *Journal of Visual Communication and Image Representation*, 72: 102912.

Cai, B., X. Xu, and K. Jia. 2016. DehazeNet: An end-to-end system for single image haze removal. *IEEE Trans-IP*, 25(11): 5187–5198.

Chu, H. L., Y. X. Li, Z. M. Zhou, et al. 2013. Optimized fast dehazing method based on dark channel prior. *Acta Electronica Sinica*, 41(4): 791–797.

Dudhane, A., and S. Murala. 2020. RYF-Net: Deep fusion network for single image haze removal. *IEEE Trans-IP*, 29, 628–640.

Fan, X., Y. Wang, X. Tang, et al. 2016. Two-layer Gaussian process regression with example selection for image dehazing. *IEEE Transactions on CSVT*, 27: 2505–2517.

Fang, S., J. Q. Zhang, Y. Cao, et al. 2010. Improved single image dehazing using segmentation. *Proceedings of the ICIP*, 3589–3592.

Fang, W., and B. H. Liu. 2013. Image dehazeing using multiscale dark channel prior. *Chinese Journal of Stereology and Image Analysis*, 18(3): 230–237.

Gan, J. J., and C. X. Xiao. 2013. Fast image dehazing based on accurate scattering map. *Journal of Image and Graphics*, 18(5): 583–590.

Golts, A., D. Freedman, and M. Elad. 2019. Unsupervised single image dehazing using dark channel prior loss. IEEE *Transactions on IP*, 29, 2692–2701.

Guo, F., and Z. X. Cai. 2012. Objective assessment method for the clearness effect of image defogging algorithm. *Acta Automatica Sinica*, 38(9): 1410–1419.

Hasler, D., and S. E. Suesstrunk. 2003. Measuring colorfulness in natural images. *Proceedings of the Human Vision and Electronic Imaging VIII, SPIE 5007*, 87–95.

Hautière, N., J. P. Tarel, D. Aubert, et al. 2008. Blind contrast enhancement assessment by gradient rationing at visible edges. *Image Analysis and Stereology Journal*, 27(2): 87–95

He, K. M., J. Sun, and X. O. Tang. 2009. Single image haze removal using dark channel prior. *Proceedings of the CVPR*, 1956–1963.

He, K. M., J. Sun, and X. O. Tang. 2011. Single image haze removal using dark channel prior. *IEEE-PAMI*, 33(12): 2341–2353.

He, K. M., J. Sun, and X. O. Tang. 2013. Guided image filtering. *IEEE-PAMI*, 35(6): 1397–1409.

Huang, K. Q., Q. Wang, and Z.-Y. Wu. 2006. Natural color image enhancement and evaluation algorithm based on human visual system. *Computer Vision and Image Understanding*, 103: 52–63.

Huang, S. C., D. W. Jaw, B. H. Chen, et al. 2020. Single image snow removal using sparse representation and particle swarm optimizer. *ACM Transactions on Intelligent Systems and Technology*, 11(2): 1–15.

Jobson, D. J., Z. Rahman, and G. A. Woodell. 1997. Properties and performance of a center/surround retinex. *IEEE-IP*, 6(3): 4511–462.

Kang, H.-J., and Y.-H. Kim. 2015. FPGA implementation for enhancing image using pixel-based median channel prior. *International Journal of Multimedia and Ubiquitous Engineering*, 10(9): 147–154.

Kuanar, S., K. R. Rao, D. Mahapatra, et al. 2019. Night time haze and glow removal using deep dilated convolutional network. Computer Vision and Pattern Recognition arXiv: 1902.00855.

Li, B., X. Peng, Z. Wang, et al. 2017a. Aod-net: All-in-one dehazing network. *Proceedings of the ICCV*, 4780–4788

Li, C. Y., and J. C. Guo. 2018. A cascaded convolutional neural network for single image dehazing. *IEEE Access*, 6: 24877–24887.

Li, J. T., and Y.-J. Zhang. 2017. Improvements and subjective and objective performance evaluation of image haze removal algorithm. *Optics and Precision Engineering*, 25(3): 735–741.

Li, Y., S. D. Youb, M. S. Brownc, et al. 2017b. Haze visibility enhancement: A survey and quantitative benchmarking. *Computer Vision and Image Understanding*, 165, 1–16.

Liao, Y., Z. Su, X. Liang, et al. 2018. HDP-Net: Haze density prediction network for nighttime dehazing. *Advances in Multimedia Information Processing-PCM*, 469–480.

Liu, C. Y., Q. Wang, and X. J. Bi. 2020. Research on rain removal method for single image based on multi-channel and multi-scale CNN. *Journal of Electronics & Information Technology*, 42(9): 2286–2292.

Long, J., R. E. Shelhame, and T. Darrell. 2014. Fully convolutional networks for semantic segmentation. *IEEE Trans-PAMI*, 39(4): 640–651.

Long, W., J. X. Fu, Y. Y. Li, et al. 2016. Algorithm about dense fog image dehazing based on atmospheric extinction coefficient and guided filtering. *Journal of Sichuan University (Engineering Science Edition)*, 48(4): 175–180.

Miao, Q. G., and Y. N. Li. 2017. Research status and prospect of image dehazing. *Computer Science*, 44(11): 1–8.

Narasimhan, S. G., and S. K. Nayar. 2003. Contrast restoration of weather degraded images. *IEEE-PAMI*, 25(6): 713–724.

Ngo, D., S. Lee, T. M. Ngo, et al. 2021. Visibility restoration: A systematic review and meta-analysis. *Sensors*, 21(8): 1–41.

Park, J., D. K. Han, and H. Ko. 2020. Fusion of heterogeneous adversarial networks for single image dehazing. *IEEE Transactions on IP*, 29: 4721–4732.

Park, T. H., and I. Eom. 2021. Sand-dust image enhancement using successive color balance with coincident chromatic histogram. *IEEE ACCESS*, 9: 19749–19760.

Pei, S. C., and T. Y. Lee. 2012. Nighttime haze removal using color transfer preprocessing and dark channel prior. *Proceedings of the ICIP*, 957–960.

Ren, W., S. Liu, H. Zhang, et al. 2016. Single image dehazing via multi-scale convolutional neural networks. *Proceedings of the ECCV*, 154–169.

Santra, S., R. Mondal, and B. Chanda. 2018. Learning a patch quality comparator for single image dehazing. *IEEE Transactions on IP*, 27: 4598–4607.

Shi, D.-F., B. Li, W. Ding, et al. 2013. Haze removal and enhancement using transmittance-dark channel prior based on object spectral characteristic. *Acta Automatica Sinica*, 39(12): 2064–2070.

Shi, Z., M. M. Zhu, and B. Guo. 2017. A photographic negative imaging inspired method for low illumination night-time image enhancement. *Multimedia Tools and Applications*, 76(13): 15027–15048.

Singh, D. and V. Kumar. 2018. Comprehensive survey on haze removal techniques. *Multimedia Tools and Applications*, 77:9595–9620.

Song, Y. C., H. B. Luo, B. Hui, et al. 2016. Haze removal using scale adaptive dark channel prior. *Infrared and Laser Engineering*, 45(9): 286–297.

Song, C. M., X. Hong, and D. K. Liu. 2020. Rain removal method for traffic surveillance video in joint spatial-frequency domain. *Pattern Recognition and Artificial Intelligence*, 33(9): 852–866.

Tang, C. M., Y. C. Dong, X. Sun. 2018. Image restoration algorithm for single nighttime weakly illuminated haze image. *Journal of Computer-Aided Design and Computer Graphics*, 55(6): 95–102.

Wang, P., D. Bicazan, and A. Ghosh. 2014. Rerendering landscape photographs. *Proceedings of the CVMP*, 13: 1–6.

Wang, S., Y. Z. Pan, Y. Liu, et al. 2013. Image quality improvement of laser active imaging in fog. *Infrared and Laser Engineering*, 42(9): 2392–2396.

Wang, Z., A. C. Bovik, H. R. Sheikh, et al. 2004. Image quality assessment: From error visibility to structural similarity. *IEEE-IP*, 13(4): 600–612.

Wu, D., and Q. S. Zhu. 2015. The latest research progress of image dehazing. *Acta Automatica Sinica*, 41(7): 221–239.

Xie, C.H., W. W. Qiao, Z. Liu, et al. 2016. Single image dehazing using kernel regression model and dark channel prior. *Signal, Image and Video Processing*, 11: 1–8.

Yang, A. P., H. P. Liu, Y. Q. He, et al. 2016. Single image dehazing based on dark channel fusion and wiener filtering. *Journal of Tianjin University (Science and Technology)*, 49(6): 574–580.

Yang, A. P., N. Wang. 2018. Night time image de-hazing algorithm by structure-texture image decomposition. *Laser and Optoelectronics Progress*, 55(6): 95–102.

Yu, M. J., and H. F. Zhang. 2014. Single-image dehazing based on dark channel and incident light assumption. *Journal of Image and Graphics*, 19(12): 1812–1819.

Zhang, Y.-J. 2017. *Image Engineering, Vol.1: Image Processing*. Germany: De Gruyter.

Zhao, X.Z., D. H. Xie, and K. J. Pan. 2013. Color image quality assessment algorithm based on color structural similarity. *Journal of Computer Applications*, 33(6): 1715–1718.

## CHAPTER 6

Image Reconstruction from Projection

*I*MAGE RECONSTRUCTION FROM *projection* is a special kind of image processing method. Here, the reconstruction from projection refers to the process of reconstructing the image of an object from multiple (radial) projection results of the object. At this time, the input is (a series of) projection image, and the output is a reconstruction image. Through the reconstruction from projection, one can directly see the spatial distribution of a certain characteristic of the original projected object from the reconstructed image, which is much more intuitive than observing the (original) projection image. If the projection is regarded as an image degradation process, then reconstruction is an image restoration process.

The image reconstruction from projection is closely related to *computed tomography* (CT) technology. In many CT systems, an X-ray emitter and a receiver move in opposite directions, and a cross-sectional image can be obtained by means of the projection results obtained from the penetrating object. Many techniques use similar projections to reconstruct images, such as synthetic aperture radar (SAR), magnetic resonance imaging (MRI), and so on.

Mathematically, Radon established the connection between the projection image and the reconstruction image as early as 1917 (*Radon transform*) and pointed out that this problem can be solved by using the inverse transformation method. However, the calculation of the Radon inverse transform is technically an ill-posed problem, and a small error in the calculation of the transformation function will cause a large error in the reconstruction function. Therefore, the practical reconstruction algorithm based on Radon theory has been researched and improved in recent years, and some typical basic methods are shown in the following sections. It is worth pointing out that obtaining CT images is also considered to be the first successful example of obtaining images by solving a mathematical problem belonging to inverse and ill-posed problems (Bertero and Boccacci 1998).

In addition to the analytical algorithms based on Radon transform, the image reconstruction algorithms also has iterative algorithms represented by solving linear equations. The former can be further divided into direct Fourier transform reconstruction algorithm and indirect back-projection reconstruction algorithm.

DOI: 10.1201/9781003241416-6

The contents of each section of this chapter are arranged as follows.

Section 6.1 introduces some typical projection reconstruction forms and procedures, including not only various CT (transmission, emission, reflection) but also electrical impedance tomography (EIT), MRI, and so on.

Section 6.2 analyzes and discusses the principles of 2-D and 3-D projection reconstructions, the basic model is discussed first, and then the central layer theorem obtained from the Radon transform is introduced, thus establishing the basis of the reconstruction methods in the following sections.

Section 6.3 introduces the inverse Fourier transform reconstruction method realized with the help of the central layer theorem. In principle, the method is straightforward, and the amount of calculation required is comparatively small, although the quality of the reconstructed image is relatively poor.

Section 6.4 summarizes the principle, step, and characteristics of a large class of inverse projection reconstruction methods first and specifically introduces several inverse projection reconstruction methods that are easier to implement with software and hardware as well as have more accurate and clear reconstruction effects.

Section 6.5 introduces the iterative reconstruction method as opposed to the analytical inverse transformation reconstruction method and the inverse projection reconstruction method. It can directly obtain the numerical solution through iterative calculation. Typical methods include algebraic reconstruction and maximum likelihood-maximum expectation reconstruction.

Section 6.6 gives an example of a comprehensive reconstruction method that combines the inverse Fourier transform reconstruction method, the inverse projection reconstruction method, and the series expansion iterative reconstruction method.

Section 6.7 provides a brief introduction of some technique developments and promising research directions in the last year.

6.1 PROJECTION RECONSTRUCTION FORMS

If the data collected or measured by the sensor has an integral form of the spatial distribution of a certain interesting physical property of the object, then the reconstruction from the projection method can be used to obtain images inside the object that reflect different physical properties (Kak and Slaney 1988). There are many forms of reconstruction from projection methods (Committee 1996), some of the most common and typical methods can be classified according to the (spatial) relationship between the emitter, receiver, and object. If the emission source and the receiver are on both sides of the object, the radiation emitted by the emission source penetrates the object and captured by the receiver at the other side, this is called transmission type. If the emission source is inside the object and the receiver is outside the object, the radiation emitted by the emission source penetrates the object from the inside to the outside and is then received by the receiver, this is called the emission type. If the emission source and the receiver are on the same side of the object, the radiation emitted by the emission source hits the object and is reflected back to be picked up by the receiver, this is called reflection type.

6.1.1 Transmission Tomography

In *transmission computed tomography* (TCT, CT for short), the radiation emitted by the emitter penetrates the object to be examined and reaches the receiver. When the ray passes through the object, part of it is absorbed by the object along the trajectory, and the remaining part is received by the receiver. Since each part of the object absorbs rays differently, the ray intensity obtained by the receiver reflects the total absorption of the rays by each part of the object. Different absorption of rays reflects the material characteristics of each part of the object, which can help determine the category and nature of the material.

6.1.1.1 CT Value

If I_0 represents the emitting intensity of the ray source, $A(s)$ represents the linear attenuation coefficient/factor at the object point s along the ray direction, L represents the ray of radiation, and I represents the intensity of the ray penetrating the object, then

$$I = I_0 \exp\left\{-\int_L A(s)\,ds\right\} \tag{6.1}$$

If the object is uniform, then

$$I = I_0 \exp\left\{-AL\right\} \tag{6.2}$$

where L is the length of the ray inside the object and A represents the linear attenuation coefficient of the object (the unit is the reciprocal of the length unit).

In practice, the gray value in the image formed by CT reflects the attenuation coefficient value relative to water (as a reference), which is called CT value:

$$CT = k\frac{A - A_w}{A_w} \tag{6.3}$$

Among them, A_w is the linear attenuation coefficient of water, and k is the normalized coefficient (generally taken as 1000). The unit of CT value is HU (Hounsfield Unit). For water, CT = 0 HU; for air, CT = −1000 HU; for bones, CT = 1000 HU.

6.1.1.2 CT System

After decades of development, the structure of the CT system has already seven generations. The scanning imaging structures of the CT system from the first to the fourth generation are shown in Figure 6.1. The circle in the figure represents the region to be imaged. The dashed line arrow passing through the emission source (X-ray tube) indicates that the emission source can move in the direction of the arrow, and the dashed curve arrow from one emission source to another indicates that the emission source can move along the curve (rotation). The first-generation system is shown in Figure 6.1a, in which the emitter and receiver are one-to-one, move toward each other (generating parallel projected beams) to cover the entire region to be imaged, and at the same time rotate in a circle to obtain

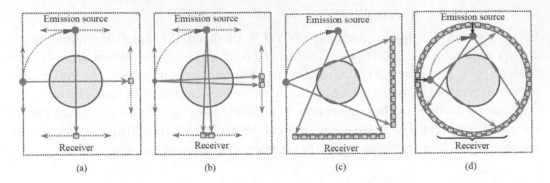

FIGURE 6.1 Schematic diagram of scanning imaging structure of CT system; (a) the first-generation system; (b) the second-generation system; (c) the third-generation system; (d) the fourth-generation system.

projections in multiple directions. The second-generation system is shown in Figure 6.1b, in which there are several receivers (distributed in a narrow sector) corresponding to each emission source, and they also move toward each other to cover the entire region to be imaged, and at the same time, they rotate in a circle to obtain projections in multiple directions. The third-generation system is shown in Figure 6.1c, where each emission source corresponds to a receiver array (which can be distributed on a straight line or on a wide fan-shaped arc). Both can cover the entire region to be imaged, so the emission source does not need to (translational) move, just rotate. The fourth-generation system is shown in Figure 6.1d, where the receiver forms a complete ring, and there is no movement during operation, only the emission source rotates.

The structure of the fifth-generation system is similar to that of the fourth-generation system. It only uses the electron beam rotation to realize the rotation of the emission source. In the electron beam system, the focus point is moved. In addition, the *fan-beam projection* modes are used in systems after the third generation, which can shorten the projection time as much as possible and reduce the image distortion caused by the movement of the object during the projection period and the harm to the patient. Recently, many systems have adopted the spiral scanning projection method, that is, when the scanning bed on which the human body is located is automatically translated at a constant speed, X-rays are used to continuously rotate and scan the human body to obtain spiral scan data and obtain a 3-D image with a certain thickness. This kind of system is also often called the sixth-generation system, and the data obtained is often called volume data. There is also a seventh-generation system now, also known as a multi-slice CT scanner. It is similar to that obtained by stacking the multi-slice CT scan planes in the fourth-generation system. Since rays are emitted and received in 3-D space, the seventh-generation system has a relatively high utilization rate of rays, which can improve scanning efficiency and reduce the amount of rays.

6.1.2 Emission Tomography

In *emission computed tomography* (ECT), the emission source is placed inside the object being inspected. In general, radioactive ions are injected into the object and their radiation is received from the outside of the object so that the movement and distribution of the ions in the object can be understood, so as to obtain physiological information. There are two main types of ECT in common use: positron emission CT (PET) and single-photon emission CT (SPECT). Both PET and SPECT obtain images reflecting the spatial distribution information of radioactive ions in the imaging object. Relatively, SPECT can use reagents that have a long life (half-value period) and are relatively easy to obtain, while PET uses an accelerator because of the short life of the ions used.

6.1.2.1 Positron Emission CT

The history of *positron emission tomography* (PET) can be traced back to the 1950s when imaging of radioactive materials was first used. A schematic diagram of the PET imaging system for emission tomography is shown in Figure 6.2.

PET uses radioactive ions that emit positrons when attenuated. The emitted positrons quickly collide with the negative electrons inside the object and annihilate to produce a pair of photons that are emitted in opposite directions. Therefore, the two opposite receivers will collect the two photons generated by a pair of positive and negative electrons and they can determine a ray.

If two photons are recorded by a pair of receivers at the same time, then the annihilation that produces these two photons must occur on the straight line connecting the two receivers. To avoid the influence of scattering, the tomographic reconstruction method is generally used to calculate the trajectory of positron emission after receiving 100,000 or more annihilation events. The projected record data of the event can be represented as

$$P = \exp\left(-\int A(s)\,ds\right) \cdot \int f(s)\,ds \tag{6.4}$$

In the equation, P is the projection data; $A(s)$ is the linear attenuation coefficient for γ rays; $f(s)$ is the distribution function of the isotope. Compared with the CT described above and the MRI described below, PET has great sensitivity and has the ability to detect and display nano-molar (one-billionth molar concentration) precision. However, the resolution of PET imaging is not as good as that of CT, and the noise is more obvious.

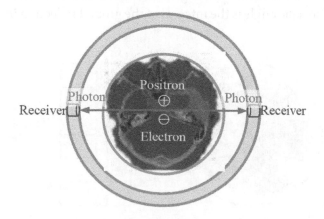

FIGURE 6.2   Schematic diagram of PET imaging system.

6.1.2.2 Single-Photon Emission CT

Single-photon emission CT (SPECT) combines nuclear medicine imaging technology and tomographic reconstruction technology. Any radioactive ion that can generate γ rays during attenuation can be used in SPECT. The structure of the SPECT imaging system is shown in Figure 6.3. When radioactive materials are injected into objects, different materials (such as tissues or organs) will emit γ rays after being absorbed. To determine the direction of the ray, a collimator that can prevent the deviation of the ray is used to directionally collect photons to determine the direction of the ray. Only γ-rays in a certain direction can pass through the collimator to reach the crystal, where γ-ray photons are converted into lower-energy photons and further converted into electrical signals by the photomultiplier. These electrical signals provide the position where the photon interacts with the crystal, so the 3-D distribution of the radioactive material is transformed into a 2-D projection image.

The sensitivity S of general emission tomography can be represented as

$$S \propto \frac{Ae^n k}{4\pi r^2} \tag{6.5}$$

In the equation, A is the area of the receiver; e is the efficiency of the receiver (n is 1 for SPECT and 2 for PET); k is the attenuation coefficient (usually 0.2–0.6); and r is the radius of the section. In general, the ratio of the sensitivity of PET to the sensitivity of SPECT is about 150 divided by the resolution. When the resolution is 7.5 mm, for example, the ratio is about 20. The sensitivity of SPECT is lower than that of PET because it requires a collimator made of lead to determine the direction of the rays, which limits the solid angle of the tomographic imaging device.

6.1.3 Reflection Tomography

Reflection computed tomography (RCT) also uses the principle of projection reconstruction. A common example is a radar system, where the radar image is produced with the echoes reflected by the object. For example, in *forward-looking radar* (FLR), the radar transmitter emits radio waves from the air to the ground. The intensity of the echo received by the radar receiver at a specific angle is the integral of the ground reflection in a scanning phase.

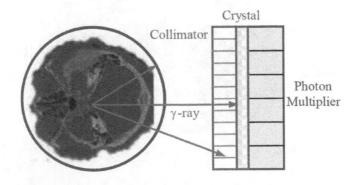

FIGURE 6.3 Schematic diagram of SPECT imaging system.

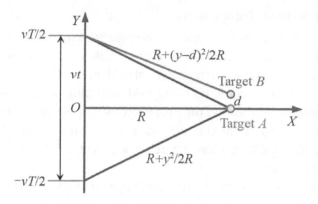

FIGURE 6.4   Schematic diagram of non-focus synthetic aperture radar imaging.

A schematic diagram of non-focus *synthetic aperture radar* (SAR) imaging is shown in Figure 6.4.

In SAR imaging, the radar is moving and the target is not moving (the relative movement between them is used to generate a larger relative aperture to improve the lateral resolution). Let v be the moving speed of the radar (carrier) along the Y-axis, T be the effective accumulation time, and λ be the wavelength of the radio wave. Considering the distribution of two point targets along the direction of radar movement, Target A is located on the center line (X-axis) of the radar aperture front view (the radar beam direction is perpendicular to the direction of radar movement), and the displacement between Target B and Target A is d. The shortest distance between the radar and Target A is R, which is defined as time zero at this moment, $t = 0$. Set the change in distance before and after $t = 0$ as δR. If $R \gg \delta R$, then $\delta R = (y - d)^2/2R$. The two-way (radio wave propagating back and forth between the antenna and the target) of the echo signal at Target A leads the phase is

$$\theta_A(t) = -\frac{4\pi y^2}{2R\lambda} = -\frac{4\pi}{\lambda}\frac{v^2 t^2}{2R} \tag{6.6}$$

The two-way of the echo signal at Target B leads the phase is

$$\theta_B(t,d) = -\frac{4\pi}{\lambda}\frac{(vt-d)^2}{2R} \tag{6.7}$$

If the frequency of the transmitted signal is high enough, the echo signal can be considered continuous, and the time period $-T/2 \sim T/2$ can be integrated to process the echo signal $\exp[j\theta_B(t, d)]$. Further, suppose it is uniform emission within the integration time, then the echo response at Target B is

$$E(d) = \int_{-T/2}^{T/2} \exp\left[-\frac{j4\pi}{2R\lambda}(vt-d)^2\right]dt \tag{6.8}$$

6.1.4 Electrical Impedance Tomography

Electrical impedance tomography (EIT) uses AC electric fields to excite objects. This method is more sensitive to changes in conductance or reactance. By injecting a low-frequency current into the object and measuring the electric potential field on the surface of the object (calculate the boundary voltage of the electric potential field according to the conductivity distribution using finite element) and then use the image reconstruction algorithm to reconstruct the distribution or change image of the conductance and reactance of the internal region of the object (i.e., the conductivity distribution of the electric potential field is estimated based on the boundary measurement value).

Currently, EIT is the only method that can image conductance. Because different biological tissues or organs have different electrical impedance characteristics under different physiological and pathological conditions, EIT images can reflect the pathological and physiological information carried by the tissues or organs. EIT does not use nuclide or radiation, only requires a little of current, is non-toxic and harmless, and can be used as a non-damage detection technology for long-term, continuous image monitoring of patients.

The working modes of commonly used EIT systems are divided into two categories: injection current type and induced current type. The injection current EIT uses injection excitation and measurement technology to measure the impedance distribution information of the imaging region: a constant AC excitation is applied to the driving electrode on the surface of the object, and the equivalent impedance of the imaging region reflects the amplitude of the voltage signal measured on the different measuring electrodes value and phase. Using demodulation technology can demodulate part of the information in the measured signal that reflects the impedance distribution of the imaging region. The induced current EIT uses an excitation coil that is not in contact with the surface of the object for AC excitation to generate an induced current (eddy current) inside the imaging target. The induced current field is detected from the surface, and the corresponding impedance distribution or change inside the object is calculated.

Figure 6.5 shows two images reconstructed by injection current EIT, where the gray scale everywhere depends on the value of electrical impedance.

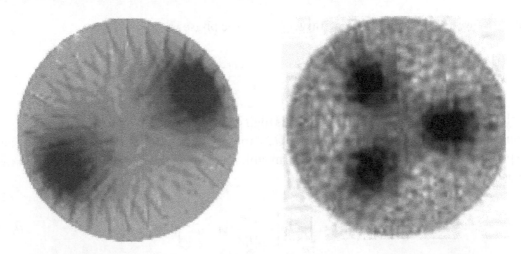

FIGURE 6.5   Result images of electrical impedance tomography.

From a mathematical point of view, EIT is similar to various CTs because they all need to process external data to obtain images that reflect the internal structure of the object, and the imaging is often performed on a 2-D cross-section through the object. The difference is that EIT uses the diffusion of current to obtain the distribution of conductance, which is different from CT. EIT has some attractive features, including safety and simplicity of the technology used for EIT imaging. However, compared with CT, PET, SPECT, MRI, and other technologies, the resolution of EIT is poor. The resolution of EIT depends on the number of electrodes, but the number of electrodes that can simultaneously contact an object is often limited. The main disadvantage of the EIT imaging method stems from its nonlinear ill-conditioned problem. If the measurement has a small error, it may cause a great influence on the calculation of the conductance.

6.1.5 Magnetic Resonance Imaging

Magnetic resonance imaging (MRI) was called *nuclear magnetic resonance* (NMR) in the early days. Its working principle is as follows. Hydrogen nuclei and other nuclei with an odd number of protons or neutrons contain protons with a certain magnetic momentum or spin. If they are placed in a magnetic field, they will make precession in the magnetic field like a whipping top in the earth's gravitational field. Under normal circumstances, protons are randomly arranged in a magnetic field. When a resonance field signal of appropriate strength and frequency acts on an object, the protons absorb energy and turn to the direction that intersects the magnetic field. If the resonance field signal is removed at this time, the energy absorbed by the proton will be released and can be detected by the receiver. Based on the detected signal, the density of protons can be determined. By controlling the intensity of the resonance field signal and the magnetic field used, a signal along a line passing through the object can be detected every time. In other words, the detected signal is the integral of the MRI signal along a straight line.

Each MRI imaging system includes a magnetic field subsystem, a transmitting/receiving subsystem, a computer image reconstruction subsystem, and a display subsystem. In the magnetic field subsystem, there are a longitudinal core magnetic field, a non-uniform magnetic field, and a transverse radio frequency magnetic field. Under their combined action, the imaging object will generate a magnetic resonance signal, which can be measured by the detection coil in the detection device. Assuming that the action time of the radio frequency field is much shorter than the transverse and longitudinal relaxation time constants of the spin nuclei, the magnetic resonance signal can be represented as

$$S(t) = \iiint\limits_{V} R(x,y,z) f(x,y,z) \exp\left[j\theta \int_{0}^{t} w(x,y,z,\tau)\mathrm{d}\tau \right] \mathrm{d}x\,\mathrm{d}y\,\mathrm{d}z \qquad (6.9)$$

In the equation, $R(x, y, z)$ is the nuclear spin density distribution function weighted by physical parameters such as the transverse and longitudinal relaxation time constants; $f(x, y, z)$ is the sensitivity function of the radio frequency receiving coil for magnetic resonance signals distribution; $w(x, y, z, t)$ is the function of the spatial distribution of Larmor frequency of nuclear spin precession with time, where $w(x, y, z, t) = g[B_0 + B(x, y, z, t)]$, g

is the gyromagnetic ratio of the nucleus, B_0 is the main magnetic field strength, $B(x, y, z, t)$ is the time-varying non-uniform magnetic field; V is the volume of space in which the imaging object is located.

MRI reconstructs the spin density distribution function of the object based on the magnetic resonance signal generated by the time-varying non-uniform magnetic field and the radio frequency magnetic field and their excitation. Mathematically, MRI is regarded as an inverse problem, that is, solving the integral Equation (6.9) of $R(x, y, z)$ under the conditions of known $S(t)$, $w(x, y, z, t)$, and $f(x, y, z)$. The earliest proposed MRI method designed the non-uniform magnetic field as a linear gradient magnetic field, thereby simplifying the integral Equation (6.9) to the Radon transform (see Section 6.2) and then reconstructing the spin density image of the object by solving the Radon inverse transform.

6.2 PRINCIPLES OF RECONSTRUCTION FROM PROJECTION

Although there are many ways of reconstruction from projection, the basic models and reconstruction principles they are based on are relatively similar.

6.2.1 Basic Model

A simple *model of image reconstruction from projection* is shown in Figure 6.6. Here, the image $f(x, y)$ is used to represent the distribution of a certain physical quantity (to be measured) on the 2-D plane. The material to be reconstructed by projection is limited to an infinitely thin plane so that the gray value of the reconstructed image at any point is proportional to the relative linear attenuation coefficient inherent in the point where the ray is projected.

For the convenience of discussion (and also in line with the actual situation), let $f(x, y)$ be 0 outside a circle Q centered on the origin of the coordinate system. Now consider that a straight line from the emission source to the receiver intersects $f(x, y)$ in Q on the plane. This line can be determined by two parameters: (i) The distance s from the origin; (ii) The angle θ between it and the Y-axis. If $g(s, \theta)$ is used to denote the integral of $f(x, y)$ along a straight line (s, θ), with the help of coordinate transformation, it can get

$$g(s,\theta)= \int_{(s,\theta)} f(x,y)\mathrm{d}t = \int_{(s,\theta)} f(s\cos\theta-t\sin\theta,\ s\sin\theta+t\cos\theta)\ \mathrm{d}t \qquad (6.10)$$

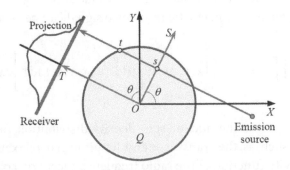

FIGURE 6.6   Schematic diagram of reconstruction from projection.

This integral is the projection of $f(x, y)$ along the t direction, where the integral limit depends on s, θ, and Q. When the radius of Q is 1, set the upper and lower limits of the integral to t and $-t$ respectively, then

$$t(s) = \sqrt{1 - s^2} \qquad |s| \leq 1 \tag{6.11}$$

If the line (s, θ) falls outside Q (does not intersect with Q), then

$$g(s, \theta) = 0 \qquad |s| > 1 \tag{6.12}$$

It can be seen that the integral equation represented by Equation (6.10) is defined and computable.

In the actual projection reconstruction environment, $f(x, y)$ is used to denote the object to be reconstructed, and the integral path determined by (s, θ) corresponds to a ray from the emitter to the receiver. The integral measurement value obtained by the receiver is $g(s, \theta)$. Under these definitions, reconstruction from projection can be described as: for a given $g(s, \theta)$, it is needed to determine $f(x, y)$. Mathematically, it is to solve the integral Equation (6.10).

It should be noted that a function $f(x, y)$ defined in a finite interval can be uniquely determined by an infinite number of projections but not necessarily uniquely determined by any finite number of projections (Herman 1980).

6.2.2 Radon Transform

The problem of solving the integral Equation (6.10) can be made with the help of *Radon transform*. Refer to Figure 6.7, the Radon transform $R_f(s, \theta)$ of $f(x, y)$ is defined as the line integral along line l (the line equation is $s = x\cos\theta + y\sin\theta$):

$$R_f(s, \theta) = \int_{-\infty}^{\infty} f(x, y) \, dl = \int_{-\infty}^{\infty} \int_{-\infty}^{\infty} f(x, y) \delta(s - x\cos\theta - y\sin\theta) \, dx \, dy \tag{6.13}$$

It can be proved that the 2-D Fourier transform of $f(x, y)$ is equivalent to the result of Radon transform and then 1-D Fourier transform of $f(x, y)$ (Zhang 2009). That is (where

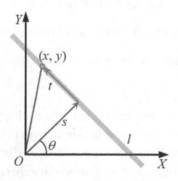

FIGURE 6.7 The coordinate system used to define the Radon transform.

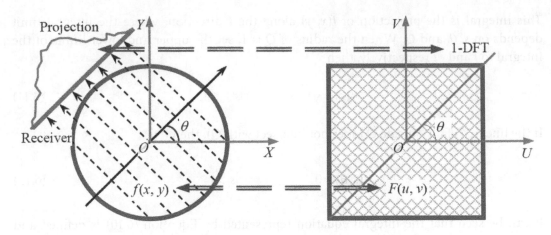

FIGURE 6.8   Schematic diagram of the central layer theorem.

$\mathcal{R}$ represents the Radon transform, $\mathcal{F}$ represents the Fourier transform, and the number in the subscript brackets represents the dimensionality of the transform)

$$\mathcal{F}_{(1)}\{\mathcal{R}[f(x,y)]\}=\mathcal{F}_{(1)}\{R_f(s,\theta)\}=\mathcal{F}_{(2)}[f(x,y)]=F(u,v) \qquad (6.14)$$

The equation above is also called the *central layer theorem*, that is, the 1-D Fourier transform of the projection result of $f(x, y)$ along a fixed angle corresponds to a section/ layer of the 2-D Fourier transform of $f(x, y)$ along the equal angle, as shown in Figure 6.8.

6.3 INVERSE FOURIER TRANSFORM RECONSTRUCTION

Inverse Fourier transform reconstruction is a transform-based reconstruction method, which is the first method to be applied in reconstruction from projection.

6.3.1 The Basic Steps and Definitions

The transform reconstruction method mainly includes the following three steps:

1. Establish a mathematical model in which the known quantity and the unknown quantity are functions of continuous real numbers.

2. Using the inverse transform formula to solve the unknown quantity.

3. Adjust the inverse transform formula to meet the needs of discrete and noisy applications.

Note that in step (2) above, there can theoretically be multiple equivalent formulas to solve the unknown quantity. In step (3), since different approximations can be used for discretization, the theoretically equivalent methods will have different results when applied to actual data. In specific applications, the measured data corresponds to the estimated value $g(s, \theta)$ at many discrete points (s, θ), and the reconstructed image is also a discrete 2-D array.

In the following discussion, first consider the case of uniform sampling on both s and θ. Suppose the projection is performed on N angles with a difference of $\Delta\theta$, and M ray measurements with a spacing of Δs are used in each direction (corresponding to a certain projection angle), and the integers M^+ and M^- are defined as

$$
\left\{
\begin{array}{ll}
M^+ = (M-1)/2 & \\
& M \text{ is odd} \\
M^- = -(M-1)/2 & \\
& \\
M^+ = (M/2) - 1 & \\
& M \text{ is even} \\
M^- = -M/2 &
\end{array}
\right.
\tag{6.15}
$$

Refer to the model in Figure 6.6, in order to ensure that a series of rays $\{(m\Delta s, n\Delta\theta): M^- \leq m \leq M^+, 1 \leq n \leq N\}$ cover the unit circle Q, it is needed to choose $\Delta\theta = \pi/N$ and $\Delta s = 1/M^+$. At this time, $g(m\Delta s, n\Delta\theta)$ is the ray data of parallel projection. Suppose that the image region is covered by a right-angled grid, where K^+ and K^- (K is the number of points in the X direction) are defined in a similar way to Equation (6.15), and L^+ and L^- (L is the number of points in the Y direction) are also defined in a similar way to Equation (6.15). According to these definitions, a reconstruction algorithm is to estimate $f(k\Delta x, l\Delta y)$ at $K \times L$ sampling points through $M \times N$ measured values $g(m\Delta s, n\Delta\theta)$.

6.3.2 Fourier Transform Projection Theorem

The basis of the transformation method is the *Fourier transform projection theorem*. Let $G(w, \theta)$ be the (1-D) Fourier transform of $g(s, \theta)$ corresponding to the first variable s, namely

$$
G(w,\theta) = \int_{(s,\theta)} g(s,\theta) \exp\left[-j2\pi ws\right] ds
\tag{6.16}
$$

$F(u, v)$ is the 2-D Fourier transform of $f(x, y)$:

$$
F(u,v) = \iint_Q f(x,y) \exp\left[-j2\pi(xu+yv)\right] dx dy
\tag{6.17}
$$

Then, the following Fourier transform projection theorem can be proved:

$$
G(w,\theta) = F(w\cos\theta, w\sin\theta)
\tag{6.18}
$$

That is, the Fourier transform of $f(x, y)$ projected at the angle θ is equal to the value of the Fourier transform of $f(x, y)$ in the Fourier space (w, θ). In other words, the Fourier transform of $f(x, y)$ projected on a straight line at an angle of θ with the X-axis is a cross-section of the Fourier transform of $f(x, y)$ at the orientation angle θ.

The above results were also involved in the previous discussion of the Radon transform (see Sub-section 6.2.2). The 1-D Fourier transform of the projection can obtain the polar

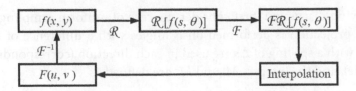

FIGURE 6.9   Flowchart of direct inverse Fourier transform reconstruction.

coordinate grid defined in Fourier space. In this way, interpolation is needed to obtain $F(u, v)$ in the rectangular coordinate system, and then $f(x, y)$ can be obtained through 2-D inverse Fourier transform. The whole process can be seen in Figure 6.9, where $\mathcal{R}$ stands for Radon transform, $\mathcal{F}$ stands for Fourier transform, and $\mathcal{F}^{-1}$ stands for inverse Fourier transform.

Although this method looks the simplest and most intuitive, it requires interpolation and 2-D inverse Fourier transform, so the amount of calculation will be quite large. In addition, due to the need to use 2-D transformation, the image cannot be reconstructed according to the obtained partial projection data, and the image must be reconstructed after all the projection data are obtained.

6.3.3 Model Reconstruction

To test the correctness of the reconstruction formula and grasp the influence of each parameter in the reconstruction algorithm on the reconstruction effect, people often design and synthesize various *phantom model* images for experiments. A commonly used experimental image is the Shepp-Logan head model image (Shepp and Logan 1974). Figure 6.10 shows an improved result image (size 115×115, 256 gray levels), and the parameters of each part

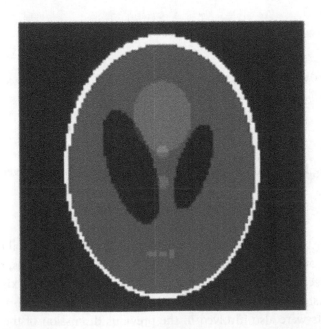

FIGURE 6.10   Improved Shepp-Logan head model image.

TABLE 6.1   Parameters of the Improved Shepp-Logan Head Model Image

Serial Number of Ellipses	X-axis Center Coordinate	Y-axis Center Coordinate	Half-Length of Short-Axis	Half-Length of Long-Axis	Angle between Y-axis and Long-Axis	Relative Density
A (Big ellipse outside)	0.0000	0.0000	0.6900	0.9200	0.00	1.0000
B (Big ellipse inside)	0.0000	−0.0184	0.6624	0.8740	0.00	−0.9800
C (Right inclined ellipse)	0.2200	0.0000	0.1100	0.3100	−18.00	−0.2000
D (Left inclined ellipse)	−0.2200	0.0000	0.1600	0.4100	18.00	−0.2000
E (Top big ellipse)	0.0000	0.3500	0.2100	0.2500	0.00	0.1000
F (Middle-high ellipse)	0.0000	0.1000	0.0460	0.0460	0.00	0.1000
G (Middle-low ellipse)	0.0000	−0.1000	0.0460	0.0460	0.00	0.1000
H (Bottom-left ellipse)	−0.0800	−0.6050	0.0460	0.0230	0.00	0.1000
I (Bottom-middle ellipse)	0.0000	−0.6060	0.0230	0.0230	0.00	0.1000
J (Bottom-right ellipse)	0.0600	−0.6050	0.0230	0.0460	0.00	0.1000

(suppose the side length of the image is 1, the coordinate origin is at the center of the picture) are listed in Table 6.1 (Toft 1996). The contrast of the original Shepp-Logan image is relatively small, and the small ellipse in the picture is not clear. The improved image adjusts the density of each ellipse so that the contrast of each part is enhanced, and the visual effect is better.

In actual reconstruction, it is necessary to obtain enough projections in many directions to reconstruct the spatial image. Figure 6.11 shows an example of a set of results obtained by the inverse Fourier transform reconstruction method with the help of the model image in Figure 6.10. Among them, from Figure 6.11a–e are the 2-D frequency space images obtained by performing 4 projections, 8 projections, 16 projections, 32 projections, and 64 projections of Figure 6.10 along the circumference of the equal angle. It can be seen from Figure 6.11 that the radioactivity distribution in the frequency space gradually gathers toward the center with the increase of the number of projections, which will lead to a relatively lack of high-frequency information, and the error when interpolating into the rectangular coordinate system is also relatively large.

Figure 6.12a–e are the reconstruction result images corresponding to Figure 6.11a–e in sequence. It can be seen from Figure 6.12 that the quality of the reconstructed image (including the effects of unevenness and blurring) has improved with the increase of the number of projections, but it is still not very clear (this is limited by the inverse Fourier transform reconstruction method used). In addition, the number of projections in practical applications is always limited.

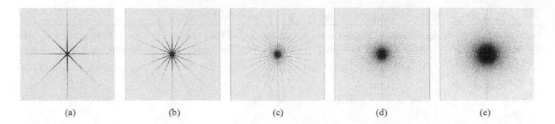

FIGURE 6.11 The 2-D frequency space image obtained using the inverse Fourier transform reconstruction; (a) the 2-D frequency space image obtained by performing 4 projections; (b) the 2-D frequency space image obtained by performing 8 projections; (c) the 2-D frequency space image obtained by performing 16 projections; (d) the 2-D frequency space image obtained by performing 32 projections; (e) the 2-D frequency space image obtained by performing 64 projections.

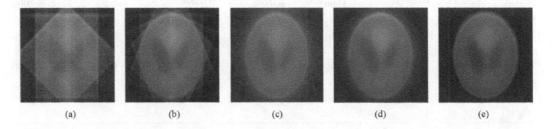

FIGURE 6.12 The result of inverse Fourier transform reconstruction; (a) the reconstruction result image corresponding to Figure 6.11a; (b) the reconstruction result image corresponding to Figure 6.11b; (c) the reconstruction result image corresponding to Figure 6.11c; (d) the reconstruction result image corresponding to Figure 6.11d; (e) the reconstruction result image corresponding to Figure 6.11e.

6.4 BACK-PROJECTION RECONSTRUCTION

Back-projection reconstruction is also a kind of analytical reconstruction method, which is currently the most used in actual reconstruction from projection.

6.4.1 Principles of Back-Projection Reconstruction

The principle of *back-projection* is to reverse the projections obtained from various directions to various positions in that direction. If such a back-projection is performed on each of the multiple projection directions and the results are superimposed, it is possible to establish a corresponding distribution on the plane. Let's take a look at Figure 6.13 first. Figure 6.13a shows the schematic diagrams of horizontal projection and horizontal back-projection, respectively. During projection, the emitter emits uniform rays. Due to the different density of the penetrating object, the responses obtained by each receiver are different; the back-projection returns the responses uniformly in the projection direction. Figure 6.13b gives a schematic diagram of vertical projection and vertical back-projection, respectively, which have a similar effect as the horizontal effect.

Looking at Figure 6.14 now, Figure 6.14a shows the object density distribution; Figure 6.14b and c correspond to the horizontal and vertical back-projection results, respectively; Figure 6.14d shows the effect of superimposing the horizontal and vertical back-projections, Figure 6.14e shows the effect of superimposing more back-projection

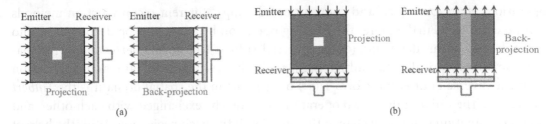

(a)   (b)

FIGURE 6.13 Projection and back-projection; (a) the schematic diagrams of horizontal projection and horizontal back-projection; (b) the schematic diagrams of vertical projection and vertical back-projection.

results. From this series of figures, it can be seen that as the back-projection results continue to be superimposed, it will more and more accurately reflect the relative density distribution of the original object.

Strictly, back-projection is not the inverse operation of projection. If the image is represented as a vector f and the result of the projection is represented as a vector g, then the projection matrix A satisfies $g = Af$. The inverse projection matrix B is the companion matrix of the projection matrix A (when A is a real square matrix, B is its transpose A^T).

Back-projection can form an image that is closer to the physical strength of the original object from the projection data obtained from different directions but is somewhat blurry than the desired image. This is because there is a density distribution in the 2-D Fourier domain (i.e., (u, v) plane) that is inversely proportional to $|w| = (u^2 + v^2)^{1/2}$. To correct this density distribution, the 1-D Fourier transform $G(w, \theta)$ of the projection data $g(s, \theta)$ can be filtered, that is, the projection data is multiplied by $|w| = (u^2 + v^2)^{1/2}$ in the frequency domain. This operation is called ramp-filtering in projection reconstruction. Back-projecting the filtered data can get a more accurate reconstructed image.

The two main operations of reconstruction are *filtering* and *back-projection*. Because multiplication in the frequency domain is equivalent to convolution in the spatial domain, filtering in the frequency domain (w domain) can also be achieved by *convolution* in the spatial domain (s domain). Therefore, it can also be said that the two main operations of reconstruction are convolution and back-projection. In addition, the order of filtering/convolution and back-projection can also be reversed. By changing the order of different

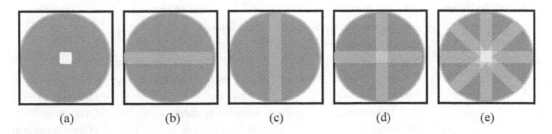

(a)   (b)   (c)   (d)   (e)

FIGURE 6.14 Superposition result of back-projections; (a) the object density distribution; (b) the horizontal back-projection result; (c) the vertical back-projection result; (d) the effect of superimposing the horizontal and vertical back-projections; (e) the effect of superimposing more back-projection results.

operations (back-projection and convolution/filtering), different reconstruction methods can be obtained. Furthermore, the filtering operation here can also be decomposed into two sub-operations: derivation (operation) and Hilbert transform. *Derivation* in the spatial domain is equivalent to multiplying $j2\pi w$ in the frequency domain, and convolution with the inverse Fourier transform $1/(\pi s)$ of $-j\mathrm{sgn}(w)$ in the spatial domain is the *Hilbert transform*. The order of these two operations can also be exchanged with each other, and their combination can also exchange the order with the back-projection. With the help of these sequence operations, a variety of reconstruction methods with different characteristics and suitable for different purposes can be obtained, as shown in Table 6.2 (Zeng 2009).

6.4.2 Convolutional Back-Projection Reconstruction

Let's first introduce the convolutional back-projection reconstruction method in detail, which is the most typical method in the back-projection reconstruction.

6.4.2.1 Continuous Formula Derivation

The formula of the *convolutional back-projection reconstruction* method can also be derived from the Fourier transform projection theorem. However, here the data obtained by each projection is diffused back to the image against the image acquisition direction, and there is no need to store the complex frequency space map like the inverse Fourier transform method.

First, calculate the inverse transformation of Equation (6.18) in the polar coordinate system:

$$f(x,y) = \int_0^{\pi} \int_{-\infty}^{\infty} G(w,\theta)\exp\left[j2\pi w\left(x\cos\theta + y\sin\theta\right)\right]|w|\,dw\,d\theta \tag{6.19}$$

If $G(w, \theta)$ is substituted into Equation (6.16), the formula of $f(x, y)$ reconstructed from $g(s, \theta)$ is obtained. In practical applications, as in the inverse Fourier transform reconstruction method, a window W needs to be introduced in the Fourier space. According to the sampling theorem, $G(w, \theta)$ can only be estimated when the bandwidth is limited as $|w| < 1/(2\Delta s)$. If the following is defined ($s = x\cos\theta + y\sin\theta$):

TABLE 6.2   List of Steps of Various Back-Projection Reconstruction Methods

Method Order Number	First Step	Second Step	Third Step
1	(Spatial domain) Convolution	Back-projection	—
2	(Frequency domain) Filtering	Back-projection	—
3	Back-projection	(Spatial domain) Convolution	—
4	Back-projection	(Frequency domain) Filtering	—
5	Back-projection	Derivation	Hilbert transform
6	Back-projection	Hilbert transform	Derivation
7	Derivation	Back-projection	Hilbert transform
8	Derivation	Hilbert transform	Back-projection
9	Hilbert transform	Back-projection	Derivation
10	Hilbert transform	Derivation	Back-projection

$$h(s) = \int_{-1/(2\Delta s)}^{1/(2\Delta s)} |w| W(w) \exp[j2\pi ws] \, dw \tag{6.20}$$

Then substituting Equation (6.19) and exchanging the order of integration of s and w can get a windowed image:

$$f_W(x,y) = \int_0^\pi \int_{-1/(2\Delta s)}^{1/(2\Delta s)} G(w,\theta) W(w) \exp[j2\pi w(x\cos\theta + y\sin\theta)] |w| \, dw \, d\theta$$

$$= \int_0^\pi \int_{-1}^1 g(s,\theta) h(x\cos\theta + y\sin\theta - s) \, ds \, d\theta \tag{6.21}$$

It can also be done by decomposing the above equation into the following two sequences of operations:

$$g'(s',\theta) = \int_{-1}^1 g(s,\theta) h(s'-s) \, ds \tag{6.22}$$

$$f_W(x,y) = \int_0^\pi g'(x\cos\theta + y\sin\theta, \theta) \, d\theta \tag{6.23}$$

In the equations, $g'(s', \theta)$ is the convolution result of the projection of $f(x, y)$ in the direction of θ angle and $h(s)$, which can be called the projection convolved in the direction of angle θ, and $h(s)$ is called the convolution function. The process represented by Equation (6.22) is a convolution process, and the process represented by Equation (6.23) is called *back-projection* process, so the process of convolution back-projection reconstruction is shown in Figure 6.15, where $\mathcal{R}$ stands for Radon transform. Because the parameter in $g'(\cdot)$ is the parameter of a ray passing through (x, y) at an angle of θ, so $f_W(x, y)$ is the integration of the projection of the convolution result of all rays passing through (x, y).

6.4.2.2 Discrete Calculation

In practice, the back-projection process represented by Equation (6.23) can be approximated by the following equation:

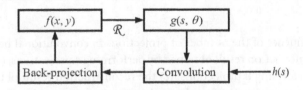

FIGURE 6.15 Convolutional back-projection reconstruction flowchart.

$$f_W\left(k\Delta x, l\Delta y\right) \approx \Delta\theta \sum_{n=1}^{N} g'\left(k\Delta x \cos\theta_n + l\Delta y \sin\theta_n, \theta_n\right) \qquad (6.24)$$

For each θ_n, $g'(s', \theta_n)$ needs to be calculated for $K \times L$ values of s'. Because K and L are generally very large, the workload would be very large if they are directly calculated. A practical method is to calculate $g'(m\Delta s, \theta_n)$ for $M^- \leq m \leq M^+$, and then obtain $K \times L$ values of g' by interpolation based on M values of g'. The convolution of Equation (6.22) is completed in the discrete domain by two steps: first, a discrete convolution, and the result is represented by g'_C; then, an interpolation, and the result is represented by g'_I. They are respectively given by the following two equations:

$$g'_C\left(m'\Delta s, \theta_n\right) \approx \Delta s \sum_{m=M^-}^{M^+} g(m\Delta s, \theta_n)\, h\left[(m'-m)\Delta s\right] \qquad (6.25)$$

$$g'_I\left(s', \theta_n\right) \approx \Delta s \sum_{n=1}^{N} g'_C\left(m\Delta s, \theta_n\right) I(s' - m\Delta s) \qquad (6.26)$$

where $I(\bullet)$ is an interpolation function.

Figure 6.16 shows a set of examples obtained by using the convolutional back-projection reconstruction method for the model image in Figure 6.10. Figure 6.16a–e are the reconstruction results obtained by performing 4 projections, 8 projections, 16 projections, 32 projections, and 64 projections, respectively, on the equal angle along the circumference of Figure 6.10. It can be seen from these figures that when the number of projections is relatively small, there are obvious bright lines along the projection direction in the reconstructed image, which shows the result of influence of the number of projections in convolutional back-projection reconstruction. The contrast of each image in Figure 6.16 is stronger and clearer than that of each corresponding image in Figure 6.12.

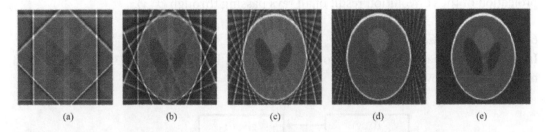

(a)   (b)   (c)   (d)   (e)

FIGURE 6.16 The influence of the number of projections in convolutional back-projection reconstruction; (a) the reconstruction result obtained by performing 4 projections; (b) the reconstruction result obtained by performing 8 projections; (c) the reconstruction result obtained by performing 16 projections; (d) the reconstruction result obtained by performing 32 projections; (e) the reconstruction result obtained by performing 64 projections.

6.4.2.3 Reconstruction from Fan-Beam Projection

In practical applications, it is often necessary to shorten the projection time as much as possible, so as to reduce the image distortion caused by the movement of the object during the projection and the harm to the patient. *Fan-beam projection* is an effective method. There are two main types of geometric measurement commonly used, which correspond to the third-generation CT system and the fourth-generation CT system in Figure 6.1c and d, respectively.

To reconstruct in the case of fan-beam projection, the central projection can be transformed into parallel projection and then the technology for parallel projection reconstruction can be used in reconstruction. The following discusses how to adjust the parallel projection reconstruction formula derived above for the fan-beam projection situation when the receivers are arranged at equal angular intervals on an arc.

As shown in Figure 6.17, the ray specified by (s, θ) in the previous discussion can be regarded as one of the rays specified by (α, β) here, where α is the scatter angle between the source ray and the center ray, β is the angle between the line connecting the source and the coordinate origin with the Y-axis, which determines the emitting direction of the source. The line integral $g(s, \theta)$ is now denoted as $p(\alpha,\beta)$ (for $|s| < D$, D is the distance from the source to the origin). It is assumed that the source is outside the object, so for all $|\alpha| > \delta$, it has $p(\alpha,\beta) = 0$, where δ is the angle between the ray tangent to the object and the center ray. From Figure 6.17, the following set of relationships can be obtained:

$$s = D\sin\alpha \tag{6.27}$$

$$\theta = \alpha + \beta \tag{6.28}$$

$$g(s,\theta) = p(\alpha,\beta) \tag{6.29}$$

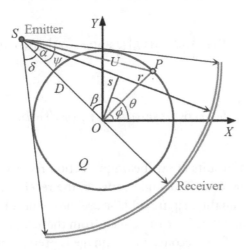

FIGURE 6.17   Schematic diagram of fan-beam projection.

In addition, suppose U is the distance from the source to the point P to be reconstructed (the position of P can be represented by r and ϕ), and ψ is the angle between the line from the source to P and the central emission line, as shown in the figure:

$$U^2 = \left[r\cos(\beta-\phi)\right]^2 + \left[D+r\sin(\beta-\phi)\right]^2 \tag{6.30}$$

$$\psi = \arctan\left[\frac{r\cos(\beta-\phi)}{D+r\sin(\beta-\phi)}\right] \tag{6.31}$$

So it can get

$$r\cos(\theta-\phi)-s = U\sin(\psi-a) \tag{6.32}$$

Following Equations (6.27)– (6.32), then Equation (6.21) can be written as

$$f_W(r\cos\phi, r\sin\phi) = \frac{1}{2}\int_{-\infty}^{\infty}\int_{-\infty}^{\infty}\int_{0}^{2\pi} g(s,\theta)\exp\{j2\pi w[r\cos(\theta-\phi)-s]\}W(w)|w|\,d\theta\,ds\,dw \tag{6.33}$$

Replace (s, θ) with (α, β):

$$f_W(r\cos\phi, r\sin\phi) = \frac{D}{2}\int_{-\infty}^{\infty}\int_{-\delta}^{\delta}\int_{-\alpha}^{2\pi-\alpha} p(\alpha,\beta)\cos\alpha\exp\left[j2\pi wU\sin(\psi-\alpha)\right]W(w)|w|\,d\beta\,d\alpha\,dw \tag{6.34}$$

Substituting Equation (6.20) in it, and changing the upper and lower limits of the integral of β to 2π and 0, respectively, Equation (6.34) can be decomposed in a similar way to the decomposition of Equation (6.21) into Equations (6.22) and (6.23) with two steps:

$$p(\psi,\beta) = \int_{-\delta}^{\delta} p(\alpha,\beta)\,h\left[U\sin(\psi-\alpha)\right]\cos\alpha\;d\alpha \tag{6.35}$$

$$f_W(r\cos\phi, r\sin\phi) = \frac{D}{2}\int_{0}^{2\pi} p(\psi,\beta)\,d\beta. \tag{6.36}$$

Figure 6.18 shows a set of results of fan-beam projection reconstruction with the help of the model image in Figure 6.10. The angle between the receivers in fan-beam projection affects the reconstruction quality. Figure 6.18a–e are the results obtained when the interval angle is 5°, 1°, 0.5°, 0.1°, and 0.05°. It can be seen from these figures that when the angle is less than 0.5°, the quality of the reconstructed image is pretty well, and the improvement of further reducing the angle is not obvious.

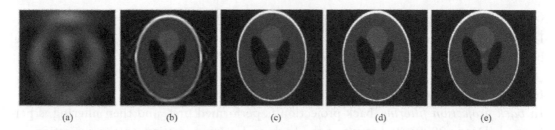

(a)   (b)   (c)   (d)   (e)

FIGURE 6.18 The influence of the interval angle in fan-beam convolutional back-projection reconstruction; (a) the result obtained when the interval angle is 5°; (b) the result obtained when the interval angle is 1°; (c) the result obtained when the interval angle is 0.5°; (d) the result obtained when the interval angle is 0.1°; (e) the result obtained when the interval angle is 0.05°.

6.4.2.4 Comparison of Inverse Fourier Transform Reconstruction Method and Convolutional Back-Projection Reconstruction Method

Both the inverse Fourier transform reconstruction method and the convolutional back-projection reconstruction method are based on the Fourier transform projection theorem. The difference is that when deriving the inverse Fourier transform reconstruction equation, the 2-D inverse Fourier transform is represented in rectangular coordinates; when deriving the convolutional back-projection reconstruction equation, the 2-D inverse Fourier transform is represented in polar coordinates. Although they seem to have the same stem, the inverse Fourier transform reconstruction method is rarely used in practice, while the convolutional back-projection reconstruction method is mostly practical. The two main reasons are as follows.

1. The basic algorithm of convolutional back-projection reconstruction is easy to implement with software and hardware, and can reconstruct accurate and clear images with high data quality. The inverse Fourier transform reconstruction method requires 2-D interpolation, so it is not easy to implement and the reconstructed image quality is poor. However, the inverse Fourier transform reconstruction method requires a relatively small amount of calculation, so it is more attractive when the amount of data and the image size are large. In the research of radio astronomy, the inverse Fourier transform reconstruction method has been widely used. This is because the measured data directly corresponds to the Fourier transform sampling points of the target spatial distribution. In addition, in MRI, the Fourier transform of the projection can be directly measured, so the inverse Fourier transform reconstruction method can be used directly.

2. The convolutional back-projection reconstruction equation derived during parallel projection can be modified in different ways to apply to the case of fan-beam projection (Equation (6.34) gives an example). However, the inverse Fourier transform reconstruction equation derived during parallel projection cannot be suitably modified for fan-beam projection while maintaining the original efficiency. At this time, it is necessary to use 2-D interpolation to reorganize the fan-beam projection data in the projection space to reconstruct the image using the parallel projection algorithm (Lewitt 1983).

6.4.3 Other Back-Projection Reconstruction Methods

In addition to the convolution back-projection reconstruction method, two other typical back-projection methods are introduced below.

6.4.3.1 Back-Projection Filtering

In *back-projection filtering*, back-projection is performed first, and then filtering is performed (Deans 2000). The result of the back-projection operation on the projection is a blurred image, which is the result of 2-D convolution of the real image with the inverse Fourier transform of $1/w = 1/(u^2 + v^2)^{1/2}$. Let the blurred image obtained by back-projecting the projection result be

$$b(x, y) = \mathcal{B}\big[R_f(p, \theta)\big] = \int_0^\pi R_f\big(x\cos\theta + y\sin\theta, \theta\big)\mathrm{d}\theta \tag{6.37}$$

Then the real image and the blurred image are related by the following equation (using $\otimes_{(2)}$ to represent 2-D convolution):

$$b(x, y) = f(x, y) \otimes_{(2)} \frac{1}{z} = \int_{-\infty}^{\infty}\int_{-\infty}^{\infty} \frac{f(x', y')\mathrm{d}x'\mathrm{d}y'}{\Big[(x-x')^2 + (y-y')^2\Big]^{1/2}} \tag{6.38}$$

To derive the above equation, it can start from Equation (6.14):

$$\mathcal{R}\big[f(x, y)\big] = \mathcal{F}_{(1)}^{-1}\mathcal{F}_{(2)}\big[f(x, y)\big] \tag{6.39}$$

Then use back-projection to get

$$b(x, y) = \mathcal{B}\big[R_f(x, y)\big] = \mathcal{B}\mathcal{F}_{(1)}^{-1}\mathcal{F}_{(2)}\big[f(x, y)\big] \tag{6.40}$$

Note that the 1-D inverse Fourier transform in the above equation is an operation on radial variables in Fourier space, which means that $F(u, v)$ must first be converted to polar coordinates $F(w, \theta)$. The variable w is the radial variable in Fourier space, $w^2 = u^2 + v^2$. If the 1-D inverse Fourier transform of $F(w, \theta)$ is $f(s, \theta)$, then

$$b(x, y) = \mathcal{B}\big[f(s, \theta)\big] = \mathcal{B}\int_{-\infty}^{\infty} F(w, \theta)\exp(\mathrm{j}2\pi sw)\mathrm{d}w \tag{6.41}$$

If s is mapped to $x\cos\theta + y\sin\theta$, it gets

$$b(x, y) = \int_0^\pi \int_{-\infty}^{\infty} F(w, \theta)\exp\big[\mathrm{j}2\pi w\big(x\cos\theta + y\sin\theta\big)\big]\mathrm{d}w\,\mathrm{d}\theta$$

$$= \int_0^{2\pi}\int_{-\infty}^{\infty} \frac{1}{w} F(w, \theta)\exp\big[\mathrm{j}2\pi wz\cos(\theta - \phi)\big]w\,\mathrm{d}w\,\mathrm{d}\theta \tag{6.42}$$

Among them, $x = z\cos\phi$ and $y = z\sin\phi$ are replaced; radial integration is performed on the positive part of w. Note that the representation on the right side of the equation is a 2-D inverse Fourier transform:

$$b(x, y) = \mathcal{F}_{(2)}^{-1}\left\{|w|^{-1} F\right\} \tag{6.43}$$

According to the convolution theorem:

$$b(x, y) = \mathcal{F}_{(2)}^{-1}\left\{|w|^{-1}\right\} \otimes_{(2)} \mathcal{F}_{(2)}^{-1}\{F\} \tag{6.44}$$

Because the first term on the right side of the equal sign is equal to $|z|^{-1}$, Equation (6.38) is verified.

According to Equation (6.39), the reconstruction algorithm can be obtained by taking 2-D Fourier transform:

$$\mathcal{F}_{(2)}\left[b(x, y)\right] = |w|^{-1} F(u, v) \tag{6.45}$$

Or it can be written as

$$F(u, v) = |w| \mathcal{F}_{(2)}\left[b(x, y)\right] \tag{6.46}$$

Replace b with $\mathcal{B}[F(u, v)]$ and take the 2-D inverse Fourier transform of the above equation to get

$$f(x, y) = \mathcal{F}_{(2)}^{-1}\left\{|w| \mathcal{F}_{(2)}\mathcal{F}[F(u, v)]\right\} \tag{6.47}$$

This is the basic equation used to perform back-projection filtering on the projection to achieve reconstruction. Introduce 2-D window function:

$$G(u, v) = |w| W(u, v) \tag{6.48}$$

The Equation (6.47) can be written as

$$f(x, y) = \mathcal{F}_{(2)}^{-1}\left\{G(u, v)\mathcal{F}_{(2)}\mathcal{B}[F(u, v)]\right\} = \mathcal{F}_{(2)}^{-1}[G(u, v)] \otimes_{(2)} \mathcal{B}[F(u, v)] = g(x, y) \otimes_{(2)} b(x, y) \tag{6.49}$$

Once the window function is determined, $g(x, y)$ can be obtained by 2-D inverse Fourier transform, and then the reconstruction can be realized by 2-D convolution with the back-projection.

The processes of implementing the above algorithm in the space domain and in the frequency domain are shown in the left and right parts of Figure 6.19, respectively, where $\mathcal{R}$ stands for Radon transform, $\mathcal{F}$ stands for Fourier transform, and $\mathcal{B}$ stands for back-projection.

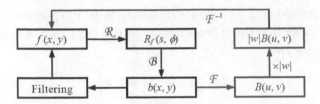

FIGURE 6.19   Back-projection filtering reconstruction flowchart.

Figure 6.20 shows an example of a set of images obtained by using back-projection filtering reconstruction, where the original image used is still shown as in Figure 6.10. In Figure 6.20, the reconstruction results obtained by performing 4 projections, 8 projections, 16 projections, 32 projections, and 64 projections at the equal angle along the circumference are shown in Figure 6.20a–e, respectively. The result is better than Figure 6.12.

6.4.3.2 Filtered Back-Projection

Filtered back-projection (FBP) is also called *back-projection of filtered projection*. The basic idea of this method is: the attenuation in each projection (caused by the object absorption) is related to the object structure along each projection line. If only one projection is used, the absorption at each position along the direction cannot be obtained, but the measurement of the absorption value can be evenly distributed in this direction. If such assignment can be made to each of the multiple directions, the absorption value can be superimposed to obtain the characteristic value reflecting the object structure. This reconstruction method is equivalent to collecting enough projections and performing Fourier space reconstruction, but the amount of calculation is much less.

The FBP reconstruction method can be regarded as an approximate computer realization method of Radon inverse transformation. It uses the inverse Fourier transform to convert the calculation of the w function into the calculation of the radial quantity s. The implementation processes of this algorithm in the space domain and in the frequency domain are shown in the left and right parts of Figure 6.21, respectively, where $\mathcal{R}$ stands for Radon transform, $\mathcal{F}$ stands for Fourier transform, and $\mathcal{B}$ stands for back-projection.

(a)   (b)   (c)   (d)   (e)

FIGURE 6.20   Reconstruction result of back-projection filtering reconstruction; (a) the reconstruction result obtained by performing 4 projections; (b) the reconstruction result obtained by performing 8 projections; (c) the reconstruction result obtained by performing 16 projections; (d) the reconstruction result obtained by performing 32 projections; (e) the reconstruction result obtained by performing 64 projections.

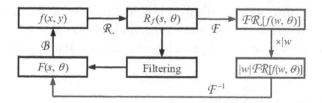

FIGURE 6.21   Flowchart of filtered back-projection reconstruction.

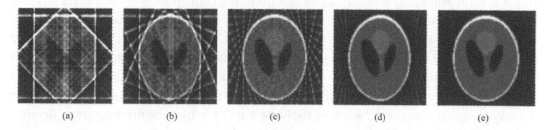

FIGURE 6.22   Reconstruction result of filtered back-projection reconstruction; (a) the reconstruction result obtained by performing 4 projections; (b) the reconstruction result obtained by performing 8 projections; (c) the reconstruction result obtained by performing 16 projections; (d) the reconstruction result obtained by performing 32 projections; (e) the reconstruction result obtained by performing 64 projections.

Figure 6.22 shows a set of examples obtained by the FBP reconstruction method with the help of the model image in Figure 6.10. Figure 6.22a–e are the reconstruction results obtained by performing 4 projections, 8 projections, 16 projections, 32 projections, and 64 projections on the equal angle along the circumference of Figure 6.10, respectively. It can be seen from these figures that the effect of FBP reconstruction and effect of convolutional back-projection reconstruction are relatively close, but the contrast of the reconstructed image for FBP reconstruction is stronger than that of convolutional back-projection reconstruction, especially when the number of projections is relatively small.

It needs to be pointed out that with the increase in the number of projections, the main structure of the image becomes more and more obvious, but the original density of the region is now no longer uniform and becomes gradually weaken from the center to the periphery. In addition, the edges of the original clearer regions have become a little blurry. The main reason here is that the projections from various directions in the FBP are more densely superimposed in the central region than in the surrounding regions. This effect is somewhat similar to that produced by an out-of-focus optical system, where the point spread function is proportional to the reciprocal of the frequency (or the distance from the center of frequency transformation).

6.5 ITERATIVE RECONSTRUCTION

The *iterative reconstruction* method is different from the previous methods based on inverse transform or back-projection. It is modeled in the discrete domain from the beginning, and the solution is iterative. This kind of method performs reconstruction in the space domain and is relatively easy to adjust to adapt to the new application environment.

It is often used in reconstruction with new physical principles and new data acquisition methods, as well as in 3-D reconstruction. With multiple iterations, images can be reconstructed from fewer projections (< 10), and it is also more suitable for reconstruction work in incomplete projections.

6.5.1 Iterative Reconstruction Model

According to the basic model in Sub-section 6.2.1, the input data for reconstruction is the projection integral along each ray, and the sum of the contribution of each pixel position along the ray to the linear attenuation coefficient (weighted by the length of the actual path) is equal to the measured absorption value, that is, the projection result. When the projection is known, the integral of each ray can provide an equation, which together form a set of homogeneous equations. The number of unknowns in these equations is the number of pixels in the image plane, and the number of equations is the number of line integrals. In this way, reconstruction can be seen as solving a set of homogeneous equations. Iterative reconstruction is to use iteration to solve such a problem.

The model of iterative reconstruction can be introduced with the help of Figure 6.23, where the object to be reconstructed is placed in a rectangular coordinate grid, the emitter and receiver are considered to be point-like, and the line between them corresponds to a ray (suppose there are M rays in total). Arrange each pixel (grid) from 1 to N in the scanning order (N is the total number of grids). Inside the j-th pixel, the ray absorption coefficient can be regarded as a constant x_j, and the length of the intersection of the i-th ray and the j-th pixel is a_{ij}, which represents the weight of the contribution of the j-th pixel along the i-th ray.

If y_i is used to represent the total measured value along the ray direction (the sum of the measured values of each pixel on the path), then

$$y_i \approx \sum_{j=1}^{N} x_j a_{ij} \qquad\qquad i=1, 2, \cdots, M \qquad\qquad (6.50)$$

Written in matrix form:

$$y = Ax \qquad\qquad (6.51)$$

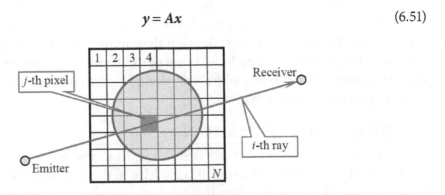

FIGURE 6.23   Schematic diagram of iterative reconstruction.

In the equation, y is the measurement vector, x is the image vector, and the $M \times N$ matrix A is the projection matrix. To obtain high-quality images, both M and N need to be at least on the order of 10^5, so A is a very large matrix. Consider an image with a size of 256×256. To solve Equation (6.51), the number of rays must be at least equal to the number of pixels, so $N \times M \approx 4.3 \times 10^9$. It is a challenge to store the entire matrix with so many elements in the computer. In addition, it can be proved that to calculate the inverse of a matrix with D elements, the number of operations required is $D^{3/2}$. Therefore, for an image of 256×256, the number of operations will reach about 2.8×10^{14}, which also poses a challenge to the computing power of the computer.

6.5.2 Algebraic Reconstruction Technique

Although A is a very large matrix, since it only intersects a few pixels for each ray, there are often less than 1% of the elements in A that are not zero. Therefore, in practice, iterative techniques are often used for reconstruction. *Algebraic Reconstruction Technology* (ART) (Gordon 1974) is also called iterative algorithm or optimization technique, and is the first iterative reconstruction method that has been applied.

6.5.2.1 Basic Algorithm

The basic algebraic reconstruction algorithm is relatively simple. First initialize an image vector $x^{(0)}$ as the starting point of the iteration, and then iterate as follows:

$$x^{(k+1)} = x^{(k)} + \frac{y_i - a^i \cdot x^{(k)}}{\left\| a^i \right\|^2} a^i \tag{6.52}$$

Among them, y_i is the value measured by the i-th receiver; $a^i = [a_{i1}, a_{i2}, \ldots, a_{iN}]^T$ is a vector, "$\bullet$" means the inner product, so $a^i \cdot x^{(k)}$ corresponds to the projection of i-th ray; $\|a^i\|^2 = \Sigma_j a^2_{ij}$ is the sum of the lengths of intersection of each pixel and the ray along the i-th ray; the product of a^i and the fraction is equivalent to back-projecting the value of the fraction along the i-th ray.

The algebraic reconstruction algorithm is an iterative operation based on rays because it considers one ray at a time and updates the image once. To understand the geometric meaning of the algorithm more intuitively, Equation (6.52) can be rewritten as:

$$x^{(k+1)} = x^{(k)} - \left[\frac{a^i \cdot x^{(k)}}{\left\| a^i \right\|} - \frac{y_i}{\left\| a^i \right\|} \right] \frac{a^i}{\left\| a^i \right\|} \tag{6.53}$$

Refer to Figure 6.24. The calculation process of this method can be described as: each time a ray is taken, the value of the pixel that intersects the ray in the image is changed, thereby updating the current image vector $x^{(k)}$ to $x^{(k+1)}$. In the specific operation, the difference between the measured value and the currently calculated projection data is proportional

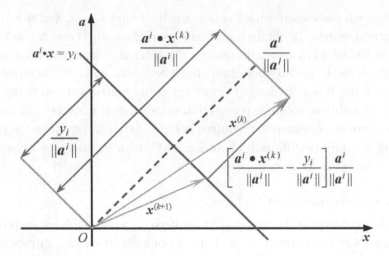

FIGURE 6.24 The geometric explanation of the iterative reconstruction calculation process.

to a_{ij} and is redistributed to each pixel through which the ray passes. The main steps of the iteration here include:

1. Calculate the projection value of the previous round (or initial estimation) iteration.

2. Compare the calculated projection value with the actual measured value.

3. Back-project the difference between the above two values back to the image space.

4. The image is updated by correcting the currently estimated image value.

The solution of this algorithm can be explained with the help of a geometric explanation as shown in Figure 6.25. The three straight lines (L_1, L_2, L_3) in the figure represent 3

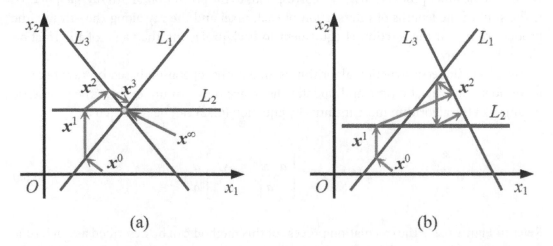

(a)   (b)

FIGURE 6.25 Schematic diagram of iterative solution of basic algebraic reconstruction algorithm; (a) The three straight lines have a common intersection point; (b) The three straight lines have no common point of intersection.

rays, which also correspond to the three equations of the homogeneous equation system. The three lines in Figure 6.25a have a common intersection point, which means that the system is compatible, and the intersection point is the solution of the system. The three straight lines in Figure 6.25b have no common point of intersection, which means that these equations are incompatible, that is, there is no solution. The image considered in the figure has only two pixels, which constitutes a 2-D coordinate system. The basic idea of the algebraic reconstruction algorithm is to start from any initial value x^0, and perform vertical projection to each straight line in turn to obtain x^1, x^2,.... One iteration of the algorithm is defined as one projection to each straight line. If the equations are compatible, the algorithm will gradually converge, and the final result of the iterative projection x^∞ is the common intersection of the straight lines. If the system of equations is incompatible, the "solution" of the algorithm will jump back and forth between the straight lines, failing to converge.

The ART uses line-by-line iteration, which avoids directly inverting the matrix and thus reduces the amount of calculation; moreover, only one row of data in the matrix is used in each iteration, which also saves storage space.

6.5.2.2 Relaxed Algebraic Reconstruction Technique

Relaxed algebraic reconstruction technique is an improvement of basic algebraic reconstruction technique. Add a relaxation factor r $(0 < r < 2)$ to control the convergence rate in the iterative Equation (6.52) of the basic algorithm to get the iterative equation of the relaxation algebraic reconstruction algorithm (when $r = 1$ it is the Equation (6.52))

$$x^{(k+1)} = x^{(k)} + r^{(k)} \frac{y_i - a^i \cdot x^{(k)}}{\left\| a^i \right\|^2} a^i \tag{6.54}$$

The main steps of the algorithm are (take $r = r^{(k)}$:

1. Assign an initial value to each pixel of the image, $x^{(k)} = x^{(0)}$, and initialize the pointer $i = k = 0$.

2. $i = i + 1$, use Equation (6.50) to calculate the estimated value y_i' of the i-th projection.

3. Calculation error $\Delta_i = y_i - y_i'$.

4. Calculate the correction factor $c_i = \Delta_i a^i / \| a^i \|^2$.

5. Modify and update the image, $x^{(k+1)} = x^{(k)} + r c_i$.

6. $k = k + 1$, return to Step (2), and repeat Step (2) to Step (5) until $i = M$, complete one round of algorithm iteration.

7. The iteration result of the previous round of algorithm is the initial pixel value, $i = k = 0$, repeat Step (2) to Step (6) until the result meets the convergence requirements.

6.5.2.3 Simultaneous Algebraic Reconstruction Technology

Simultaneous algebraic reconstruction technology (SART) is also an improvement of the basic algebraic reconstruction technique.

The basic algebraic reconstruction technique uses a line-by-line iterative update method, that is, every time a ray is calculated, the pixel values related to the ray are updated once. This is equivalent to using only the value of a certain row of the system matrix for each calculation, which can avoid directly seeking the inverse of the system matrix, so as to greatly reduces the computational complexity and space complexity. In addition, the error is back-projected to avoid the error concentration. However, the basic algebraic reconstruction algorithm only considers one ray when correcting the image, and can only guarantee that the projection result of this ray is accurate each time, which causes the result to oscillate near the optimal value and the convergence speed is slow.

The SART considers all rays along a projection angle together, that is, uses the measured values of all rays passing through the same pixel to update the value of this pixel (the result does not change with the order of using the ray measured values). In other words, in the simultaneous algebraic reconstruction technique, one iteration involves multiple rays, and the average value of them can be used to suppress the influence of some interference factors. When repairing a pixel, it also takes into account all the rays that interact with the pixel. The reconstruction result is smoother than the ART algorithm and can better suppress banding artifacts. Its iterative equation can be written as

$$x^{(k+1)} = x^{(k)} + \frac{\sum\limits_{i \in I_\theta} \left[\dfrac{y_i - a^i \cdot x^{(k)}}{\left\| a^i \right\|^2} a^i \right]}{\sum\limits_{i \in I_\theta} a^i} \tag{6.55}$$

Among them, I_θ represents the set of rays corresponding to a certain projection angle.

The main iterative steps of the simultaneous algebraic reconstruction technique include:

1. Initialize an image vector $x^{(0)}$ as the starting point of the iteration.

2. Calculate the projection value of the i-th projection under a projection angle θ.

3. Calculate the difference between the actual measured value and the projected value.

4. $i = i + 1$, repeat Step (2) to Step (3), and add up all the projection differences in this projection direction.

5. Calculate the correction value for the image vector $x^{(k)}$.

6. Correct the image vector $x^{(k)}$, that is, update $x^{(k+1)}$.

7. $k = k + 1$, repeat Step (2) to Step (6) until all projection angles are completed, that is, a round of iteration is completed.

8. The result of the previous iteration is the initial value, repeat Step (2) to Step (7) until the final convergence.

6.5.2.4 *Some Characteristics of the Series Expansion Technique*

The algebraic reconstruction technique introduced above uses the method of series expansion, also known as the *series expansion technique*. The general transformation method requires much less calculation than the series expansion technique, so most practical systems use the transformation method. But compared with the transformation method, the series expansion technique has some unique advantages (Censor 1983):

1. Since reconstruction in the space domain is easier to adjust to adapt to new application environments, the series expansion technique is more flexible and is often used in reconstruction with new physical principles and new data acquisition methods.

2. The series expansion technique can reconstruct relatively high-contrast images (especially for materials with sudden changes in density).

3. With multiple iterations, the series expansion technique can be used to reconstruct images from fewer projections (< 10).

4. The series expansion technique is more suitable than the transformation method for ECT system.

5. The series expansion technique is more suitable for 3-D reconstruction than the transformation method (also because it is more flexible in the space domain, it is easy to generalize).

6. The series expansion technique is more suitable for incomplete projection than the transformation method. This is because the transformation method requires uniform sampling of each projection and assignment of each sampling point, so the incomplete projection must be complete first. The series expansion technique will transform the reconstruction problem into the problem of solving the linear equations by the relaxation method, and the missing projection value is regarded as a missing equation, so this problem can be ignored.

6.5.3 Maximum Likelihood-Maximum Expectation Reconstruction Algorithm

The ART algorithm uses the difference between the measured value and the projection data as a correction factor, and adjusts the projection data by means of addition (or subtraction). The algorithm described below uses the ratio of the measured value to the projection data as the correction factor, and iteratively updates with the help of multiplication. It is a statistical iterative reconstruction algorithm, which generally adopts the Poisson noise model (the radiation of photons satisfies the Poisson random process), or only uses non-negative constraints. Non-negativity is an important feature of the algorithm. If there is no negative value in the original image, there will be no negative value in the result of the iteration.

The objective function of the algorithm is a likelihood function, that is, the joint probability density function of Poisson random variables. The reconstructed image of the algorithm should maximize the likelihood function. Since it is difficult to obtain the extreme value of the Poisson likelihood function through the general method of obtaining partial derivatives, some random variables in the objective function should be replaced with their expected values (i.e., statistical mean values) to simplify the solution. This is a "E" (expectation) step. The next step is to calculate the maximum value of the likelihood function (represented by the expected value), which is a "M" (maximization) step. Therefore, the essence of the reconstruction algorithm is to use the maximum expected value to find the maximum likelihood function, so it is called the *maximum likelihood-maximum expectation* (ML-EM) reconstruction algorithm.

The iterative equation of the ML-EM algorithm can be written as:

$$x^{(k+1)} = \frac{\mathcal{B}\left[y_i / x^{(k)}\right]}{\mathcal{B}[1]} \tag{6.56}$$

In the equation, $\mathcal{B}$ represents back-projection; **1** is a vector whose elements are all 1, and the number of elements is the same as that of the projection data vector.

Write out the Equation (6.56), for the j-th pixel, it gives:

$$x_j^{(k+1)} = \frac{x_j^{(k)}}{\sum_i a_{ij}} \sum_i a_{ij} \frac{y_i}{\sum_l a_{il} x_l^{(k)}} \tag{6.57}$$

Among them, the summing of l is a projection operation, and the summing of i is a back-projection operation.

The main steps of the algorithm are:

1. Assign an initial value to each pixel of the image, $x^{(k)} = x^{(0)}$, and initialize the pointer $i = k = 0$.

2. Use Equation (6.50) to calculate the estimated value y_i' of all projections, $i = 1, 2, ..., M$.

3. Calculate each error $\Delta_i = y_i / y_i'$, $i = 1, 2, ..., M$.

4. Calculate the correction factor $c = ||\Delta_i a^i|| / ||a^i||$.

5. Use all rays passing through each pixel to correct and update the image, $x^{(k+1)} = x^{(k)} \times c$ to complete an iteration of the algorithm.

6. $k = k + 1$, the result of the previous round iteration of algorithm is the initial pixel value, and Step (2) to Step (5) are repeated for a new round of iteration until the result meets the convergence requirements.

An example of the calculation steps of the ML-EM algorithm is given below. Suppose that the projection results (measured values) obtained for a 2×2 image are as follows (the initial pixel iteration values in the image are all 1):

$$
\begin{array}{cc}
4 & 0 \\
\begin{bmatrix} 1 & 1 \end{bmatrix} & 8 \\
\begin{bmatrix} 1 & 1 \end{bmatrix} & 4
\end{array}
$$

An iteration using the ML-EM algorithm includes the following steps:

1. Calculate the projection of the current image, get

$$\begin{array}{cc} 2 & 2 \end{array}$$
$$\begin{bmatrix} 1 & 1 \\ 1 & 1 \end{bmatrix} \begin{array}{c} 2 \\ 2 \end{array}$$

2. Calculate the ratio of the given measurement value to the projection data of the current image to get

$$(4 \quad 0)/(2 \quad 2) = (2 \quad 0) \qquad\qquad (8 \quad 4)/(2 \quad 2) = (4 \quad 2)$$

3. The ratio value is back-projected to obtain

$$\begin{array}{cc} 2 & 0 \end{array}$$
$$\begin{bmatrix} 6 & 4 \\ 4 & 2 \end{bmatrix} \begin{array}{c} 4 \\ 2 \end{array}$$

4. Perform back-projection on the constant 1 to get

$$\begin{array}{cc} 1 & 1 \end{array}$$
$$\begin{bmatrix} 2 & 2 \\ 2 & 2 \end{bmatrix} \begin{array}{c} 1 \\ 1 \end{array}$$

5. Calculate the ratio of the image obtained in Step (3) to the image obtained in Step (4), that is, divide the corresponding pixel to obtain

$$\begin{bmatrix} 6 & 4 \\ 4 & 2 \end{bmatrix} \Big/ \begin{bmatrix} 2 & 2 \\ 2 & 2 \end{bmatrix} = \begin{bmatrix} 3 & 2 \\ 2 & 1 \end{bmatrix}$$

6. Multiply the result of Step (5) with the corresponding pixel of the current image (equivalent to array multiplication instead of matrix multiplication) to get

$$\begin{bmatrix} 1 & 1 \\ 1 & 1 \end{bmatrix} \times \begin{bmatrix} 3 & 2 \\ 2 & 1 \end{bmatrix} = \begin{bmatrix} 3 & 2 \\ 2 & 1 \end{bmatrix}$$

It can be proved that after each iteration of the ML-EM algorithm, the sum of the new projection results is equal to the sum of the original projection results.

In the ART algorithm, after each ray is projected, the image is updated once. If there are a total of M rays, the image will be updated M times in one iteration of the algorithm. In the maximum likelihood reconstruction algorithm, the image will only be updated once after M rays are projected. In addition, there is an *ordered subsets-expectation maximization* (OS-EM) reconstruction algorithm, which divides the data into multiple subsets. The algorithm visits each subset in a given order, and calculates the maximum value of the expected value according to the subset. In this way for updating the image, it can speed up the convergence.

6.6 COMBINED RECONSTRUCTION

The different methods introduced in Sections 6.3–6.5 can be combined to form a comprehensive reconstruction method. Here, "comprehensive" is sometimes reflected in the derivation of the equation, sometimes in the method of realization, and sometimes in the actual application.

Here is an example: *iterative transform reconstruction* technology. It is also called continuous ART, which is based on continuous orthogonal projection in Hilbert space. From the perspective of continuous derivation and then discretization, this method can be regarded as a transform method, but its iterative calculation nature and discrete representation of images have many similarities with the series expansion technique (Lewitt 1983).

Refer to Figure 6.26, let $f(x, y)$ be 0 outside the object region Q, and $L(s, \theta_n)$ is the length of the intersection of the straight line (s, θ_n) and Q. The reconstruction work can be described as: Given a projection $g(s, \theta_n)$ of a function $f(x, y)$, where s can take all real numbers, θ_n is a set of N discrete angles, it is needed to recover $f(x, y)$. For $i \geq 0$, the image $f^{(i+1)}(x, y)$ produced in step $(i+1)$ can be iteratively obtained from the current estimated image $f^{(i)}(x, y)$:

$$f^{(i+1)}(x,y) = \begin{cases} 0 & (x,y) \notin Q \\ f^{(i)}(x,y) + \dfrac{g(s,\theta_n) - g^{(i)}(s,\theta_n)}{L(s,\theta_n)} & \text{otherwise} \end{cases} \tag{6.58}$$

where $n = (i \bmod N) + 1$, $s = x\cos\theta_n + y\sin\theta_n$, $g^{(i)}(s, \theta_n)$ is the projection of $f^{(i)}(x, y)$ along θ_n, $f^{(0)}(x, y)$ is a given initial function. It can be proved that the image sequence $\{f^{(i)}(x, y); i = 1, 2,...\}$ will converge to an image that satisfies all projections.

$g(\cdot, \theta_n)$ in Equation (6.58) is a "semi-discrete" function because one of its two independent variables takes a value in a finite set, and the other takes a value in an infinite set. Now use the method in Section 6.3 to derive its discrete form. To estimate $g(s, \theta_n)$ from the sample $g(m\Delta s, \theta_n)$, an interpolation function $q(\cdot)$ can be introduced such that

$$g(s,\theta_n) \approx \sum_{m=M}^{M+} g(m\Delta s, \theta_n) q(s - m\Delta s) \tag{6.59}$$

Similarly, to estimate $f(x, y)$ from the sample $f(k\Delta x, l\Delta y)$, a basis function $B(x, y)$ can be introduced such that

$$f(x,y) \approx \sum_{k=K^-}^{K^+} \sum_{l=L^-}^{L^+} f(k\Delta x, l\Delta y) B(x - \Delta x, y - l\Delta y) \tag{6.60}$$

Now replace f in Equation (6.60) with $f^{(i)}$ and substitute it into Equation (6.10), it gives

$$g^{(i)}(s,\theta) = \sum_{k,l} f^{(i)}\left(k\Delta x, l\Delta y\right) G_{k,l}^{(B)}(s,\theta) \qquad (6.61)$$

where

$$G_{k,l}^{(B)}(s,\theta) = \int B\left(s \times \cos\theta - t \times \sin\theta - k\Delta x,\ s \times \sin\theta + t \times \cos\theta - l\Delta y\right) dt \qquad (6.62)$$

According to the interpolation principle introduced above, the continuous ART can be discretized. Using Equations (6.59) and (6.61), Equation (6.58) can be written as discrete variables:

$$f_{k,l}^{(i+1)} = \begin{cases} 0 & \left(k\Delta x, l\Delta y\right) \notin Q \\ f_{k,l}^{(i)} + \dfrac{\sum\limits_{m}\left[g(m\Delta s,\theta_n) - \sum\limits_{k,l} f_{k,l}^{(i)} \times G_{k,l}^{(B)}(m\Delta s,\theta_n)\right] \cdot q\left[s_{k,l}(\theta_n) - m\Delta s\right]}{L\left[s_{k,l}(\theta_n),\theta_n\right]} & \text{otherwise} \end{cases}$$

$$(6.63)$$

where $n = (i \bmod N)+1$, $s_{k,l}(\theta) = (k\Delta x)\cos\theta + (l\Delta y)\sin\theta$, and

$$f_{k,l}^{(i)} = f^{(i)}\left(k\Delta x, l\Delta y\right) \qquad (6.64)$$

According to Equation (6.63), the reconstruction can be carried out through discrete iterations.

6.7 SOME RECENT DEVELOPMENTS AND FURTHER RESEARCH

In the following, some technique developments and promising research directions in the last years are briefly overviewed.

6.7.1 Metal Artifact Reduction

Computed tomography (CT) has been widely used for clinical diagnosis. If metal implants exist in a scanned object, when X-rays pass through these metals, the attenuation of photons is much higher than that of normal tissues in the human body, resulting in distortions of the measured projection data.

6.7.1.1 Metal Artifact

The above mentioned distortions cause metal artifacts in the imaging result. How to develop effective methods for *metal artifact reduction* (MAR) has been considered.

Common distortion phenomena include (Wang et al. 2020):

1. Beam hardening

The X-ray in the CT system has a continuous energy spectrum. The attenuation of X-rays is related to the materials passed through and the energy of photons. In general, the greater the atomic number of a material, the stronger the attenuation of X-rays; the higher the energy of the photon, the less attenuation through the same substance. When the X-ray beam enters the human body, the low-energy X-ray will be absorbed first. As the X-ray beam passes through the human body, the average energy of the X-ray will become higher and higher, that is, the rays will become harder. This phenomenon is called the *beam hardening effect*. Due to the beam hardening effect, the attenuation of the ray intensity with the penetration distance are no longer linear. When the average energy of the ray reaches a certain level, the attenuation of the X-ray by the substance is no longer obvious. Beam hardening will cause more photons to reach the detector region, resulting in an underestimation of the attenuation coefficient. The CT image reconstructed from such detection data cannot truly reflect the internal states of the measured object, and the artifact appears as the black in the middle with white edges around.

2. Nonlinear partial volume artifacts

The nonlinear partial volume effect means that each pixel value in the CT image is not the real attenuation coefficient of each region, but the average attenuation coefficient of human body. Assuming that the incident X-ray intensity is I_0, the emitted intensity after the ray passing through the materials with the attenuation coefficients A_1 and A_2 are respectively I_1 and I_2, where I_1 and I_2 are detected by the same detection unit, the detector will count the average value of I_1 and I_2 as detection value to calculate the attenuation coefficient A_d:

$$A_d = -\ln \frac{I_1/I_0 + I_2/I_0}{2} \tag{6.65}$$

In the reconstruction phase, the average value A_r of the attenuation coefficients A_1 and A_2 is used:

$$A_r = \frac{A_1 + A_2}{2} = -\ln \sqrt{I_1/I_0 + I_2/I_0} \tag{6.66}$$

If $A_d \neq A_r$, then from the triangle inequality, $A_d < A_r$ can be obtained. This situation occurs when the edge of a metal object crosses certain projection lines, resulting in a change in the attenuation coefficient perpendicular to the propagation direction of X-ray. Since the density of this region measured by the detector is no longer a linear function of attenuation, there will be inconsistencies in the projection data, resulting in errors in the density estimation of the image, and nonlinear partial volume effects appears. In this case, the reconstructed CT image shows some dark streak artifacts, that is, the in images severely affected by sparse-view sampling in images.

3. Scattering

When X-ray photons collide with electrons in the substance, X-ray photons transfer part of their energy to the electrons, causing the electrons to leave the atoms, and the path of the X-ray photons will also be deflected and scattered. Scattering makes the X-ray photons detected by the detector include scattered photons in addition to the initial photons that travel along a straight line. Like beam hardening, more photons reach the normal region of the detector, resulting in distortion of the detection value. The low-frequency scattering signal hardly contributes for reflecting the internal attenuation information of the measured object but increases the noise, which will reduce the contrast and signal-to-noise ratio of the CT image

4. Photon starvation

When X-ray attenuation is too large after passing through the scanned part of object, the detector can only detect a few photons, and the projection process will generate more noise, which will increase the noise after filtering, and the finally reconstructed CT image will have fringe artifacts. The main reason for producing photon starvation is that the dose of X-ray is too low.

5. Motion artifacts

Motion artifacts are mainly caused by the spontaneous movement (breathing, etc.) and non-spontaneous movement (gastrointestinal motility, etc.) of the tested patient. These movements will make the discontinuous of measurement data, and the projection data affected by the metal increases due to the movement. Shorter scan time can reduce artifacts due to motion, but this will place higher requirements on the time resolution of the CT scan system.

6.7.1.2 Classical MAR Methods

Classical MAR methods are mainly in two categories.

1. Interpolation-based methods

The MAR method based on projection domain data is quite simple. This type of method usually needs to obtain the trajectory of metal artifacts in the projection domain through image segmentation and forward projection, as well as treat the data in the metal trajectory as data missing and fill it by interpolation. After the projection domain data is repaired, the method of *filtered back-projection* (FBP) is used to get the CT image after removing the artifacts, the general flowchart is shown in Figure 6.26.

2. Iterative-based methods

Although the FBP method-based on analytical reconstruction has high computational efficiency and fast reconstruction speed, when there is metal implant occlusion and insufficient projection data, the reconstruction quality is not high, and metal artifacts cannot be removed well. It is related to the mathematical assumptions of the FBP method. The FBP method is based on the line integral model, does not take into account the statistical characteristics of the measured data, and assumes that the data is noise-free and all response lines have the same weight.

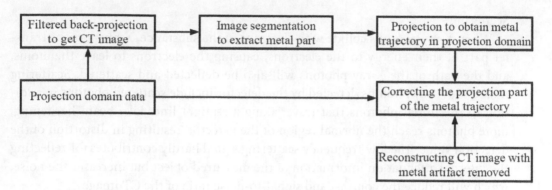

FIGURE 6.26   Flowchart of interpolation-based methods.

To solve the shortcomings of the FBP method, the iterative method can be used. The iterative method is a method of continuous revision and gradual improvement. It has a good effect on the problems of projection data truncation, limited angle scanning, uneven projection interval, and de-noising.

In the field of CT reconstruction, iterative reconstruction methods are mainly divided into two types: algebraic iteration and statistical iteration. The ART and SART methods discussed in Sub-section 6.5.2 are both typical algebraic iteration methods. On the other side, the statistical iteration method uses a statistical model based on data observations, assuming that the detected photons obey a Poisson distribution, with the minimum mean square error, maximum likelihood function, maximum posterior probability, etc. as the objective function, and the maximum expected value, conjugate iteration, etc. as the iteration method. The ML-EM method discussed in Sub-section 6.5.3 is a typical statistical iteration method.

Each of analytical reconstruction methods and iterative reconstruction methods has obvious shortcomings. Analytical reconstruction algorithms may introduce additional artifacts in the repair of projection data, while the speed of iterative reconstruction algorithms is slow. To combine the advantages of the two types of reconstruction algorithms, the original CT image can be first segmented. According to the strength of the artifacts, different reconstruction strategies are used for the parts of the image with different degrees of degradation. The part with serious artifacts adopts iterative reconstruction algorithm with better de-noising effect, and vice versa, the analytical reconstruction algorithm with faster calculation speed is used for other degradation situations (Van Slambrouck and Nuyts 2012).

In recent years, with the continuous improvement of hardware computing power, iterative reconstruction algorithms have had more applications. The multiple projections and back-projection calculations required in the iterative process have high parallelism and can be easily accelerated by GPU (Serrano et al. 2020; Pérez et al. 2020).

6.7.1.3 Deep Learning-Based MAR Methods
In recent years, deep learning-based MAR methods have developed rapidly. For example:

1. To suppress the effect of beam hardening caused by metal implants, a U-Net-based projection domain data correction method has been proposed to make the projection domain data more continuous (Park et al. 2018).

2. Similar to image restoration, the metal trajectory part of the projection domain can be regarded as missing data, and the partial convolution method is used to repair the metal trajectory part (Liu et al. 2018). Partial convolution is a method of updating, at the same time, both mask and the image to be repaired. Assuming that the corresponding mask value of the part to be repaired is 1, as the update progresses, the part with the mask of 1 becomes less and less, until all are 0, at which time the image repair is completed (Pimkin et al. 2019).

3. In the image domain, with the help of convolutional neural network (CNN) to extract fine features from a large amount of image data, an open processing framework (*convolutional neural network based metal artifact reduction*, CNNMAR) is proposed (Zhang and Yu 2018). It stacks the original uncorrected image, beam hardening corrected image, and linear interpolation corrected image as the input of CNN, adjust the network weights through the supervised training process, and finally map these three types of images to CT images without metal artifacts.

4. In the projection domain, a CNN to interpolate the projection data on the metal trajectory in the projection domain is trained (Claus et al. 2017). The repaired projection data is visually superior to the linear interpolation result, and there are fewer streak artifacts and banding artifacts in the reconstructed CT image.

5. The projection domain and image domain can also be combined. For example, an end-to-end dual domain network combines projection domain and image domain information (*dual domain network*, DuDoNet) has been proposed (Lin et al. 2019). The network as a whole is composed of three modules. In the first module, the projection data is roughly repaired by linear interpolation, and then the data is enhanced by the network of the projection domain. The second module is the reconstruction layer, which is the key to end-to-end training. To suppress the generation of secondary artifacts, the L_1 loss between the same label images is applied after the reconstruction is completed. The third module uses the U-Net network structure to enhance the reconstructed image and further remove artifacts.

    In the projection domain enhancement stage of DuDoNet, the data in the metal trajectory is regarded as missing, and the internal details of the metal are completely lost, which may cause the reconstruction result to be too smooth. In addition, the projection domain and the image domain are both based on linear interpolation, which will introduce new artifacts and make the learning process difficult, especially when the metal implant is large. As a result, the data missing is more serious, and the missing information cannot be recovered in the subsequent steps. The improved DuDoNet++ (Lyu et al. 2020) directly uses the original artifact data in both the projection domain and the image domain, and the projection data of the metal part is used in the projection domain enhancement stage. In this way, the contrast between the various tissues in the reconstructed CT image is stronger, and the details of the structure near the metal are also more complete.

6. The foregoing are all methods based on supervised learning, but it is difficult to obtain matched training data in clinical practice. The method based on unsupervised

learning can learn from the idea of image style transfer (it can be seen as a conversion from one type of data distribution to another type of data distribution), and treat the MAR problem as a conversion from an artifact CT image to an artifact-free CT image. For example, the *artifact disentanglement network* (ADN) is used to decouple the artifact CT image into the artifact-free image domain and the pure noise domain, and then perform the reconstruction (Liao et al. 2019).

The ADN learning process imposes many constraints. These constraints are controlled by the loss function, which is represented by multiple GANs against the generation loss, reconstruction loss, artifact consistency loss, and overall cycle consistency loss. Too many constraints make the parameters need to be fine-tuned, and also increase the difficulty of network training. There is an approach called β-cycleGAN (Lee et al. 2020) that uses another generative model β-VAE and introduces the attention mechanism. This approach simplifies the complexity of the network compared to ADN, controls the degree of entanglement by controlling the hyper-parameter β, and has better interpretability.

6.7.2 4-D Cone-Beam CT Reconstruction

To directly achieve 3-D imaging, cone-beam geometry can be used. The 3-D cone-beam scanning CT system uses flat-panel detectors, and each projection is derived from a point (see Figure 6.27), which can be regarded as an extension of the fan-beam system (refer to Sub-sections 6.1.1 and 6.4.2). To improve the image resolution along the object axis, spiral scanning can be used. At this time, the object is rotated and moved upward along the object axis. With spiral CT, there is no need for traditional layer-by-layer imaging but uniform (isotropic) resolution can be obtained in all three space directions.

6.7.2.1 Cone-Beam CT Reconstruction

Due to the limited maximum size of the flat-panel detector, the scanning field of view is limited, and CT images of large-size objects cannot be obtained. A common way to expand the scanning field of view is to use *detector off-centered scanning*. There are two corresponding reconstruction approaches.

One approach is to rearrange the fan-beam projection data into parallel-beam projection data, and then use the conjugate relationship of the parallel-beam projection data to fill

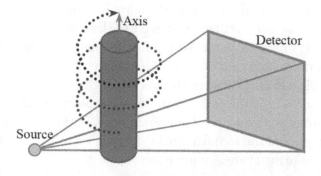

FIGURE 6.27   Cone-beam geometry and spiral scanning.

in the missing projection data, and use the parallel-beam reconstruction algorithm to get CT reconstruction image. The other approach is to divide the projection data. One part of the projection data is sampled twice in conjugate, and the rest part of the projection data is sampled only once. The projection data sampled twice and sampled once are normalized to make their contribution to the reconstructed image equal. Then, the Parker type function to weight the repeatedly sampled projection data is applied, followed by the using of standard fan-beam reconstruction and cone-beam reconstruction algorithms to obtain the CT image.

Another way to expand the scanning field of view is to use *turntable off-centered scanning*. There are also two corresponding reconstruction approaches that correspond to that of the detector off-centered scanning, that is, rearranging fan-beam projection data into parallel-beam projection data, and using parallel-beam reconstruction algorithm to obtain CT reconstructed images; as well as using Parker type functions to weight resampled projection data, then use fan-beam and cone-beam reconstruction algorithms to obtain CT images.

A reconstruction algorithm using scanning mode with multiple off-centered processes on one side of the turntable and generalized to the cone-beam case has been proposed (Chen et al. 2020). Its procedure flow mainly includes:

1. According to the cone-beam rearrangement algorithm, the projection data is rearranged into oblique parallel-beam projection data. The oblique parallel beams obtained in this way are not on the same plane but their projections on the horizontal plane are parallel to each other.

2. Splicing oblique parallel beams into complete oblique parallel-beam projection data. This needs to be stitched in the interval where the oblique parallel beam projection data is located to recombine into a complete oblique parallel beam projection.

3. Analyze the redundancy of projection data and perform normalization processing. The problems of projection data include projection data truncation and uneven sampling, so it is necessary to use Parker type functions to weight the projection data so that their contributions to the reconstructed image are equal.

4. The PFDK (Parallel FDK) algorithm is used to reconstruct the weighted oblique parallel beam projection data to obtain the reconstructed image. The FDK (Feldkamp-Davis-Kress) algorithm is a FBP-type algorithm that solves the CCB reconstruction problem approximately. The PFDK reconstruction algorithm includes three steps: cosine weighting, filtering, and back-projection.

A computationally efficient reconstruction algorithm for circular cone-beam CT using shallow neural networks has been proposed in (Lagerwerf et al. 2020).

6.7.2.2 4-D Cone-Beam CT

Modern complex radiation therapy (RT) techniques enable highly precise target irradiation but also rely on highly accurate target localization (Madesta et al. 2020). To minimize uncertainties during treatment delivery, different imaging systems are employed before and during the course of the treatment to frequently control the target position, leading to the term of *image guided RT* (IGRT). The cone-beam scanning mode has higher ray utilization, the reconstructed voxel size is isotropic, and the volume imaging has significant advantages. The current clinical standard to acquire a three-dimensional *cone-beam computed tomography* (3-D CBCT; using imaging devices integrated directly into treatment machines) before the individual treatment fractions to evaluate residual patient setup errors and target position shifts by comparison of the 3-D CBCT images to treatment planning 3-D CT images. 3-D image guidance is, however, insufficient to counter uncertainties inherent to thoracic and abdominal lesions, which are known to exhibit breathing-induced motion amplitudes during treatment up to several centimeters and significant inter-fraction motion variability. To increase dose application accuracy and precision for moving targets, it has been recommended to acquire time-resolved, that is, 4-D (= 3-D + t; instead of aforementioned 3-D CBCT data) CBCT images to verify that tumor and organ motion patterns at the time of treatment correspond to the treatment planning situation and the related treatment planning 4-D CT.

However, integration of 4-D CBCT into clinical 4-D RT workflows is hampered by low quality of the individual phase images, that is, the 3-D CBCT images that represent the anatomy of the patient at different breathing phases, which leads to unreliable error-prone, target localization, and motion quantification.

The low image quality of current *4-D CBCT phase images* is inherent to the CBCT data acquisition procedure and its combination with standard reconstruction approaches. While a typical patient breathing cycle length is about 4s, CBCT projection data acquisition time is defined by the duration of a full rotation of the linear accelerator gantry, which is in the order of 60s. For 4-D CBCT image reconstruction, the acquired projection data are binned according to associated breathing phase information derived from a simultaneously recorded breathing signal.

6.7.2.3 4-D Cone-Beam CT Reconstruction

To solve the problem, a self-contained deep learning-based boosting technique has been proposed to perform 4-D cone-beam CT reconstruction (Madesta et al. 2020).

The main idea of the boosting framework is to learn the relationship between low-quality, artifact-containing 3-D CBCT images and high-quality 3-D CBCT images of exactly the same patient geometry and breathing state. Such an image pair does not be affected by breathing phase differences and with an image appearance not being biased toward a specific breathing phase. Moreover, the low-quality images are supposed to closely resemble 4-D CBCT phase image characteristics in terms of image quality and contained streak artifacts.

Specifically, a specific projection selection scheme is designed to reconstruct pseudo-time-averaged CBCTs of phase image-inherent image quality, serving as low-quality images; high-quality images are corresponding 3-D time-average CBCTs reconstructed using all available projection data. After training a CNN to transform low-quality into high-quality average CBCTs, the network can be applied to boost reconstructed 4-D CBCT phase images to reduce the streaking artifacts while maintaining the temporal and motion information represented by the phase images.

For image reconstruction, a deep learning-based boosting framework is applied. Boosting is achieved by learning the relationship between so-called sparse-view pseudo-time-average CBCT images obtained by a projection selection scheme introduced to mimic phase image sparse-view artifact characteristics and corresponding time-average CBCT images obtained by full view reconstruction. The employed CNN is based on the *residual dense network* (RDN) (Zhang et al. 2020). The underlying hypothesis is that the RDN learns the appearance of the streaking artifacts that is typical for 4-D CBCT phase images—and removes them without influencing the anatomical image information.

The main RDN component is a *residual dense block* (RDB), which is illustrated in Figure 6.28. In Figure 6.28, the convolutional layers (Conv.) are indicated in red together with filter dimensions in parentheses and the total number of filters after parentheses. A rectified linear unit (ReLU, in green) is applied element-wise after every convolutional layer. To merge the skip connections with the output of the preceding layer, concatenation layers (blue) are integrated to stack the inputs along the channel axis. Eventually, the output of the residual branch is added to the input of the RDB by element-wise addition (⊕). Densely connected convolutional layers use concatenated feature maps of all preceding layers as input to subsequent layers. Extracted features are therefore globally available to subsequent network parts. To control the RDB output features, a 1×1 convolution is applied to the concatenation of the preceding RDB's output and the resulting feature maps of the considered RDB. Since it is difficult for neural networks with increasing depth to learn the identity function, a local skip connection is implemented, which is added to the output tensor yielded by local feature fusion.

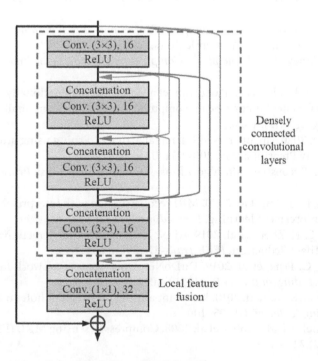

FIGURE 6.28　Illustration of a residual dense block (RDB).

In addition, start from the point of view that CBCT data with sparse-view, a 4-D cone-beam CT reconstruction method is also proposed by (Den Otter et al. 2020). By the way, compressed-sensing has been proposed also for accelerating the MRI data acquisition (CS-MRI) (Lustig et al. 2008). A deep reinforcement learning-based approach with meaningful pixel-wise operations to make the reconstruction process transparent has been recently proposed (Li et al. 2020).

REFERENCES

Bertero, M., and P. Boccacci. 1998. *Introduction to Inverse Problems in Imaging.* UK, Bristol: IOP Publishing Ltd.

Censor, Y. 1983. Finite series-expansion reconstruction methods. *Proceedings of IEEE*, 71: 409–419.

Chen, Y. B., S. T. Li, and X. Jin. 2020. A PFDK-based reconstruction algorithm for industrial CT with multiple cone-beam scans of off-centered rotation. *Chinese Journal of Stereology and Image Analysis*, 25(3): 224–233.

Claus, B. E. H., Y. Jin, L. A. Gjesteby, et al. 2017. Metal-artifact reduction using deep-learning based sinogram completion: Initial results. *Fully 3D 2017 Proceedings*, 631–635.

Committee on the Mathematics and Physics of Emerging Dynamic Biomedical Imaging. 1996. *Mathematics and Physics of Emerging Biomedical Imaging.* Washington, D.C.: National Academic Press.

Deans, S. R. 2000. Radon and Abel transforms. In: Poularikas A. D., Ed. *The Transforms and Applications Handbook*, 2nd Ed. New York: CRC Press (Chapter 8).

Den Otter, L. A., K. L. Chen, J. Guillaume, et al. 2020. 4D cone-beam CT reconstruction from sparse-view CBCT data for daily motion assessment in pencil beam scanned proton therapy (PBS-PT). *Medical Physics*, 47(12): 6381–6387.

Gordon, R. 1974. A tutorial on ART (algebraic reconstruction techniques). *IEEE Trans-NS*, 21: 78–93.

Herman, G. T. 1980. *Image Reconstruction from Projection – The Fundamentals of Computerized Tomography.* Bethesda, MD: Academic Press, Inc.

Kak, A. C., and M. Slaney. 1988. *Principles of Computerized Tomographic Imaging.* New York: IEEE Press.

Lagerwerf, M. J., D. M. Daniel, W. J. Palenstijn, et al. 2020. A computationally efficient reconstruction algorithm for circular cone-beam computed tomography using shallow neural networks. *Journal of Imaging*, 6(12): 1–26.

Lee, J., J. Gu, J. C. Ye. 2020. Unsupervised CT metal artifact learning using attention-guided beta-CycleGAN. arXiv Preprint arXiv: 2007.03480.

Lewitt, R. M. 1983. Reconstruction algorithms: Transform methods. *Proceedings of IEEE*, 71: 390–408.

Li, W. T., X. D. Feng, H. T. An, et al. 2020. MRI reconstruction with interpretable pixel-wise operations using reinforcement learning. *Proceedings of the AAAI*, 792–799.

Liao, H., W. A. Lin, S. K. Zhou, et al. 2019. ADN: Artifact disentanglement network for unsupervised metal artifact Reduction. *IEEE Trans-MI*, 39(3): 634–643.

Lin, W. A., H. Liao, C. Peng, et al. 2019. DuDoNet: Dual domain network for CT metal artifact reduction. *Proceedings of the CVPR*, 10512–10521.

Liu, G., F. A. Reda, K. J. Shih, et al. 2018. Image inpainting for irregular holes using partial convolutions. *Proceedings of the ECCV*, 85–100.

Lustig, M., D. L. Donoho, J. M. Santos, et al. 2008. Compressed sensing MRI. *IEEE Signal Processing Magazine*, 25(2):72–82.

Lyu, Y., W. A. Lin, J. Lu, et al. 2020. DuDoNet++: Encoding mask projection to reduce CT metal artifacts. ArXiv Preprint ArXiv: 2001.00340.

Madesta, A., T. Sentker, T. Gauer, et al. 2020. Self-contained deep learning-based boosting of 4D cone-beam CT reconstruction. *Medical Physics*, 47(11): 5619–5631.

Park, H. S., S. M. Lee, H. P. Kim, et al. 2018. CT sonogram-consistency learning for metal-induced beam hardening correction. *Medical Physics*, 45(12): 5376–5384.

Pérez, T. A. V., J. M. H. López, E. Moreno-Barbosa, et al. 2020. Efficient CT image reconstruction in a GPU parallel environment. *Tomography*, 6(1): 44.

Pimkin, A., A. Samoylenko, N. Antipina, et al. 2019. Multi-domain CT metal artifacts reduction using partial convolution based inpainting. ArXiv Preprint ArXiv: 1911.05530.

Serrano, E., J. Garcia-Blas, J. Carretero, et al. 2020. Accelerated iterative image reconstruction for cone - beam computed tomography through big data frameworks. *Future Generation Computer Systems*, 106: 534–544.

Shepp, L. A., and B. F. Logan. 1974. The Fourier reconstruction of a head section. *IEEE Trans-NS*, 21: 21–43.

Toft, P. 1996. The Radon Transform: Theory and Implementation. PhD thesis, Technical Univ. of Denmark.

Van Slambrouck, K. and J. Nuyts. 2012. Metal artifact reduction in computed tomography using local models in an image block-iterative scheme. *Medical Physics*, 39(11): 7080–7093.

Wang, T., W. Xia, Y. S. Zhao, et al. 2020. Review of metal artifact reduction in computed tomography. *Chinese Journal of Stereology and Image Analysis* 25(3): 207–223.

Zeng, G. S. 2009. *Medical Image Reconstruction – A Conceptual Tutorial*. Beijing: Higher Education Press.

Zhang, Y., and H. Yu. 2018. Convolutional neural network based metal artifact reduction in X-ray computed tomography. *IEEE Trans-MI*, 37(6): 1370–1381.

Zhang, Y.-J. 2009. *Image Engineering: Processing, Analysis, and Understanding*. Singapore: Cengage Learning.

Zhang, Y., Y. Tian, Y. Kong, et al. 2020. Residual dense network for image restoration. *IEEE Transactions on Pattern Analysis and Machine Intelligence*, 43, 2480–2495.

## CHAPTER 7

Image Watermarking

Dıgıtal watermark is a kind of digital mark. Image watermark is a special type of digital watermark, which can be secretly embedded in digital visual products (such as digital images, digital videos, digital photos, electronic publications, etc.) to help identify the owner, content, usage rights, and integrity of the product, and so on. Some people call digital watermarking technology as digital fingerprinting technology. More in-depth discussion can be seen in Regazzoni et al. (2021), Wu et al. (2021).

Watermark is a kind of secret information that is embedded into digital data by distributors for copyright tracking. This kind of information can be images, symbols, text, and so on. Normally, this kind of information is not displayed to the outside world. When the attacker launches an attack, the information can not be destroyed by the attack. When someone maliciously infringes on its copyright, the data holder can completely extract the original watermark embedded in the data through a series of extraction algorithms, in order to declare their ownership of the data.

Image watermarking has many important utilizations, such as:

1. Protect the copyright of image products. The watermark generally contains basic information such as the copyright owner's mark or code and the user code that can prove that the user legally owns the data. This information is embedded in the image product to establish a corresponding relationship between the image product and its owner or user. The copyright is protected to prevent illegal pirated copying, and it also avoids the copyright problem of non-authors arbitrarily claiming image works.

2. Protect the transmitted data from being modified. Processing the transmitted data will change the data. If the watermark is combined with the data, the watermark will also change when the data is changed, and the change of the data can be judged by the change of the watermark.

3. Copy protection or reproduction protection. A typical application is the protection of DVD players. In addition, the use of image watermarking technology can be used for

DOI: 10.1201/9781003241416-7

document anti-counterfeiting, avoiding imitation and duplication of citizen documents, and protecting citizens' interests and social stability.

4. The use of images or videos can be monitored with the help of watermarks, and the watermarked images or videos can be tracked when and where they are used. For example, use programs that search for web pages to monitor images or videos placed on the Internet, discover the location of illegal users, or collect royalties from users. The watermark here is equivalent to the digital fingerprint of the image product, and it can be used to track piracy authorized copy source.

5. Help identify the authenticity of image products or perform content authentication on image products. The use of image watermarking can not only protect image products from being easily tampered with but also judge whether tampering has occurred and possibly estimate the location of the tampering. For example, an electronic seal is a specific application to protect the authenticity and integrity of an electronic document, in which a fragile watermark is used.

This chapter discusses image digital watermarking technology, hereinafter referred to as *image watermarking*. The work in this domain mainly includes the embedding and detection (extraction) of watermarks, as well as the research on the characteristics of watermarks. Adding a watermark to an image can also be regarded as a special image encoding process, that is, incorporating a watermark into an image. Adding a digital watermark to an image as an image technology can be divided into the spatial methods performed in the image space domain and the transform domain methods performed in the image transform domain according to its different processing domains. Since many international standards on image representation and coding use discrete cosine transform (DCT) (such as JPEG, MPEG-1, and MPEG-2) and discrete wavelet transform (DWT) (such as JPEG-2000, MPEG-4, H.265, etc.), many image watermarking work in transform domains such as DCT domain and DWT domain.

The contents of each section of this chapter will be arranged as follows.

Section 7.1 gives a general introduction to watermark and watermarking technology. The embedding and detection of watermarks are modeled, some important characteristics of watermarks are analyzed, and different classification methods of watermarking are also discussed.

Section 7.2 discusses watermark measurement standards. Aiming at the three important characteristics of watermarking, namely, saliency, robustness, and security, the corresponding measurement methods and indicators are respectively analyzed.

Section 7.3 introduces the embedding and detection of watermarks in the DCT domain. After analyzing the basic principles and characteristics, the realization methods of meaningless watermark and meaningful watermark are introduced separately, and the effects of watermarking are also evaluated.

Section 7.4 introduces the embedding and detection of watermark in the DWT domain. After giving the characteristics of the wavelet domain and the watermarking process, a method of watermarking in the wavelet domain is given based on the analysis of the human visual characteristics, and the effect of the watermarking is evaluated.

Section 7.5 provides a brief introduction of some technique developments and promising research directions in the last year.

7.1 OVERVIEW OF WATERMARKING

An *image watermark* is a signal that contains special information (an image watermark is also an image in many cases). Generally, it must be embedded in the image to be protected in advance, and then extracted when needed. As a special signal, it needs to meet certain characteristics according to different application requirements.

7.1.1 Embedding and Detection of Watermark

The use of watermarks to protect digital products requires two operations: for protection, the watermark needs to be added into the digital product before it is used, which is generally called *watermark embedding*; to verify or indicate copyright, it is necessary to extract the embed watermark from the digital product, which is generally called *watermark detection*.

Suppose the original image is $f(x, y)$, the watermark is $W(x, y)$, and the image embedded with the watermark is $g(x, y)$, the watermark embedding process can be represented as:

$$g = E(f, W) \tag{7.1}$$

where $E(\bullet, \bullet)$ represents the embedding function. If the image $h(x, y)$ to be detected is given (it may be a degraded version of the image $g(x, y)$ embedded in the watermark, such as affected by transmission, etc.), the possible watermark to be verified $w(x, y)$ is:

$$w = D(f, h) \tag{7.2}$$

where $D(\bullet, \bullet)$ is the detection function. Consider the correlation function $C(\bullet, \bullet)$ of the original watermark and the possible watermark. If T is a (pre-determined) threshold, then when:

$$C(W, w) > T \tag{7.3}$$

it is considered that the watermark exists, otherwise it is considered that the watermark does not exist. In addition, to give a binary judgment of existence or non-existence, a corresponding degree of confidence can also be given according to the degree of correlation.

The embedding and detection processes of the watermark can be introduced with the help of Figure 7.1. By adding the watermark to the original image by embedding, the watermark embedded image can be obtained. Performing the relevant inspection on the image to be detected, it can judge whether the watermark is embedded in the image and get confidence in the obtained judgment. The detection of the watermark here requires both the original image and the original watermark (not for all watermark detection) and is carried out according to the previous hypothesis test. However, the method of watermark detection and the method of watermark embedding may not completely correspond to each other.

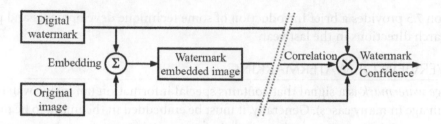

FIGURE 7.1 Schematic diagram of watermark embedding and detection.

From the perspective of signal processing, the process of embedding a watermark can be seen as a process of superimposing a weak signal under a strong background; and the process of detecting a watermark is a process of detecting a weak signal in a noisy channel. From the perspective of digital communication, the process of embedding a watermark can be seen as a process of transmitting a narrowband signal using spread spectrum communication technology on a wideband channel.

The embedding of the watermark often adopts the method of numerical superposition. In the early watermark embedding in the spatial domain, the watermark value was used to adjust the gray value of image pixels. For example, embedding the watermark on the least important lowest bit (least significant bit, LSB) plane of pixel of randomly selected image points is called the LSB method. The advantage of this method is that it can ensure that the embedded watermark is invisible. The disadvantage is that the watermark is only at the lowest bit position, which will be affected by various filtering and quantization, and the robustness is poor. There is also a simple statistical-based spatial watermark embedding method (called patchwork) that arbitrarily selects several pairs of image pixels in the image while increasing the brightness value of one pixel, the brightness value of the other pixel is correspondingly reduced (this can make the average brightness of the entire image remain unchanged). Through this adjustment process, the watermark embedding is completed. To increase the anti-noise ability of the watermark, the pixel pair can also be expanded into the image block region, and the watermark can be embedded by increasing the brightness value of all pixels in a region and correspondingly reducing the brightness value of all pixels in the corresponding region. The spatial method is relatively intuitive and has a small amount of calculation, but it is more sensitive to image coordinate transformation.

7.1.2 Watermark Characteristics

The watermark embedded in the image should have certain characteristics according to the purpose of use. The three most important ones are first introduced below.

7.1.2.1 Saliency

The *saliency* (significance) of a watermark measures the (imperceptible) perceptibility or (difficult) perceptibility of the watermark. For image watermarking, it means invisibility or hiddenness. In certain application domains, it is also called transparency. There are two meanings here: one is that the watermark itself is not easily noticed by the receiver or user, and the other is that the addition of the watermark does not affect the visual quality of the original product. From the perspective of human perception, the embedding of image watermarks should be based on the premise that no perceptible distortion of the original image is made.

Image watermark is a special kind of watermark. For general digital products, a visible mark can be added to the product to indicate its ownership, but for images, this may affect the visual quality and integrity of the image. Therefore, image watermarks often refer to invisible watermarks, that is, watermarks are certain to the copyright owner, but hidden to ordinary users.

7.1.2.2 Robustness

Robustness is also called reliability. It means that the image watermark resists external interference as well as guarantees its own integrity and the accuracy to be detected accurately under the condition that the image is distorted (this generally means that the distortion does not exceed the limit that makes the image unusable). There can be many kinds of external interference with the image, which are often divided into two categories from the perspective of discussing the robustness of the watermark. The first category is conventional image processing methods (not specific for watermark), such as sampling, quantization, digital/analog conversion and analog/digital conversion, scanning, low-pass filtering, transforming, geometric correction, lossy compression coding, printing, and so on. The ability of an image watermark to resist these external interferences is more often expressed as robustness. The second category refers to malicious attack modes (specific for watermarks), such as illegal detection and decoding of watermarks, resampling, cropping, and special displacements, scale changes, and so on. The ability of image watermark resists these external interferences is also commonly called the ability to resist attack (see the security described below).

Contrary to the robustness required in copyright protection applications, vulnerable watermarks or *fragile watermarks* (refer to watermarks with very limited robustness) can be used when authenticating or verifying whether the original image has been altered or damaged. The fragility watermark itself is the sign information that is related or not related to the image content. After embedding the fragile watermark into the image, when the image content needs to be authenticated, it can be judged whether the image content is true and complete according to the extraction result of the watermark. The fragile watermark is used to detect whether the data protected by the watermark has been changed, not to transmit indelible copyright information. The fragile watermark is sensitive to external processing (so it is also called sensitivity), and it will change as the image is modified (vulnerable). In this way, the change in the image can be determined according to the detected watermark change, and the conclusion of determining whether the image has been changed can be reached.

In actual applications, image authentication can be divided into two situations: (i) Accurate authentication; (ii) Fuzzy authentication. The former generally regards an image as a whole, and any changes to it are not allowed. The fragile watermark described above can be used for this purpose. The latter generally refers to allowing the image to have a certain degree of distortion without changing the semantic content of the image. In this way, malicious tampering with obvious changes to the image content cannot be authenticated, but common image operations (such as filtering, enhancement, and compression, etc.) are still allowed. At this time, a semi-fragile watermarking technology is needed. Semi-fragile watermarking has both robustness and vulnerability. It is vulnerable to malicious tampering and attacks, but it is robust (semi-robust) under normal image processing.

The robustness of the watermark should have nothing to do with the original image content and its application. But it depends on the following points.

1. The amount of embedded information

    It directly affects the robustness of the watermark. In general, the more information that is embedded, the lower the robustness of the watermark. Some people use the *payload*, which is the new data added based on the original data, to represent it.

2. Embedding strength of watermark

    The embedding strength corresponds to the amount of embedded data, also called data capacity, which is related to but not equivalent to the amount of embedded information. In practice, a balance needs to be made between the embedding strength of watermark (related to the robustness of the watermark) and the visibility of the watermark. Generally, a stronger embedding is needed to increase the robustness, but this will increase the possibility of the watermark being perceived.

3. The size and nature of the image

    The size of the image has a direct impact on the robustness of the embedded watermark. For example, very small images do not have much commercial value, but the watermarking software program still needs to be able to recover the watermark from them, which helps to resist mosaic attacks (see below). For printing applications, high-resolution images are required, but people also want to protect these images after they are resampled for use on the network. In addition to the size of the image, the nature of the image also has an important impact on the robustness of the watermark. For example, methods with high robustness for scanned natural images may have unexpectedly low robustness when faced with computer-synthesized images.

7.1.2.3 Security

Security mainly refers to the ability of the watermark itself that is hard to be copied, tampered with, and forged, as well as the ability of watermark that is hard to be illegally detected and decoded. The latter is also called undetectable or concealed, that is, to prevent anyone other than the owner from determining or judging whether a watermark is embedded in the image. It is closely related to the saliency and robustness introduced earlier.

7.1.2.4 Other Characteristics

In addition to the above three important characteristics, other characteristics need to be considered according to the requirements of specific applications.

1. Complexity

    Low complexity refers to the low computational load and fast computational speed for watermarking (embedding and detection). The image has a large amount of data, so low complexity (such as low codec calculations) is particularly important for the application of image watermarking.

2. Uniqueness

It is also called certainty. That is to say, from the detection or judgment result of the watermark, the uniqueness of the ownership can be clearly determined, or the watermark should clearly reflect or indicate the identity of the owner. There should be no ambiguity that may cause multiple ownership disputes. A unique watermark has the effect of a certificate, which can provide complete and reliable evidence of the ownership of the copyrighted information product.

3. Universal/generality

Refers to whether the same watermarking technology can be applied to different product media, including audio, animation, image, video, and so on.

Some of the above-mentioned characteristics are mutually restrictive and competitive, and the choice needs to be weighted against the pros and cons according to the needs of practical applications. For example, robustness requires increasing the strength of the watermark, and if the strength of the watermark is too high, the watermark will be visible, which in turn will reduce the security of the watermark and, at the same time, lead to a reduction in the visual quality of the product.

7.1.3 Watermark Classification

There are many different classification methods for watermark and watermarking technology according to usage, technology, characteristics, and so on. Some classifications based on watermark characteristics are discussed below.

7.1.3.1 Publicity Classification

Considering the publicity of watermarks, watermarks can be divided into the following four types.

1. Private watermark

The detection of this type of watermark needs to provide the original digital product, which can be used as a reminder to find the location of the watermark embedded or to distinguish the watermark part from the embedded watermark image. The detector used at this time is also called a detector with auxiliary information.

2. Semi-private watermark

The detection of this type of watermark does not need to use the original digital product, but it must provide information about whether there is a watermark in the original digital product.

3. Public watermark (blind watermark)

The detection of this type of watermark neither requires the provision of original digital products nor requires the provision of digital products with embedded watermarks. This watermark can be detected directly from the received digital product. In contrast to this blind watermark, the first two types of watermarks can be called non-blind watermarks.

4. Asymmetric watermark (public key watermark)

The watermark is that any user can see/know but it cannot be removed. At this time, the keys used in the watermark embedding process and the watermark detection process are different.

7.1.3.2 Perceptual Classification

Considering the perception of the watermark (the visibility of the image watermark), the watermark can be divided into the following two types.

1. Perceptible watermark

Perceptible watermarks are visible, such as visible icons overlaid on images (such as those used to mark web images to prevent commercial use). Another example of a visible watermark is the logo of a TV station seen in the upper left and/or right corners of the TV screen. This kind of watermark makes it clear at a glance that this is a channel of a certain TV station, and that it is a broadcast program of a certain TV station. Such a watermark not only proves the attribution of the product but also does not hinder the appreciation of the programs. Another important application of perceptible watermark is to distribute a product with a perceptible digital watermark on the Internet before the digital product is sold. The watermark is often copyright information, which provides clues to find the original high-resolution work. When consumers buy, the perceptible watermark can be removed with professional software after payment.

2. Imperceptible watermark

Imperceptible watermarks (invisible watermarks for image), like the invisible text of invisible ink technology, are hidden in digital products. This kind of watermark often indicates the identity of the original work, and counterfeiters should not easily remove it. It is mainly used to prevent illegal copying and to identify the authenticity of products. A digital signature (adding a watermark) to a digital file cannot be directly attached to the image in a visible form because it can easily be erased or replaced, and it also affects the viewing value and use-value of the original work. It also cannot be implemented with a cryptographic digital signature because in this way, it will make the image appear in an unreadable form. The digital watermark of each genuine copy of the original work can be unique to identify the characteristics of the person who obtained the copy (recipient, legal consumer); it can also be that multiple copies have the same digital watermark, which is often the characteristics of the producer or the issuer. Digital watermarks that are not easily perceptible cannot prevent legal products from being copied illegally, but because digital watermarks exist in products, they can be used as evidence in court.

7.1.3.3 Meaning/Content Classification

Considering the meaning or content of the embedded watermark itself, watermarks can be divided into the following two types.

1. Meaningless watermark

    Meaningless watermarks often use pseudo-random sequences (Gaussian sequence, binary sequence, uniformly distributed sequence) to represent the presence or absence of information. The pseudo-random sequence is composed of pseudo-random numbers, which are more difficult to imitate and can ensure the security of the watermark. For meaningless watermarks, hypothesis testing is often used to detect:

    No watermark (n is noise):

    $$H_0 : g - f = n \tag{7.4}$$

    With watermark:

    $$H_1 : g - f = w + n \tag{7.5}$$

    Using a pseudo-random sequence as a watermark can only give two conclusions: "Yes" and "No", which is equivalent to one bit of secret information put into the digital product. Pseudo-random sequence cannot represent specific information and has certain limitations in its use.

2. Meaningful watermark

    Meaningful watermarks are visible (text strings, seals, icons, images, etc.), and they have precise meanings in themselves. Meaningful watermarks can provide much more information than meaningless watermarks, but the requirements for their embedding are much higher, and the detection situation is much more complicated. For example, if the watermark is a text string, the detection result may be that a part of the text is detected and/or only a part of the detected text is correct, in addition to the detected and undetected judgment results.

7.2 WATERMARK MEASUREMENT INDEX

For watermark and watermarking technology, the quality of watermark and the performance of watermarking technology must also be considered, which requires a measurement index for watermark. There are different measurement indicators for different characteristics of watermarks, including many *benchmark measurement* methods to measure the performance of watermarking. Since the different characteristics of watermarks are related, some watermark measurement indicators may be used when measuring different watermark characteristics; while in order to measure a certain watermark characteristic, multiple measurement indicators may also be used.

The following mainly discusses three important characteristics of watermarking.

7.2.1 Saliency/Perception Measurement

For image watermarks, the measurement of its *saliency* is mainly judged from the perspective of perception (invisibility).

7.2.1.1 Perception Benchmark Metrics

The measurement of perception can adopt the scheme of benchmark measurement. A typical benchmark measurement method (Kutter and Petitcolas 1999) is to fix the payload to 80 bits and use the distortion measure for the visual quality measure (Branden and Farrell 1996). The distortion measure considers the contrast sensitivity and mask characteristics of the human visual system (HVS), and counts the points that exceed the visual threshold (e.g., *just a noticeable difference*, JND).

One indicator closely related to saliency is fidelity. The *fidelity* of a watermark-embedded image can be judged by comparison with the original (non-watermarked) image. If it is considered that the watermarked image may be degraded during transmission, the fidelity of the watermarked image needs to be judged by the difference between its result after transmission and the result after transmission of the original image.

7.2.1.2 Objective Distortion Metrics

The above benchmark measurement used to measure the invisibility of an image watermark is based on a subjective index, but the fidelity can also be measured with an objective distortion metric. If $f(x, y)$ is used to represent the original image and $g(x, y)$ is used to represent the image embedded with the watermark, here the image size is all $N \times N$, then different *distortion measures* can be defined. This includes the following (1)–(6) for difference distortion metrics, (7) and (8) for correlation distortion metrics, and (9) and (10) for other distortion metrics.

1. Average absolute difference:

$$D_{\text{aad}} = \frac{1}{N^2} \sum_{x=0}^{N-1} \sum_{y=0}^{N-1} \left| g(x,y) - f(x,y) \right| \tag{7.6}$$

2. Mean squared error:

$$D_{\text{mse}} = \frac{1}{N^2} \sum_{x=0}^{N-1} \sum_{y=0}^{N-1} \left| g(x,y) - f(x,y) \right|^2 \tag{7.7}$$

3. L^p norm:

$$D_{L^p} = \left\{ \frac{1}{N^2} \sum_{x=0}^{N-1} \sum_{y=0}^{N-1} \left| g(x,y) - f(x,y) \right|^p \right\}^{1/p} \tag{7.8}$$

When $p=1$, the average absolute difference is obtained; when $p=2$, the root mean square error is obtained.

4. Laplacian mean squared error:

$$D_{\text{Lmse}} = \frac{\displaystyle\sum_{x=0}^{N-1}\sum_{y=0}^{N-1}\left[\nabla^2 g(x,y) - \nabla^2 f(x,y)\right]^2}{\displaystyle\sum_{x=0}^{N-1}\sum_{y=0}^{N-1}\left[\nabla^2 f(x,y)\right]^2} \tag{7.9}$$

5. Signal-to-noise ratio:

$$D_{\text{snr}} = \frac{\displaystyle\sum_{x=0}^{N-1}\sum_{y=0}^{N-1}\left[f^2(x,y)\right]}{\displaystyle\sum_{x=0}^{N-1}\sum_{y=0}^{N-1}\left[g(x,y) - f(x,y)\right]^2} \tag{7.10}$$

6. Peak signal-to-noise ratio (PSNR):

$$D_{\text{psnr}} = \frac{N^2 \displaystyle\max_{x,y}\left\{f(x,y)\right\}}{\displaystyle\sum_{x=0}^{N-1}\sum_{y=0}^{N-1}\left[g(x,y) - f(x,y)\right]^2} \tag{7.11}$$

7. Normalized cross-correlation:

$$C_{\text{ncc}} = \frac{\displaystyle\sum_{x=0}^{N-1}\sum_{y=0}^{N-1} g(x,y) f(x,y)}{\displaystyle\sum_{x=0}^{N-1}\sum_{y=0}^{N-1} f^2(x,y)} \tag{7.12}$$

8. Correlation quality:

$$C_{\text{cq}} = \frac{\displaystyle\sum_{x=0}^{N-1}\sum_{y=0}^{N-1} g(x,y) f(x,y)}{\displaystyle\sum_{x=0}^{N-1}\sum_{y=0}^{N-1} f(x,y)} \tag{7.13}$$

9. Histogram similarity:

$$O_{\text{hs}} = \sum_{l=0}^{L-1} \left| H_g(l) - H_f(l) \right| \tag{7.14}$$

10. Global sigma signal-to-noise ratio:
Here it is needed to decompose the image into $n \times n$ blocks, let $B = (N \times N)/(n \times n)$, then:

$$O_{\text{gssnr}} = \frac{\displaystyle\sum_{b=1}^{B} \sigma_b^2(f)}{\displaystyle\sum_{b=1}^{B} \left[\sigma_b^2(g) - \sigma_b^2(f) \right]^2} \tag{7.15}$$

where

$$\sigma_b(f) = \sqrt{\frac{1}{n^2} \sum_{b=1}^{B} f^2(x,y) - \left[\frac{1}{n^2} \sum_{b=1}^{B} f(x,y) \right]^2} \tag{7.16}$$

$$\sigma_b(g) = \sqrt{\frac{1}{n^2} \sum_{b=1}^{B} g^2(x,y) - \left[\frac{1}{n^2} \sum_{b=1}^{B} g(x,y) \right]^2} \tag{7.17}$$

7.2.2 Robustness Measurement

In general, the robustness of the watermark is related to the visibility of the watermark and the *payload*. To evaluate different watermarking methods fairly, a certain amount of image data can be determined first, and as many watermarks as possible that will not affect the visual quality are embedded in it. Then, the watermarked data is processed or attacked, and the performance of the watermarking method is estimated by measuring the proportion of errors. It can be seen that the benchmark method for measuring watermark performance will be related to the selected payload, visual quality measurement, and processing or attack methods.

There is a typical robustness benchmark measurement method (Fridrich and Miroslav 1999), in which the payload is fixed at 1 bit or 60 bits; the visual quality measurement uses a spatial masking model (Girod 1989). This model is based on the HVS and accurately describes the situation where visual distortion/degradation/artifacts are generated in the edges and smooth regions. The intensity of the watermark is adjusted so that less than 1% of the pixels can see a change according to the above model. The selected processing methods and related parameters are shown in Table 7.1. The ratio of visual distortion is a function of the related processing parameters.

TABLE 7.1   Processing Methods and Related Parameters Used to Determine Robustness

Serial Number	Processing Operation	Parameter
1	JPEG compression	Quality factor
2	Blurring	Mask size
3	Adding noise	Noise amplitude
4	Gamma correction	Gamma index
5	Pixel swap	Mask size
6	Mosaic (filtering)	Mask size
7	Median filtering	Mask size
8	Histogram equalization	

7.2.3 Security and Watermark Attack

The security of the watermark mainly considers the resistance to malicious attacks on the watermark.

7.2.3.1 Attack type

Attacks on watermarks are unauthorized operations and are often divided into three types.

1. Detection: For example, a user of a watermarked product tries to detect a watermark that should be detected by the owner. This is also called a *passive attack*.

2. Embedding: For example, a user of a watermarked product attempts to embed a watermark that should be embedded by the owner. This is also called a *forgery attack*.

3. Deletion: For example, a user of a watermarked product attempts to delete a watermark that should be deleted by the owner. This is also called a *deletion attack* and can be further divided into *remove attack* and *masking attack*.

The above types of attack methods may also be used in combination. For example, one may first try to delete the original watermark on the product and then try to embed another watermark (belong to the attacker), this is called a *substitution attack*.

7.2.3.2 Typical Attack Examples

A few typical examples of *watermark attacks* are as follows.

1. IBM attack

   This is an attack method against the reversible watermarking algorithm, which can produce ambiguity. Suppose the original image is I, and the image with watermark W_A is $I_A = I + W_A$. When attacking, the attacker will first generate his own watermark W_F and then create a fake original image $I_F = I_A - W_F$. Accordingly, the attacker can claim that he owns the copyright of the image I_A because he can use his forged original image I_F to detect the watermark W_F from the real original image I. Although the original author can use the real original image I to detect its watermark W_A from the forged original image I_F, it still produces a situation that cannot be distinguished and explained. An effective way to prevent this attack is to use an irreversible watermark embedding algorithm.

2. Mosaic attack

This attack method first divides the image into many small images and then puts them together on the HTML page to form a complete image. General web browsers can organize these images without leaving any gaps in the middle of the images so that the overall effect of such a pieced-together image will look the same as the original image. At this time, the normally used Internet automatic infringement detector including a digital watermarking system and a Web crawler cannot detect infringements. As mentioned earlier, if the detector can detect watermarks from very small images, this attack can be prevented.

3. Collusion attack

The so-called collusion attack (also called multicopy attack) is to use different watermarked versions of the same original data set to generate an approximate data set, and use this to approximate and restore the original data. The purpose of this is to make the detection system unable to detect the existence of a copyright watermark in this approximate data set. One of the easiest ways to achieve this collusion attack is to average the different versions. For example, many copies of the same work will have different watermarks. When watermarking is used as a method to identify purchasers, it may be attacked by many purchasers. At this time, multiple users can use their own legal copies of the watermark to destroy the watermark or form different legal watermarks to frame a third party by averaging the same data.

7.2.3.3 Watermark Attack Analysis

To resist watermark attacks, it is necessary to analyze watermark attacks when designing the watermark system. It is to simulate attacks on the designed watermark system to test its robustness against watermark attacks. The purpose of the attack is to make the corresponding watermark system unable to recover the watermark signal correctly, or the detection tool cannot detect the existence of the watermark signal. In this way, the design of the watermark system can be improved by analyzing the weaknesses of the system and the reasons for its vulnerability.

There is a tool used to simulate attacks, called StirMark, which is a watermark attack software. People can use it to evaluate the anti-attack ability of different watermark algorithms by examining whether the watermark detector can extract or detect watermark information from the attacked watermark carrier. StirMark can simulate many processing methods and attack methods, such as geometric distortion (stretching, shearing, rotation, etc.), nonlinear A/D and D/A conversion, print output, scanner scanning, resampling attacks, and so on. In addition, StirMark can also combine various processing methods and attack means to form new attacks.

7.3 DCT DOMAIN WATERMARK

Although the embedding of image watermarks can be carried out in the spatial domain, that is, the image domain, most techniques for the embedding of image watermarks are carried out in the transform domain. Typical representatives of transform domain algorithms use transform technology to realize the superposition of watermark signals in the frequency domain and use techniques such as spread spectrum communication to effectively encode the watermark signals to improve robustness and invisibility. Some also appropriately use filtering techniques for watermarking. The high-frequency noise introduced by the signal is eliminated, which increases the resistance to low-frequency filtering attacks.

The main advantages of the transform domain methods include:

1. The energy of the watermark signal can be widely distributed to all pixels in image, which helps to ensure invisibility.

2. It can be more convenient to combine certain characteristics of the HVS, which is conducive to improving the robustness.

3. The transform domain method is compatible with most international standards, and can directly implement the watermarking algorithm in the compressed domain (the watermark at this time is also called bit stream watermark) to improve efficiency.

The *discrete cosine transform* (DCT) domain is a common transform domain. The DCT domain watermark has first been applied in practice.

7.3.1 Features and Principles

In the DCT domain, images are often decomposed into direct current (DC) components and AC (alternating current) components. From the perspective of robustness (under the premise of ensuring the invisibility of the watermark), the watermark signal should be embedded in the part of image that is most important to humans (Cox et al. 2002). Therefore, the DC component is more suitable for embedding watermarks than the AC component. On the one hand, compared with the AC coefficient, the absolute amplitude of the DC coefficient is much larger, so the perceived capacity is large; on the other hand, according to the signal processing theory, the image with an embedded watermark is most likely to encounter the signal processing process, such as grayscale transformation, compression, low-pass filtering, sub-sampling, interpolation, and so on, that has a greater impact on the AC component than on the DC component. If the watermark is embedded in the AC component and the DC component at the same time, the confidentiality of the embedding can be enhanced by using the AC component, and the amount of embedded data can be increased by using the DC component.

AC components in the DCT domain are divided into high-frequency components and low-frequency components. The high-frequency components are related to the invisibility of the watermark, but it is not enough if robustness is considered. On the other hand, the low-frequency components are more important when considering robustness, but they have a greater impact on visual observation. *Spread spectrum* technology can reconcile the contradiction between the two, and it allows low-energy signals to be embedded in various frequency bands. Spread spectrum technology also provides the possibility of using a key to control the pseudo-noise generator to protect the secret of the watermark. Applying spread spectrum technology to hidden information (watermark) can match the frequency band by changing the image before transmitting the watermark (Kutter and Hartung 2000).

In practice, there are some other advantages in using watermarks in the DCT domain. The embedding rules in the DCT domain are often more robust than the JPEG and MPEG compression methods that use DCT so that the watermarks can be better prevented from being affected by JPEG or MPEG compression. The research results of visual distortion in source coding in the DCT domain can also be used to predict the influence of watermark on carrier image.

In the DCT domain, a semi-fragile watermark can also be embedded. Many semi-fragile watermarking algorithms have been proposed in the DCT domain to resist JPEG compression.

7.3.2 Meaningless Watermarking Algorithm

The following introduces a *meaningless watermarking* scheme that comprehensively utilizes DC and AC coefficients of DCT (Zhang et al. 2001).

7.3.2.1 Watermark Embedding

The flowchart of the *watermark embedding* algorithm can be seen in Figure 7.2. Before embedding the watermark, the image is preprocessed. The original image is divided into small blocks, and all small blocks are divided into two types according to the texture classification: small blocks with simple texture or small blocks with complex texture. Besides, DCT is performed on each small block, through the analysis of the DCT coefficient of each small block, the intensity of blocks can be classified. Combined the results of the above two classifications, the small blocks in the image are divided into three categories: (i) Blocks with low intensity and simple texture; (ii) Blocks with high intensity and complex texture; (iii) Other blocks that do not meet the above two types of conditions. According to the principle of invisibility, the amount of watermark embedded in small blocks of Type (i) should be less, and the amount of watermark embedded in small blocks of Type 2 can be more, while the amount of watermark embedded in small blocks of Type 3 is in the middle.

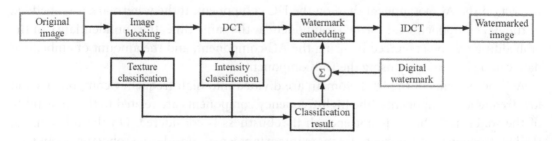

FIGURE 7.2   DCT domain watermark embedding process.

It has been proved that the watermark composed of Gaussian random sequence has the best robustness (Cox et al. 2002). Therefore, a random sequence $\{g_m: m=0, 1, 2, \ldots, M-1\}$ that obeys the Gaussian distribution $N(0, 1)$ is generated as the watermark. The length M of the sequence should be considered in accordance with the robustness and invisibility of the watermark and should match the number of DCT coefficients used. If four DCT coefficients are used for each small block i, namely $F_i(0, 0)$, $F_i(0, 1)$, $F_i(1, 0)$, and $F_i(1, 1)$, then the sequence length M can be taken as four times the number of blocks in the image. The sequence is multiplied by an appropriate stretching factor according to the classification result of the image block, and then the DCT coefficients are embedded. Different embedding equations are used for DC and AC coefficients: linear equations are used for AC coefficients, and nonlinear equations are used for DC coefficients. The embedding results are:

$$F_i'(u,v) = \begin{cases} F_i(u,v)\times(1+ag_m) & m=4i & (u,v)=(0,0) \\ F_i(u,v)+bg_m & m=4i+2u+v & (u,v)\in\{(0,1),(1,0),(1,1)\} \\ F_i(u,v) & \text{otherwise} \end{cases}$$

$$(7.27)$$

Among them, a and b are stretch factors. According to Weber's law, ag_m should be less than 0.02 theoretically. In practice, for blocks with simple texture, $a=0.005$; for blocks with complex texture, $a=0.01$. The value of the stretch factor b is selected according to the previous classification of the blocks. The first category selects 3, the second category selects 9, and the third category selects 6. Finally, IDCT is performed on the image after coefficient adjustment in the DCT domain to obtain a watermarked image.

A set of example results obtained by using the above method to embed the watermark is shown in Figure 7.3, where Figure 7.3a is the 512×512 Lena image, and Figure 7.3b is the image after the watermark is embedded. Comparing the watermarked image with the original image, it is difficult to find the presence of the watermark from the visual effect point of view. From the difference image in Figure 7.3c, it can be seen that there is almost

(a) (b) (c)

FIGURE 7.3 Comparison for images before and after watermark embedding.

no difference between the two images, which indicates that the watermark embedded in this algorithm has better invisibility.

7.3.2.2 Watermark Detection

The flowchart of the *watermark detection* algorithm can be seen in Figure 7.4. The detection of watermark adopts the hypothesis correlation detection method. That is, the result of subtracting the image to be tested from the original image is subjected to block DCT, and then the correlation detection is made between the watermark sequence to be tested and the original watermark to determine whether the image to be tested contains a watermark.

The specific steps of watermark detection are as follows:

1. Calculate the difference image between the original image $f(x, y)$ and the to-be-tested image $h(x, y)$, in which watermark may be embedded:

$$e(x,y) = f(x,y) - h(x,y) = \bigcup_{i=0}^{N-1} e_i(x',y') \quad 0 \le x',y' < 8 \tag{7.28}$$

2. Calculate DCT for each small block (8×8) of the difference image:

$$E_i(u',v') = \text{DCT}\{e_i(x',y')\} \quad 0 \le x',y' < 8 \tag{7.29}$$

3. Extract possible watermark sequences from small blocks of DCT image:

$$w_i(u',v') = \{g_j, j = 4i + 2u' + v'\} = E_i(u',v') \tag{7.30}$$

4. Calculate the correlation between the possible watermark and the original embedded watermark with the following function:

$$C(W,w) = \sum_{j=0}^{4N-1}(w_j g_j) \Bigg/ \sqrt{\sum_{j=0}^{4N-1} w_j^2} \tag{7.31}$$

If $C(W, w) > T$, it indicates that the required watermark is detected; otherwise, it is considered that there is no watermark. When selecting the threshold T, both false detection and

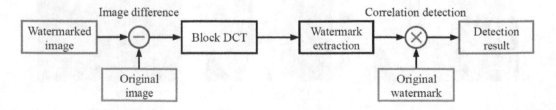

FIGURE 7.4 Watermark detection process.

false alarm must be considered. When the random sequence satisfies the Gaussian distribution, the probability of $C(W, w) > T$ is the probability that the absolute value of the watermark sequence is greater than the product of the threshold and the variance. For $N(0, 1)$ distribution, if the threshold is 5, the probability that the absolute value of the watermark sequence is greater than 5 will be less than or equal to 10^{-5}.

7.3.2.3 Watermark Performance

This meaningless watermark has a certain degree of robustness. The test results of several common image processing operations and interference on the watermarked Lena image can be seen in Figure 7.5. Figure 7.5a is the result image (PSNR = 19.4 dB) after compressing the watermarked image by retaining only the first four DCT coefficients (with obvious distortion). Figure 7.5b is the result image of mean filtering the watermarked image with 5×5 mask (PSNR = 21.5 dB). Figure 7.5c is the result image of 2:1 sub-sampling in both the horizontal and vertical directions (take one pixel in a small region of 2×2, PSNR = 20.8 dB) of the watermarked image, and Figure 7.5d is the result image (PSNR = 11.9 dB) after adding Gaussian noise to the watermarked image, the effect of noise is more obvious). In these four cases, the image has large distortion, but the watermark can be detected correctly.

This kind of meaningless watermark has better uniqueness. In theory, given a random sequence as a watermark, other sequences that can be generated by the same probability distribution can also be used as a watermark. According to this idea, the uniqueness of the watermark can be tested. Here, consider generating 10,000 random sequences from a Gaussian distribution that satisfies $N(0, 1)$, select one sequence as the embedded watermark, and test the other sequences as the contrast watermark. The test results are shown in Table 7.2, where only the maximum correlation values among the 9,999 fake watermarks

(a)　　　　　　　(b)　　　　　　　(c)　　　　　　　(d)

FIGURE 7.5 Example of checking the robustness of watermark to various image processing operations.

TABLE 7.2 Test Results on the Uniqueness of the Watermark

Image Processing Operation	Original Image	Compression	Mean Filtering	Sub-sampling
Correlation with real watermark	114.5	12.4	13.8	23.6
Correlation with fake watermarks (Max)	3.82	3.98	4.59	3.58

for each operation are listed. Since the correlation results obtained with real watermarks and fake watermarks are quite different, it is easy to distinguish real watermarks from fake watermarks.

7.3.3 Meaningful Watermarking Algorithm

In many appraisal or identification applications, the information that is often used includes the name, label, or icon of the owner or company. To represent these contents, a meaningful (multi-bit) watermark is needed. On the one hand, it will be able to directly represent the owner's information, and it will not be easily forged or tampered with. On the other hand, the technology of meaningful watermarking is also much more complicated.

7.3.3.1 Watermark Design

The following introduces an algorithm that can be used for *meaningful watermarking* obtained by improving the above-mentioned watermarking scheme (Zhang et al. 2001). Its specific steps include:

1. Construct a symbol set (meaningful symbols).

2. Each symbol corresponds to a binary sequence.

3. Let the occurrence of "0" and "1" in the binary sequence obey the Bernoulli distribution.

4. Extend the binary sequence to the length of an integral multiple of the number of symbols.

5. Add the extended sequence to the coefficients of the DCT block.

Specifically, a set of 64 symbols can be used. Each symbol corresponds to a 32-bit sequence. In such a 32-bit sequence, let the occurrence of 0 and 1 satisfy the Bernoulli distribution. If 0 and 1 are coded as −6 and 6, respectively, the Hamming distance between any two symbols will be greater than 16, and the entire sequence is quite random. When detecting the watermark, the degree of matching between the extracted symbol and each symbol in the symbol set can be calculated, and the symbol corresponding to the largest matching result is the detected symbol.

7.3.3.2 Watermark Embedding

According to the channel coding theorem, if the dimensionality of the filter is increased but the signal power and noise probability remain unchanged, the number of symbols that can be embedded in the image will decrease. Therefore, in this algorithm, the number of symbols that can be embedded in the image must be determined first, and then these symbols are repeatedly embedded into each DCT block according to the principle of spread spectrum communication. According to the number of symbols embedded in the image, the dimension of the matching filter can be automatically determined to maximize the use of the channel capacity. In practice, the 32-bit sequence can be repeatedly extended according to the number of image blocks. If the first 4 coefficients are used for embedding for each image block, the maximum number of bits that can be embedded for an image of 512×512 is 4×(512×512)/(8×8)=16,384. This number of bits corresponds to 512 symbols. When the number of symbols to be embedded is less than 512, the symbols can be expanded repeatedly. For example, when there are only two symbols to be embedded, each bit can be repeated 16,384/64=256 times.

The specific steps of *watermark embedding* are as follows:

1. Decompose the original image $f(x, y)$ into 8×8 image blocks, and mark each block as B_i, $i=0, 1, \ldots, N-1$:

$$f(x,y)=\bigcup_{i=0}^{N-1}B_i =\bigcup_{i=0}^{N-1}f_i\left(x',y'\right) \quad 0\leq x',y'<8 \tag{7.32}$$

2. Calculate DCT for each block:

$$F_i\left(u',v'\right)=\mathrm{DCT}\left\{f_i\left(x',y'\right)\right\} \quad 0\leq x',y'<8 \tag{7.33}$$

3. Extend the sequence corresponding to each symbol to a sequence of $32M$ (where M is the number of symbols to be embedded);

4. According to the length L of the symbol sequence to be embedded, choose a suitable matching filter dimension. For example, assuming that $2^N\leq L\leq 2^{N+1}$, the dimensionality can be calculated as 2^{13-N} using the actual data above;

5. Embed the extended sequence into the extended DCT block. Let $W=\{w_i|w_i=0, 1\}$ be the extended sequence corresponding to meaningful symbols, the watermark can be represented as:

$$F_i' =\begin{cases} F_i+s & w_i =1 \\ F_i-s & w_i =0 \end{cases} \quad F_i \in D \tag{7.34}$$

where D represents the first four DCT coefficients, and s is the strength of the watermark (in the specific case above $s=6$).

7.3.3.3 Watermark Detection

The first three specific steps for detecting meaningful watermarks are the same as those for detecting meaningless watermarks. In the fourth step, suppose that for the i-th extraction, w_i^* is the intensity of the extracted signal; w_i^k is the output of the k-th matching filter, and the correlation between them is:

$$C_k\left(w^*,w^k\right)=\sum_{i=0}^{M-1}\left(w_i^* \cdot w_i^k\right)\bigg/ \sqrt{\sum_{i=0}^{M-1}\left(w_i^*\right)^2} \tag{7.35}$$

where M is the dimension of the matched filter. For a given j, $1 \leq j \leq 64$, if:

$$C_j\left(w^*, w^j\right) = \max\left[C_k\left(w^*, w^k\right)\right] \quad 0 \leq k \leq 64 \tag{7.36}$$

then the symbol corresponding to j is the detected symbol.

7.3.3.4 The Robustness of Watermark

This meaningful watermark has been tested for robustness against low-pass filtering, subsampling, and JPEG compression. Lena image, Flower image, and Person image have been used for test.

1. Robustness to low-pass filtering

   A watermark sequence with eight symbols is embedded in each experimental image. Low-pass filtering uses 3×3, 5×5 and 7×7 masks, respectively. Figure 7.6 shows the results of several low-pass filtering. Figure 7.6a and b are the results of 5×5 and 7×7 mask filtering on the Lena image, respectively. Figure 7.6c and d shows the results of 5×5 and 7×7 mask filtering for the Flower image.

   For meaningful watermarking, it is necessary not only to correctly detect each symbol but also to correctly detect the position of each symbol. Table 7.3 shows the corresponding test results for all three images, where the correct symbol number refers to both the symbol correct and the position correct. The table also lists the *peak signal-to-noise ratios* (PSNR) of the three watermarked images after low-pass filtering to indicate image quality.

| (a) | (b) | (c) | (d) |

FIGURE 7.6   Several low-pass filtering results.

TABLE 7.3   Test Results on the Robustness of Low-Pass Filtering

	3×3		5×5		7×7	
Image	**# Correct Symbols**	**PSNR (dB)**	**# Correct Symbols**	**PSNR (dB)**	**# Correct Symbols**	**PSNR (dB)**
Lena	8	25.6	8	21.5	3	19.4
Flower	8	31.4	8	25.6	3	22.5
Person	8	19.3	4	12.4	1	9.4

It can be seen from Figure 7.6 and Table 7.3 that as the size of the mask increases, the image becomes more blurred, and the watermark's ability to resist low-pass filtering also decreases. Since the details of the Lena image and the Flower image are less than those of the Person image, all symbols can still be detected correctly after using 5×5 mask filtering, but at this time, the symbols embedded in the Person image cannot be detected correctly.

2. Robustness to sub-sampling

In this experiment, a sequence of eight symbols is also embedded for each experimental image. Three sub-sampling rates are considered, namely (in both horizontal and vertical directions) 1:2 sub-sampling, 1:4 sub-sampling, and 1:8 sub-sampling. Figure 7.7 shows several sub-sampling results. Figure 7.7a and b are the results of partial Lena image with 1:2 and 1:4 sub-sampling, respectively. Figure 7.7c and d shows the results of partial Person images with 1:2 and 1:4 sub-sampling, respectively. Comparing the two sets of images, the Person image is more affected by sub-sampling.

Table 7.4 shows the corresponding test results. The table also lists the PSNR of the three watermarked images after sub-sampling to indicate image quality. Compared with the case of low-pass filtering, the image distortion caused by the three types of sub-sampling is much more serious.

3. Robustness against JPEG compression

In this experiment, the size of the symbol sequence embedded in each experimental image varied from 1 to 128. Table 7.5 shows the corresponding test results. The value given in the table is the lowest value of the image PSNR when the entire

(a) (b) (c) (d)

FIGURE 7.7   Several sub-sampling results.

TABLE 7.4   Test Results of Robustness to Sub-sampling

	1:2		1:4		1:8	
Image	**# Correct Symbols**	**PSNR (dB)**	**# Correct Symbols**	**PSNR (dB)**	**# Correct Symbols**	**PSNR (dB)**
Lena	8	20.8	4	15.5	1	12.0
Flower	8	24.2	5	17.2	1	13.5
Person	8	12.8	0	6.6	0	4.6

TABLE 7.5 Test Results on the Robustness of JPEG Compression

Image	1	2	4	8	16	32	64	128
Lena	23.4	25.4	26.5	27.2	28.3	30.5	34.5	36.5
Flower	15.4	20.4	20.6	20.6	21.6	22.2	35.3	38.3
Person	23.3	24.3	25.8	26.7	26.8	26.8	26.9	38.4

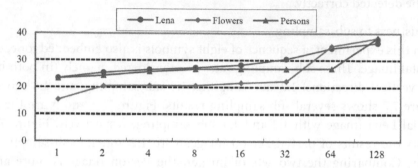

FIGURE 7.8   The relationship between the length of the embedded symbol sequence and the PSNR of the image.

symbol sequence can be detected correctly. The relationship between the length of the embedded symbol sequence and the noise level can be seen from the table. Since the dimension of the matching filter is automatically adjusted, the noise level that can be tolerated is also different for symbol sequences of different lengths. The relationship between the length of the embedded symbol sequence of the three experimental images and the PSNRs of the images is shown in Figure 7.8.

By the way, the semi-fragile watermark algorithm based on the DCT domain is usually proposed to resist JPEG compression.

7.4 DWT DOMAIN WATERMARK

In recent years, many international standards for image coding have adopted DWT, such as JPEG-2000, MPEG-4, H.265, and so on, so the DWT domain image watermarking method has also received more attention. The advantage of directly embedding the watermark in the DWT domain is that the information obtained in the compression can be reused so that no decoding is needed to embed the watermark in the compressed domain, which can reduce the relatively large number of calculations for embedding the watermark in the DWT domain to a certain extent.

7.4.1 Features and Process

Compared with DCT domain image watermarking, the superiority of DWT domain image watermarking technology comes from a series of characteristics of the wavelet transform:

1. Wavelet transform has multi-scale space-frequency characteristics, and the image decomposition can be continuously carried out from low resolution to high resolution. This helps to determine the distribution and location of the watermark to

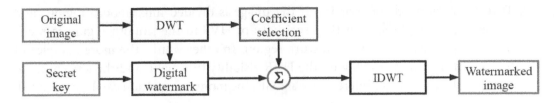

FIGURE 7.9   Wavelet domain watermark embedding process.

improve the robustness of the watermark and ensure invisibility. In contrast, DCT cannot decompose the image differently and only transforms the image as a whole to the frequency domain.

2. DWT has a fast algorithm, which can transform the image as a whole, and has good resistance to external interference such as filtering and compression processing. The DCT transform needs to divide the image into blocks, so the mosaic phenomenon will occur.

3. The multiresolution characteristics of DWT can better match the characteristics of the HVS, and it is easy to adjust the watermark embedding strength to adapt to the human visual characteristics, so as to better balance the contradiction between watermark robustness and invisibility. Therefore, wavelet watermarking algorithms often use some characteristics of HVS and masking effects.

The wavelet domain image watermarking method generally adopts the method of multi-resolution decomposition of the image and then selects the appropriate coefficient to add the watermark at the corresponding level after the decomposition. The basic embedding process can be seen in Figure 7.9. First, DWT is performed on the original image, and a certain number of coefficients are selected from the transformed coefficients for watermark embedding. A secret key can be added to the watermark and then embedded, which can increase the security of the watermark. After the coefficients of the DWT are embedded in the watermark, the inverse DWT is performed to return to the image domain to obtain the image embedded with the watermark.

7.4.2 Human Visual Characteristics

Wavelet transform has multi-scale space-frequency characteristics, which corresponds to the characteristics of the *human visual system* (HVS). In wavelet domain watermarking, some characteristics of the HVS, especially masking or masking effects (different sensitivity to different intensity/brightness ratios) are often combined. Common HVS characteristics and masking effects include:

1. Luminance masking characteristics: The human eye is less sensitive to noise added to high-brightness regions. This shows that the higher the image background brightness, the larger the *contrast sensitivity threshold* (CST) of the HVS, and the more additional information can be embedded.

2. Texture masking characteristics: If the image is divided into smooth regions and dense texture regions, then the sensitivity of HVS to the smooth region is much higher than that of the dense texture region. In other words, the more complex of texture in the image, the higher the HVS visibility threshold, and the less ability to perceive the presence of interference signals, the more information can be embedded.

3. Frequency characteristics: The human eye has different sensitivity to diverse spatial frequency components of the image. Experiments have shown that after transforming an image from the spatial domain to the frequency domain, the human eye is less sensitive to high-frequency content, and the low-frequency component corresponds to the smooth region in the image. Relatively, the human eye has a higher resolving power in the low-frequency region.

4. Phase characteristics: The human eye is less sensitive to changes in phase than to changes in mode. For example, in the watermarking technology based on discrete Fourier transform, the watermark information is often embedded in the phase component, and it is not easy to find.

5. Directional characteristics: The human eye has direction selection ability when observing a scene, and it is more sensitive to the characteristic changes in the horizontal and vertical directions than to the characteristic changes in the oblique direction. In addition, HVS has the most sensitivity to light intensity changes in the horizontal and vertical directions and the least sensitivity to light intensity changes in oblique directions.

With the help of HVS characteristics and the basic idea of the visual masking effect method, the *just noticeable difference* (JND) derived from the visual model, also known as the minimum noticeable difference (Branden and Farrell 1996) is used as a visual threshold and is used to determine the maximum intensity of the watermark signal that can be tolerated in each part of the image, so as to avoid the watermark embedding destroying the visual quality of the image. In other words, the human visual model is used to determine the modulation mask associated with the image to obtain the best watermarking performance. This method can not only improve the invisibility of the watermark but also improve the robustness of the watermark.

The following specifically introduces the visual threshold determined according to the visual masking characteristics of the human eye (Barni et al. 2001). Suppose that the image is decomposed by an L-level wavelet ($3L+1$ sub-images are obtained), and the visual threshold based on the human visual masking characteristics in the wavelet domain can be represented as $T(u, v, l, s)$, where u and v represent the position of the wavelet coefficients in wavelet space, the integer l ($0 \leq l \leq L$) represents the wavelet decomposition level, $s \in \{LH, HL, HH\}$ represents the direction of the high-frequency sub-image (LH, HL, HH represent the three sub-images obtained after wavelet decomposition: horizontal low frequency and vertical high frequency, horizontal high frequency and vertical low frequency, as well as horizontal high frequency and vertical high frequency, respectively). Three considerations for visual masking effects are as follows.

1. The human eye is not very sensitive to the noise of high-frequency sub-images in different directions and different levels, and it is also not very sensitive to the noise of sub-images in the 45° direction (such as HH sub-images). The sensitivity of different sub-images to noise is inversely proportional to the masking factor of the sub-image. Assuming that the masking factor of the sub-images in the s direction of layer l is $D(l, s)$, then $D(l, s)$ can be estimated by the following equation:

$$D(l,s) = D_l \times D_s \qquad (7.37)$$

Among them, D_l and D_s consider the masking characteristics of sub-images with different decomposition scales and different decomposition directions:

$$D_l = \begin{cases} 1 & l=0 \\ 0.32 & l=1 \\ 0.16 & l=2 \\ 0.1 & l=3 \end{cases} \qquad (7.38)$$

$$D_s = \begin{cases} \sqrt{2} & s \in HH \\ 1 & \text{otherwise} \end{cases} \qquad (7.39)$$

D_l takes a larger value for high-frequency sub-images, and a smaller value for low-frequency sub-images; D_s takes a larger value for sub-images in the 45° direction, and a smaller value for sub-images in other orientations. A large $D(l, s)$ indicates that the sub-image is less sensitive to noise, and more watermarks can be superimposed on it.

2. The human eye has different visual sensitivity to noise in different brightness regions and is usually the most sensitive to medium grayscales (the Weber ratio remains constant at 0.02 in a wide range around medium gray scales). The sensitivity decreases nonlinearly in both directions: toward low grayscales and high grayscales. In practical applications, this nonlinearity can be represented by a quadratic curve with respect to grayscale. For example, for a 256-level grayscale image, the grayscale range is divided into three parts. It can be considered that the dividing line between low grayscale and medium grayscale is at the grayscale of 85 (take the threshold $T_1 = 85$), while the dividing line between high grayscale and medium grayscale is at the gray level of 170 (take the threshold $T_2 = 170$). The normalized sensitivity curve should be as shown in Figure 7.10, where the horizontal axis is the gray level axis. In the low gray level region, the sensitivity increases in the form of a quadratic function with the increase in gray level; in the high gray level region, the sensitivity decreases in the

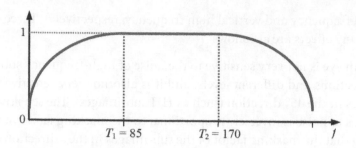

FIGURE 7.10 The normalized sensitivity curve of human eyes to different brightness.

form of a quadratic function with the increase in gray level; in the middle gray level region, the sensitivity remains constant.

Further, define the masking factor with the help of the sensitivity curve. Consider dividing the image into small blocks, the average gray value of the block is m, and the masking factor of each point of the block to noise is $B(u, v)$:

$$B(u,v)=\begin{cases} \dfrac{(0.2-0.02)[m-T_1]^2}{T_1^2}+0.02 & m \leq T_1 \\[2mm] 0.02 & T_1 < m \leq T_2 \\[2mm] \dfrac{(0.2-0.02)[m-T_2]^2}{(255-T_2)^2}+0.02 & m > T_2 \end{cases} \tag{7.40}$$

The $B(u, v)$ curve obtained in this way is a downward convex curve, which is similar to inverting the curve in Figure 7.10 up and down. It can be seen from the $B(u, v)$ curve that the lower and higher gray levels are less sensitive to noise, and more watermarks can be superimposed.

3. The human eye is more sensitive to noise in the smooth region of the image and less sensitive to noise in the texture region. For this reason, the entropy value of the image region can be calculated. A smaller entropy value indicates a corresponding (gray-scale) smooth region, and a larger entropy value indicates a corresponding image texture region. Therefore, the texture masking effect of the block can be calculated according to the entropy value of the image block region. The entropy value of the block is denoted as H, the entropy value of the block is normalized and multiplied by the coefficient k to match with other masking effect factors, that is, the block image texture masking effect factor is obtained:

$$H(u,v)=k\frac{H-\min(H)}{\max(H)-\min(H)} \tag{7.41}$$

More watermarks can be superimposed in regions with large masking effects.

Considering the above three characteristics comprehensively, the value of the visual masking characteristic in the wavelet domain can be represented by the following equation (Barni et al. 2001):

$$T(u,v,l,s)=D(l,s)B(u,v)H(u,v) \tag{7.42}$$

The visual threshold $T(u, v, l, s)$ of the human visual masking characteristics given by Equation (7.42) comprehensively considers the sensitivity of the HVS at different resolutions and different directions, as well as the masking effects of image block under different brightness for contrast and different density of textures. According to the visual threshold, the intensity of watermark embedding and the invisibility of the embedded watermark can be controlled to ensure that the intensity of the embedded watermark is increased as much as possible on the premise that the watermark is invisible, so as to improve the robustness of the watermark.

7.4.3 Wavelet Watermarking Algorithm

The following is a discussion of the watermark embedding and detection processes in a wavelet watermarking algorithm (Wang et al. 2005).

7.4.3.1 Watermark Embedding

Here, a real random sequence with Gaussian distribution $N(0, 1)$ and length M is selected as the watermark W, that is, $W=\{w_1, w_2, ..., w_M\}$.

The specific process of the *watermark embedding* algorithm is as follows:

1. To prevent the influence of image shearing on watermark extraction, the watermark is first randomly permutated. A typical method (Hsu and Wu 1999) is to first use the key K_1 (which can include the author's identification code) as a seed to generate a random sequence W of length M, and then adjust the position of each element in W to obtain a new digital watermark sequence $Z=\{z_1, z_2, ..., z_M\}$. This latter step can also be seen as establishing a correspondence between the elements in the two sequences W and Z and replacing the corresponding elements.

2. Determine the wavelet base and perform an L-level fast wavelet transform on the original image $I(x, y)$ to obtain a lowest frequency sub-image and $3L$ different high-frequency sub-images respectively.

3. Calculate the visual threshold $T(u, v, l, s)$ of the human visual masking characteristics in the high-frequency sub-image according to Equation (7.25). Then according to $T(u, v, l, s)$, the wavelet coefficients in the high-frequency sub-image are arranged in descending order, and then the first N wavelet coefficients are selected as the watermark insertion position.

4. Embed the watermark as follows (that is, the first N wavelet coefficients are modulated by the watermark sequence):

$$S(u,v) = J(u,v) + qz_i \qquad (7.43)$$

Among them, $J(u, v)$ and $S(u, v)$ represent the (first N) wavelet coefficients of the original image and the watermark embedded image, respectively; q is the embedding intensity coefficient, and $q \in (0, 1]$; z_i is the i-th watermark component of the watermark sequence of length M. Here, embedding is carried out in the DWT domain. In the process of embedding the watermark, a secret key K_2 for extracting the watermark information is generated at the same time, and the key records the position of the first N wavelet coefficients used to embed the watermark information.

5. The high-frequency sub-images with the watermark embedded are combined with the low-frequency sub-images to perform a fast inverse wavelet transform to obtain the space image $G(x, y)$ with an embedded watermark.

The permutation described above is performed for the image block based on the variance of the image block. The variance of the image block can be regarded as a measure of the visibility of the image block. The variance of the image blocks can be used to rank the image blocks to determine the number of watermarks that can be embedded. The watermark image (binary image is considered here) can also be divided into blocks and ranked according to the number of watermark pixels (gray value 1) in each block. According to the two rankings, the corresponding relationship between the two sets of block images is established, and the permutation is performed accordingly.

A schematic diagram is shown in Table 7.6 (Hsu and Wu 1999), where the left two columns give the variance corresponding to the image block, the middle two columns give the number of watermark pixels in each watermark block, and the right two columns indicate the correspondence relationship for the embedding of each watermark block into each image block.

7.4.3.2 Watermark Detection

The process of *watermark detection* can be approximately regarded as the reverse process of the above-mentioned watermark embedding.

TABLE 7.6   Image Block Permutation Schematic

Image Block Pointer	Image Block Variance	Watermark Block Pointer	Watermark Pixel Number	Watermark Block Pointer		Image Block Pointer
0	40	1	10	0		0
3	30	2	8	1		1
1	20	3	5	2		2
2	10	0	2	3		3

1. First, select the wavelet base used in the embedding process, and perform L-level wavelet decomposition for both the original watermark embedded image $G(x, y)$ and the watermark image $D(x, y)$ to be detected (here the image $D(x, y)$ to be tested may be different with the original watermark embedded images $G(x, y)$), to obtain one lowest frequency sub-image and $3L$ high-frequency sub-images for each of these two images.

2. According to the secret key K_2 generated in the watermark embedding process, the important coefficient set $\{I_i, i = 1, 2, ..., P\}$ is obtained from the wavelet high-frequency sub-image of the original image $I(x, y)$. Take the address of these values as the index, the corresponding coefficients are selected from the high-frequency sub-images of the wavelet image to be measured $D(x, y)$ as the important coefficient set to be measured $\{D_i, i = 1, 2, ..., P\}$. The values of I_i and D_i are sequentially one-to-one compared to extract the watermark information Z. When the difference between I_i and D_i is greater than a certain threshold, it can be considered that the watermark component z_i exists at that position, and its value is set to 1, otherwise it is set to 0.

3. Perform the reverse operation of the watermark embedding Step (1) to obtain the watermark sequence to be judged $W' = \{w_1', w_2', ..., w_M'\}$.

The quantitative evaluation of the similarity between the watermark sequence to be tested and the original watermark can be done using the normalized correlation coefficient C_N:

$$C_N(W, W') = \frac{\sum_{i=1}^{L} (w_i - W_m)(w_i' - W_m')}{\sqrt{\sum_{i=1}^{L} (w_i - W_m)^2} \sqrt{\sum_{i=1}^{L} (w_i' - W_m')^2}} \tag{7.44}$$

In the above equation, W and W' are the original watermark sequence and the watermark sequence to be judged, respectively; and W_m and W_m' are the mean values of W and W', respectively. $C_N \in [-1, 1]$. If the value of C_N exceeds a certain threshold, it is determined that W and W' are related watermark sequences, that is, there is a previously embedded watermark in the image. The judgment threshold can be obtained by a posteriori estimation of the statistical value of the image embedded with the watermark.

Figure 7.11 shows a set of experimental results of watermark distribution and invisibility. The watermark used here is a random sequence with Gaussian distribution $N(0, 1)$ and length $M = 1000$. Figure 7.11a is the original image, Figure 7.11b is the watermarked image (PSNR = 38.52 dB), and Figure 7.11c is the absolute difference (image) of the two images. It can be seen from Figure 7.11:

1. From the visual effect, the difference between the two images before and after embedding the watermark cannot be seen, which shows that the embedded watermark of this algorithm has good invisibility. The normalized correlation coefficient calculation

(a)   (b)   (c)

FIGURE 7.11   Watermark distribution and invisibility effect.

TABLE 7.7   Wavelet Domain Watermarking Resistance to Some Image Processing and Attacks

Processing/Attacks	PSNR/dB	Normalized Correlation Coefficient C_N
Sharpening	34.19	0.969
Median filtering	32.00	0.689
2×2 Mosaic	29.62	0.531
JPEG Compression (Compression ratio 37:1)	27.15	0.299
Mean filtering	19.35	0.908
Gaussian noise	16.78	0.537

result for the two images is 0.999, indicating that the two images are highly correlated, which is consistent with the subjective feeling that the two images are very similar.

2. It can be seen from the difference image that the watermark embedding strength is larger in the texture region, low-brightness region, and high-brightness region, while it is relatively weaker in the smooth region and medium-brightness region of the image. The watermark embedding strength has the property of adaptive adjustment.

7.4.3.3 Wavelet Domain Watermark Performance Test

Lena image is still used for the robustness test of the above wavelet domain watermarking algorithm. The resistance of the embedded watermark to some image processing and attacks is shown in Table 7.7. If the decision threshold is selected as 0.2, the watermark can be well detected according to the normalized correlation coefficient value.

7.5 SOME RECENT DEVELOPMENTS AND FURTHER RESEARCH

In the following, some technique developments and promising research directions in recent years are briefly overviewed.

7.5.1 Zero-Watermarking

As discussed in Section 7.1.2, saliency (perception) and robustness are two important characteristics of watermarking. They are also closely related. Increasing the amount of watermark embedded is beneficial to increase the robustness of the watermark against attacks, but at the same time, it is also possible to increase the saliency of the watermark, making it easier for the watermark to be discovered/perceived and the watermark to be attacked. *Zero-watermarking* is a special watermark method proposed for solving this problem. It can be used to resolve the contradiction between the saliency and robustness of the invisible image watermark.

7.5.1.1 Basic Principle

Many watermarking methods are implemented by embedding (additional) watermark data into the carrier image. For image watermarking, the embedding of the watermark is equivalent to a certain amount of processing on the image. The spatial domain watermarking method directly modifies the image, and the frequency-domain watermarking method modifies the image indirectly. Although many methods take into account the characteristics of the HVS, the image alteration caused by the embedded watermark information is not perceived as much as possible, but after all, the image is artificially modified, resulting in the possibility of detecting the watermark from the image. This will reduce the robustness of the watermark. This also shows that there is a certain contradiction between the saliency (visual perception) and robustness of the watermark.

The main idea of zero-watermarking is to use the image's own characteristics to construct the watermark information, instead of modifying the image to change the image's own characteristics. Since there is no modification of any data in the original image, this kind of watermark related to the image but not added to the image can be called "zero-watermark" (Wen et al. 2003).

The zero-watermarking method uses the internal characteristics of the original carrier image to construct a "zero-watermark" and store it in the information database of *intellectual property right* (IPR) center. When the watermark needs to be authenticated, it is restored with the saved data to achieve authentication. This not only ensures the integrity of the original carrier image (the carrier image itself is not modified, so this kind of watermark has no effect on the image quality) but also solves the contradiction between the robustness and saliency of the watermarking algorithm (there is no limit to the amount of watermark data, so increasing robustness does not increase saliency or perception).

7.5.1.2 Watermark Generation

The general watermarking method includes two stages: watermark embedding and watermark detection (see Section 7.1.1). The zero-watermark method also includes two similar functional stages, except that the watermark is not directly embedded into the original carrier image (copyrighted image), but only the original carrier image is used for watermark generation (construction). Therefore, the first stage of zero-watermarking is often referred to as *watermark generation* or watermark construction. The zero-watermark generation process is shown in Figure 7.12. The input is the original carrier image and the original watermark image (with copyright information), and the output is the generated zero-watermark image. The feature vector extracted from the original carrier image and the encrypted watermark after encrypting the original watermark image are combined

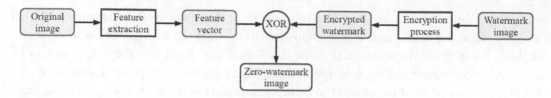

FIGURE 7.12   Schematic diagram of zero-watermark generation.

through XOR (mapping/masking) to construct a zero-watermark image. This is somewhat similar to the process of signal modulation, that is, the encrypted watermark image is modulated using the feature vector of the original image, but the original image itself is not changed.

The construction of a zero-watermark (image) sequence can be described as follows (Wen et al. 2003). Select part of the data from the original image (one can also select all the data), perform feature extraction (further discussion and examples below), and select M values from the result to form the feature sequence F (this sequence forms also a feature vector):

$$F(i) = \{f(i)\,|\,1 \leq i \leq M\} \qquad (7.45)$$

Then the random generator is used to generate a random sequence R that also has M value numbers and is reproducible according to the seed (the seed of the random generator can be used as the key to encrypt the watermark):

$$R(i) = \{r(i)\,|\,1 \leq i \leq M\} \qquad (7.46)$$

Now use the random number in the sequence R as the index of F to generate the sequence F':

$$F'(i) = \{f'(i)\,|\,1 \leq i \leq M\} = \{r[f(i)]\,|\,1 \leq i \leq M\} \qquad (7.47)$$

According to the sequence F', the watermark sequence W can be generated by mapping. If the i-th number in F' is positive, then the i-th number in the corresponding watermark sequence W has value 1, otherwise it has value −1. The binary watermark sequence W generated in this way can be expressed as:

$$W(i) = \{w(i)\,|\,1 \leq i \leq M\} \qquad (7.48)$$

where $w(i) = \{-1, 1\}$. The generated zero-watermark needs to be registered in the information database of the IPR center so that it can be used to verify the ownership of the original image when needed. Such a zero-watermark is closely related to the original image and can be used to protect the original image.

7.5.1.3 Watermark Verification

The second stage of the zero-watermarking method is to extract the zero-watermark image and verify it by comparing it with the zero-watermark registered in the IPR database, so this stage is often called *watermark verification*, and its flow chart can be seen in Figure 7.13. Among them, the input is the image that needs to be verified (the result of the original carrier image being transmitted through the network or undergone various processing) and the zero-watermark image, which is combined to form the watermark that needs to be verified, and the output is the binary judgment whether the watermark in the input image and the original watermark are consistent, this judgment can also be given by a corresponding degree of confidence based on the degree of correlation. The decryption process of the watermark here is the reverse process of the watermark generation process.

The operation on the image to be verified is the same as the operation on the original carrier image in the watermark generation, and the corresponding data of the carrier image is still used for feature extraction (Wen et al. 2003). First, find the coordinate positions of the M values used in the construction process, and use the values at these positions to form the sequence E (but note that the pixel values of these positions may have some changes after network transmission/processing):

$$E(i) = \{e(i) | 1 \leq i \leq M\} \tag{7.49}$$

Then the key is input to get the random sequence R of Equation (7.46), and get the changed sequence E' according to the sequence R:

$$E'(i) = \{e'(i) | 1 \leq i \leq M\} = \{e[r(i)] | 1 \leq i \leq M\} \tag{7.50}$$

According to the sequence E', the detected watermark sequence W' can be mapped out. If the i-th number in E' has a positive value, then the i-th number in the corresponding watermark sequence has value 1, otherwise, it has value −1. The binary watermark sequence W' obtained in this way can be expressed as:

$$W'(i) = \{w'(i) | 1 \leq i \leq M\} \tag{7.51}$$

where $w'(i) = \{-1, 1\}$.

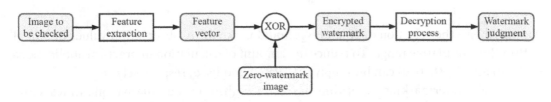

FIGURE 7.13   Schematic diagram of zero-watermark verification.

The relevant calculation and verification of the watermark can be carried out as follows (T is a pre-determined threshold according to Equation (7.3)):

$$C(W, W') > T \tag{7.52}$$

In the generation and verification of zero-watermark, the processes of feature extraction and encryption are very important to the performance of zero-watermarking. People have conducted in-depth research and proposed many methods. The following are examples of some typical ideas and methods.

7.5.1.4 Feature Extraction: Higher-Order Statistics

The cumulative quantity is the coefficient of the Taylor series expansion of the second characteristic function of the random variable, and the *higher-order statistic* quantity refers to the cumulative quantity of the third order and above. Compared with second-order cumulative quantities such as correlation function and power spectrum, high-order cumulative quantities can provide more random signal information. An important property of higher-order cumulative quantities is that the third-order and above third-order cumulative quantities of Gaussian processes are zero, which makes them an effective mathematical method for extracting signals from noise. Algorithms that use high-order cumulative quantities have good robustness.

In practice, what is sought first is the estimated value of the higher-order cumulative quantity. The estimation methods of the third-order cumulative quantity and the fourth-order cumulative quantity are given below (Wen et al. 2003):

Assuming that $\{x(n)\}$ is a stationary random signal (taking real values for the image), $n = 0, 1, ..., N-1$, the third-order cumulative quantity is estimated as:

$$C_{3x}(t_1, t_2) = \frac{1}{N} \sum_{n=N_1}^{N_2} [x(n)x(n+t_1)x(n+t_2)] \tag{7.53}$$

The fourth-order cumulative quantity is estimated as

$$C_{3x}(t_1, t_2, t_3) = \frac{1}{N} \sum_{n=N_1}^{N_2} [x(n)x(n+t_1)x(n+t_2)x(n+t_3)] \tag{7.54}$$

Among them, the selection of N_1 and N_2 should make the N observation values of $x(n)$ all within the cumulative range. To reduce the amount of calculation in practical applications, $C_{3x}(t_1, 0)$ and $C_{4x}(t_1, 0, 0)$ can be simply calculated and used, respectively.

The zero-watermarking algorithm based on high-order cumulative quantities shows good performance in the four image processing tasks: filtering, histogram equalization, dithering, and contrast enhancement under the influence of three geometric distortions: rotation, scaling, and clipping. These algorithms also have strong anti-Gaussian noise, anti-multiplicative noise, and anti-JPEG compression capabilities (Wen et al. 2003).

7.5.1.5 Feature Extraction: Singular Values and Extension

Singular value decomposition (SVD) is an effective tool for matrix diagonalization. Consider the image I of $N \times N$ in size, perform SVD on it and get

$$I = U \times S \times V^{\mathrm{T}} \tag{7.55}$$

where U and V are both orthogonal matrices of $N \times N$ (U is called the left singular value matrix, V is called the right singular value matrix), S is the diagonal matrix of $N \times N$, and the element values on the diagonal are λ_i ($i = 1, 2, \ldots, r$) and $\lambda_1 \geq \lambda_2 \geq \ldots \geq \lambda_r > 0$, r is the rank of matrix I.

After SVD, the corresponding orthogonal matrix represents the geometric structure of the image, and the singular matrix represents the brightness information of the image. When a small disturbance is applied to the image, the singular value of the image will not be excessively affected, so it has better stability. However, there is no one-to-one correspondence between the image and the singular value vector, so different images may have the same singular value vector, but their structures are not the same. This will cause the watermark information to be extracted from images that have never embedded the watermark information when using the singular value vector to embed the watermark information, causing false alarms when extracting the watermark. In addition, due to the inherent characteristics of SVD, serious diagonal distortion problems will occur when extracting watermarks (Xiao et al. 2019).

Boost normed-SVD (BN-SVD) introduces a power parameter β based on SVD, and its function is to obtain the diagonal gray level equalization after SVD. Consider the image I of $N \times N$, and perform BN-SVD on it, and get

$$I = U \times S^{\beta} \times V^{\mathrm{T}} \qquad 0 < \beta < 1 \tag{7.56}$$

where U, V, and S are the same as in Equation (7.55).

The advantages of BN-SVD include (Xiao et al. 2019):

1. It amplifies the singular value of the image, reduces the sensitivity of the image matrix when it is attacked, and improves the robustness of the algorithm to a certain extent.

2. It limits the singular value to a certain range, equalizes the grayscale in the diagonal direction, and can solve the problem of diagonal distortion.

3. It specializes the singular value vector so that it has a one-to-one correspondence with the image. In this regard, the singular value can represent the characteristics of the image, thereby can solve the problem of false alarm.

A further improvement to the BN-SVD method is to first perform wavelet transformation on the original image, then perform non-negative matrix decomposition on the low-frequency sub-bands, and finally perform the BN-SVD on the decomposed feature matrix (Xiao et al. 2020).

7.5.1.6 Video Zero-Watermarking

The zero-watermarking method can be used not only for images but also for videos (in this case, motion information can be used). For example, there is a video zero-watermarking algorithm (Yi and Feng 2020) for against re-compression of 3D-HEVC. The main steps are as follows:

1. Use the depth image of the *I*-frame in the video to segment the foreground and background. The human eye is less sensitive to changes in complex texture regions and fast-moving targets in the video. Therefore, the flat, static, and foreground regions in the video are more likely to cause perceptual changes when they are attacked. Selecting these regions helps limit the degree of modification of pirated videos in these regions so that the zero-watermark information can be better preserved.

2. Choose a suitable 16×16 block in the non-*I*-frame texture image in the video for the construction of zero-watermark. Perform 8×8 *all phase biorthogonal transform* (APBT) on these blocks and take their DC coefficients to form a coefficient matrix (the DC value in the flat, static region that passes through the APBT is more stable than in other regions).

3. Perform *SVD* on the coefficient matrix, and use the *most significant bit* (MSB) of the largest singular value as the final feature information to improve the robustness of the algorithm.

4. XOR the obtained feature information with the video watermark to generate a zero-watermark and register the zero-watermark to ensure security.

7.5.1.7 Video Zero-Watermark Based on CNN and a Self-Organizing Map

Recent deep learning techniques have also been used in video-watermarking. For example, a robust video zero-watermarking based on *deep convolutional neural network* (DCNN) and *self-organizing map* (SOM) in *polar complex exponential transform* (PCET) domain is proposed (Gao et al. 2021).

The watermarking process starts by extracting the content features of each video frame by DCNN and then some significant frames are selected as the input of SOM for clustering analysis. The frame with the highest entropy value in each cluster is selected as the keyframe. By introducing CNN and SOM into the keyframe selection, significant frames are chosen adaptively and the robustness of the scheme against inter-frame attacks is improved. Then, the PCET is applied to all selected keyframes to abstract invariant moments, which are scrambled by a chaotic logistic map and reduced in dimensions by SVD. By adopting PCET and SVD to extract strong and essential features of keyframes, the robustness of resisting intra-frame attacks and the distinguishability of zero-watermarking is enhanced. In the following, a binary sequence is generated by comparing adjacent values of the obtained compact PCET moments, which is permuted to produce a binary matrix as the features extracted from the original video. Finally, a bitwise exclusive-OR operation is imposed on the binary matrix and the encrypted watermark by the chaotic map to generate a zero-watermark signal. For improving the security, three chaotic sequences to scramble obtained PCET moments, to permute extracted binary sequence, and to encrypt original watermark are generated, respectively.

7.5.2 More Extensive Watermarking Technology

Watermarking technology has been deeply studied and widely used in recent years. Many watermarking methods also consider the characteristics of different media and different fields. Here are a few examples.

7.5.2.1 Database Watermarking

Database watermarking technology embeds watermark information into the database. In addition to requiring the watermark to be extracted by the publisher without damage during the detection stage, it also needs to modify the utilization value of the original data as little as possible in the process of embedding in the database to ensure that the original information can be normally exploited by the user. Therefore, in the research of database watermarking, great attention is paid to the distortion-free watermarking technology (zero-watermarking technology is a typical example) that can ensure the integrity of data to the greatest extent (Wang et al. 2019).

For databases, the use of watermarking technology not only requires proof of copyright but also requires more piracy tracking and tracing to the source. At this time, some people prefer to use the term database fingerprint technology. Database fingerprint technology is an extension of database watermarking technology, which embeds different mark information, called fingerprints, into the database using database watermarking technology. Generally, database fingerprint technology embeds different meaningful character strings for different users and then distributes the database embedded with different fingerprint information to different users in turn. If other pirated databases are found in the market, the source of the pirated databases can be determined according to the fingerprint information in the database, so as to achieve the effect of protecting copyright.

There are many types of databases. In addition to the common relational databases, there are also non-relational databases. There are also many data types in the database. In addition to numerical data, there is also categorical data. This is a data type that reflects the category of things. It has a limited number of unordered values, so it is discrete data. The database watermarking used for categorical data should hide the watermark in the categorical data. At this time, the requirement for watermarking technology is no longer to minimize the changes to the data like for the numerical data but to minimize the changed data items. Because the data types in the database are often complex and diverse, it is necessary to have a general and efficient database watermarking algorithm to break through the limitations of the data types in the traditional database watermarking algorithm.

7.5.2.2 3-D Mesh Watermarking

A 3-D mesh model consists of a collection of vertices and connections between these vertices.

As the embedded watermarking algorithm changes the original model data, it is unsuitable for the fields of computer-aided manufacturing and medicine, which require precise 3-D models. The really-applied *3-D mesh watermarking* techniques are all distortionless watermarking techniques (including zero-watermarking technique).

Compared with an image or video, the features in a 3-D model are more complex and diverse; thus, the selection of a signature watermark remains a harsh challenge. A new proposed zero-watermarking technique has three stages (Lee et al. 2021):

1. Feature extraction

    In this stage, the vertices with the spherical coordinates of the 3-D mesh model are first obtained, then the angles are divided into bins and the skewed distribution of the angle in spherical coordinates is used for extracting the features. It has a series of steps: (i) Convert the Cartesian coordinates of all vertices to spherical coordinates and arrange the vertices in ascending order, (ii) Partition the sorted vertices into bins, (iii) Permute the order of the angle partitions by the pseudo-random number sequence, (iv) Normalize the angles of all vertices for each bin within the range [0, 1], (v) Calculate the skewness value of angle for the bin, (vi) Repeat Step (iv) and Step (v) until all bins have been completed. The skewness value of each bin is obtained.

2. Watermark construction

    In this stage, the watermark is constructed by using the extracted features. The sign of the skewness value that has higher stability is used to produce the watermark. If the sign is positive, the corresponding feature value is 1; if the sign is negative, the corresponding feature value is 0. The watermark used to protect the copyright of the owner is formed by the vector of all feature values.

3. Zero-watermark detection

    The detection procedure for watermark consists of two steps: watermark extraction and correlation analysis. The watermark extraction has the same flow as the watermark construction. The correlation analysis measures the strength of association between the extracted watermark and the original one to verify the copyright of the model owner.

The flow chart of feature extraction and watermark construction is given in Figure 7.14.

7.5.2.3 Bio-Medical Signal Data Watermarking

Embedding watermark into digital media (signal, image, etc.) can not only protect the copyright but also give a means of data hiding. This function has been considered in biomedical

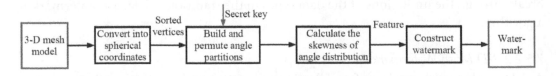

FIGURE 7.14 Flow chart of feature extraction and watermark construction.

signal data sharing. In the case of sharing bio-medical signals through an open network, it should be noted that the distortion of the signal at the time of receiving should be minimum. To solve this problem, machine learning algorithms can be used at the receiver side for real-time feature extraction and binary classification of the received signal.

In addition, the Coronavirus pandemic has been declared a global health emergency by the *World Health Organization* (WHO). During these times, a lot of significant patient data is stored in the local server of the medical center and distributed from one center to other hospitals via an unsecured network. However, this may lead to a high risk of data security and privacy in the current advanced healthcare systems.

To solve these issues, *data hiding* techniques are used to provide confidentiality, integrity, and authenticity requirements for medical data. A comparison of three types of data hiding techniques (watermarking, steganography, and cryptography) is shown in Table 7.8 (Sharma et al. 2021). It is seen that watermarking technique can be used for hiding data efficiently within a cover bio-medical signal.

There are different types of biomedical signals, such as *electrocardiography* (ECG), *electroencephalography* (EEG), *electromyogram* (EMG), *electrooculography* (EOG), and *photoplethysmography* (PPG).

1. An ECG signal is a graphical representation generated by the electrical activity of the heart. One ECG signal consists of various cardiac cycles and each cycle is composed of a P wave followed by a QRS complex and a T wave.

   The maximum energy is concentrated in the QRS complex portion. Watermarking and steganography are used to embed data into 1-D and 2-D ECG signals to provide secure transmission over a public network. The secret data can be marked within the QRS region or non-QRS region of the signal as per the requirements. To avoid any distortion of the original signal, a non-QRS region is used to embed the watermark.

   To improve the imperceptibility, a lossless dual watermarking technique has been proposed to securely transmit the ECG signal and patient ID and avoid diagnosis mismatching (Nambakhsh et al. 2010). In this technique, ECG signal and patient ID are considered as watermarks that are embedded into PET image using multiresolution

TABLE 7.8 Comparison of Three Types of Data Hiding Techniques

Property	Watermarking	Steganography	Cryptography
Definition	The secret data, also called watermark, is embedded within the cover media	By manipulating and scrambling the pixels, the secret data is embedded within host data	Meaningful content is transformed into encoded form to provide security
Purpose of use	Proof the ownership, i.e., authentication purpose and to provide robustness	To provide confidentiality and is highly secure	Maintain the integrity of the data. Provides data secrecy, information uprightness, verification and non-repudiation
Cover image selection	Here the cover image should be related with the embedded message	The cover image may be or may not be related with the embedded message	There is no need of relating cover image with embedded message

wavelet transform. Further, the texture feature extraction method is used to identify the locations for imperceptibly and robustly concealing the marks.

2. EEG is a medical technique for recording electrical signals generated from the brain. EEG signals can be used as a cover signal in telemedicine due to their large size. The frequency ranges of the EEG signals are defined from 0.01 to 100 Hz. To perform the embedding in the frequency domain, the EEG signal is first converted into a 2-D matrix and then decomposed into sub-bands like HH, HL, LH, and LL. The embedding of secret data is mainly performed in the HH sub-bands.

An imperceptible and blind watermarking technique based on pattern recognition to securely transmit secret data marked within EEG signals using DWT is proposed (Duy et al. 2016). Patient information and signature are used as watermarks and to increase security, Arnold transform is used to scramble the mark. Further, the watermarked data is embedded within the decomposed signal using the mean value relationship of the coefficients. On the receiver side, *support vector data description* (SVDD) is used to efficiently extract the mark. The suggested scheme can handle different types of common attacks.

3. EMG signal analysis is performed to measure and record the biceps muscle activity during exercise. EMG signals are also used as diagnostic tools to detect various diseases of muscles by recording electrical signals of muscles. Using this EMG signal, the reason for muscle weakness can be detected, whether it is caused by the breakdown of a nerve attached to the muscle or neurological disorder.

A bio-medical signal-based blind watermarking technique has been proposed (Dey et al. 2014) where EMG signal is used as a cover signal. The self-recovered watermarking method uses spread spectrum and *stationary wavelet transformation* (SWT). Self-authentication verifies the integrity and source of confidential information. A blind recognition of surface EMG based on watermarking has been proposed (Yina and Dawei 2012). To provide more security, Arnold transformation is used to scramble the secret image. DWT is used to decompose the EMG signal. Synchronization codes are used to get the embedding locations and then embedding is done using adaptive coefficients.

4. EOG is a medical test to detect any abnormality in human eyes by monitoring the movement of the eyeball without rapid movement during the sleep period and with rapid eye movement in another case. The EOG signal is the graphical representation of the electrical response of the sensitive rods and cons cells as well as motor nerves present inside the eye.

To verify the integrity of the EOG signal and to reduce the computation time and complexity, blind watermarking has been proposed (Dey 2012b). The mean value of the blink frequency and blink interval of the EOG signal are used as a watermark. The watermark is concealed using a different expansion algorithm.

Another blind watermarking technique is also proposed (Dey et al. 2012c) to provide data authenticity along with access control in the EOG signal. The frequency-domain techniques are used to imperceptibly embed the grayscale mark image. It is imperceptible and can provide security against unauthorized access and copying.

5. PPG is a very sensitive and uncomplicated medical diagnostic tool to detect various types of cardiovascular diseases. PPG is a non-invasive method where a light source and a photodetector are used at the surface level of the skin to measure the variation of relative blood volume in the blood vessels. Various cardiovascular diseases like atherosclerosis and arterial stiffness can be detected from the second derivative of the PPG signal.

A reversible and blind watermarking technique where patient data is embedded within the PPG signal has been proposed to securely and imperceptibly embed the EPR into the transformed PPG signal and to ensure the authenticity of the PPG signal when transmitted over an open channel (Dey et al. 2012a). It uses a binary image as a watermark. The PPG signal is cropped according to the marked size and then decomposed using the lifting wavelet transform method. The watermark image is embedded within the decomposed signal using a pseudo-random sequence.

7.5.2.4 Watermarking in Different Application Domains

In recent years, with in-depth research on watermarking technology, watermarking technology has also been widely used in other special digital image fields, such as medical images, remote sensing images, and digital maps. Since the structures of these digital images are different from those of common digital images, the requirements for the integrity and transparency of the original information content are relatively high.

1. Medical field

   Medical images are mainly divided into B-ultrasound images, X-photos, CT images, and so on. This type of digital information often contains some important disease information, which provides an important basis for doctors for diagnosing. If the medical information is maliciously tampered with, it will affect the doctor's judgment. Therefore, how to ensure the integrity and security of medical information is a constant challenge in the field of medical imaging. To prevent medical data from being maliciously modified, it is usually necessary to perform effective identity verification. For example, a robust non-blind medical image watermarking scheme has been proposed (Mala et al. 2015), which performs the multiple-level fractional wavelet transform on the image by using *fractional wave packet transform* (FR-WPT), and embed the watermark in the modified reference image. Through the test, it is found that this method has better robustness in the test results on mammograms.

2. Remote sensing field

   Remote sensing images are mainly used for real-time monitoring and statistical investigation. Due to the sensitive characteristics of its information, the transparency and completeness of remote sensing maps need to be taken into consideration for copyright protection. For example, a non-blind watermarking algorithm based on *quaternion wavelet transform* (QWT) and tensor decomposition has been proposed (Li et al. 2019). The image features can be better preserved by QWT, and better transparency can be obtained when applied to color remote sensing images. In addition, an improved compressed sensing watermarking algorithm has been applied to remote sensing images (Tong et al. 2019). It uses boosted wavelet transform, Hadamard matrix, and ternary watermark sequence to improve the robustness of the algorithm and achieve good results.

3. Map copyright field

With continuous development and progress, the application range of maps has become more and more extensive. For example, the flat maps used in Baidu Maps and Google Maps are essentially two-dimensional vector maps. Since maps often contain some information such as coordinates, locations, and directions, the copyright protection of such digital images mainly considers the transparency and safety of the map information. A 2-D vector graph reversible watermarking algorithm based on reversible contrast mapping has been proposed (Tong et al. 2019). It first selects the coordinates of the vertices and then selects the position where the watermark can be embedded according to the data accuracy requirements, to use the reversible contrast for embedding the encrypted watermark into the selected relative coordinates with the mapping conversion. The map coordinate information after the watermark embedding is consistent with the original information.

REFERENCES

Barni, M., F. Bartolini, and A. Piva. 2001. Improved wavelet-based watermarking through pixel-wise masking. *IEEE-IP*, 10(5):783–791.

Branden, C. J. and J. E. Farrell. 1996. Perceptual quality metric for digitally coded color images. *Proceedings of EUSIPCO-96*, 1175–1178.

Cox, I. J., M. L. Miller, and J. A. Bloom. 2002. *Digital Watermarking*. Amsterdam, The Netherlands: Elsevier Science.

Dey, N., D. Biswas, A. B. Roy, et al. 2012a. Analysis of photoplethysmographic signals modified by reversible watermarking technique using prediction-error in wireless telecardiology. *Proceedings of 47th ANC*, 1–6.

Dey, N., D. Biswas, A. B. Roy, et al. 2012b. DWT-DCT-SVD based blind watermarking technique of gray image in electrooculogram signal. *Proceedings of ISDA*, 680–685.

Dey, N., G. Dey, S. Chakraborty, et al. 2014. *Feature Analysis of Blind Watermarked Electromyogram. Signal in Wireless Telemonitoring*. Springer Int Publ.

Dey, N., P. Maji, P. Das, et al. 2012c Embedding of blink frequency in electrooculography signal using difference expansion based reversible watermarking technique. *Transactions on Electronics and Communications*, 57(71): 1–6.

Duy, T.P., D. Tran, and W. Ma. 2016. A proposed pattern recognition framework for EEG based smart blind watermarking system. *Proceedings of ICPR*, 955–960.

Fridrich, J. and G. Miroslav. 1999. Comparing robustness of watermarking techniques. *SPIE*, 3657: 214–225.

Gao, Y. M., X. B. Kang, and Y. J. Chen. 2021. A robust video zero-watermarking based on deep convolutional neural network and self-organizing map in polar complex exponential transform domain. *Multimedia Tools and Applications*, 80: 6019–6039.

Girod, B. 1989. The information theoretical significance of spatial and temporal masking in video signals. *SPIE*, 1077, 178–187.

Hsu, C.-T. and J.-L. Wu. 1999. Hidden digital watermarks in images. *IEEE T-IP*, 8(1): 58–68.

Kutter, M. and F. A. P. Petitcolas. 1999. A fair benchmarking for image watermarking systems. *SPIE*, 3657: 226–239.

Kutter, M. and F. Hartung. 2000. Introduction to watermarking techniques. In: Katzenbeisser S., and Petitcolas F. A. P., Eds. *Information Hiding Techniques for Steganography and Digital Watermarking*. Boston, MA: Artech House, Inc. (Chapter 5).

Lee, J.-S., C. Liu, Y.-C. Chen, et al. 2021. Robust 3D mesh zero-watermarking based on spherical coordinate and Skewness measurement. *Multimedia Tools and Applications*, 80, 1–16.

Li, D. S., X. Y. Che, W. Luo, et al. 1999. Digital watermarking scheme for color remote sensing image based on quaternion wavelet transform and tensor decomposition. *Mathematical Methods in the Applied Sciences*, 42(14): 4664–4678.

Mala, S. P., J. Devappa, and E. Kaliyamoorthy. 2015. Application of fractional wave packet transform for robust watermarking of mammogram. *International Journal of Telemedicine and Applications*, 2015, 1–8.

Nambakhsh, M., A. Ahmadian, and H. Zaidi. 2010. A contextual based double watermarking of PET images by patient ID and ECG signal. *Computer Methods Programs Biomedicine*, 104(3): 418–425.

Regazzoni, F., P. Palmieri, and F. Smailbegovic. 2021. Protecting artificial intelligence IPs: A survey of watermarking and fingerprinting for machine learning. *CAAI Transactions on Intelligence Technology*, 6, 180–191.

Sharma, N., A. Anand, and A. K. Singh. 2021. Bio-signal data sharing security through watermarking: A technical survey. *Computing*, 1–35.

Tong, D. Y., N. Ren, and C. Q. Zhu, 2019. Secure and robust watermarking algorithm for remote images based on compressive sensing. *Multimedia Tools and Applications*, 78(12): 16053–16076.

Wang, C. D., L. Yang, F. J. Wan, et al. 2019. Survey on database watermarking models and algorithms. *Acta Electronica Sinica*, 47(4): 214–216.

Wang, Z. M., Y.-J. Zhang, and J. H. Wu. 2005. A wavelet domain watermarking technique based on human visual system. *Journal of Nanchang University (Natural Science)*, 29(4): 400–403.

Wen, Q., T. F. Sun, and S. X. Wang. 2003. Concept and application of zero-watermark. *Acta Electronica Sinica*, 31(2): 214–216.

Wu, D. Y., J. Y. Zhang, W. Y. Rong, et al. 2021. Survey of digital image watermarking technology. *High Technology Letters*, 31(2): 148–162.

Xiao, Z. J., D. Jiang, H. Zhang, et al. 2019. Adaptive zero-watermarking algorithm based on boost normed singular value decomposition. *Journal of Image and Graphics*, 24(1): 1–12.

Xiao, Z. J., Q. Y. Ning, H. Zhang, et al. 2020. Adaptive zero-watermarking algorithm based on block NMF and boost normed singular value decomposition. *Application Research of Computers*, 37(4): 1144–1153.

Yi, Y. C. and G. Feng. 2020. A video zero-watermarking algorithm against recompression coding for 3D-HEVC. *Journal of Signal Processing*, 36(5): 778–786.

Yina, G. and Z. Dawei. 2012. Single channel surface electromyography blind recognition model based on watermarking. *Journal of Vibration and Control*, 18, 42–47.

Zhang, Y., T. Chen, and J. Li. 2001. Embedding watermarks into both DC and AC components of DCT. *SPIE*, 4314: 424–435.

## CHAPTER 8

Image Super-Resolution

I MAGE *SUPER-RESOLUTION* (SR), ALSO known as *super-resolution image reconstruction* (SRIR), refers to the use of image processing methods to convert existing *low-resolution* (LR) images into *high-resolution* (HR) images through software algorithms (emphasizing unchanged imaging hardware equipment). The SR technology makes full use of the information resources in the acquired image, or fully excavates the hidden information in the image, and the cost is lower than the method of using high-performance hardware to obtain HR images.

Image SR technology has been widely used in many domains, such as:

1. Use SR technology to produce cheap HR digital cameras/camcorders, which can also be used to print high-quality images or stop-frame playback.

2. Due to the influence of the distance and angle between the camera and the observation object in the surveillance video, the resolution of some objects is not high enough. Use SR technology to get an effective zoomed image.

3. Convert ordinary and general NTSC format low-definition TV signals into high-definition TV signals and play them without distortion.

4. In medical applications such as CT and MRI, SR technology can be used to reconstruct high-quality clear images from multiple images with limited resolution.

5. In the application of satellite imagery such as remote sensing and earth resource satellites, the use of SR technology can enhance the resolution of the object with the help of multiple LR images in the same region.

Image super-resolution has received widespread attention in recent years. Research on image SR is still ongoing, and many new tools and technologies are also being continuously introduced. Technologies based on deep learning, machine learning, sparse representation, and locally constrained linear coding have all received attention.

DOI: 10.1201/9781003241416-8

The contents of each section of this chapter will be arranged as follows.

Section 8.1 introduces the principle of image SR, gives a basic model and classifies existing technologies, and focuses on the SR reconstruction technology based on a single image and the SR reconstruction technology based on multiple images.

Section 8.2 introduces learning-based SR technology, including example-based single-frame SR, example-based multi-frame SR, methods combined with total variation regularization, and learning-based methods.

Section 8.3 introduces SR reconstruction based on sparse representation. Based on the reconstruction process, the three main modules, namely sparse coding, dictionary learning, and image reconstruction, are discussed in detail.

Section 8.4 introduces the SR reconstruction with locally constrained linear coding, which has even more advantages than the SR reconstruction based on sparse representation. Based on the detailed description of each step of the method, it is extended from single-frame reconstruction to multi-frame reconstruction, and a number of experimental results are given.

Section 8.5 provides a brief introduction to some technique developments and promising research directions in the last year.

8.1 PRINCIPLE OF IMAGE SR

The term "super-resolution" is generally believed to have appeared in 1990 (although related work began in the 1980s) (Tekalp 1995). Initially, it was mainly referred to technologies that could improve the resolution of optical imaging systems. Now, SR generally represents a method of enlarging the spatial scale of an originally small image or video and increasing its resolving power. Some SR technologies have broken the diffraction limit of imaging systems, and some technologies have improved the resolution of digital image sensors.

8.1.1 Basic Model and Technology Classification

Various SR technologies hope to obtain HR images from LR images, or more precisely, to restore HR images from single or multiple degraded, aliased LR images. Therefore, SR reconstruction is not simply to enlarge an image or to interpolate an image. It must be carried out based on a certain model and considering the characteristics of the entire image. SR technology can also be regarded as a typical technology that combines image multi-scale representation for image processing, especially image restoration.

8.1.1.1 Image Observation Model

The imaging model on which the SR technology is based is generally called the *image observation model*, which describes the relationship between the desired ideal image and the obtained or observed real image. In SR reconstruction, the observed image is (a series of) LR image, and the ideal image is the desired HR image.

There is a degradation process from the desired HR ideal image *f* to the actual LR observation image *g*. Degradation factors can include sub-sampling, atmospheric blur (such as fog, etc.), imaging blur (such as the blur caused by camera movement, the blur caused by the optical limit of the imaging sensor), geometric motion, projection, and additional noise

FIGURE 8.1   The degradation process of high-resolution images to low-resolution images.

(such as the noise of the imaging sensor itself), etc. In this way, the image model of SR technology can often be represented as

$$g = SBTf + n \qquad (8.1)$$

In the equation, S represents the sub-sampling matrix, B represents the blur matrix, T represents the distortion matrix (including various motions that make the pixel coordinates relatively offset), and n represents noise. The corresponding degradation process from HR image to LR image is shown in Figure 8.1, that is, each matrix acts on the image in turn, and finally noise is superimposed.

It can be seen from the above imaging model that there are many influencing factors in the image degradation process, and each factor may also have a different mode of action and effect. So SR reconstruction is a typical ill-conditioned (inverse) problem. This is very similar to many image restoration problems. Especially when the input is only a single LR image, this becomes a problem of solving underdetermined equations. In most cases, the HR images obtained are for observation, and this ill-conditioned problem can be relieved by the characteristics of the human visual mechanism, so the image SR technology has been applied in many aspects.

8.1.1.2 SR Technology Identification

Image SR technology is similar to image restoration technology on a theoretical basis. If $H = SBT$, the image model of SR technology becomes a typical image restoration model, so some people also call SR technology the second-generation image restoration technology (Park et al. 2003). The main difference between traditional image restoration technology and SR technology is that the former does not increase the number of pixels in the processed image.

Some special cases of image restoration are also special cases of SR reconstruction. For example, the image degradation model with additive noise

$$g = f + n \qquad (8.2)$$

can be regarded as a special case of SR reconstruction without distortion, blur, and sub-sampling. For another example, the degradation model when the image is affected by blur is:

$$g = Bf + n \qquad (8.3)$$

This can be regarded as a special case of SR reconstruction with only blur and noise, without distortion and sub-sampling. SR can improve the sharpness of the image, which is also the main purpose of image de-blurring or deconvolution (to eliminate the influence of the point spread function on the image).

In addition, the image model for image interpolation or image magnification can be represented as

$$g = S^{-1}f + n \tag{8.4}$$

There are similar forms here, but blur and distortion are not considered. However, general interpolation cannot recover the high-frequency information lost in the image sub-sampling process, so image interpolation and image super-resolution reconstruction are still different.

Image sharpening can enhance high-frequency information, but it only enhances the existing high-frequency components, while SR technology can estimate HR details that are not shown in the original image. This can be described by the changes in the amplitude A of different spatial frequencies p in Figure 8.2. Figure 8.2a corresponds to the image sharpening technology. The raising of the curve indicates that the existing high-frequency components have been elevated. Figure 8.2b corresponds to SR technology. The curve moves toward high frequency, indicating that not only the original high-frequency components are strengthened, but also some high-frequency components that did not previously exist have been added.

Finally, it should be noted that although image stitching can combine multiple images into a larger image, it contains more pixels but does not provide finer details, so it cannot be regarded as a SR technology.

8.1.1.3 Technology Classification

There are many SR implementation technologies, which can be divided into different categories according to different classification criteria.

First, according to the domain of processing, SR technology can be divided into frequency-domain-based methods and spatial-domain-based methods. The frequency-domain method is mainly based on Fourier transform and inverse transform for image

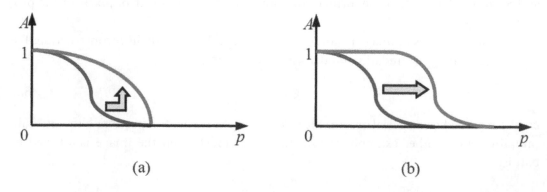

(a)   (b)

FIGURE 8.2   The difference between image sharpening and super-resolution.

restoration. Take the typical anti-aliasing reconstruction method, as an example. Since the image details are reflected by high-frequency information, eliminating the spectral aliasing in the LR image can obtain more masked high-frequency information, thereby increasing the image detail, so as to improve the resolution of the image. Spatial methods often use the local information about the image to increase the number and tightness of pixels. Relatively, the frequency-domain method has clear principles, convenient theoretical derivation, and low computational complexity; however, the frequency-domain method is only suitable for the case of spatially invariant noise, and can only handle the situation where there is only overall motion in the image without local motion. It is also difficult to use prior information for the process in the frequency domain. In recent years, most of the methods for achieving SR are based on the spatial domain. There are many types of spatial domain methods, which can comprehensively consider various degradation factors and are highly flexible; however, spatial domain methods are often complicated in design (see below) and have high computational complexity.

Second, according to the number of LR images used, SR technology can be divided into *single-image-based super-resolution* (SISR) and *multi-image-based super-resolution* (MISR). The method based on a single image is also often called *super-resolution restoration* because it is based on the principle of image restoration. The early SR technology was mainly based on a single image, and what improved or restored was the resolving power of the image, but the general effect was not ideal. Recent research mainly focuses on methods based on multiple images, which rely on redundant information for reconstruction. The multiple images here can be either a group of still images, a series of images (video), or multiple series of images (video). The output of SR based on a single image is generally still a single image, while the output of SR based on multiple images can be a single image or a series of images (usually a video). If the input and output are both videos, it is often called video super-resolution. It can be seen that the choice of different methods mainly depends on the requirements of the actual application. For further details on the SR based on a single image and the SR based on multiple images, see Sections 8.1.2 and 8.1.3, respectively.

Finally, according to the characteristics of the technology itself, SR technology can be divided into *reconstruction-based super-resolution* and *learning-based super-resolution*. This is mainly used for SR based on multiple images. The reconstruction-based method mainly has two key steps: registration and reconstruction. During registration, LR multi-frame images are used as data consistency constraints, so that the relative displacement or motion of sub-pixel precision between other LR images and the reference LR images can be obtained. During reconstruction, the prior knowledge of the image can be used to optimize the target image. The learning-based method (see Section 8.2) considers that LR images contain information for reasoning and predicting the corresponding HR images. In this way, a LR image set can be trained to produce a learning model from which high-frequency detail information of the image can be derived. Some technologies now combine reconstruction-based methods with learning-based methods.

The above classification is summarized in Figure 8.3.

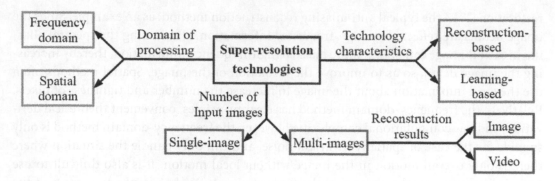

FIGURE 8.3   Super-resolution technology classification.

The following is a summary of the method based on a single image and the method based on multiple images, respectively. The learning-based methods and reconstruction-based methods will be introduced in the subsequent sections.

8.1.2   SR Restoration Based on Single Image

The method based on a single image uses the information contained in a LR image itself or can also use prior information obtained from other similar images, to estimate the content that a HR image should have, so as to enlarge the image (increase or improve the resolution) without introducing blur.

8.1.2.1   Image Enlargement

One result of processing using SR technology is an increase in image resolution (increase in the size of image or the number of pixels), that is, the image is enlarged and includes more pixels. There are many ways to enlarge an image.

When an integer magnification factor is used to magnify the image, the calculation of the pixel gray level is divided into two steps. For example, considering that the magnification factor is 2, the first step is to convert the input image into an array, in which a zero is added between any two original data along the row or column, and the results obtained are shown in Figure 8.4a and b; the second step is to convolve the zero-inserted image with the discrete interpolation kernel as shown in Figure 8.4c.

For larger enlargement factors and more precise interpolation, the discrete interpolation convolution kernel shown in Figure 8.5 can also be used. Figure 8.5a–c corresponds

$$
\begin{bmatrix} a & b \\ c & d \end{bmatrix}
\qquad
\begin{bmatrix} a & 0 & b \\ 0 & 0 & 0 \\ c & 0 & d \end{bmatrix}
\qquad
\begin{bmatrix} 1 & 1 \\ 1 & 1 \end{bmatrix}
$$

(a)   (b)   (c)

FIGURE 8.4   Example of image enlargement.

$$\frac{1}{4}\begin{bmatrix} 1 & 2 & 1 \\ 2 & 4 & 2 \\ 1 & 2 & 1 \end{bmatrix} \qquad \frac{1}{16}\begin{bmatrix} 1 & 3 & 3 & 1 \\ 3 & 9 & 9 & 3 \\ 3 & 9 & 9 & 3 \\ 1 & 3 & 3 & 1 \end{bmatrix} \qquad \frac{1}{64}\begin{bmatrix} 1 & 4 & 6 & 4 & 1 \\ 4 & 16 & 24 & 16 & 4 \\ 6 & 24 & 36 & 24 & 6 \\ 4 & 16 & 24 & 16 & 4 \\ 1 & 4 & 6 & 4 & 1 \end{bmatrix}$$

(a)　　　　　　(b)　　　　　　　　(c)

FIGURE 8.5   Some convolution kernels for discrete interpolation.

to the kernels of 3 × 3, 4 × 4, and 5 × 5, respectively. For even larger kernels, the effective calculation can also be achieved through filtering in the frequency domain without convolution.

8.1.2.2   SR Restoration

The earliest SR technology is to restore the information lost in a single image due to exceeding the limit of the transfer function of the optical system. To this end, it is necessary to estimate the spectral information of the image above the diffraction limit and perform spectral extrapolation. This process can also be considered as an inverse process of image degradation, which can be implemented by linear deconvolution or blind deconvolution. At this time, it is necessary to use the prior knowledge of the point spread function and the object to restore the image information beyond the diffraction limit of the imaging system, so it is also called SR restoration.

Similar to Equation (8.1), SR restoration based on a single image can be introduced with the help of the following model:

$$g = DSf + n \tag{8.5}$$

In the equation, S represents the sub-sampling matrix, D represents the diffraction (corresponding to blur) matrix, and n is generally set as additive white noise. Because only a single image is considered here, there is no distortion matrix T compared with Equation (8.1).

It is often impossible to directly solve Equation (8.5) in practice. On the one hand, the matrix DS is often singular, that is, irreversible; on the other hand, the order of the matrix DS is often very large and the calculation is complicated. According to the above model, sub-sampling and diffraction classification processing can be considered. If $Sf = e$, then Equation (8.5) is equivalent to

$$g = De + n \tag{8.6}$$

$$e = Sf \tag{8.7}$$

Solve the Equation (8.6) needs to eliminate noise and to make interpolation while solving Equation (8.7) can use a gradient iteration method (such as the gradient descent method).

8.1.3 SR Reconstruction Based on Multiple Images

The SR technology based on multiple images (or sequence of images) needs to use multiple images acquired from the same scene, with some offsets. Such multiple images can be obtained by three types of methods:

1. Use one camera to shoot multiple images at different positions.

2. Use multiple cameras placed in different positions to shoot at the same time.

3. Use a camera that moves relative to the scene to shoot continuously.

The multiple images here should be multiple slightly different LR images (sub-pixel offset between each other, pixel offset would be useless). They contain similar but not completely different complementary information, so the total information of multiple images is more than the information of any one of them. It can also be understood that each LR image contains less detailed information, but if a series of LR images containing different parts of the detailed information can be obtained, an image with higher resolution and containing more information can be obtained by complementing each other. It should be pointed out that although generally increasing the number of input images can further increase the magnification, the magnification has a certain upper limit and the resolution cannot be increased indefinitely.

According to the above analysis, by combining the non-overlapping information in multiple LR images, a higher-resolution (large-size) image can be constructed. This type of SR method is generally called *super-resolution reconstruction*. Reconstruction-based SR technology usually includes the following steps:

1. Image preprocessing, including registration, etc.

2. Image degradation model establishment.

3. Image restoration and reconstruction, including de-noising, de-blurring, HR image estimation, etc.

If multiple LR images are obtained from image sequences, SR reconstruction can be achieved with the help of motion detection technology. The core idea here is to exchange time bandwidth for the spatial resolution to achieve the conversion from time resolution to spatial resolution. Of course, if the object does not move at all and is the same in all frames, no additional information can be obtained. On the other hand, if the object moves too fast so that it looks very dissimilar in different frame images, it is also very difficult to achieve SR reconstruction at this time.

8.1.3.1 Typical Method

Typical SR reconstruction algorithms include the following (all are spatial methods).

1. Non-uniform interpolation method

   The process of this method is shown in Figure 8.6. The desired image is regarded as having a high resolution, and different LR observation images are regarded as

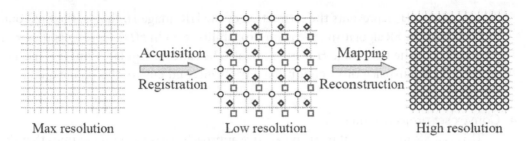

Max resolution   Low resolution   High resolution

FIGURE 8.6   Non-uniform interpolation process.

sampling at different positions on it. First, obtain the sampled values equivalent to the non-uniformly spaced sampling grid points on the desired image from the registered LR image, and then interpolate and map these sampled values to obtain the sampled values on the SR image sampling grid points. The HR image reconstructed in this way will have problems such as noise and blur, and it needs to be repaired through image restoration technology. This method is more intuitive in principle.

2. Iterative back-projection method

This method uses an initial estimated value of the output image as the current result, then projects it onto the LR image, and adjusts the projection according to the difference between the obtained LR image and the actual observed image until convergence, so as to obtain the final output SR image. The advantage of the iterative back-projection method is that it is intuitively easy to understand, but it does not consider the influence of noise and is very sensitive to high-frequency noise. In addition, this method is not easy to incorporate a priori constraints.

3. Maximum posterior probability method

This is a probability-based algorithm framework, which is currently the most used method in practical applications and scientific research. Many specific SR algorithms can be classified into this probabilistic framework. It has better flexibility and robustness.

The basic idea of this method is to maximize the posterior probability of HR images on the premise that LR images are known. According to the Bayesian principle, the posterior probability of a HR image is equal to the product of the conditional probability of the appearance of a LR image and the prior probability of an ideal HR image. It is worth pointing out that the problem of SR reconstruction is considered to be an ill-conditioned problem, and it needs to be transformed into a healthy problem by restricting it with the aid of prior conditions. This method can directly introduce various prior knowledge of image. The reconstruction quality is better, and the existence and uniqueness of the solution can be guaranteed. However, this method has higher computational complexity and slower convergence speed.

If H represents a HR image, and L_1, L_2, ..., L_n represent multiple LR images, the idea of the maximum posterior probability algorithm can be represented by the following equation:

$$H_R = \arg\max[p(H \mid L_1, L_2, ..., L_n)] = \arg\max[\ln p(L_1, L_2, ..., L_n \mid H) + \ln p(H)] \quad (8.8)$$

Among them, H_R represents the estimation of the HR image H, that is, the final output result of the SR algorithm; the prior probability term $\ln p(H)$ represents the prior probability of the HR image H, which can also be called a regular term. It is used to control the occurrence of ill-conditioned problems and ensure the image quality of the final result.

4. Convex set projection method

This is a SR method that uses an iterative approach. This method assumes that the SR reconstructed image exists in a vector space, and the desired ideal properties of the SR reconstruction solution, such as positive definiteness, energy boundedness, data reliability, and smoothness, can be calculated as constraints. The set of these conditions constitutes a convex set in the vector space, and the image is projected into these convex sets, which is called *projection onto convex sets* (POCS). By intersecting these sets, the SR solution space can be finally obtained.

The process of projection onto convex sets is a process of searching from any point in a given vector space until a solution that satisfies all convex constraint sets is found. The principle of projection onto convex sets method is simple and intuitive, and the form is relatively flexible. It can easily add prior information, and can well maintain the edges and details of HR images. Its disadvantages include high computational complexity, slow convergence speed, and the solution is often not unique (a set of solutions), strong dependence on the initial value, and low convergence stability.

In principle, the method of projection onto convex sets and the posterior probability method have some complementarity. Combining these two approaches provides a maximum posterior probability-projection onto convex sets method (Park et al. 2003).

8.1.3.2 Video SR

There is a special case of SR reconstruction based on multiple images, that is, the input for the SR reconstruction is a LR video, and the desired result is a HR video, which is often called *video super-resolution*. The reconstruction-based SR discussed above can be regarded as a special case of video SR, but the goal of the former is to generate a HR single-frame image to make the originally blurred part of the image clearer; while the latter's effect is to obtain continuous HR multi-frame images, which can enhance the visual experience of the output video. If one considers visual effects, one can not only enhance the image resolution in space but also increase the frame rate in time to make the output video smoother, which is also called *spatio-temporal super-resolution*.

An intuitive idea of obtaining video SR is to use the reconstruction-based SR algorithms to reconstruct each HR video frame image in turn, and then concatenate the obtained results into a video sequence. However, specially designed video SR methods often consider both the intra-frame spatial scale enlargement of the frame image and the inter-frame motion compensation based on the registration of the frame sequence.

The existing video SR methods can be divided into two main groups: incremental video SR and simultaneous video SR. As shown in Figure 8.7a, the *incremental video*

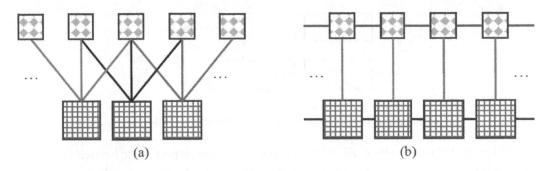

FIGURE 8.7 Schematic diagram of two video super-resolution methods.

super-resolution method inputs the LR video sequence incrementally in time sequence, and the SR operation is performed on each frame in the video sequence in turn, that is, several LR video sequences are sequentially used. LR images (upper line) are used to construct a HR image (lower line), and each HR image is obtained independently in this process. The *simultaneous video super-resolution* method inputs all LR video sequences at the same time and obtains all output video frames at once through an overall optimization process, as shown in Figure 8.7b. In practice, the calculation speed can be improved by means of estimating the motion between frames.

The above two groups of video SR methods have their own strengths. The characteristic of the incremental video SR method is that the speed is generally faster, and only a few frames of LR images need to be input for each frame of a HR image. It is more suitable for real-time or semi-real-time processing, but the quality often cannot catch up with simultaneous SR. The simultaneous SR method can better consider the consistency factors between video frames to generate higher-quality output video, but it requires the entire LR video sequence to be input at one time, which cannot meet the real-time requirements.

8.2 SR TECHNOLOGY BASED ON LEARNING

The *SR technology based on learning* is also called *image hallucination*. This kind of method is very different from traditional image processing technology. It does not directly process a given LR image to obtain a HR image but uses pre-training and learning (from the database) to find or establish the mapping relationship between (other similar) LR images and their corresponding HR images, and the high-frequency information is extracted, so that in the case of a given LR image, the corresponding HR image can be obtained through an optimization method. In this way, not only the visual effect of increased resolution can be obtained but also the texture details lost in LR images can often be restored.

8.2.1 Conventional Process

The conversional process of learning-based SR technology is shown in Figure 8.8. The input image X_i is up-sampled by an interpolation method to obtain the low-frequency part Y_o^L of the output image. The high-frequency part X_i^H of the input image X_i is extracted with a high-pass filter and used as an input for the learning-based method. In the learning-based process, the high-frequency part X_t^H of the low-resolution images in the training set and

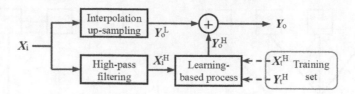

FIGURE 8.8 The conventional process of learning-based super-resolution technology.

the HR image Y_t^H need to be used. With the help of the correspondence between them (the correspondence between LR image blocks and HR image blocks is actually required), the high-frequency part Y_o^H of the output image corresponding to X_i^H is estimated. Finally, both the Y_o^L and Y_o^H are combined to get the required HR output image Y_o.

8.2.2 Example-Based Single-Frame SR

Example-based super-resolution is a typical learning-based method (Freeman et al. 2002). The basic idea is to first learn the relationship between LR images and HR images through examples, and then use this relationship to guide the SR reconstruction of LR images. The main points are as follows.

8.2.2.1 Basic Principles and Steps

First, use some reference images to learn how to sharpen the image. These reference images constitute a training set, including low, medium, and high-frequency data. The image that needs to be sharpened and enlarged is called the input image. First, the input image is increased in size through interpolation, and the high-frequency data that is missing in the enlarged image needs to be obtained with the help of a reference image. Considering the diversity of natural images, a large number of reference images are often needed to form a training set to obtain good results. Therefore, the method mainly has two independent steps: the first is to generate the training set, and the second is to construct the missing high-frequency bands in the input image after up-sampling.

8.2.2.2 Training Set Generation

Assuming that three frequency bands, low (L), medium (M), and high (H) are obtained using pyramid image decomposition, the low-frequency band and the high-frequency band are conditionally independent, which can be written as: $P(H|M, L) = P(H|M)$. In this way, only two frequency bands need to be considered, and there is no need to consider the diversity of low-frequency bands. Second, assume that the connection between the medium-band and the high-band has nothing to do with the local contrast of the image. In this way, by normalizing the contrast of each image, the difference between them can be reduced, thereby improving the effectiveness of the training set.

Generating the training set is the key to determining the SR result. A patch composed of local neighborhoods can be considered in each frequency band. Each LR patch corresponds to a HR patch. They are centered on the same pixel, but they do not necessarily have the same size. However, only partial patches do not contain enough data to estimate HR details: for an input patch, the closest LR patch can be selected from the training set, but it has been proven that its corresponding HR patch can be very different. Therefore, choosing the closest LR patch to construct the high-frequency band of the input image may lead to an inaccurate estimation of the true high-frequency band. For this reason, it is also necessary to consider the proximity in space. Two different algorithms can be used here: The Markov network algorithm and the single-pass algorithm.

8.2.2.3 Markov Network Algorithm

The *Markov network algorithm* models spatial relationships, that is, use Markov networks to learn the fine details of HR images corresponding to different regions in the LR images in the training library and then uses the learned relationships to predict the detailed information of the image. As shown in Figure 8.9, the image is divided into small patches, and each image patch corresponds to a node on the Markov network. For a given input image y, the potential scene x is estimated. Image y is composed of LR patches, which can be described by HR patches. In Figure 8.9, the connections between nodes indicate the statistical dependence between nodes. Use the training set to calculate the probability matrices S and T. S represents the horizontal connection between HR nodes, and T represents the vertical connection between HR nodes and LR nodes. According to the training library, use a propagation algorithm (such as the belief propagation interactive algorithm) to solve the Markov network. The optimal HR patch is the one that maximizes the probability of the Markov network.

8.2.2.4 Single-Pass Algorithm

The single-pass algorithm only needs three to four iterations to obtain a satisfactory high-frequency band. The overall goal of the algorithm is easy to understand: to sequentially generate the high-frequency bands required by the enlarged image. The specific steps are: once the image is preprocessed, it is divided into patches; for these patches, the HR patches are predicted according to the order of raster scanning; finally, these HR patches are added to the previous image to obtain a sharpened image that contains all frequency bands.

The prediction of HR patches is very important, and there are two constraints here.

1. Frequency constraint: The high-frequency patch must be connected to a LR patch in the training set, and this LR patch is very close to the input LR patch according to the Euclidean distance.

2. Space constraints: High-frequency patches must have continuity, that is, the new HR patches must match the previously selected ones.

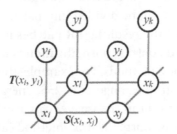

FIGURE 8.9 Markov network model for super-resolution.

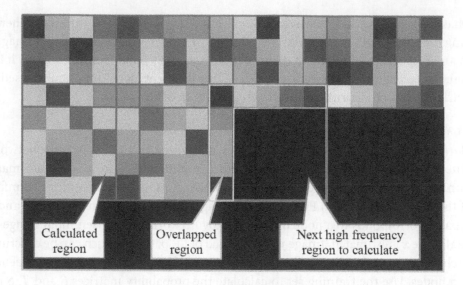

FIGURE 8.10 The region overlap of high-resolution components.

The first constraint is easily satisfied. By matching the LR patches of the image, a pair of HR patches and LR patches can be found in the training set. For the second constraint, the technique of superimposing the HR patch on the generated image can be used, as shown in Figure 8.10.

To control the relative importance of these two constraints, a weight w can be used. The training set consists of a search vector and a HR patch, as shown in Figure 8.11. The search vector includes LR patches and overlapping parts of HR patches.

Taking into account the two constraints previously described, the images that constitute the training set need to be preprocessed first. The preprocessing process and steps are shown in Figure 8.12. By first blurring and down-sampling the original images in these training sets, and finally enlarging them back to their original size by interpolation, a low-pass version of the original images can be obtained. The difference between this version and the original image is the high-frequency component. Next, use another low-pass filter to remove the lowest frequency component from the interpolated image, and the intermediate (medium) frequency component can be obtained.

Note that the interpolated image here is a degraded version of the HR image, and the input interpolated image is also so degraded. Therefore, after processing the images of the training set first, the images can be divided into patches. The size of the resulting HR patches is 5 × 5, and the size of the resulting LR patches is 7 × 7. The training set is now composed of these patches, and contrast normalization is also required for these patches. There are different normalization methods. For example, the value of each frequency band can be linearly transformed into the range of 0~255; energy image (which describes the average absolute value of each point in the image) can also be divided by each frequency band. In addition, a local contrast normalization method can also be used: each HR patch and LR patch are divided by local energy.

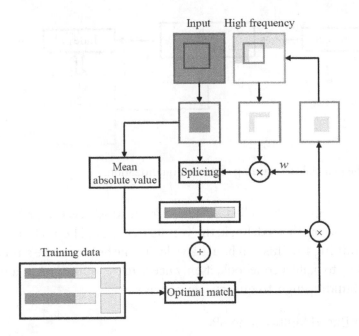

FIGURE 8.11 The flowchart of processing each region in raster order (dark gray corresponds to low frequency, light gray corresponds to high frequency).

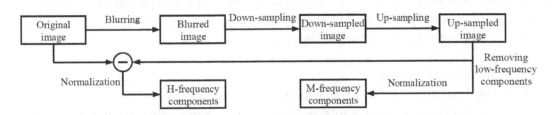

FIGURE 8.12 Preprocessing process and steps.

8.2.2.5 The Matching of Image Patches

The matching process can be carried out with the aid of Euclidean distance. Write the search vector that constitutes the training set as $V = (V_l, V_h)$, where V_l is a vector containing LR data, and V_h is a vector containing (overlapping) HR data. In this way, the matching distance can be written as

$$d^2(U,V) = |U_l - V_l|^2 + w|U_h - V_h|^2 \qquad (8.9)$$

The direct use of Equation (8.9) requires a lot of calculation. Given the input search vector, it is necessary to search the entire training set to find the best match and return to the HR patch. In general, there are often hundreds of thousands of patches in the training set, and the dimensionality of the search vector often reaches a few hundred. To this end, consider using the *training set vector quantization* (TSVQ) method. The principle of this method is shown in Figure 8.13. Instead of using all the training set vectors, a small group of search vectors can be used here to find the vector closest to an input search vector.

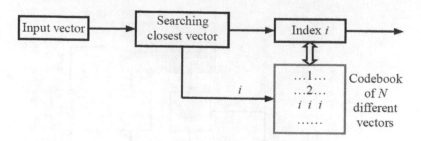

FIGURE 8.13   The principle of training set vector quantization.

The previous group can be called a codebook, in which each search vector is a code word. When calculating the codebook, the vectors in it should be as close as possible to the vectors in the training set. This can be achieved with the help of a tree structure. Although it is relatively slow to build a codebook, it only needs to be counted once, and then it can be very fast when building high-frequency components.

8.2.3 Example-Based Multi-Frame SR

The above-mentioned single-frame SR technology has been extended and improved to obtain *multi-frame SR* technology (Jeong 2015). There are three main steps: using the motion vector to determine the local region of the search for the optimal patch, adaptively selecting the optimal patch based on the LR image degradation model, and combining the optimal patch with the reconstructed image.

8.2.3.1 The Overall Process

FIGURE 8.14 shows the flowchart of this method.

In actual multi-frame input, a total of three frames are used: the current frame and the preceding and following frames. For color images, only the Y component of the color space YIQ is considered for SR reconstruction, and the color components I and Q are only inter-polated. The final SR result is obtained by combining the Y component of SR reconstruction with the interpolated I and Q components. Interpolation is performed using only the current frame. Determine the local search region through motion estimation of adjacent frames and give its position, and generate high-LR patch pairs from the local search region according to the image degradation model, and optimally synthesize HR patches from the selected patches. It is then back-projected and refined to get the final output SR result.

8.2.3.2 Specific Key Points

A few of the key points are briefly introduced below.

1. Define the local search region

    Here, the local self-similarity between neighboring video frames is used to search for patches. By using motion information, the search region of the patch is reduced as much as possible. To reduce the amount of calculation, down-sampled video frame images can be used.

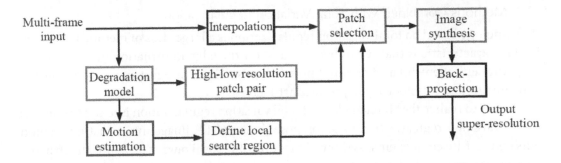

FIGURE 8.14   Example-based multi-frame super-resolution flowchart.

2. Patch search based on the degradation model

First, a LR image must be generated based on the degradation model. In this way, the patch search can eliminate the artifacts caused by interpolation during the up-sampling process. Next, the input image and its degraded version can be used to generate patch pairs in each frame. The input image provides a HR patch, and its degraded version can be regarded as a corresponding LR patch. According to the quantization direction (such as 0°, 45°, 90°, 135°, etc.), the HR and LR patch pairs in the local region are classified, so that the search time can be reduced.

3. Optimal patch combination and multi-frame image reconstruction

Combining the best patches selected from multiple frames of images to obtain a HR image, the weight used is inversely proportional to the mismatch error, that is, the greater the mismatch error, the smaller the weight.

The aforementioned method may strengthen the transition region of the edge mode when reconstructing HR images. To solve this problem, post-processing can be performed by using back-projection. This process can be seen in Figure 8.15, which is a closed-loop iteration (shown by the dotted line). First, down-sample the initially reconstructed image to the same size as the input image, and then calculate the difference between these two images. The difference image is expanded to the size of the required SR image through interpolation, and then low-pass filtering is performed. Finally, the filtering result is added to the preliminarily reconstructed image to increase naturalness.

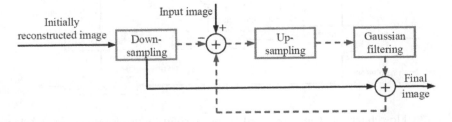

FIGURE 8.15   Flowchart of back-projection process.

8.2.4 Methods Combined with Total Variation Regularization

SR technology based on total variation regularization is a large class of methods to achieve SR. Its characteristic is that it can better maintain the edge information (the edge is still sharp after enlargement) and texture information (small texture features are not affected) in the image, and it is not easy to produce artifacts.

One way to realize the SR technology of total variation regularization is to use the method of total variation regularization to decompose the input LR image into structural components and texture components, as shown in Figure 8.16 (Yoshikawa et al. 2010). The structure component contains the low-frequency components and the edge components in the image; the texture component contains the high-frequency components in the image but does not include the edge components. HR output images can be obtained by performing up-sampling based on a total variation of structural components and performing de-blurring interpolation with smoothing and regularizing on texture components to achieve good visual effects.

One problem with the above method is that it includes two total variation regularization processes. To solve this problem, the process shown in Figure 8.17 can be used. First, the input LR image will be up-sampled using the total variation regularization similar to the aforementioned method. Then, the HR structure elements are down-sampled into LR structure elements. The LR texture component is obtained by subtracting the LR structure components from the input LR image. Using texture interpolation to up-sampling LR texture components can obtain HR texture components. On this basis, the final HR image is obtained by combining the HR structure components and the HR texture components. In the process of this method, there is only one total variation process, so the amount of calculation will be less than that of the previous method.

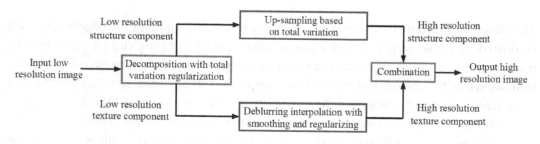

FIGURE 8.16   Flowchart of the super-resolution technology of total variation regularization.

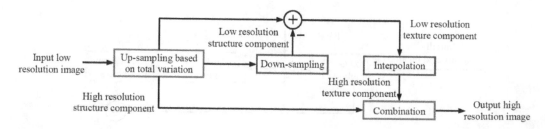

FIGURE 8.17   Flowchart of the improved super-resolution technology of total variation regularization.

8.2.5 Learning-Based Methods

The flowchart of a learning-based process is shown in Figure 8.18 (Goto et al. 2011). The input LR image X_i is divided into a low-frequency component X_i^L and a high-frequency component X_i^H. Up-sampling of X_i^L by linear interpolation method yields Y_i^H. The X_i^H is processed using a learning-based method. In the learning-based method, the LR training image X_t^H and the corresponding HR training image Y_t^H are used to estimate the required HR image Y_i^H. The estimation here is for each patch in the image. When the magnification factor is 2, one patch may include 3×3 pixels in the LR images X_i^H and X_t^H, and 6×6 pixels in the HR images Y_i^H and Y_t^H. Perform a correlation search between X_i^H and X_t^H, and each patch in X_i^H has a corresponding patch in X_t^H. Next, the corresponding patch in Y_i^H is replaced with the corresponding patch in Y_t^H. In this way, the required HR image Y_i^H is obtained. Finally, Y_i^L and Y_i^H are added to produce the output image Y_i.

The interpolation module of the texture component in Figure 8.17 can be replaced with a learning-based method similar to the above one, and the LR texture components and HR texture components in Figure 8.17 can be replaced respectively with the texture part X_t^T of the LR image and the texture part Y_t^T of the HR image, as shown in Figure 8.19.

The above method can also be combined with the learning-based method in another way. The flowchart is shown in Figure 8.20 (Yoshikawa et al. 2010). First, the input image X_i is decomposed into structure component X_i^S and texture component X_i^T by means of total variation regularization. The structure component X_i^S is up-sampled by total variation regularization to obtain the structure part Y_o^S of the output image. The texture component X_i^T,

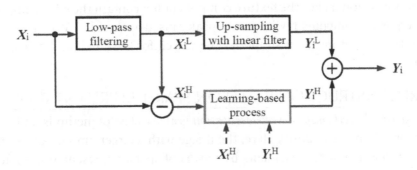

FIGURE 8.18   Basic flowchart of a learning-based method.

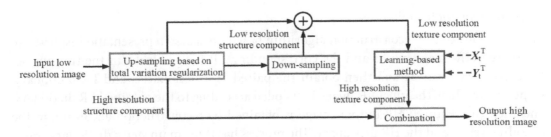

FIGURE 8.19   Flowchart of the super-resolution technology using total variation regularization combined with the learning-based method.

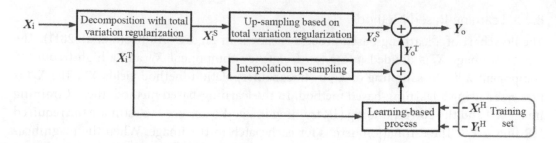

FIGURE 8.20   Flowchart of the super-resolution technology based on learning and total variation regularization.

on the one hand, is input into the learning-based process, and the texture part X_t^T of the LR image and the texture part Y_t^T of the HR image in the training set are used to establish the relationship of the high-frequency component of the texture part in the HR output image; on the other hand, it is interpolated and up-sampled to obtain the low-frequency component of the texture part in the HR output image. These two parts are combined to get the texture part Y_o^T in the HR output image. Finally, Y_o^S and Y_o^T are combined to give the required HR output image Y_o.

Combining the method based on total variation regularization with the learning-based method as above can obtain the advantages of both methods at the same time. Since the learning-based process is applied to the texture components, the quality of the texture components in the output image can be improved. In addition, the total variation regularization decomposition makes the texture component not contain the edge component, and the high-frequency component will have no peak caused by the edge. When reconstructing the edge in the output image, it simplifies the search for the patch and can speed up the calculation.

8.3   SR RECONSTRUCTION BASED ON SPARSE REPRESENTATION

SR *reconstruction based on sparse representation* is also a class of methods under the learning framework (Yang et al. 2010). Here, the image with a larger amount of information is encoded with fewer non-zero elements by means of sparse representation to achieve the effect of data compression. As the image energy is concentrated, excessive space consumption can be avoided and data utilization efficiency can be improved.

8.3.1   Reconstruction Process

The basic idea of the reconstruction algorithm based on sparse representation is: first use the paired HR image blocks and the corresponding LR image blocks in the training set for dictionary training and then obtain the paired HR dictionaries and LR dictionary, respectively. Then, the input LR image is encoded according to the obtained LR dictionary, and then the required HR output image is obtained by reconstruction according to the encoding result and the HR dictionary. The process has three main steps: dictionary training, sparse coding, and image reconstruction (Yang et al. 2010). The flowchart is shown in Figure 8.21.

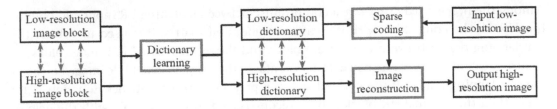

FIGURE 8.21   Flowchart of super-resolution reconstruction process based on sparse representation.

8.3.2 Sparse Coding

Let X denote the (desired) HR image, and Y denote the (input) LR image. They are divided into a series of image blocks. The image block obtained from the HR image is denoted as x, and the image block obtained from the LR image is denoted as y. Let D represent a dictionary used for *sparse coding*, where D_h is a dictionary corresponding to HR image blocks, and D_l is a dictionary corresponding to LR image blocks.

Obtaining HR X from LR Y requires certain constraints to have a unique solution. On the one hand, according to the image observation model, the obtained X should be consistent with Y. On the other hand, according to the sparse representation theory, HR x can be sparsely represented with the help of a suitable over-complete dictionary. If C is used to represent the sparse code obtained by sparse representation, then C can be obtained from y, and y can be obtained with D_l corresponding to D_h ($y = D_l C$). Specifically, x can be represented with D_h as

$$x = D_h C \tag{8.10}$$

Among them $\|C\|_0 \le K$, it means that C is sparse, that is, the number of non-zero elements in C is less than the given positive number K (C is called K sparse).

In practice, the input LR image can be first divided into a series of small blocks of fixed size, each small block may overlap to a certain extent. Then, sparse coding on the divided small block y is performed:

$$\min_{C} \left\| FD_l C - Fy \right\|_2^2 + \lambda \|C\|_1 \tag{8.11}$$

Among them, F is the feature extraction operator, and C is the code (coefficient) of y obtained according to D_l. The L_1 norm ensures the sparsity of the coding, and the Lagrangian multiplier λ is used to balance the accuracy and sparsity of the coding.

To simultaneously consider the coding accuracy and sparsity of the LR image and the reconstructed HR image, these two can be jointly coded as follows:

$$\min_{C} \left\| D'C - Fy' \right\|_2^2 + \lambda \|C\|_1 \tag{8.12}$$

where

$$D' = \begin{bmatrix} FD_l & bPD_h \end{bmatrix}^{\mathrm{T}} \qquad y' = \begin{bmatrix} Fy & bz \end{bmatrix}^{\mathrm{T}} \tag{8.13}$$

Among them, b is used to achieve a compromise between matching LR input and obtaining HR blocks compatible with its neighborhood; and matrix P is used to extract the overlapping region between the current block and the reconstructed HR image block, to ensure the continuity of reconstruction; z contains the reconstructed HR image blocks in the overlapping region. If the optimal sparse representation that satisfies Equation (8.11) is C^*, then the optimal HR block can be reconstructed from $x^* = D_h C^*$ with the help of Equation (8.10).

8.3.3 Dictionary Learning

To achieve sparse representation coding, it is necessary to build an over-complete dictionary with a larger basis function. By flexibly selecting basis functions, it is possible to use as few base functions as possible to accurately represent the image to be coded. Now it is necessary to construct a dictionary D_h corresponding to HR image blocks and a dictionary D_l corresponding to LR image blocks. Let the size of D_h be $N \times K$ and the size of D_l be $M \times K$, where N and M are the block sizes (number of pixels in the block) of the block in the HR image and the block in the LR image, respectively. If in the selection of N and M, making $K \gg N$ and $K \gg M$, then both dictionaries are over-complete. In principle, the sparse prior points out that the paired HR and LR image blocks have the same sparse representation relative to D_h and D_l, so the dictionary can be trained by directly sampling the corresponding HR and LR image blocks. However, the resulting dictionary thus obtained will be quite large and require a lot of calculations.

In practice, the training of the joint dictionary can be transformed into the following optimization problems:

$$D^* = \arg\min_{D,C} \|X - DC\|_2^2 + \lambda \|C\|_1 \qquad \text{s.t. } \|D_i\|_2^2 \leq 1 \qquad i = 1, 2, \ldots, K \qquad (8.14)$$

where

$$X = \left[\frac{1}{\sqrt{N}} X_h \quad \frac{1}{\sqrt{M}} Y_l \right]^{\mathrm{T}} \qquad D = \left[\frac{1}{\sqrt{N}} D_h \quad \frac{1}{\sqrt{M}} D_l \right]^{\mathrm{T}} \qquad (8.15)$$

where X_h is a HR image block, and Y_l is a corresponding LR image block. In the calculation of Equation (8.14), it is necessary to optimize D and C at the same time. In the actual solution process, an iterative algorithm can be used to fix one of the items and solve the other. Through repeated iterations, the solution satisfying conditions can be obtained.

8.3.4 Image Reconstruction

According to the coefficient C and the HR dictionary D_h obtained by sparse coding, the HR image block can be reconstructed by using Equation (8.10). These HR image blocks are spliced together to provide a preliminary HR image X_0.

It should be pointed out that, according to Equation (8.11), the LR image block y and the reconstructed D_iC are not the same. In addition, there is also the influence of noise, so the preliminary HR image X_0 may not be completely accurate. See Equation (8.1):

$$Y = SBX \tag{8.16}$$

Among them, S is the down-sampling matrix, and B is the blurring matrix.

Therefore, X_0 needs to be re-projected to the solution space of Equation (8.16) to obtain the final HR image X^*:

$$X^* = \arg\min_X \|SBX - Y\|_2^2 + \lambda \|X - X_0\|_2^2 \tag{8.17}$$

8.4 SR RECONSTRUCTION BASED ON LOCALLY CONSTRAINED LINEAR CODING

In the learning-based SR reconstruction algorithm, the sparse representation method has many advantages, but the technique of locally constrained linear coding can achieve better results (Bu and Zhang 2012). The following introduces a method for SR reconstruction using *locally constrained linear coding* (LLC) instead of sparse coding (Bu and Zhang 2013).

8.4.1 Locally Constrained Linear Coding

Locally constrained linear coding is also a method of encoding image representation (Wang and Zhang 2011), which focuses on local constraints rather than sparsity. It has been proved that locality can bring sparsity, but sparsity may not satisfy locality (Yu et al. 2009). In this respect, locality constraints are more important than sparsity constraints. If C is used to represent the code obtained by LLC, it satisfies

$$\min_C \sum_{i=1}^N \|x_i - DC_i\|^2 + \lambda \|v_i \cdot C_i\|^2 \quad \text{s.t. } \mathbf{1}^T C_i = 1, \forall i \tag{8.18}$$

Among them, x_i is the vector to be coded, D is the dictionary, and v_i is the weight of different codes, which is used to weigh the relationship between each element in the code and the corresponding column in the dictionary D. v_i can be calculated with the following equation:

$$v_i = \exp\left(\frac{\text{dis}(x_i, D)}{u}\right) \tag{8.19}$$

Among them, u is an adjustable parameter that controls the size of v_i; $\text{dis}(x_i, D)$ is a vector, and each element represents the Euclidean distance between x_i and each column of vectors in D.

Locally constrained linear coding has some advantages over sparse coding. Because of the addition of local constraints, the coding results obtained by locally constrained linear coding are smoother than sparse coding. In sparse coding, to meet the sparseness of coding, the results obtained from similar pixel blocks may be quite different, and the

over-completeness of the dictionary exacerbates this difference. In contrast, local constrained linear coding can ensure local smoothness and make similar pixel blocks get
similar coding, thereby ensuring the similarity of the reconstructed pixel blocks. In addition, sparse coding needs to adopt an optimization algorithm for iteration, which brings a
higher amount of calculation, while the local constrained linear coding algorithm has an
analytical solution, which can reduce computational consumption, speed up the calculation, and has a more obvious effect on large-size images.

8.4.2 SR Reconstruction Algorithm Based on Locally Constrained Linear Coding

The main steps of the algorithm are as follows:

1. Image blocking

   Properly dividing the image into blocks can reduce the computational complexity, speed up the calculation, improve the accuracy of the reconstruction, and ensure
   the effect of image reconstruction. Here, the input image can be divided into a series
   of 3×3 small blocks in the order from top to bottom and left to right. There is a
   column of overlap between adjacent pixel blocks in the same row, and a row of overlap between adjacent pixel blocks in the same column. It is to ensure the continuity
   between pixel blocks and prevent sudden changes caused by discontinuities at the
   edges of pixel blocks.

2. Joint dictionary training

   To strengthen the correlation between the HR dictionary and the LR dictionary
   in the dictionary training, the LR images in the training set are obtained by sub-
   sampling and blurring the HR images. To ensure the effect of dictionary training, the
   LR image is up-sampled and then jointly trained with the HR image, which helps to
   better find the correspondence between the two types of image.

   SR reconstruction pays more attention to recovering the high-frequency details
   of the image. Therefore, before the up-sampled LR image is divided into blocks, the
   high-frequency components are first obtained through the feature extraction matrix,
   and then the correspondence relationship between the high-frequency components is
   performed to obtain pairs of dictionaries D_h and D_l. The feature extraction operator
   can be designed as follows:

$$f_1 = [-1 \quad 0 \quad 1] \qquad f_2 = [1 \quad 0 \quad -2 \quad 0 \quad 1]$$
$$f_3 = [-1 \quad 0 \quad 1]^{\mathrm{T}} \qquad f_4 = [1 \quad 0 \quad -2 \quad 0 \quad 1]^{\mathrm{T}} \tag{8.20}$$

Among them, f_1 and f_2 are used to extract row features, and f_3 and f_4 are used to
extract column features. The feature extraction operators are convolved with the
image for training to obtain four feature images that retain edge information. These
four images are divided into blocks, and the corresponding image blocks are integrated into a vector to form the dictionary training vector. Then, the joint dictionary
training can be carried out according to Equation (8.14).

3. Locally constrained linear coding of the image

Before image coding, a preprocessing process similar to that of dictionary training is also required. That is, for an input LR image, the same Equation (8.20) is used to obtain four characteristic images. Then perform the block processing according to the aforementioned image block method, and integrate the corresponding blocks in the four images into a vector y_i, and perform local constrained linear coding with the help of the LR dictionary D_l obtained by training.

First, calculate the distance between y and each column vector of the dictionary D_l, and then obtain the encoding weight v_i similarly to Equation (8.19):

$$v_i = \exp\left(\frac{\text{dis}(y, D_1)}{u}\right) \tag{8.21}$$

Then, calculate the coefficient C_i after local constraint linear coding according to v_i:

$$C_i = \frac{[V_i + \lambda \text{diag}(v)]\backslash 1}{1^{\text{T}}[V_i + \lambda \text{diag}(v)]\backslash 1} \tag{8.22}$$

Among them, $V_i = (D - 1x_i^{\text{T}})(D - 1x_i^{\text{T}})^{\text{T}}$ is the covariance matrix. Because of the analytical solution here, it can be calculated quickly.

4. SR reconstruction

Using the coefficient C_i obtained above and the HR dictionary D_h obtained by training, the HR image block x_i can be reconstructed:

$$x_i = D_h C_i \tag{8.23}$$

The HR image blocks x_i are spliced together in the order from left to right and top to bottom, and the aliasing when the LR image is divided into blocks is taken into consideration. Then the HR image X_0 after preliminary reconstruction can be obtained.

5. Global constraints and recovery

In the above reconstruction, all constraint conditions considered are local, so each reconstructed image block is locally optimal, but it may not meet the global optimal condition. For this reason, after the initial HR image X_0 is reconstructed, it needs to be processed and restored globally. Here, X_0 can be back-projected: project X_0 onto the input LR image Y to obtain the projected image Y^+, and then map the difference between Y^+ and Y to the HR space and superimpose it on X_0. Iteratively repeat the above process to get a HR image with global constraints added.

8.4.3 Multi-Frame Image SR Reconstruction

The foregoing steps correspond to *single-frame image SR reconstruction*. Methods similar to Equations (8.12) and (8.13) can be used to integrate the data of multiple frame images into the same coding formula, perform the overall optimization, find the optimal solution, and achieve *multi-frame image SR reconstruction* (Bu and Zhang 2013). Here, since the complementary information between the images in the image sequence is used, the quality of image SR reconstruction can be improved.

First, it is necessary to perform motion estimation and inter-frame registration on the input multi-frame LR images, and then perform multi-frame SR reconstruction:

$$\min_{C_{i,j}} \left\| \tilde{D}_1 C_{i,j} - \tilde{y} \right\|_2^2 + \lambda \left\| v \cdot C_{i,j} \right\|_2^2 \quad \text{s.t.} \ I^T C_{i,j} = 1 \tag{8.24}$$

where

$$\tilde{D} = \left[\sqrt{w_1} FD \quad \cdots \quad \sqrt{w_n} FD_n \right]^T \quad \tilde{y} = \left[\sqrt{w_1} r_1 FY_1 \quad \cdots \quad \sqrt{w_n} r_n FY_n \right]^T \tag{8.25}$$

Among them, $C_{i,j}$ are the coefficients of the image block whose center point is located at (i, j) after being sparsely coded; F is the feature extraction matrix; D_l is the LR dictionary; r is the image block extraction operator, which is used to extract the image block centered at (i, j) from LR image Y; w is the weight coefficient, which is used to control the degree of constrains for each frame image on the final coding coefficient:

$$w(i, j, k, l, s, t) = \exp\left(\frac{\left\| r_{i,j} Y_s - r_{k,l} Y_t \right\|_2^2}{2u^2} \right) \tag{8.26}$$

The SR reconstruction as well as the global constraints and recovery steps after the coding coefficients are obtained can be similarly made as the single-frame SR reconstruction.

8.4.4 Reconstruction Results and Method Comparison

Some effect examples and performance comparisons of SR reconstruction based on sparse coding and locally constrained linear coding are as follows.

1. Reconstruction effect

Figure 8.22 shows a set of reconstruction effects obtained by SR reconstruction of a standard Lena image using a 1024-D dictionary. Figure 8.22a is a LR image, Figure 8.22b and c are respectively the results of sparse coding SR reconstruction and locally constrained linear coding SR reconstruction, the horizontal and vertical magnifications are both 3. The PSNR of the three pictures is 26.8270, 29.5986, and 29.6842 dB in order. The result of locally constrained linear coding SR reconstruction is better than that of sparse coding SR reconstruction.

To see clearly, the same part of the three pictures is cut and enlarged to obtain Figure 8.23. According to the subjective visual effects, it is seen that the ringing phenomenon on the edge of the hat is gradually alleviated from left to right in Figure 8.23.

FIGURE 8.22 Comparison examples of sparse coding and locally constrained linear coding reconstruction effects.

FIGURE 8.23 Local comparison of reconstruction effects between sparse coding super-resolution reconstruction and locally constrained linear coding super-resolution reconstruction.

There are more experimental results for locally constrained linear coding reconstruction. The PSNR value of the image obtained after reconstruction of a set of LR images given in Figure 8.24 can be seen in Table 8.1.

2. Anti-noise performance

To test the anti-noise performance of different algorithms, different types and intensities of noise are added to the original input LR image before SR reconstruction is performed. Figure 8.25 shows a set of examples of noise-added super-resolution reconstruction effects, where Figure 8.25a is a LR image, Figure 8.25b and c are the results of sparse coding SR reconstruction and locally constrained linear coding SR reconstruction, respectively. The added noise is Gaussian noise with a mean value of 0 and a normalized variance of 0.001. The PSNR of the three pictures is 26.4090, 28.8086, and 28.8966 dB.

The PSNR values obtained in experiments by adding other types of noise can be seen in Table 8.2. For ease of comparison, the noise-free results are also listed in the table.

3. Multi-frame image reconstruction

Here, the SR reconstruction is performed using four frames of images as an example, and the results of the single-frame SR reconstruction and the multi-frame SR

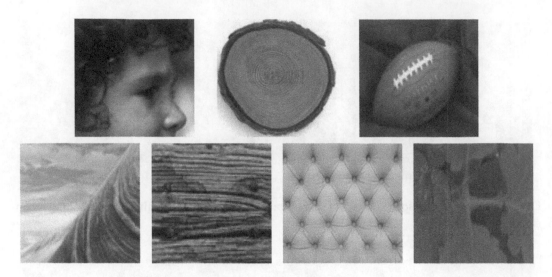

FIGURE 8.24 A set of low-resolution images.

TABLE 8.1   PSNR Value (dB) for Super-Resolution Reconstruction of Images in Figure 8.24

Image	Input Low-Resolution Image	Reconstructed Image by Sparse Coding	Reconstructed Image by Locally Constrained Linear Coding
Boy	31.2980	33.2567	33.3019
Annual ring	27.0647	28.9136	28.9913
Football	29.5038	30.7550	30.7810
Mountain	29.4152	31.6926	31.7836
Tree	15.8358	16.1866	16.3445
Grid	34.5494	37.6057	37.6887
Leaf	35.0456	37.9551	38.0160
Average	28.9589	30.9093	30.9867

FIGURE 8.25   Examples of comparison of reconstruction effects of sparse coding super-resolution reconstruction and locally constrained linear coding super-resolution reconstruction after adding noise.

TABLE 8.2   PSNR Values (dB) of Reconstruction of Lena Image after Adding Various Noises

Noise	Input Low-Resolution Image	Reconstructed Image by Sparse Coding	Reconstructed Image by Locally Constrained Linear Coding
No noise	26.8270	29.5986	29.6842
Gaussian (Variance = 0.001)	26.4090	28.8086	28.8966
Gaussian (Variance = 0.01)	22.8202	23.6923	23.7379
Pepper and Salt (Density = 0.001)	26.6695	29.2574	29.3646
Pepper and Salt (Density = 0.01)	25.3469	27.0602	27.1301

FIGURE 8.26   Examples of single-frame and multi-frame reconstruction effects.

TABLE 8.3   The Average Gradient Values after Reconstruction with Different Methods

Image	Single-Frame Sparse Coding	Multi-frame sparse coding	Single-frame LLC coding	Multi-frame LLC coding
First frame	0.0411	0.0413	0.0418	0.0422
Second frame	0.0400	0.0404	0.0403	0.0414
Third frame	0.0401	0.0400	0.0403	0.0407

reconstruction are compared, as shown in Figure 8.26. Among them, the leftmost picture is a frame in a LR video sequence, followed by the reconstruction results of single-frame sparse coding, multi-frame sparse coding (Wang and Zhang 2011), single-frame locally constrained linear coding, and multi-frame locally constrained linear coding, respectively.

Table 8.3 lists the average gradient values of the image obtained after reconstruction of three consecutive frames of images with different methods. The larger the value, the clearer the edge and more detailed information of the image, and the higher the subjective resolution.

8.5 SOME RECENT DEVELOPMENTS AND FURTHER RESEARCH

In the following, some technique developments and promising research directions in the last few years are briefly overviewed.

8.5.1 Overview of SR Based on Deep Learning

In the SR domain, many deep learning-based approaches have been proposed. A categorization of some typical *deep learning-based super-resolution* methods is listed in Table 8.4. It should be noted that there are different categorization schemes. For example, someone counts GAN-based methods are included in residual-based methods (Tang et al. 2020).

Some approaches have combined different networks (see the following descriptions).

TABLE 8.4   A Categorization of Deep Learning-Based Image Super-Resolution Techniques

#	Network	Typical Technique Example
1	CNN (Convolutional Neural Network)	SRCNN (Super-Resolution Convolutional Neural Network) ESPCNN (Efficient Sub-Pixel CNN)
2	RN (Residual Network)	VDSR (Very Deep Super-Resolution)
3	RNN (Recursive Neural Network)	DRCN (Deeply-Recursive Convolutional Network) DRRN (Deep Recursive Residual Network)
4	DCN (Dense Convolutional Network)	D-DBPN (Dense Deep Back-Projection Networks) RDN (Residual Dense Networks)
5	GAN (Generative Adversarial Network)	SRGAN (Super-Resolution using a Generative Adversarial Network)
6	NAS (Neural Architecture Search)	MoreMNAS (Multi-Objective Reinforced Evolution in Mobile NAS) ESRN (Efficient Super-Resolution Network) HNAS-SR (Hierarchical NAS for Super-Resolution)
7	Other methods	RBM (Restricted Boltzmann Machine) DBN (Deep Belief Networks) AE (Auto-Encoder): REDN (Residual Encoder-Decoder Networks)

1. Convolutional Neural Network (CNN)

Among various networks, CNN was first used for SR . *Super-resolution convolutional neural network* (SRCNN) is the earliest proposed technology (Dong et al. 2014). The basic idea is to use bi-cubic interpolation to enlarge the LR image to the target (SR) image size, and then fit the non-linear mapping through a three-layer convolutional network, finally output HR image results. SRCNN is a shallow SR CNN model with a very simple network structure, as shown in Figure 8.27. The first layer is a LR feature extraction layer, which extracts image blocks and performs feature representation; the second *layer is a low-resolution to high-resolution* (LR-HR) mapping layer, which performs non-linear mapping of features; the third layer is a HR reconstruction layer to achieve SR reconstruction.

There are already many improvements to SRCNN. For example, in view of a large amount of calculation and long reconstruction time that SRCNN needs to enlarge the LR image to the HR size and then learn the LR to HR feature mapping, *Efficient*

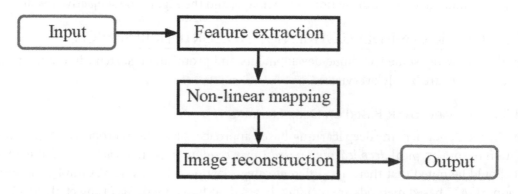

FIGURE 8.27   SRCNN model.

sub-pixel CNN (ESPCNN) uses the increase in the number of convolution kernels and sub-pixels (Shi et al. 2016). The HR feature map is obtained by convolution, and the HR image is obtained through channel reorganization. In this way, the reconstruction time of ESPCNN is only 1/10 of that of SRCNN when the reconstruction quality equivalent to SRCNN can be obtained.

2. Residual Network

Deepening the shallow network and introducing the *residual network* into the reconstruction model can improve the network performance and the accuracy of the final reconstruction result. *Very deep super-resolution* (VDSR) is a typical method following this idea (Kim et al. 2016a), and it is also an improvement to SRCNN. It takes the LR image of the target image size obtained after interpolation as the input of the network and then adds the residual error learned by the image and the network to obtain the final network output. As the network structure is deepened, the receptive field is enlarged, the loss of image information is avoided, and the details of the image can be reconstructed. By modeling the residual image, the learning speed can be improved. Using images of different multiples for mixed training, it can solve the problem of SR with different multiples.

3. Recursive Network

The *recursive network* applies the same (shared parameter) convolutional layer multiple times for repeated recursion, but it does not increase the number of parameters. *Deeply-recursive convolutional network* (DRCN) for image SR is the first method to apply recursive network structure to SR problems (Kim et al. 2016b). Its network structure corresponds to SRCNN. It can be divided into three modules: the first is an embedded network corresponding to feature extraction, the second is an inference network corresponding to feature non-linear mapping, and the third is corresponding to a reconstruction network for restoring the final reconstruction result from the feature image.

A further improvement is the *deep recursive residual network* (DRRN) (Lim et al. 2017), which combines the residual structure with the recursive module. By adopting residual learning both in global and local manners, it effectively reduces the training difficulty for the deep network.

4. Dense Connected Network

The input of each layer of the *densely connected network* (DCN) is the output of all previous layers, that is, the image features learned by each layer are directly transmitted to all layers following this layer as input. Here all the layers are connected in series, rather than simply adding up like a residual network. This structure can alleviate the problem of gradient disappearance in the entire network and has the advantages of enhancing feature propagation, supporting feature reuse, and reducing the number of parameters.

The dense connected network structure for SR is divided into four parts. First, a convolutional layer is used to learn low-level image features; then, several densely connected blocks (including BN-Relu-Conv) are used to learn high-level image features; next, several de-convolutional layers are used to learn the filtering parameters for up-sampling; finally, a convolutional layer is used to generate HR image output. A dense connection can make full use of the features of each level of the network model, so that the SR model can obtain richer feature representations, thereby improving the reconstruction effect of HR images.

Dense deep back-projection network (D-DBPN) uses an error feedback mechanism to design a series of up-sampling and down-sampling convolutional layers (Haris et al. 2018). These layers are densely connected for the circulation of feature information, which can obtain a good reconstruction effect on a larger scale. *Residual dense network* (RDN) combines the residual module and the dense module to form the residual dense module as the basic unit (Zhang et al. 2018) and uses local feature fusion to adaptively learn more effective features. This method also uses global feature fusion to fully integrate and utilize the features of different levels of the network model from low to high.

5. Generative Adversarial Network

Generative adversarial network (GAN) has powerful image generation capabilities. *Super-resolution using a generative adversarial network* (SRGAN) takes advantage of this feature (Ledig et al. 2017). The algorithm inputs LR image samples into the generator network for training and learning to generate HR images. Then, it uses the discriminator network to distinguish whether the input HR image is from the original real HR image or the generated HR image. If the discriminator cannot distinguish the authenticity of the image, it means that the generator network has generated high-quality, HR images. SRGAN mainly uses the loss function that combines perceptual loss and adversarial loss (see Section 8.5.2) to improve the authenticity of image restoration. Perceptual loss is the feature extracted by the CNN. By comparing the features of the generated image after convolution and the original image after convolution, the generated image is made as close to the original image as possible. Combining the adversarial loss, the generator and the discriminator can compete with each other so that the discriminator can extract the latent patterns that are difficult to learn from the real reference image, and force the generator to adjust the model so that the generator can produce a realistic HR image.

6. Neural Architecture Search

Neural architecture search (NAS) is a kind of method that uses reinforcement learning to find the optimal network, which can reduce the artificial influence on model design. This type of method first defines a search space, uses the corresponding controller to process the search, outputs the reconstruction result after evaluation, and automatically adjusts the reconstruction result through network training until the network converges and obtains a good reconstruction result. The NAS-based SR method usually embeds multiple SR methods into the learning of the overall network. In general, it is better than a simple combination of one or more SR methods.

The first model to apply NAS to SR tasks is *Multi-objective reinforced evolution in mobile NAS* (MoreMNAS) (Chu et al. 2019), which contains three basic components: cell-based search space, model generation controller based on related multi-objects, and an evaluator that returns multiple feedback. *Efficient super-resolution network* (ESRN) has made improvements by using three different dense residual models as cells in the search space to reduce unnecessary searches (Song et al. 2020). *Hierarchical NAS for super-resolution* (HNAS-SR) is a structural system that solves real SR hierarchical search (Guo et al. 2020). It uses a hierarchical approach to construct search spaces and controllers. The controller includes the cell layer controller and network layer controller, respectively. Different cells use the long and short-term memory method to automatically select the nodes of each layer and input them into the hierarchical network layer controller after processing.

7. Others

Many other deep learning models have also been used for image SR. For example, an image SR method using *Restricted Boltzmann machine* (RBM) has been proposed (Gao et al. 2014). In which, the visible layer of RBM is composed of LR and HR image blocks. The hidden layer represents the sparse coefficient shared by the LR and HR image dictionary pairs, and the dictionary elements are obtained through maximum likelihood estimation. The essence of this method is still sparse representation, but the dictionary construction and training process are completed through RBM.

Stacking multiple layers of RBM can form *deep belief network* (DBN) (Zhou et al. 2014). Use the hierarchical structure of DBN to learn the non-linear mapping relationship between LR and HR images, and then complete the image SR through two steps: training and reconstruction. In the training process, the HR image can be decomposed into multiple image blocks and transformed into the DCT domain, and the obtained two-dimensional DCT coefficients can be used to train DBN. During reconstruction, the LR image is interpolated to a HR size and then decomposed into image blocks and transformed into the DCT domain. In this way, the trained DBN can be used to recover the lost high-frequency information. Finally, the HR image is reconstructed by DCT inverse transformation.

Auto-encoder (AE) can also be used for image SR. For example, the symmetrical convolutional layer-deconvolutional layer can be used to form a deep residual AE network: *Residual encoder-decoder network* (REDN) (Mao et al. 2016), where each convolutional layer (used to obtain the abstraction content of the image) and the deconvolution layer (used to enlarge the feature size and restore image details) are connected by skippers to solve the problem of disappearing gradient.

8.5.2 Loss Functions and Evaluation Indicators

In image SR based on deep learning, the *loss function* is used to define the difference between the HR image generated by the SR model and the real reference image, which plays a crucial role in the optimization process based on deep learning. In addition, as more and more reconstruction methods are proposed, how to evaluate the performance of SR reconstruction methods and the visual effects of reconstructed images have also received more attention. The *evaluation indicator* has a certain connection with the loss function. A good evaluation indicator can effectively evaluate the performance of SR reconstruction methods and/or the quality of the SR reconstructed image so that the deep learning model can be optimized and improved.

8.5.2.1 Loss Functions

The early loss function is mostly based on the various norms, such as using the pixel-by-pixel *mean square error* (MSE) to obtain a higher PSNR value. However, in practice, the increases in PSNR value and the visual effect of image quality are not simply proportional. A series of other loss functions have been proposed one after another:

1. *Perceptual loss*

    To evaluate the difference in perceptual quality between different images, the perceptual distance is introduced into the SR field. Specifically, the fully trained natural image classification models, such as VGG and ResNet, are used to extract the features of different images, and then the Euclidean distance in the feature space is calculated:

$$P_{\text{loss}}(x,x') = \frac{1}{h_l w_l n_l} \sum_{i,j,k} \left[f_{i,j,k}^{(l)}(x) - f_{i,j,k}^{(l)}(x') \right]^2 \tag{8.27}$$

    where h_l, w_l, and n_l represent the numbers of height, width, and layer of the l-th feature map, respectively.

2. *Texture loss*

    Texture loss is used to describe the difference in texture styles of the generated HR image and the real reference image. The specific definition is as follows:

$$T_{\text{loss}}(x,x') = \left\| G[f(x)] - G[f(x')] \right\|_2^2 \tag{8.28}$$

    where $G(F) = FF^{\text{T}} \in \mathbb{R}^{n \times n}$, is Gram matrix (covariance matrix without mean subtraction).

3. *Adversarial loss*

    This is a proprietary loss in the GAN-based SR network model. The loss function includes two adversarial loss functions corresponding to the generator and the discriminator, respectively. The typical function form is as follows (when different GAN models are used, the loss function may be different):

$$G_{\text{loss}}^{(g)} = \sum_{i=1}^{N} -\log[D(x)] \tag{8.29}$$

$$G_{\text{loss}}^{(d)} = \sum_{i=1}^{N} -\log[D(x_i)] - \log[1 - D(x_i')] \tag{8.30}$$

The adversarial loss function is often used in combination with other loss functions. The purpose is to enable the discriminator to extract latent patterns that are difficult to learn from the real reference image through the competition between the generator and the discriminator, and to force the generator to adjust the model, so as to make the generation to produce realistic HR images.

It should be pointed out that since the training of GAN is still difficult and unstable at this time, the SR model combined with the adversarial loss may sometimes produce artificial traces and unnatural deformation. How to better apply GAN to the field of image SR reconstruction is still worthy of in-depth study.

Finally, there is no perfect theoretical basis for the selection of loss function for image SR reconstruction, and further research is needed.

8.5.2.2 Evaluation Indicators

The performance of the SR reconstruction method and the visual effect of the reconstructed image can be evaluated by objective evaluation indicators, such as PSNR and SSIM (see Section 5.5.1); can also be evaluated by subjective evaluation indicators, such as *mean opinion score* (MOS), in which the evaluation of reconstruction results is made by multiple evaluators. In MOS, the evaluation of reconstruction results produces scores from 5 to 1 (corresponding from good to bad) (Ledig et al. 2017). A comparison of them can be seen in Table 8.5 (Zhang et al. 2020).

It can be seen from Table 8.5 that objective evaluation indicators and subjective evaluation indicators have their own strengths. In practice, the application goal of SR can also be used to evaluate SR based on the application results. For example, in the classification of images, the quality of the reconstructed image can be indirectly evaluated by the accuracy of the classification results. However, this approach is only suitable for images application with a clear goal, and a certain prior knowledge of the images application is also required.

In the current environment where deep learning is widely used, it should be a promising study to learn the subjective evaluation of people with the help of neural networks to build a subjective evaluation system that can be objectively realized.

TABLE 8.5   The Advantages and Disadvantages of Several Common Subjective and Objective Evaluation Indicators

#	Advantage	Disadvantage
PSNR	Ability to measure loss between pixels	The image quality cannot be comprehensively evaluated, and its high value does not mean the high of the visual quality
SSIM	Ability to measure the statistical relationship between images	Not suitable for global image evaluation, more suitable for image local structure similarity evaluation
MOS	The evaluation results are more in line with human visual effects, with the number increase of evaluators the evaluation results are more reliable	Time-consuming, labor-intensive, costly, and subject to the influence of the evaluators when the number of evaluators is small, and discontinuous ratings can easily cause large errors

REFERENCES

Bu, S. S. and Y.-J. Zhang. 2012. Image super-resolution based on locality-constrained linear coding. *Proceedings of 16 NCIG*, 561–565.

Bu, S. S. and Y.-J. Zhang. 2013. Single-frame and multi-frame image super-resolution based on locality-constrained linear coding. *Journal of Jilin University (Engineering and Technology Edition)*, 43: 365–370.

Chu, X. X., B. Zhang, R. J. Xu, et al. 2019. Multi-objective reinforced evolution in mobile neural architecture search. https://arxiv.org/pdf/1901.01074.

Dong, C., C. C. Loy, K. He, et al. 2014. Learning a deep convolutional network for image super-resolution. *Proceedings of ECCV*, 184–199.

Freeman, W. T., T. R. Jones, and E. C. Pasztor. 2002. Example-based super-resolution. *IEEE Computer Graphics and Applications*, 22(2): 56–65.

Gao, J., Y. Guo, and M. Yin. 2014. Restricted Boltzmann machine approach to couple dictionary training for image super-resolution. *Proceedings of ICIP*, 499–503.

Goto, T., S. Suzuki, S. Hirano, et al. 2011. Fast and high quality super-resolution combined learning-based with TV regularization method. *Proceedings of the 15th IEEE International Symposium on Consumer Electronics*, 212–215.

Guo, Y., Y. Luo, Z. He, et al. 2020. Hierarchical neural architecture search for single image super-resolution. https://arxiv.org/pdf/2003.04619.

Haris, M., G. Shakhnarovich, and N. Ukita. 2018. Deep back-projection networks for super-resolution. *Proceedings of CVPR*, 1664–1673.

Jeong, S., I. Yoon, and J. Paik. 2015. Multi-frame example-based super-resolution using locally directional self-similarity. *IEEE Transactions on Consumer Electronics*, 61(3): 353–358.

Kim, J., J. K. Lee, and K. M. Lee. 2016a. Accurate image super-resolution using very deep convolutional networks. *Proceedings of CVPR*, 1646–1654.

Kim, J., J. K. Lee, and K. M. Lee. 2016b. Deeply-recursive convolutional network for image super-resolution. *Proceedings of CVPR*, 1637–1645.

Ledig, C., L. Theis, F. Huszár, et al. 2017. Photo-realistic single image super-resolution using a generative adversarial network. *Proceedings of CVPR*, 4681–4690.

Lim, B., S. Son, H. Kim, et al. 2017. Enhanced deep residual networks for single image super-resolution. *Proceedings of CVPR*, 136–144.

Mao, X. J., C. Shen, and Y. B. Yang. 2016. Image restoration using convolutional auto-encoders with symmetric skip connections. *arXiv Preprint*. arXiv:1606.08921.

Park, S. C., M. K. Park, and M. G. Kang. 2003. Super-resolution image reconstruction: A technical overview. *IEEE Signal Processing Magazine*, 20(3): 21–36

Shi, W., J. Caballero, F. Huszár, et al. 2016. Real-time single image and video super-resolution using an efficient subpixel convolutional neural network. *Proceedings of CVPR*, 1874–1883.

Song, D. H., C. Xu, X. Jia, et al. 2020. Efficient residual dense block search for image super-resolution. *Proceedings of the AAAI Conference*, 34(7): 12007–12014.

Tang, Y. Q., H. Pan, Y. P. Zhu, et al. 2020. A survey of image super-resolution reconstruction. *Acta Electronica Sinica*, 48(7): 1407–1420.

Tekalp, A. M. 1995. *Digital Video Processing*. London, UK: Prentice Hall

Wang, Y. X. and Y.-J. Zhang. 2011. Image inpainting via weighted sparse non-negative matrix factorization. *Proceedings of 18th ICIP*, 3470–3473.

Yang, J. C., J. Wright, T. S. Huang, et al. 2010. Image super-resolution via sparse representation. *IEEE-IP*, 19(11): 2861–2873.

Yoshikawa, A., S. Suzuki, T. Goto, et al. 2010. Super resolution image reconstruction using total variation regularization and learning-based method. *Proceedings of 17th ICIP*, 1993–1996.

Yu, K., T. Zhang, and Y. Gong. 2009. Nonlinear learning using local coordinate coding. *NIPS*, 1–9.

Zhang, N., Y. C. Wang, X. Zhang, et al. 2020. A review of single image super-resolution based on deep learning. *Acta Automatica Sinica*, 46(12): 2479–2499.

Zhang, Y., Y. Tian, Y. Kong, et al. 2018. Residual dense network for image super-resolution. *Proceedings of CVPR*, 2472–2481.

Zhou, Y., Y. Qu, Y. Xie, et al. 2014. Image super-resolution using deep belief networks. *Proceedings of IMCS*, 28.

Index